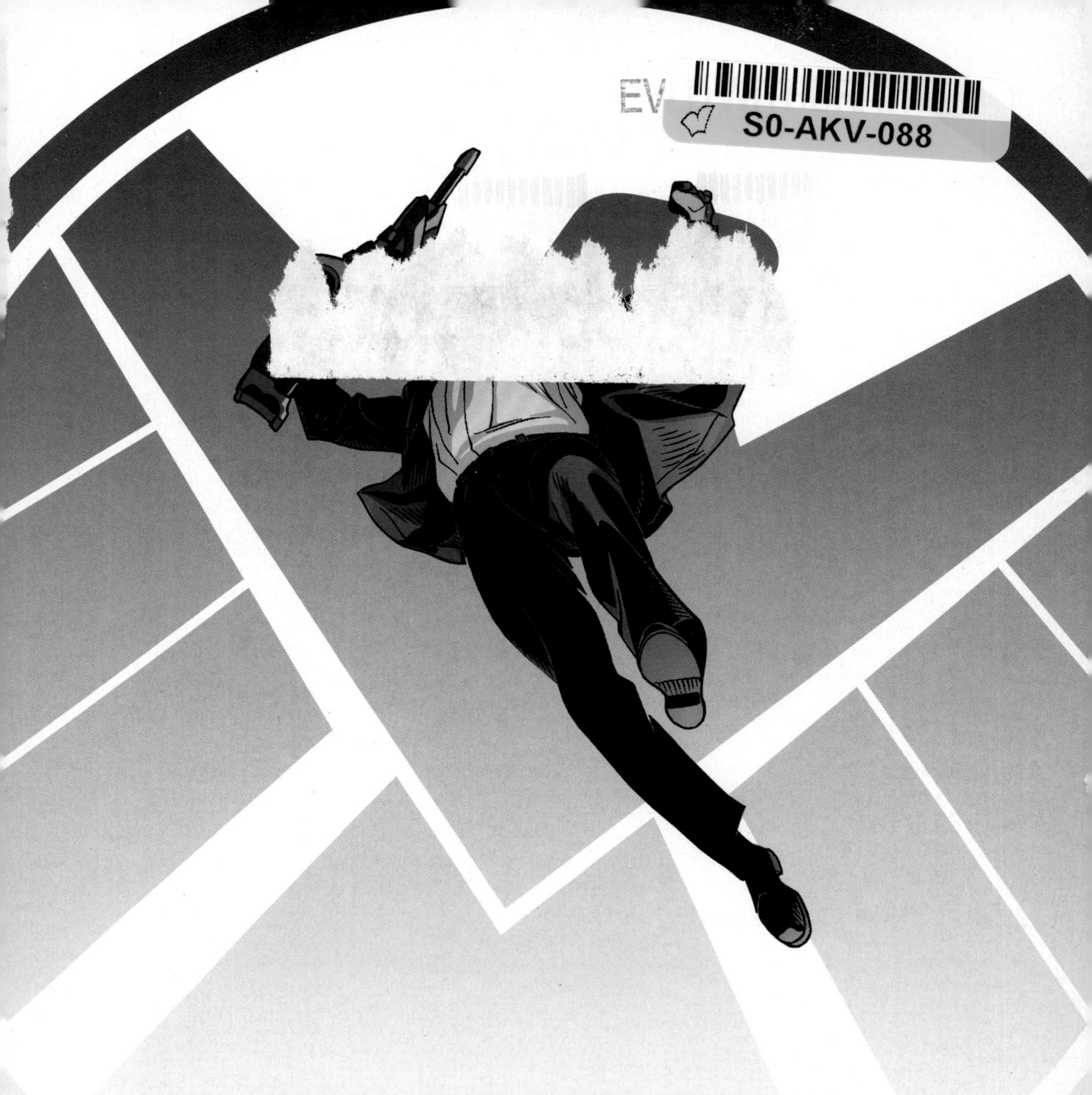

STRATEGIC HOMELAND INTERVENTION ENFORCEMENT LOGISTICS DIVISION

S.H.I.E.L.D.

PERFECT BULLETS

STRATEGIC HOMELAND INTERVENTION ENFORCEMENT LOGISTICS DIVISION

S.H.I.E.L.D.
PERFECT BULLETS

WRITER
MARK WAID

ISSUE #1
PENCILER
CARLOS PACHECO

INKERS
**MARIANO TAIBO
WITH JASON PAZ**

COLORIST
DONO SANCHEZ ALMARA

ISSUE #2
PENCILER
HUMBERTO RAMOS

INKER
VICTOR OLAZABA

COLORIST
EDGAR DELGADO

ISSUE #3
PENCILER
ALAN DAVIS

INKER
MARK FARMER

COLORIST
MATTHEW WILSON

ISSUE #4
PENCILER
CHRIS SPROUSE

INKER
KARL STORY

COLORIST
DONO SANCHEZ ALMARA

ISSUE #5
ARTIST
MIKE CHOI

COLOR ARTIST
RACHELLE ROSENBERG

ISSUE #6
ARTIST
PAUL RENAUD

COLOR ARTIST
ROMULO FAJARDO

LETTERER
VC'S JOE CARAMAGNA

COVER ART
JULIAN TOTINO TEDESCO

ASSISTANT EDITOR
JON MOISAN

EDITORS
**TOM BREVOORT
WITH ELLIE PYLE**

FITZ AND H.E.N.R.Y. STRIPS
BY **JOE QUESADA**

SPECIAL THANKS TO **JEPH LOEB
AND MEGAN THOMAS BRADNER**

S.H.I.E.L.D. CREATED BY
STAN LEE & JACK KIRBY

COLLECTION EDITOR
JENNIFER GRÜNWALD

ASSISTANT EDITOR
SARAH BRUNSTAD

ASSOCIATE MANAGING EDITOR
ALEX STARBUCK

EDITOR, SPECIAL PROJECTS
MARK D. BEAZLEY

SENIOR EDITOR, SPECIAL PROJECT
JEFF YOUNGQUIST

SVP PRINT, SALES & MARKETING
DAVID GABRIEL

BOOK DESIGNER
JAY BOWEN

EDITOR IN CHIEF
AXEL ALONSO

CHIEF CREATIVE OFFICER
JOE QUESADA

PUBLISHER
DAN BUCKLEY

EXECUTIVE PRODUCER
ALAN FINE

S.H.I.E.L.D. VOL. 1: PERFECT BULLETS. Contains material originally published in magazine form as S.H.I.E.L.D. #1-6. First printing 2015. ISBN# 978-0-7851-9362-3. Published by MARVEL WORLDWIDE, INC., a subsidiary of MARVEL ENTERTAINMENT, LLC. OFFICE OF PUBLICATION: 135 West 50th Street, New York, NY 10020. Copyright © 2015 MARVEL No similarity between any of the names, characters, persons, and/or institutions in this magazine with those of any living or dead person or institution is intended, and any such similarity which may exist is purely coincidental. **Printed in Canada.** ALAN FINE, President, Marvel Entertainment; DAN BUCKLEY, President, TV, Publishing and Brand Management; JOE QUESADA, Chief Creative Officer; TOM BREVOORT, SVP of Publishing; DAVID BOGART, SVP of Operations & Procurement, Publishing; C.B. CEBULSKI, VP of International Development & Brand Management; DAVID GABRIEL, SVP Print, Sales & Marketing; JIM O'KEEFE, VP of Operations & Logistics; DAN CARR, Executive Director of Publishing Technology; SUSAN CRESPI, Editorial Operations Manager; ALEX MORALES, Publishing Operations Manager; STAN LEE, Chairman Emeritus. For information regarding advertising in Marvel Comics or on Marvel.com, please contact Jonathan Rheingold, VP of Custom Solutions & Ad Sales, at jrheingold@marvel.com. For Marvel subscription inquiries, please call 800-217-9158. **Manufactured between 5/8/2015 and 6/15/2015 by SOLISCO PRINTERS, SCOTT, QC, CANADA.**

10 9 8 7 6 5 4 3 2 1

1. ACTIVE MISSION: PERFECT BULLETS

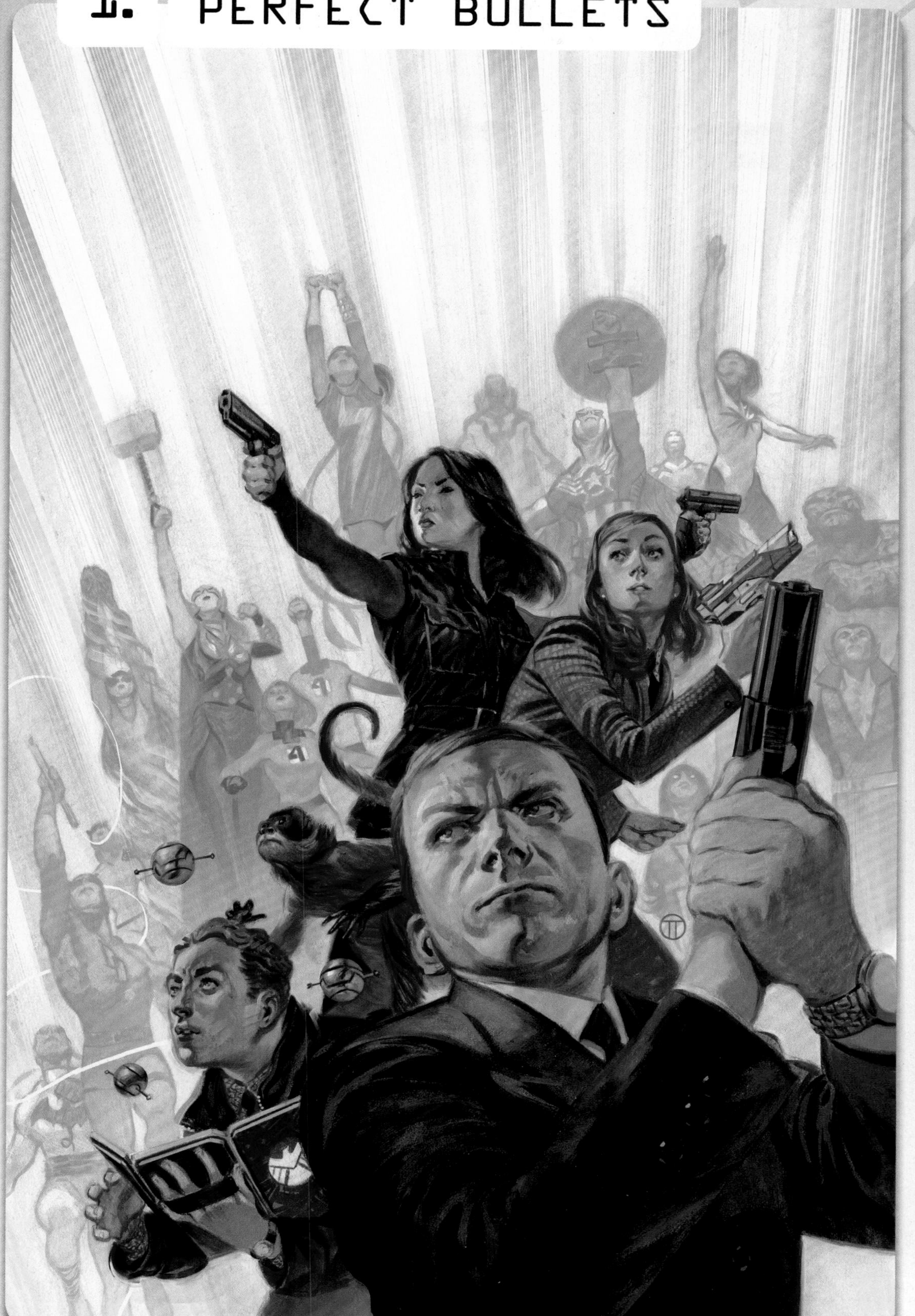

ACCESS GRANTED...

STRATEGIC HOMELAND INTERVENTION ENFORCEMENT LOGISTICS DIVISION

S.H.I.E.L.D.

PAST MISSION:

S.H.I.E.L.D., the Strategic Homeland Intervention, Enforcement and Logistics Division, mitigates and confronts threats to the security of the Earth and its people. Its highly trained agents detect and defend against any menace that might rear its ugly head against us. Among these agents is Phil Coulson—cool-headed, mild-mannered, and singularly dedicated to his work. Coulson and his fellow agents encounter mutants, monsters, villains, gods, and the best and worst of humanity on a daily basis as they endeavor to carry out S.H.I.E.L.D.'s mission.

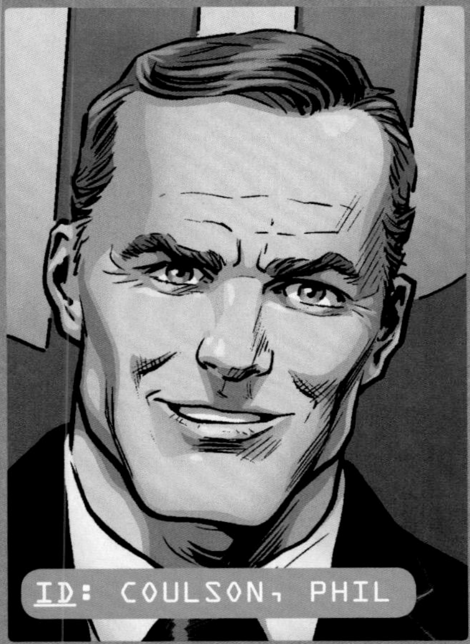
ID: COULSON, PHIL

OHIO URCHIN
PHIL COULSON,
AGE NINE.

COOOOOL.

PHIL?

The Golden Age of SUPER HEROES

PHIL! DINNER!

FIVE MINUTES, MA!

HUMAN TORCH
(Jim Hammond)
First Appearance:
New York World's
Fair, 1939
Powers: Shoots
fire, can fly,
controls h

THE AN
HUM
TOR

SYNTHETIC MAN D

THE PATRIOT
SUB-MARINER
E DESTROYER
CAPTAIN AMERICA

COLLEGE
FRESHMAN
PHIL
COULSON,
AGE
EIGHTEEN.

PHIL, C'MON! WE DON'T HAVE ENOUGH GUYS!

FIVE MINUTES, GREG.

--DOWNTOWN MANHATTAN, WHERE A BATTLE HAS ERUPTED BETWEEN THE FANTASTIC FOUR AND THE MYSTERIOUS GREEN-SKINNED BEHEMOTH KNOWN ONLY AS THE HULK--

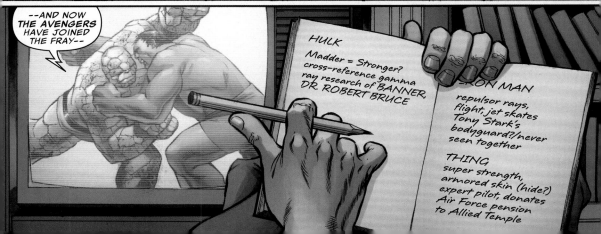

--AND NOW THE AVENGERS HAVE JOINED THE FRAY--

HULK
Madder = Stronger?
cross-reference gamma
ray research of BANNER
DR. ROBERT BRUCE

IRON MAN
repulsor rays,
flight, jet skates
Tony Stark's
bodyguard?/never
seen together

THING
super strength,
armored skin (hide?)
expert pilot, donates
Air Force pension
to Allied Temple

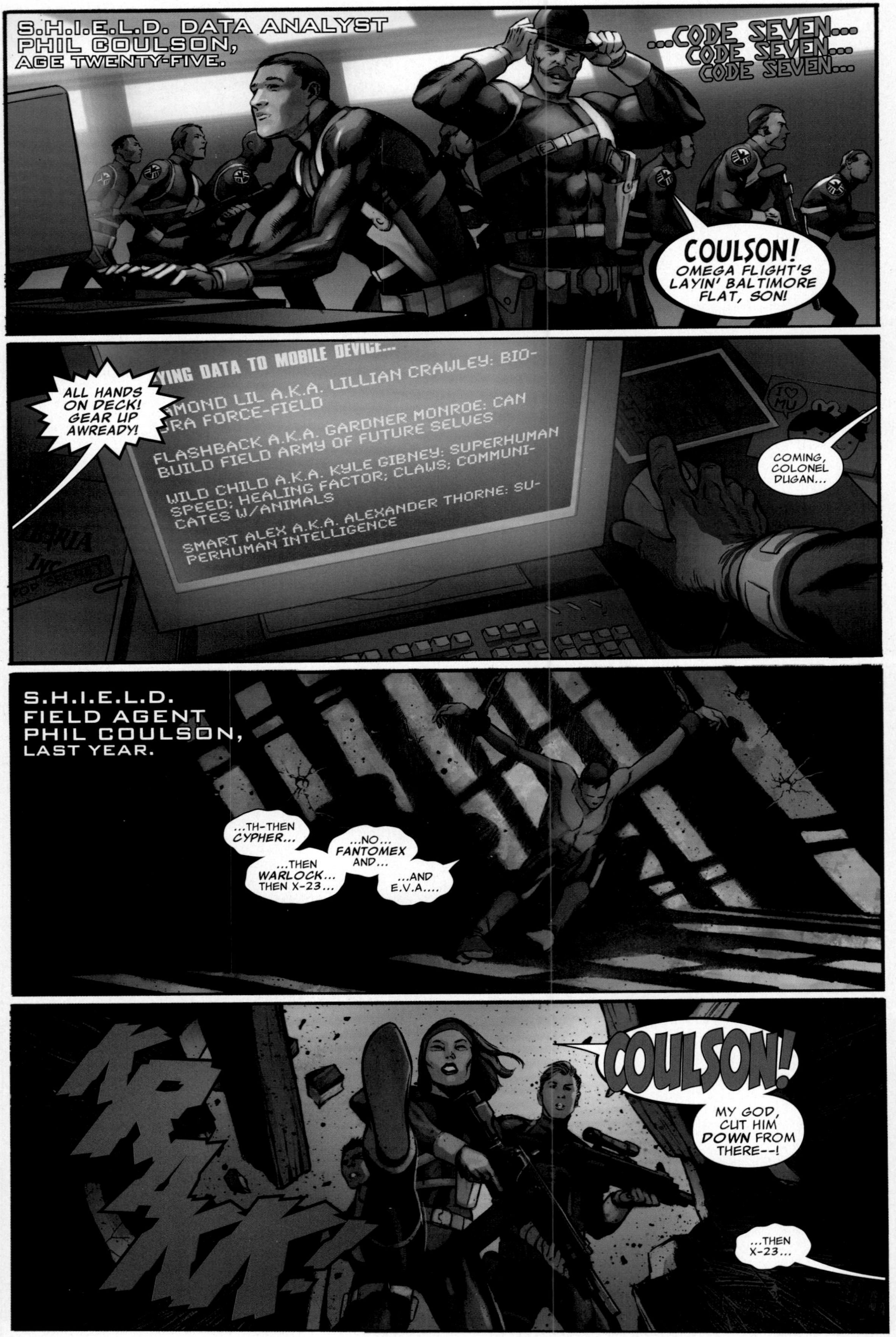
S.H.I.E.L.D. DATA ANALYST PHIL COULSON, AGE TWENTY-FIVE.
...CODE SEVEN... CODE SEVEN... CODE SEVEN...
COULSON! OMEGA FLIGHT'S LAYIN' BALTIMORE FLAT, SON!
YING DATA TO MOBILE DEVICE...
MOND LIL A.K.A. LILLIAN CRAWLEY: BIO-
RA FORCE-FIELD
FLASHBACK A.K.A. GARDNER MONROE: CAN BUILD FIELD ARMY OF FUTURE SELVES
WILD CHILD A.K.A. KYLE GIBNEY: SUPERHUMAN SPEED; HEALING FACTOR; CLAWS; COMMUNICATES W/ANIMALS
SMART ALEX A.K.A. ALEXANDER THORNE: SUPERHUMAN INTELLIGENCE
ALL HANDS ON DECK! GEAR UP AWREADY!
COMING, COLONEL DUGAN...
S.H.I.E.L.D. FIELD AGENT PHIL COULSON, LAST YEAR.
...TH-THEN CYPHER...
...THEN WARLOCK... THEN X-23...
...NO... FANTOMEX AND...
...AND E.V.A....
COULSON!
MY GOD, CUT HIM DOWN FROM THERE--!
...THEN X-23...

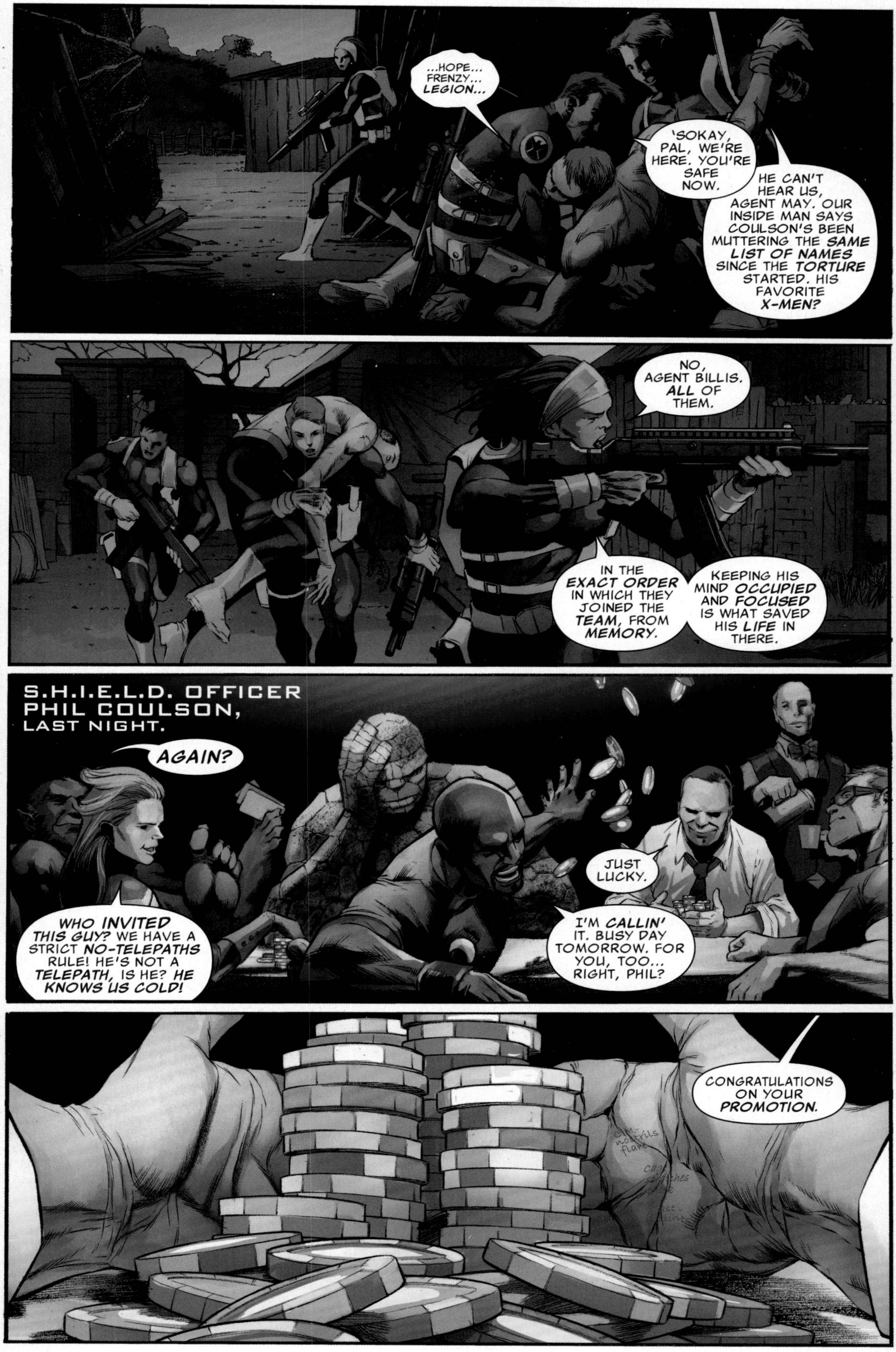
...HOPE... FRENZY... LEGION...
'SOKAY, PAL, WE'RE HERE. YOU'RE SAFE NOW.
HE CAN'T HEAR US, AGENT MAY. OUR INSIDE MAN SAYS COULSON'S BEEN MUTTERING THE SAME LIST OF NAMES SINCE THE TORTURE STARTED. HIS FAVORITE X-MEN?
NO, AGENT BILLIS. ALL OF THEM.
IN THE EXACT ORDER IN WHICH THEY JOINED THE TEAM, FROM MEMORY.
KEEPING HIS MIND OCCUPIED AND FOCUSED IS WHAT SAVED HIS LIFE IN THERE.
S.H.I.E.L.D. OFFICER PHIL COULSON, LAST NIGHT.
AGAIN?
WHO INVITED THIS GUY? WE HAVE A STRICT NO-TELEPATHS RULE! HE'S NOT A TELEPATH, IS HE? HE KNOWS US COLD!
JUST LUCKY.
I'M CALLIN' IT. BUSY DAY TOMORROW. FOR YOU, TOO... RIGHT, PHIL?
CONGRATULATIONS ON YOUR PROMOTION.

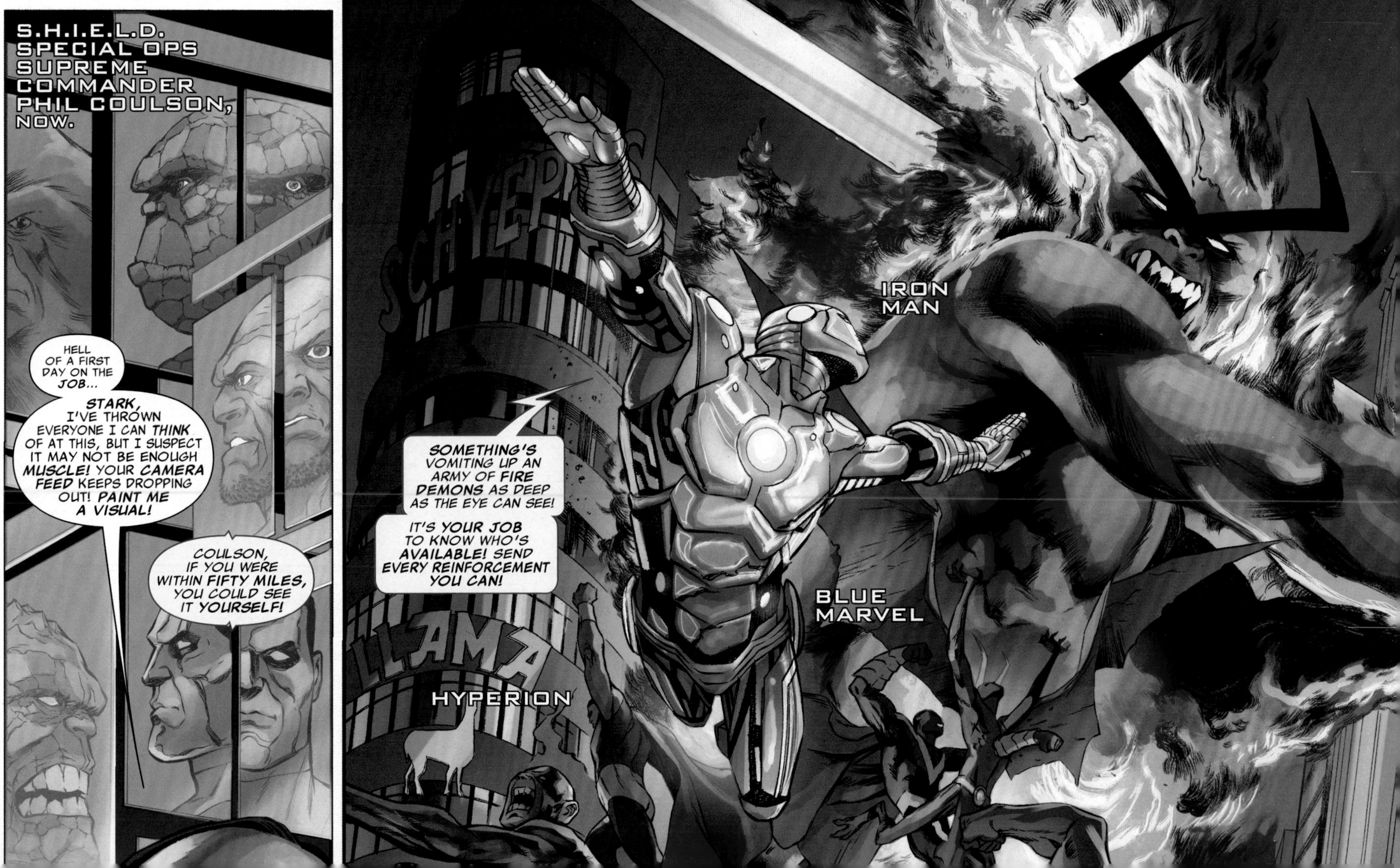
S.H.I.E.L.D. SPECIAL OPS SUPREME COMMANDER PHIL COULSON, NOW.
HELL OF A FIRST DAY ON THE JOB...
STARK, I'VE THROWN EVERYONE I CAN THINK OF AT THIS, BUT I SUSPECT IT MAY NOT BE ENOUGH MUSCLE! YOUR CAMERA FEED KEEPS DROPPING OUT! PAINT ME A VISUAL!
COULSON, IF YOU WERE WITHIN FIFTY MILES, YOU COULD SEE IT YOURSELF!
SOMETHING'S VOMITING UP AN ARMY OF FIRE DEMONS AS DEEP AS THE EYE CAN SEE!
IT'S YOUR JOB TO KNOW WHO'S AVAILABLE! SEND EVERY REINFORCEMENT YOU CAN!
IRON MAN
BLUE MARVEL
HYPERION
LLAMA

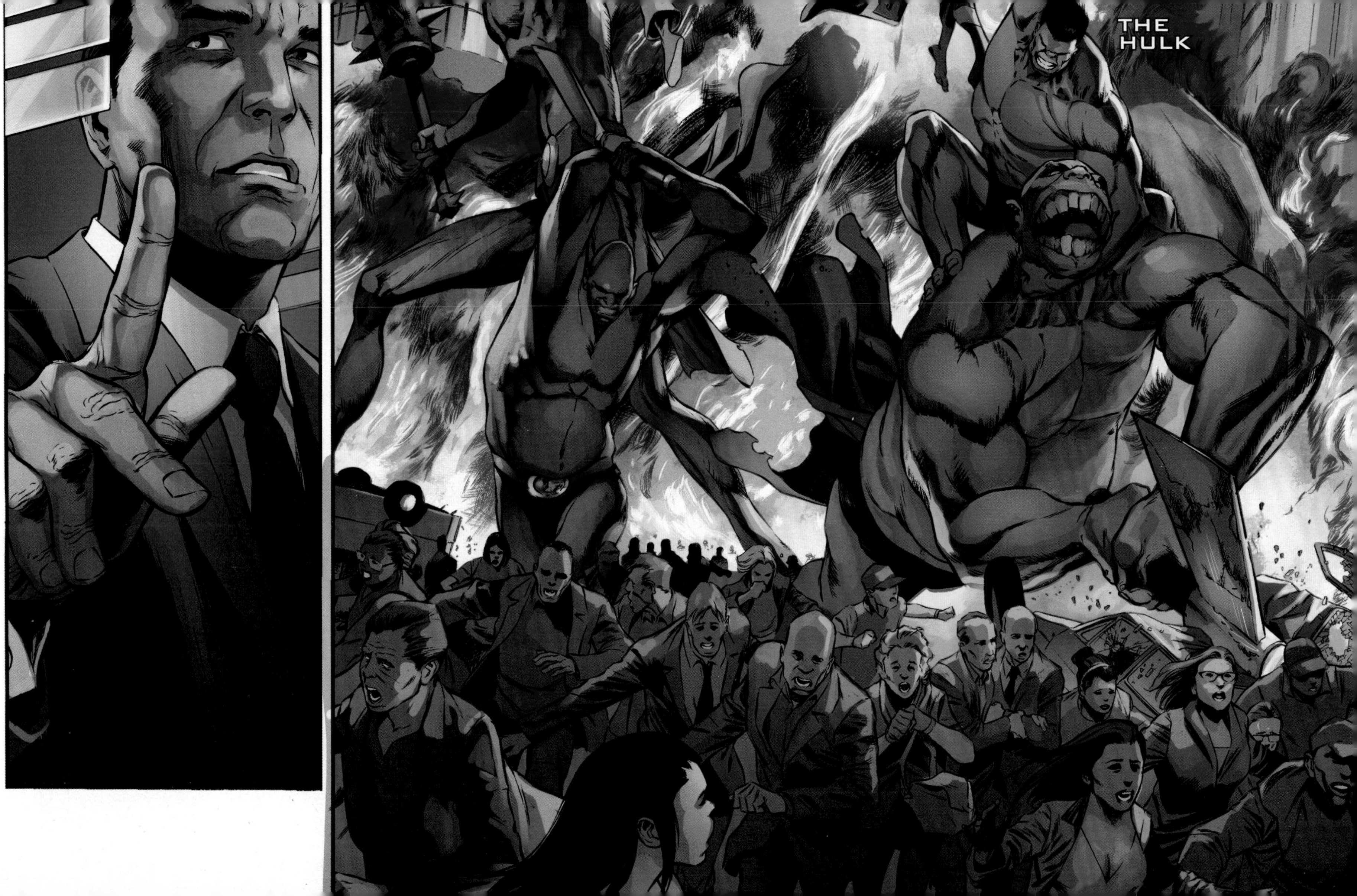
THE
HULK

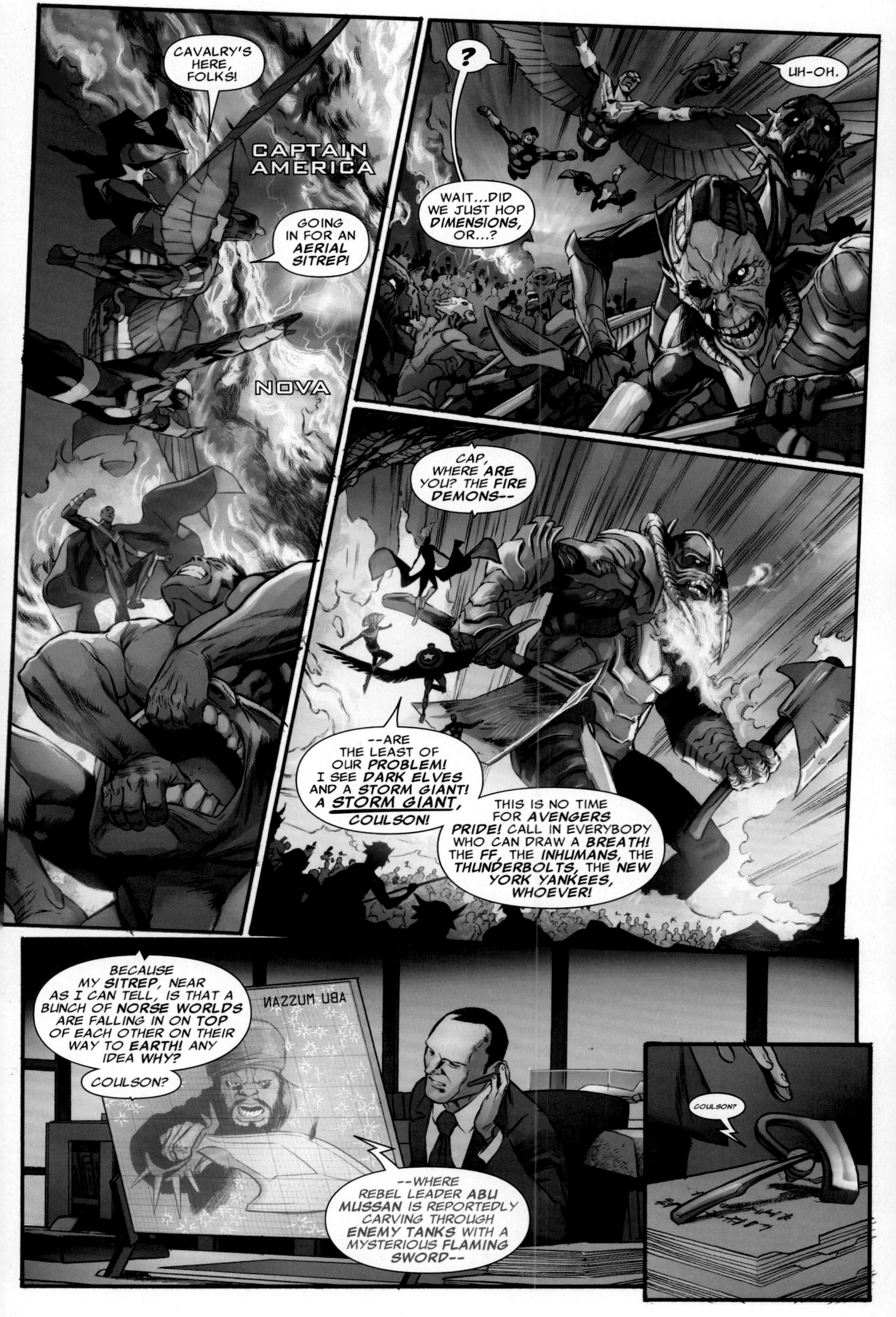
CAVALRY'S HERE, FOLKS!
CAPTAIN AMERICA
GOING IN FOR AN AERIAL SITREP!
NOVA
?
WAIT...DID WE JUST HOP DIMENSIONS, OR...?
UH-OH.
CAP, WHERE ARE YOU? THE FIRE DEMONS--
--ARE THE LEAST OF OUR PROBLEM! I SEE DARK ELVES AND A STORM GIANT! A STORM GIANT, COULSON!
THIS IS NO TIME FOR AVENGERS PRIDE! CALL IN EVERYBODY WHO CAN DRAW A BREATH! THE FF, THE INHUMANS, THE THUNDERBOLTS, THE NEW YORK YANKEES, WHOEVER!
BECAUSE MY SITREP, NEAR AS I CAN TELL, IS THAT A BUNCH OF NORSE WORLDS ARE FALLING IN ON TOP OF EACH OTHER ON THEIR WAY TO EARTH! ANY IDEA WHY?
COULSON?
ABU MUSSAN
--WHERE REBEL LEADER ABU MUSSAN IS REPORTEDLY CARVING THROUGH ENEMY TANKS WITH A MYSTERIOUS FLAMING SWORD--
COULSON?

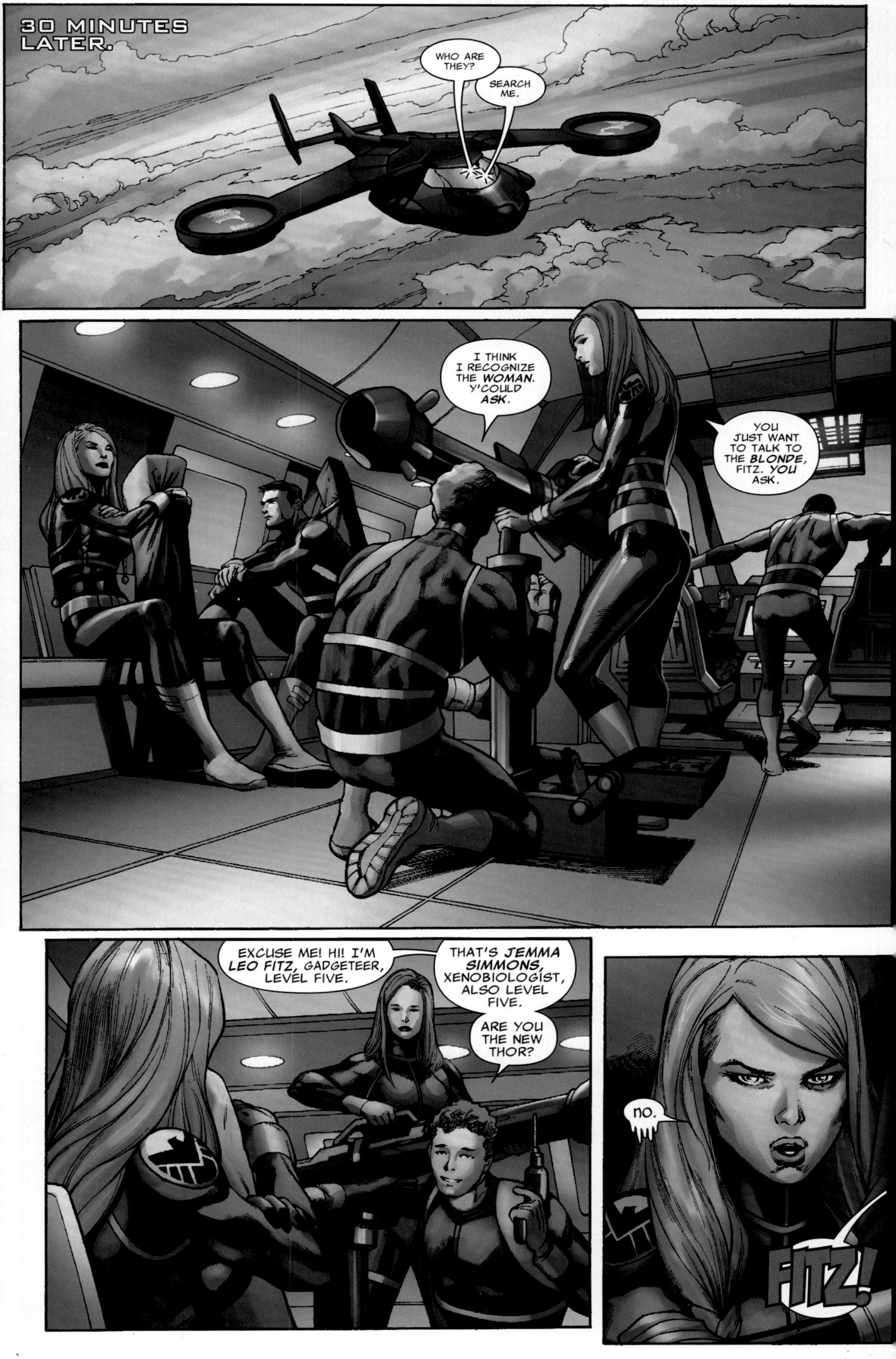
30 MINUTES LATER.
WHO ARE THEY?
SEARCH ME.
I THINK I RECOGNIZE THE WOMAN. Y'COULD ASK.
YOU JUST WANT TO TALK TO THE BLONDE, FITZ. YOU ASK.
EXCUSE ME! HI! I'M LEO FITZ, GADGETEER, LEVEL FIVE.
THAT'S JEMMA SIMMONS, XENOBIOLOGIST, ALSO LEVEL FIVE.
ARE YOU THE NEW THOR?
no.
FITZ!

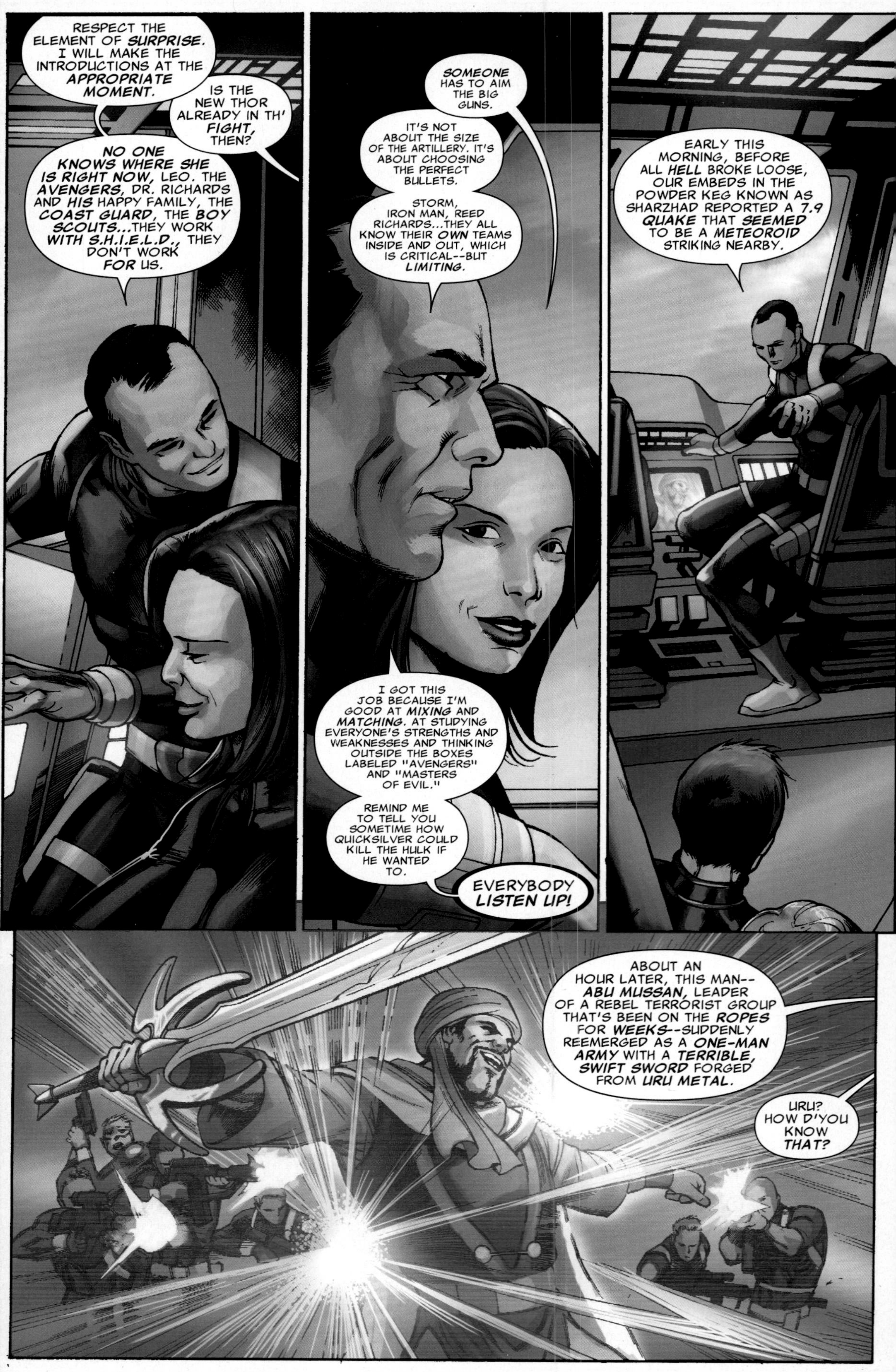

RESPECT THE ELEMENT OF SURPRISE. I WILL MAKE THE INTRODUCTIONS AT THE APPROPRIATE MOMENT.
IS THE NEW THOR ALREADY IN TH' FIGHT, THEN?
NO ONE KNOWS WHERE SHE IS RIGHT NOW, LEO. THE AVENGERS, DR. RICHARDS AND HIS HAPPY FAMILY, THE COAST GUARD, THE BOY SCOUTS...THEY WORK WITH S.H.I.E.L.D., THEY DON'T WORK FOR US.
SOMEONE HAS TO AIM THE BIG GUNS.
IT'S NOT ABOUT THE SIZE OF THE ARTILLERY. IT'S ABOUT CHOOSING THE PERFECT BULLETS.
STORM, IRON MAN, REED RICHARDS...THEY ALL KNOW THEIR OWN TEAMS INSIDE AND OUT, WHICH IS CRITICAL--BUT LIMITING.
I GOT THIS JOB BECAUSE I'M GOOD AT MIXING AND MATCHING. AT STUDYING EVERYONE'S STRENGTHS AND WEAKNESSES AND THINKING OUTSIDE THE BOXES LABELED "AVENGERS" AND "MASTERS OF EVIL."
REMIND ME TO TELL YOU SOMETIME HOW QUICKSILVER COULD KILL THE HULK IF HE WANTED TO.
EVERYBODY LISTEN UP!
EARLY THIS MORNING, BEFORE ALL HELL BROKE LOOSE, OUR EMBEDS IN THE POWDER KEG KNOWN AS SHARZHAD REPORTED A 7.9 QUAKE THAT SEEMED TO BE A METEOROID STRIKING NEARBY.
ABOUT AN HOUR LATER, THIS MAN-- ABU MUSSAN, LEADER OF A REBEL TERRORIST GROUP THAT'S BEEN ON THE ROPES FOR WEEKS--SUDDENLY REEMERGED AS A ONE-MAN ARMY WITH A TERRIBLE, SWIFT SWORD FORGED FROM URU METAL.
URU? HOW D'YOU KNOW THAT?

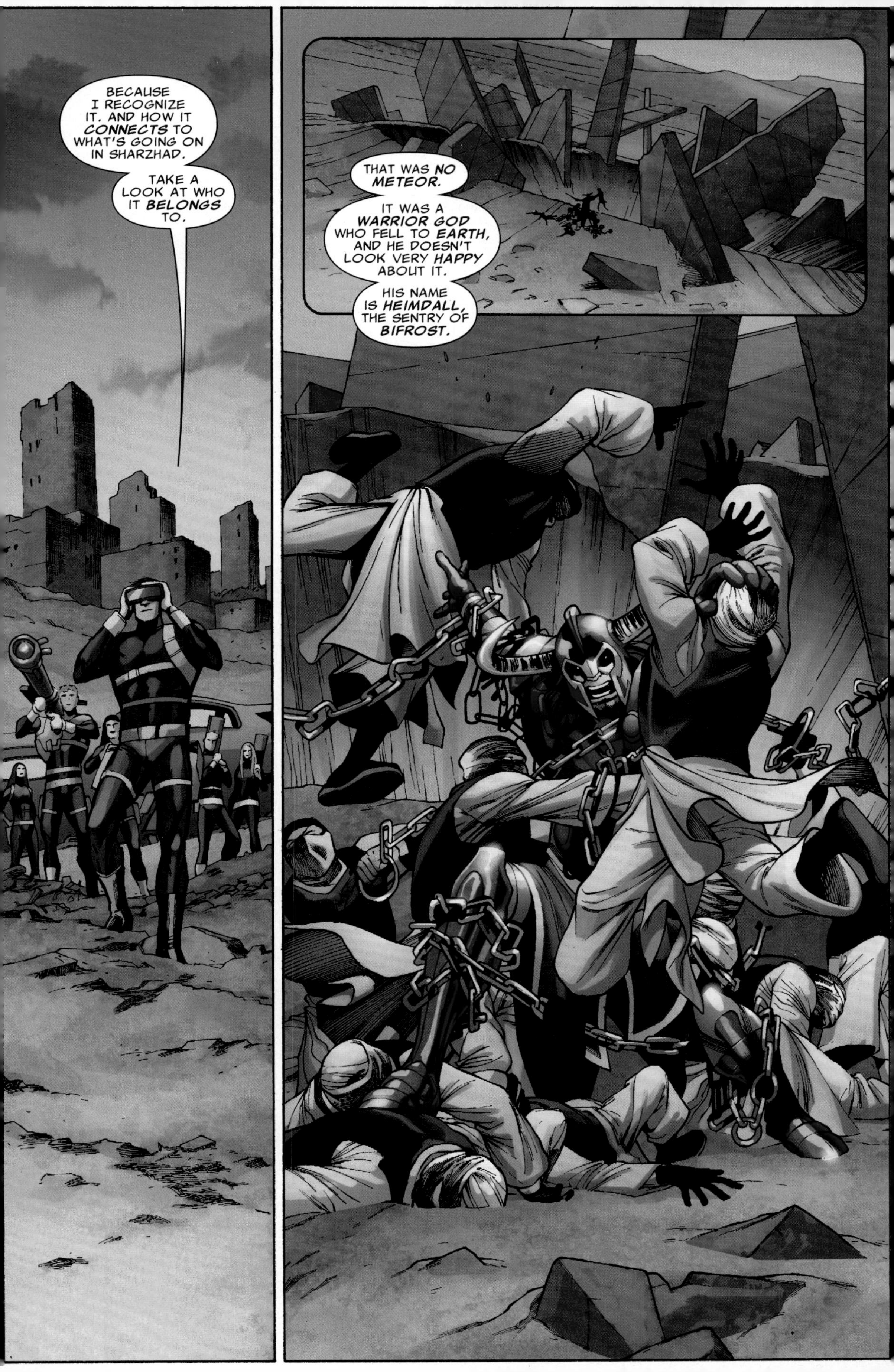

BECAUSE I RECOGNIZE IT. AND HOW IT CONNECTS TO WHAT'S GOING ON IN SHARZHAD.
TAKE A LOOK AT WHO IT BELONGS TO.
THAT WAS NO METEOR.
IT WAS A WARRIOR GOD WHO FELL TO EARTH, AND HE DOESN'T LOOK VERY HAPPY ABOUT IT.
HIS NAME IS HEIMDALL, THE SENTRY OF BIFROST.

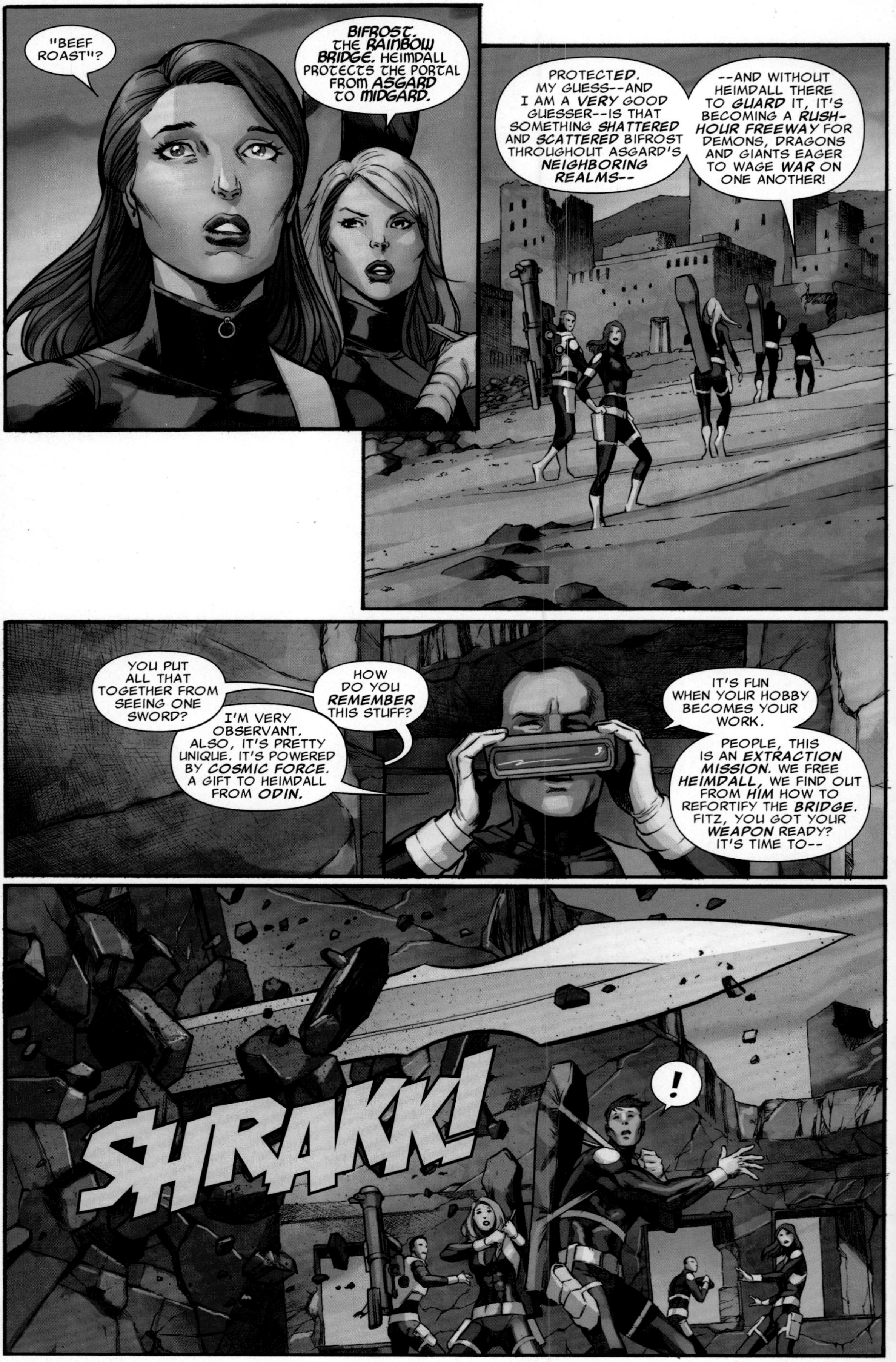
"BEEF ROAST"?
BIFROST. THE RAINBOW BRIDGE. HEIMDALL PROTECTS THE PORTAL FROM ASGARD TO MIDGARD.
PROTECTED. MY GUESS--AND I AM A VERY GOOD GUESSER--IS THAT SOMETHING SHATTERED AND SCATTERED BIFROST THROUGHOUT ASGARD'S NEIGHBORING REALMS--
--AND WITHOUT HEIMDALL THERE TO GUARD IT, IT'S BECOMING A RUSH-HOUR FREEWAY FOR DEMONS, DRAGONS AND GIANTS EAGER TO WAGE WAR ON ONE ANOTHER!
YOU PUT ALL THAT TOGETHER FROM SEEING ONE SWORD?
I'M VERY OBSERVANT. ALSO, IT'S PRETTY UNIQUE. IT'S POWERED BY COSMIC FORCE. A GIFT TO HEIMDALL FROM ODIN.
HOW DO YOU REMEMBER THIS STUFF?
IT'S FUN WHEN YOUR HOBBY BECOMES YOUR WORK.
PEOPLE, THIS IS AN EXTRACTION MISSION. WE FREE HEIMDALL, WE FIND OUT FROM HIM HOW TO REFORTIFY THE BRIDGE. FITZ, YOU GOT YOUR WEAPON READY? IT'S TIME TO--
SHRAKK!
!

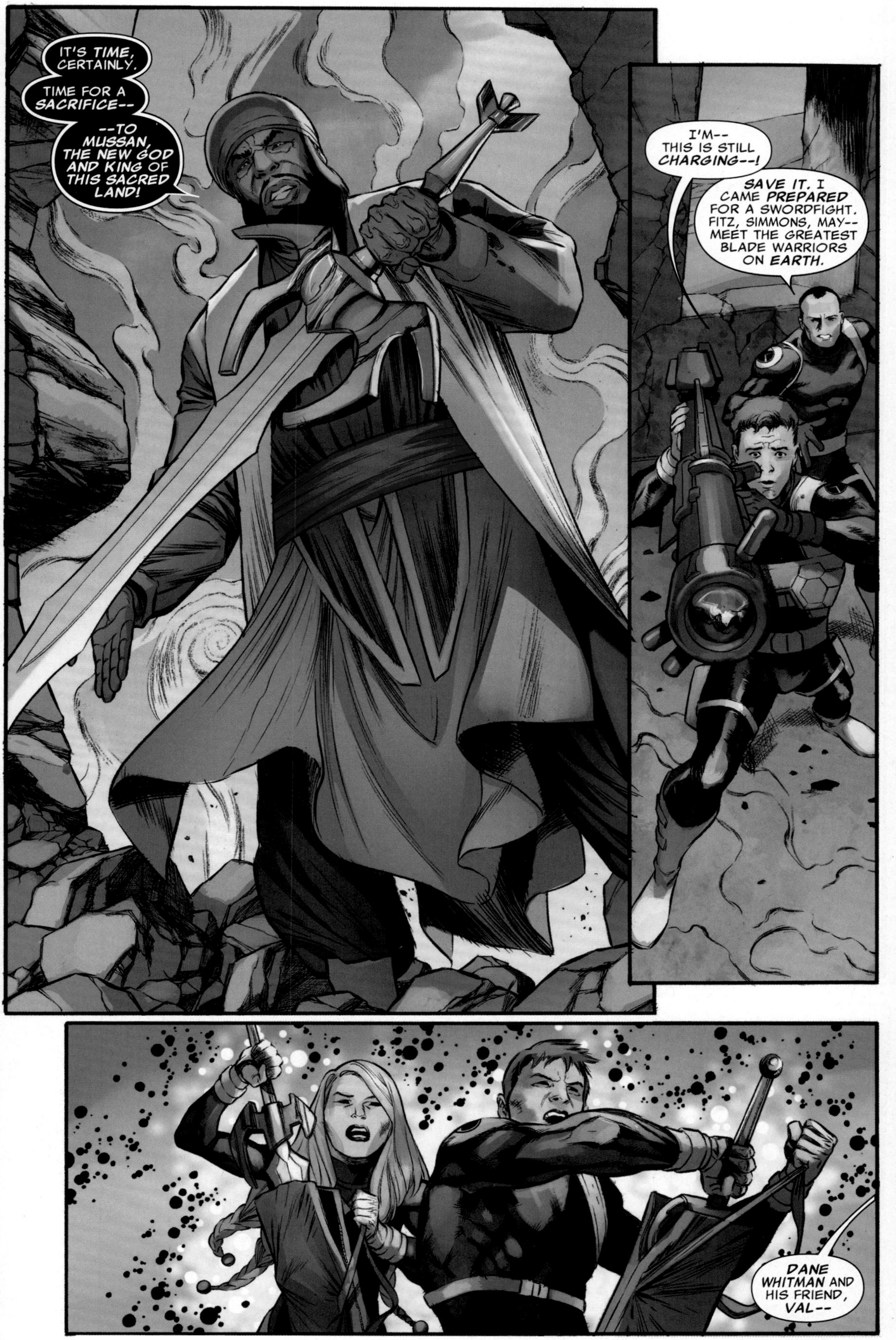
IT'S TIME, CERTAINLY.
TIME FOR A SACRIFICE--
--TO MUSSAN, THE NEW GOD AND KING OF THIS SACRED LAND!
I'M-- THIS IS STILL CHARGING--!
SAVE IT. I CAME PREPARED FOR A SWORDFIGHT. FITZ, SIMMONS, MAY-- MEET THE GREATEST BLADE WARRIORS ON EARTH.
DANE WHITMAN AND HIS FRIEND, VAL--

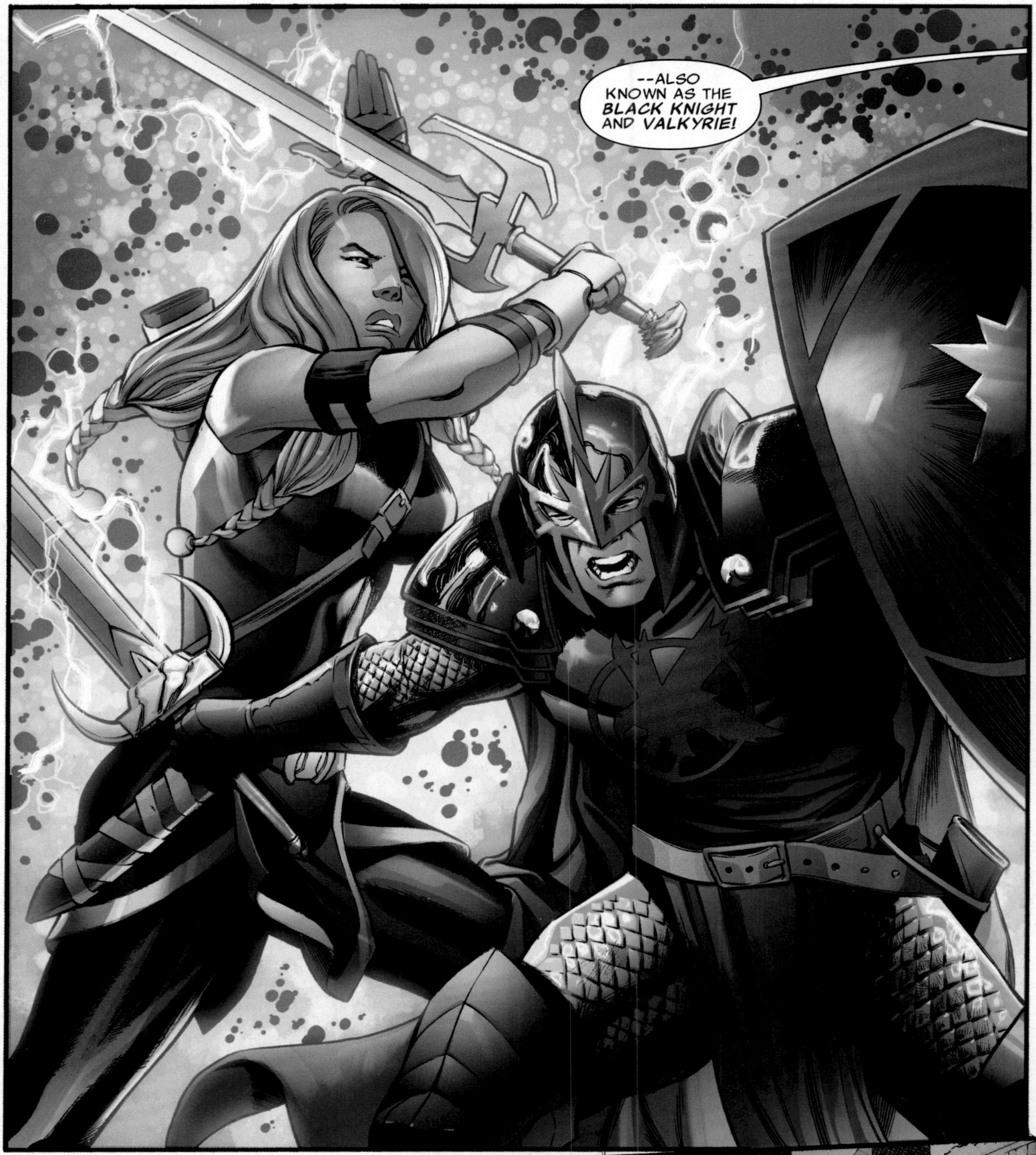
--ALSO KNOWN AS THE BLACK KNIGHT AND VALKYRIE!

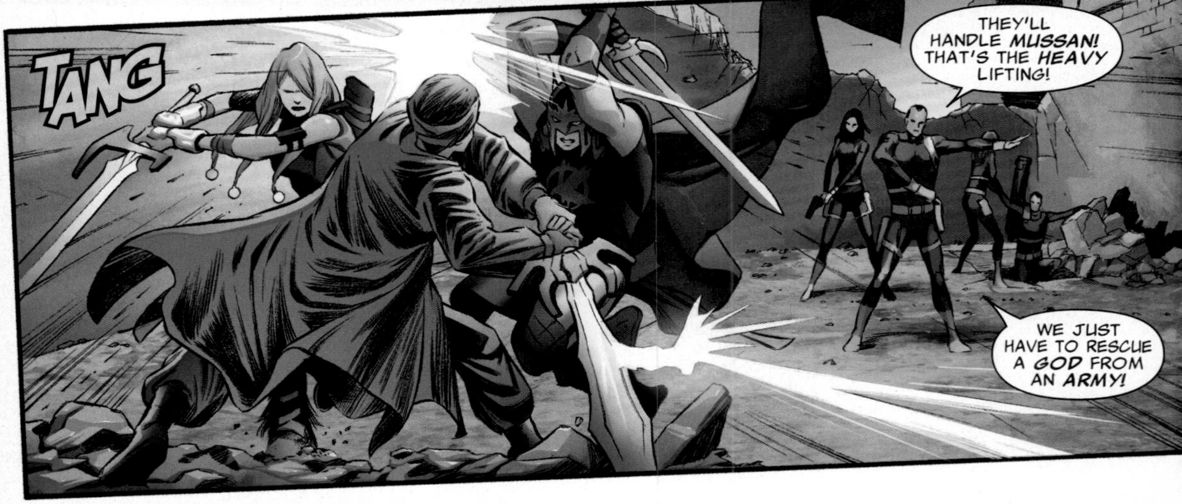
TANG
THEY'LL HANDLE MUSSAN! THAT'S THE HEAVY LIFTING!
WE JUST HAVE TO RESCUE A GOD FROM AN ARMY!

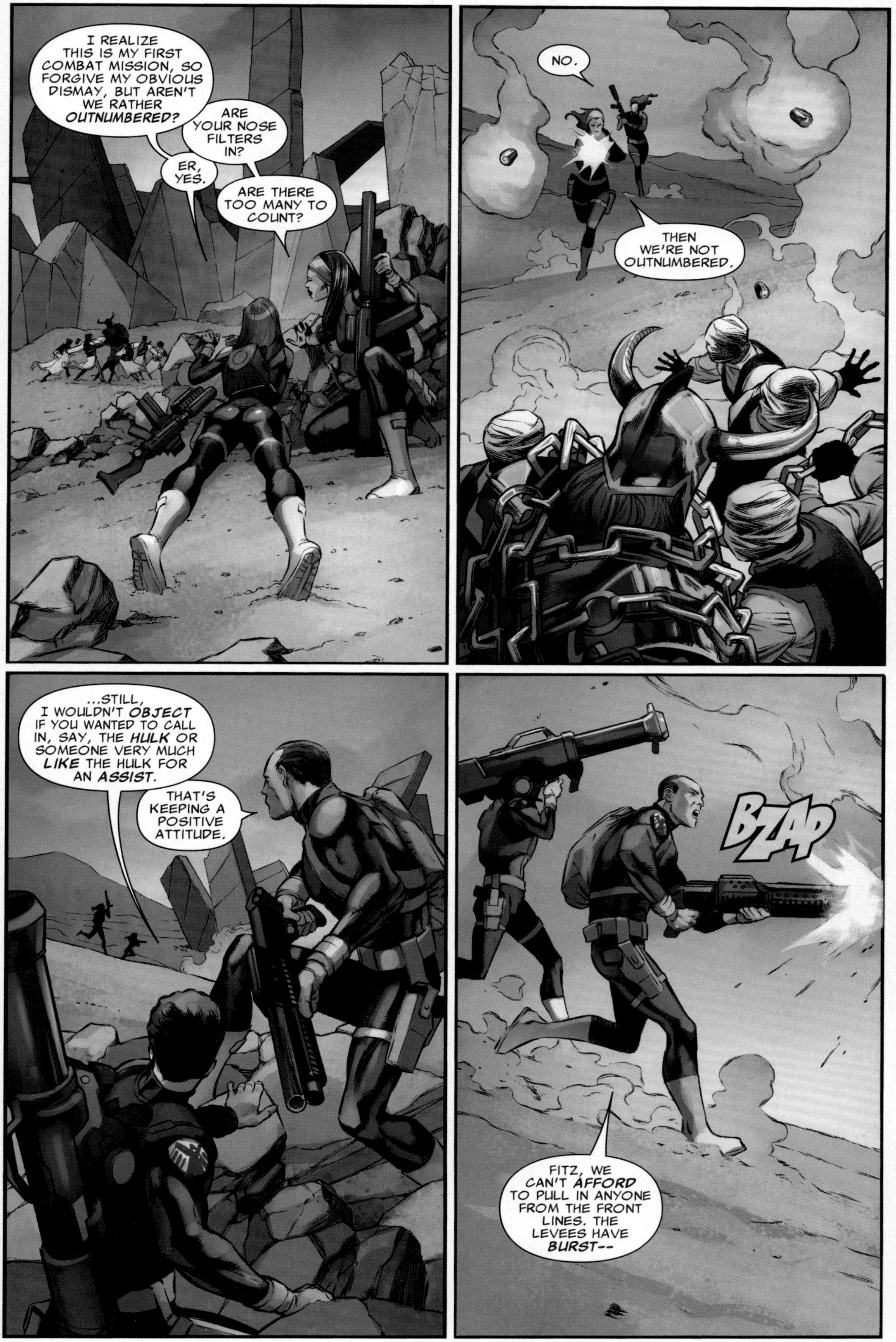
I REALIZE THIS IS MY FIRST COMBAT MISSION, SO FORGIVE MY OBVIOUS DISMAY, BUT AREN'T WE RATHER OUTNUMBERED?
ARE YOUR NOSE FILTERS IN?
ER, YES.
ARE THERE TOO MANY TO COUNT?
NO.
THEN WE'RE NOT OUTNUMBERED.
...STILL, I WOULDN'T OBJECT IF YOU WANTED TO CALL IN, SAY, THE HULK OR SOMEONE VERY MUCH LIKE THE HULK FOR AN ASSIST.
THAT'S KEEPING A POSITIVE ATTITUDE.
BZAP
FITZ, WE CAN'T AFFORD TO PULL IN ANYONE FROM THE FRONT LINES. THE LEVEES HAVE BURST--

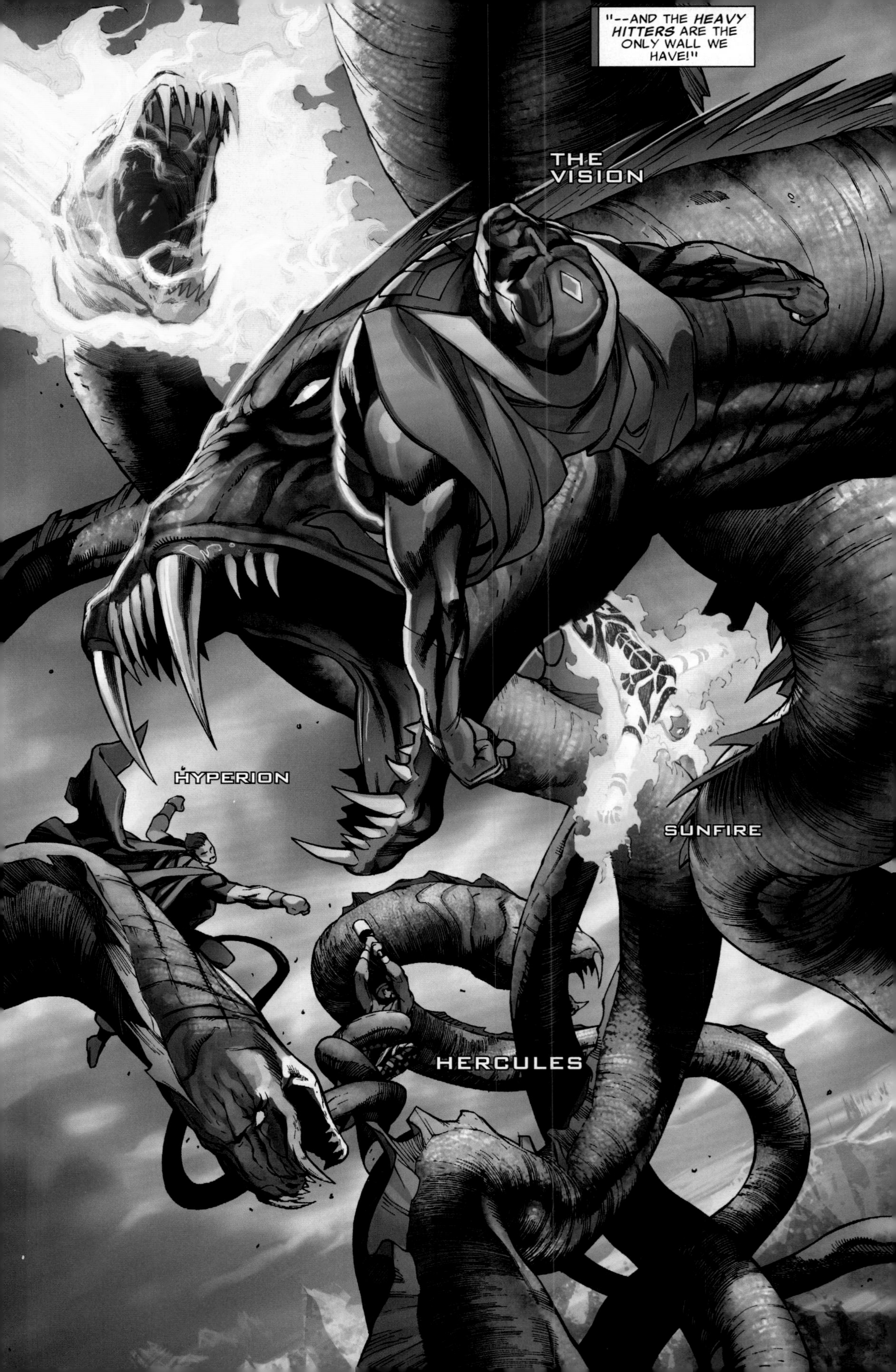
"--AND THE HEAVY HITTERS ARE THE ONLY WALL WE HAVE!"
THE VISION
HYPERION
SUNFIRE
HERCULES

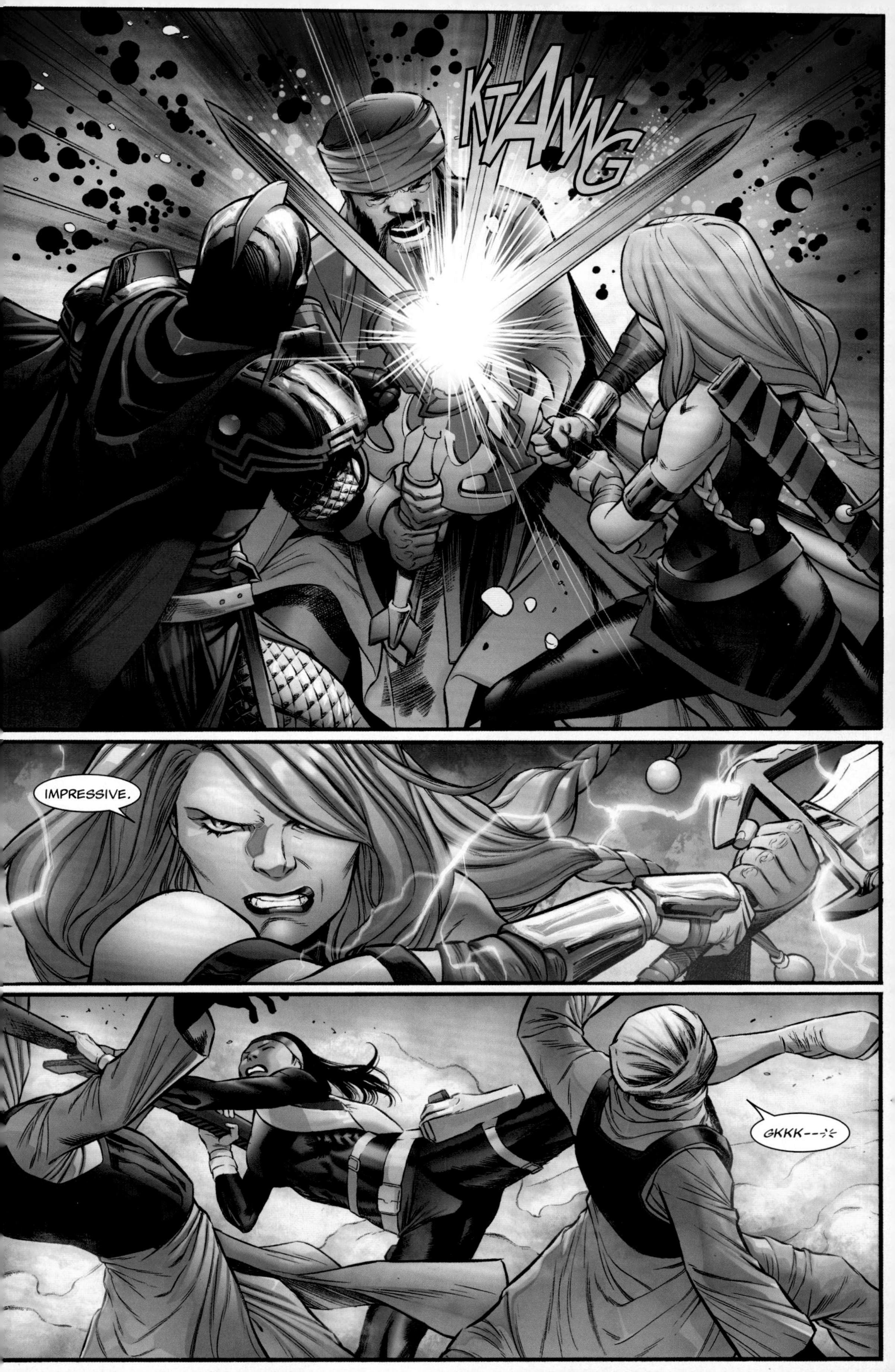
KTANNG
IMPRESSIVE.
GKKK--

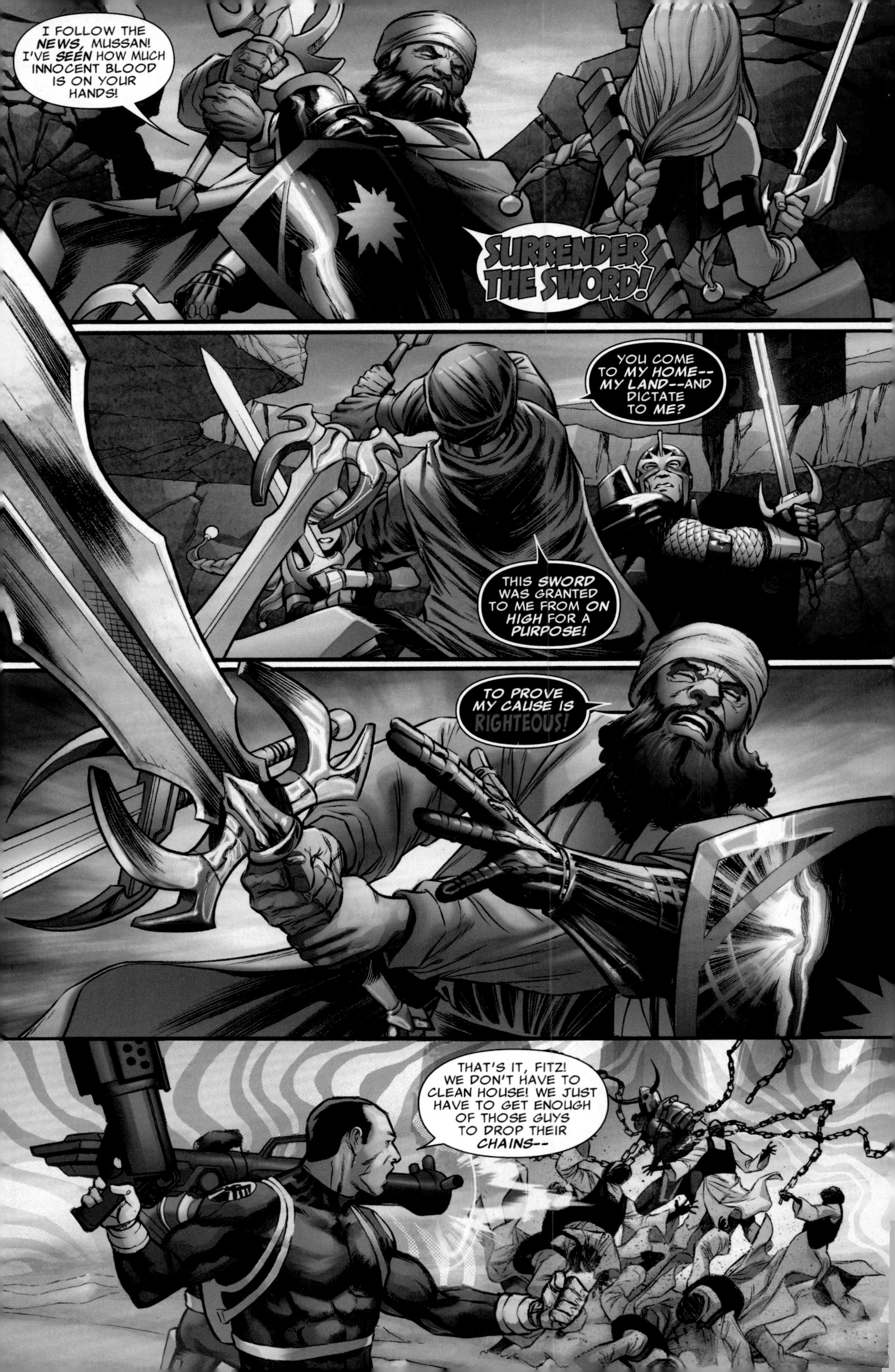
I FOLLOW THE NEWS, MUSSAN! I'VE SEEN HOW MUCH INNOCENT BLOOD IS ON YOUR HANDS!
SURRENDER THE SWORD!
YOU COME TO MY HOME-- MY LAND--AND DICTATE TO ME?
THIS SWORD WAS GRANTED TO ME FROM ON HIGH FOR A PURPOSE!
TO PROVE MY CAUSE IS RIGHTEOUS!
THAT'S IT, FITZ! WE DON'T HAVE TO CLEAN HOUSE! WE JUST HAVE TO GET ENOUGH OF THOSE GUYS TO DROP THEIR CHAINS--

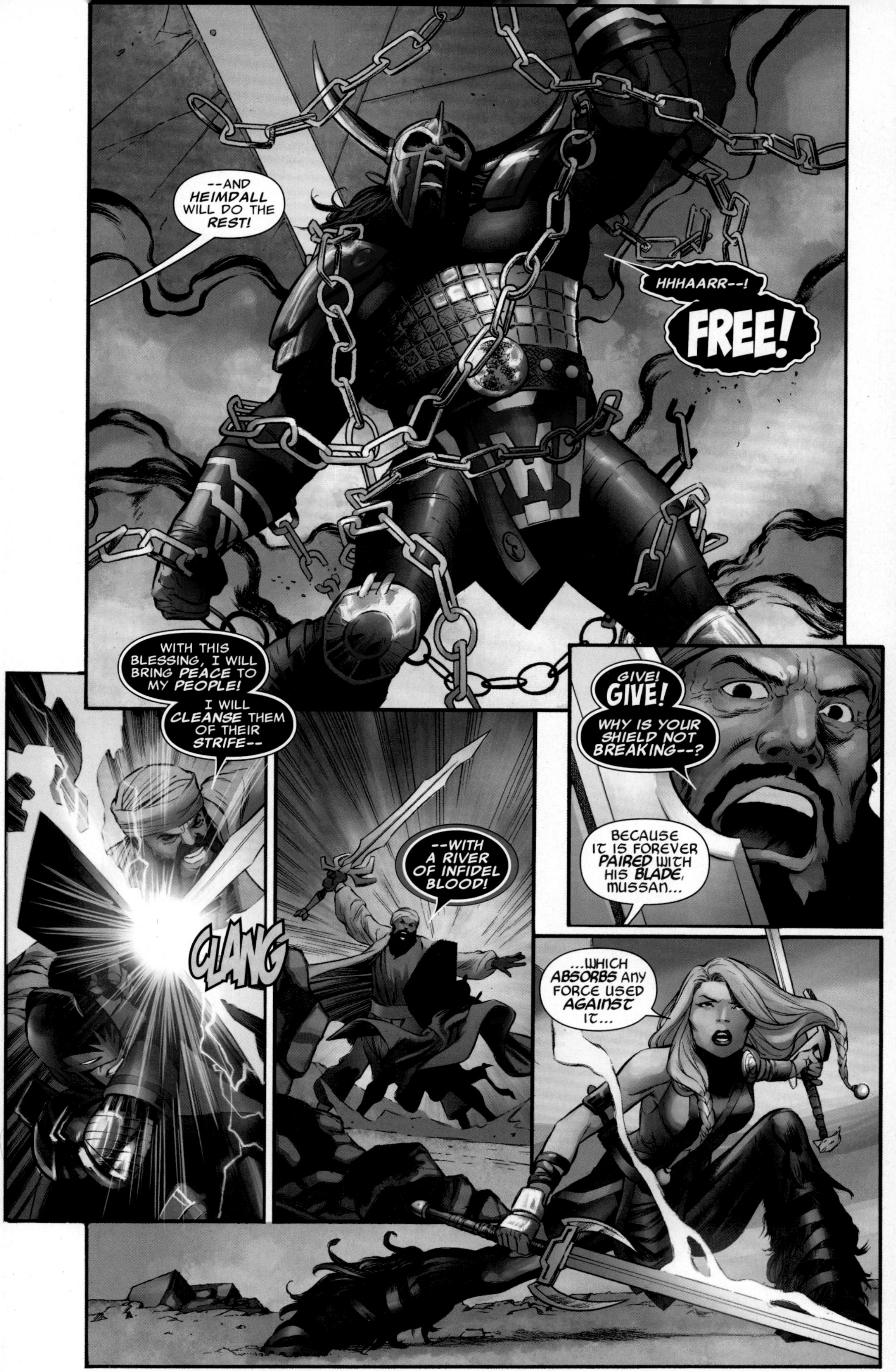
--AND HEIMDALL WILL DO THE REST!
HHHAARR--!
FREE!
WITH THIS BLESSING, I WILL BRING PEACE TO MY PEOPLE!
I WILL CLEANSE THEM OF THEIR STRIFE--
CLANG
--WITH A RIVER OF INFIDEL BLOOD!
GIVE! GIVE!
WHY IS YOUR SHIELD NOT BREAKING--?
BECAUSE IT IS FOREVER PAIRED WITH HIS BLADE, MUSSAN...
...WHICH ABSORBS ANY FORCE USED AGAINST IT...

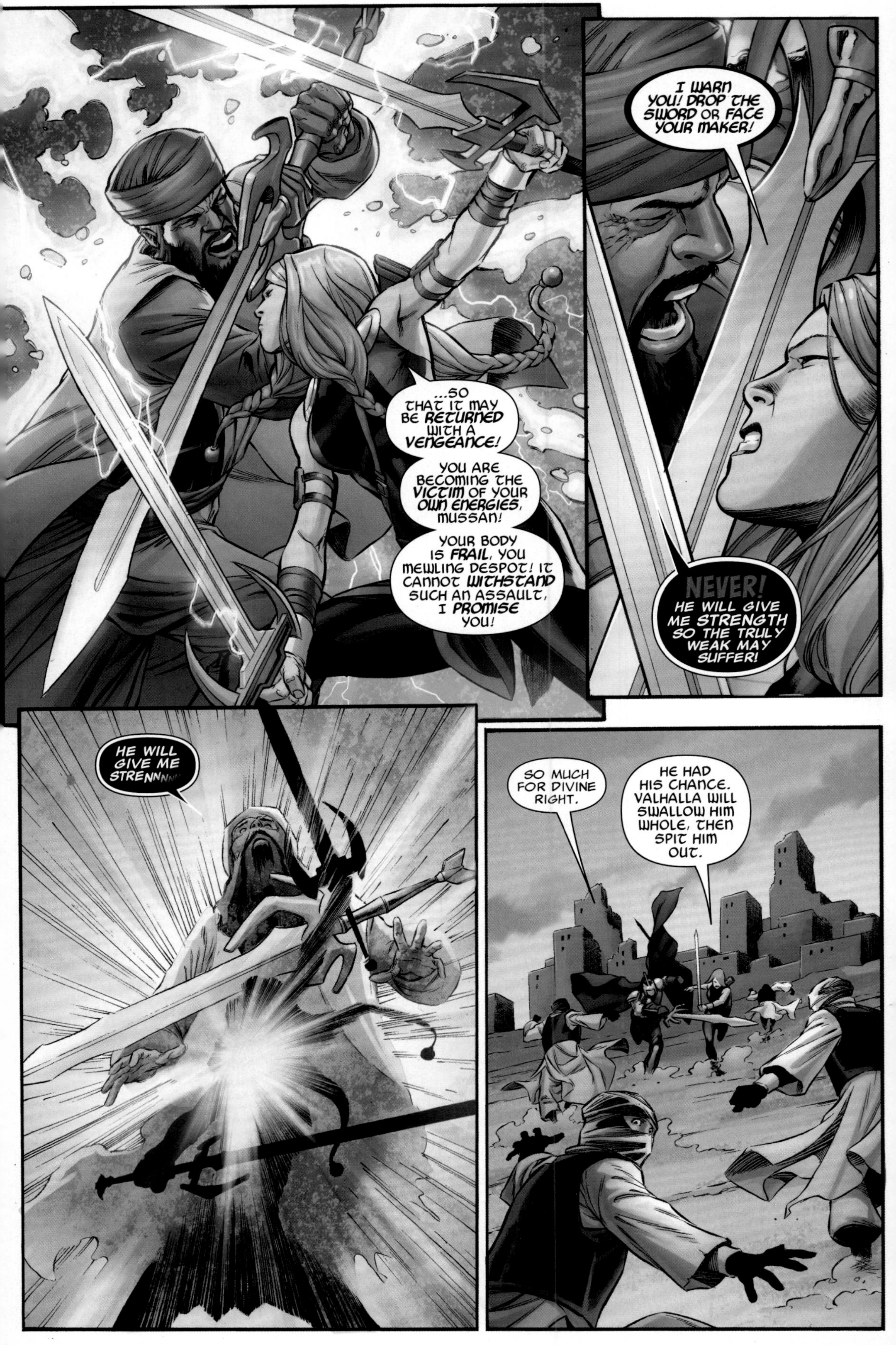
...SO THAT IT MAY BE RETURNED WITH A VENGEANCE!
YOU ARE BECOMING THE VICTIM OF YOUR OWN ENERGIES, MUSSAN!
YOUR BODY IS FRAIL, YOU MEWLING DESPOT! IT CANNOT WITHSTAND SUCH AN ASSAULT, I PROMISE YOU!
I WARN YOU! DROP THE SWORD OR FACE YOUR MAKER!
NEVER! HE WILL GIVE ME STRENGTH SO THE TRULY WEAK MAY SUFFER!
HE WILL GIVE ME STRENNNNN
SO MUCH FOR DIVINE RIGHT.
HE HAD HIS CHANCE. VALHALLA WILL SWALLOW HIM WHOLE, THEN SPIT HIM OUT.

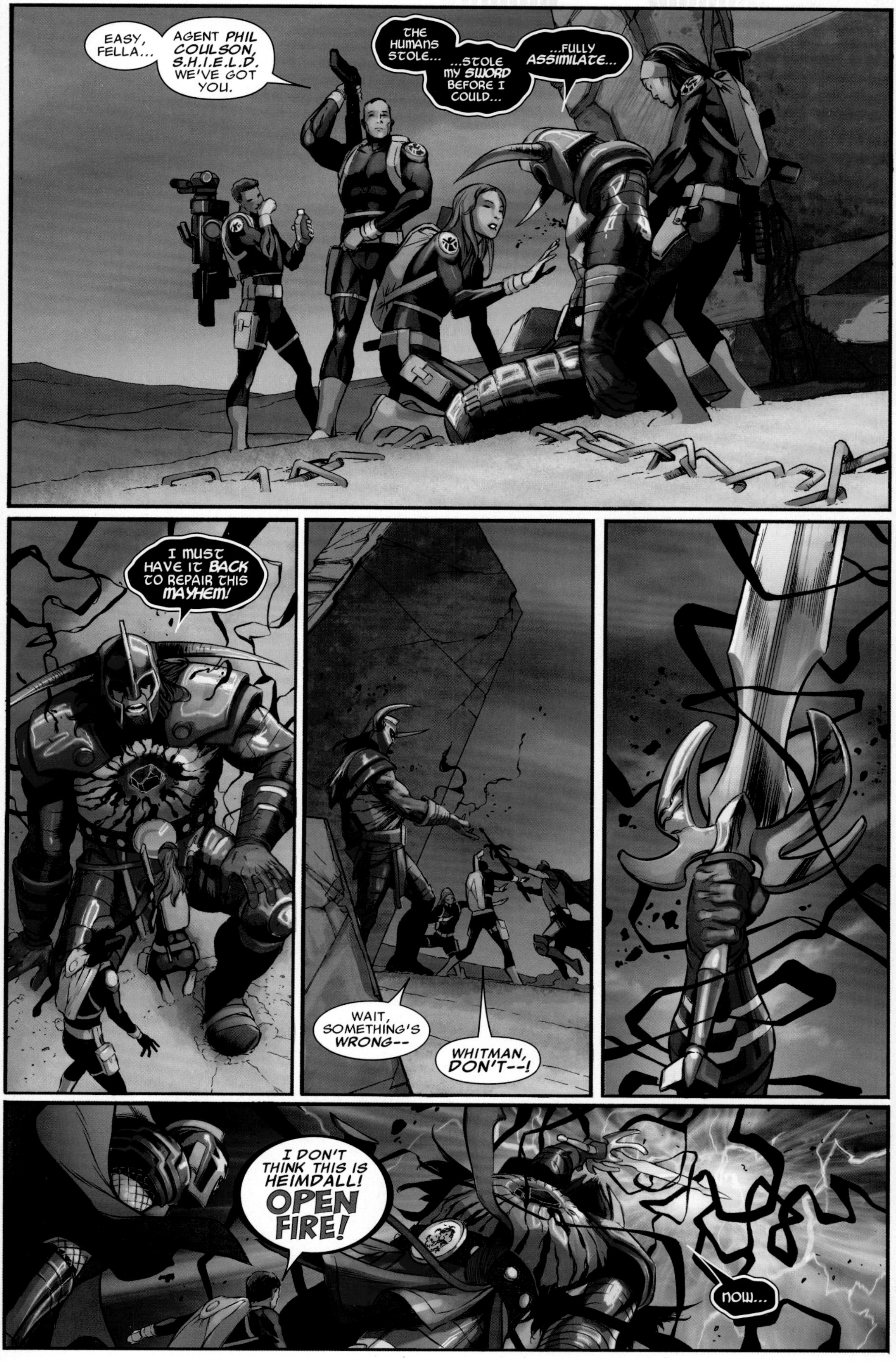
EASY, FELLA...
AGENT PHIL COULSON, S.H.I.E.L.D. WE'VE GOT YOU.
THE HUMANS STOLE...
...STOLE MY SWORD BEFORE I COULD...
...FULLY ASSIMILATE...
I MUST HAVE IT BACK TO REPAIR THIS MAYHEM!
WAIT, SOMETHING'S WRONG--
WHITMAN, DON'T--!
I DON'T THINK THIS IS HEIMDALL! OPEN FIRE!
now...

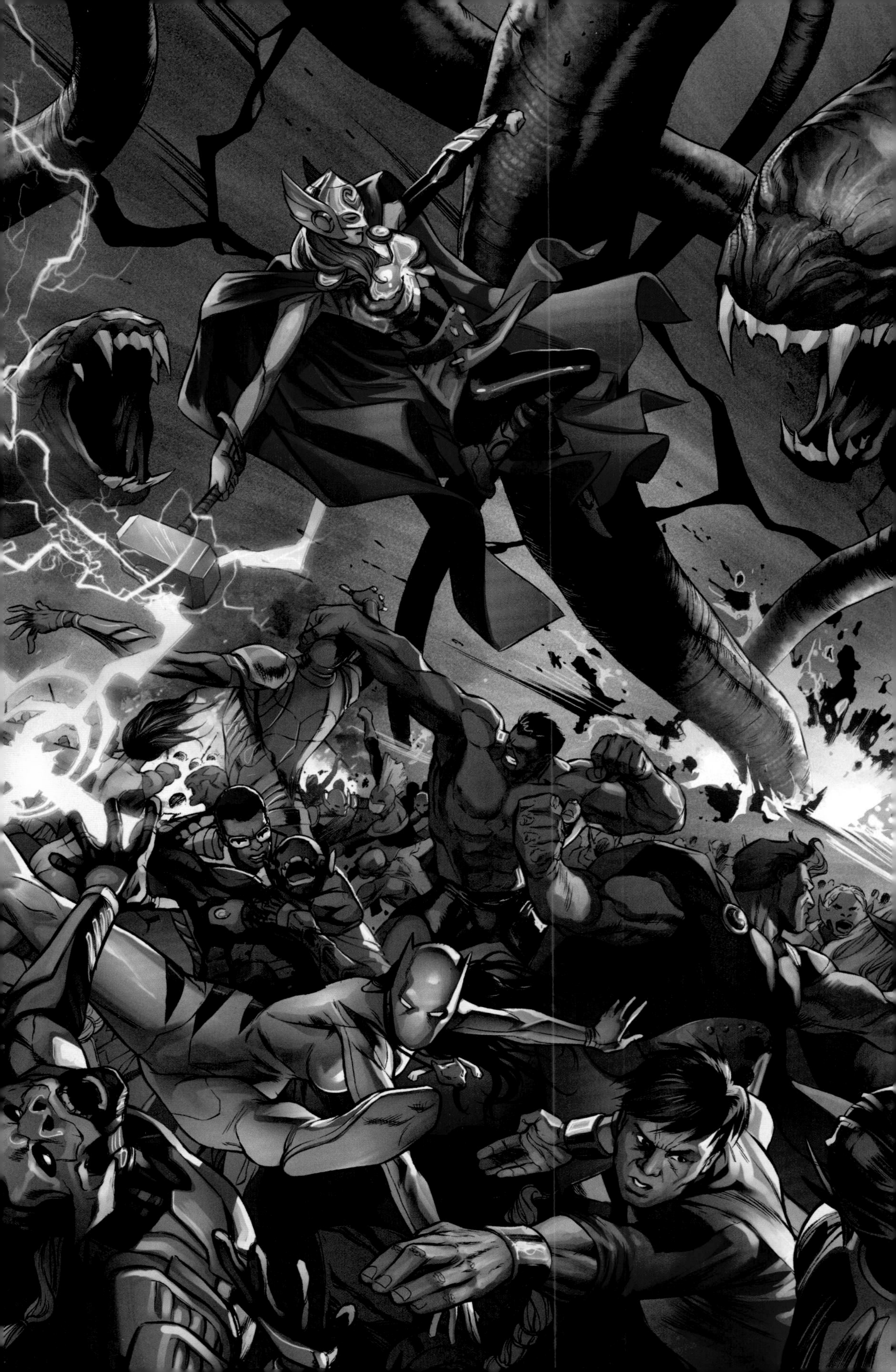

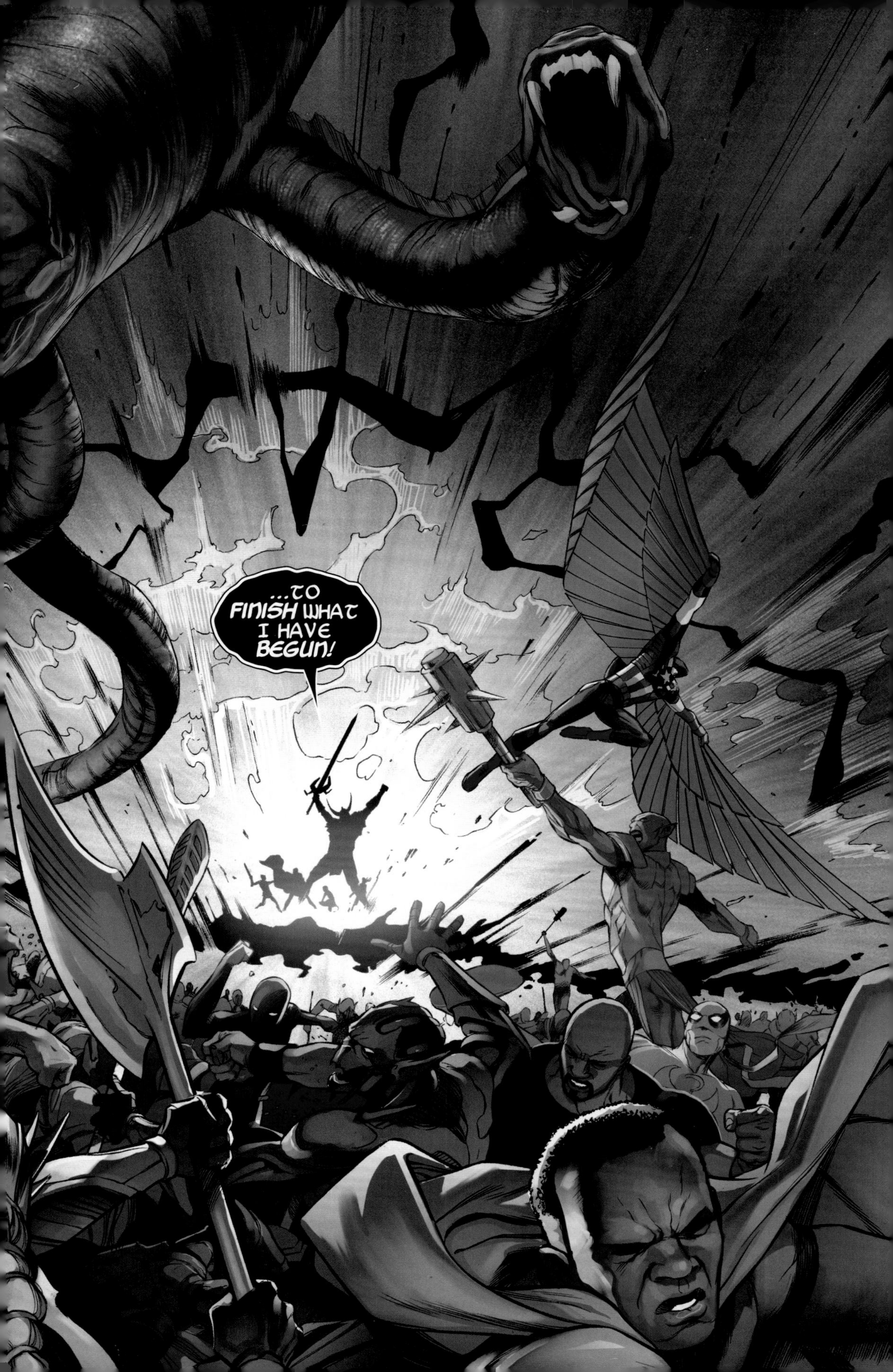
...TO FINISH WHAT I HAVE BEGUN!

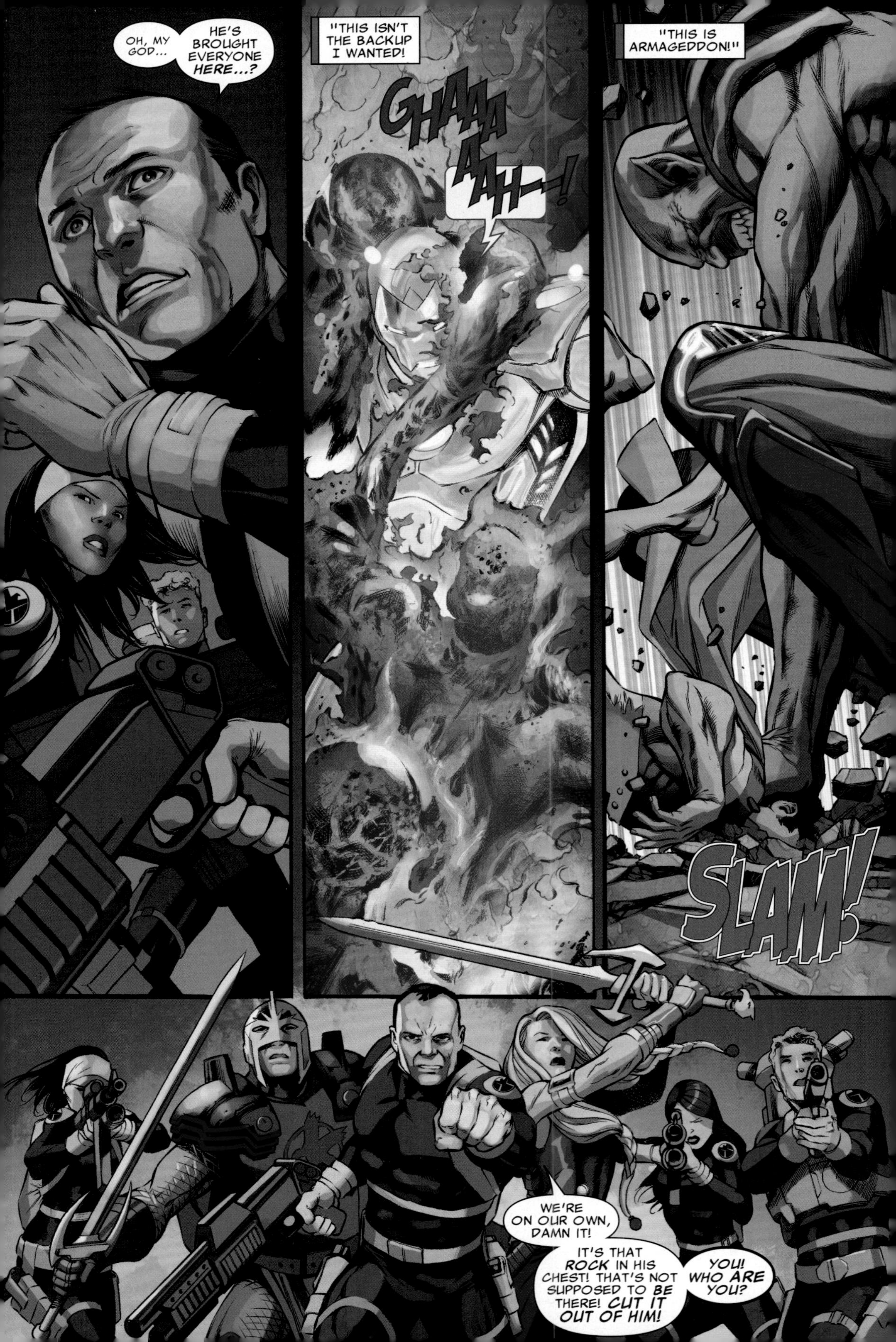
OH, MY GOD...
HE'S BROUGHT EVERYONE HERE...?
"THIS ISN'T THE BACKUP I WANTED!
GHAAAAAH--!
"THIS IS ARMAGEDDON!"
SLAM!
WE'RE ON OUR OWN, DAMN IT!
IT'S THAT ROCK IN HIS CHEST! THAT'S NOT SUPPOSED TO BE THERE! CUT IT OUT OF HIM!
YOU! WHO ARE YOU?

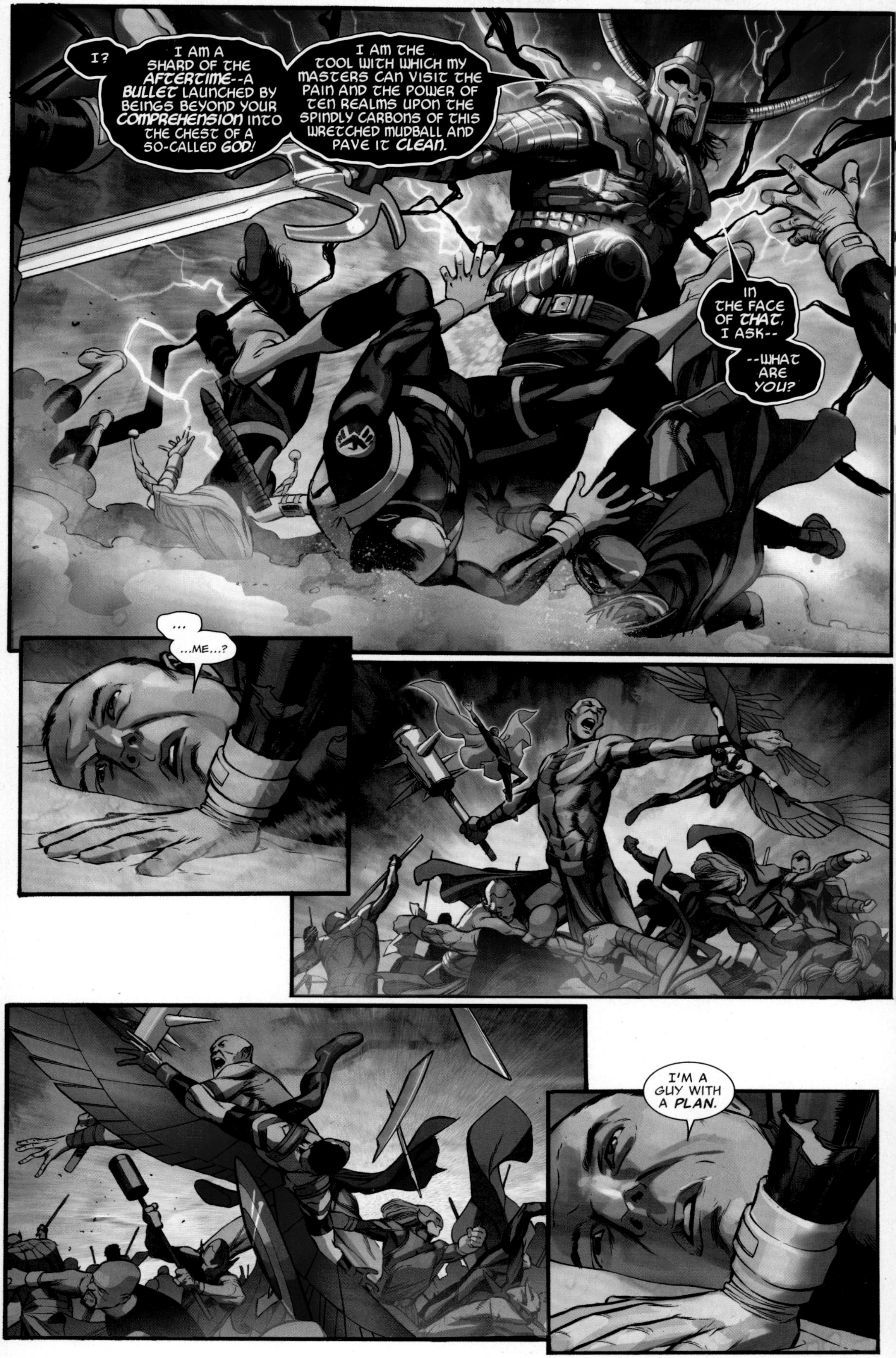
I?
I AM A SHARD OF THE AFTERTIME--A BULLET LAUNCHED BY BEINGS BEYOND YOUR COMPREHENSION INTO THE CHEST OF A SO-CALLED GOD!
I AM THE TOOL WITH WHICH MY MASTERS CAN VISIT THE PAIN AND THE POWER OF TEN REALMS UPON THE SPINDLY CARBONS OF THIS WRETCHED MUDBALL AND PAVE IT CLEAN.
IN THE FACE OF THAT, I ASK--
--WHAT ARE YOU?
...
...ME...?
I'M A GUY WITH A PLAN.

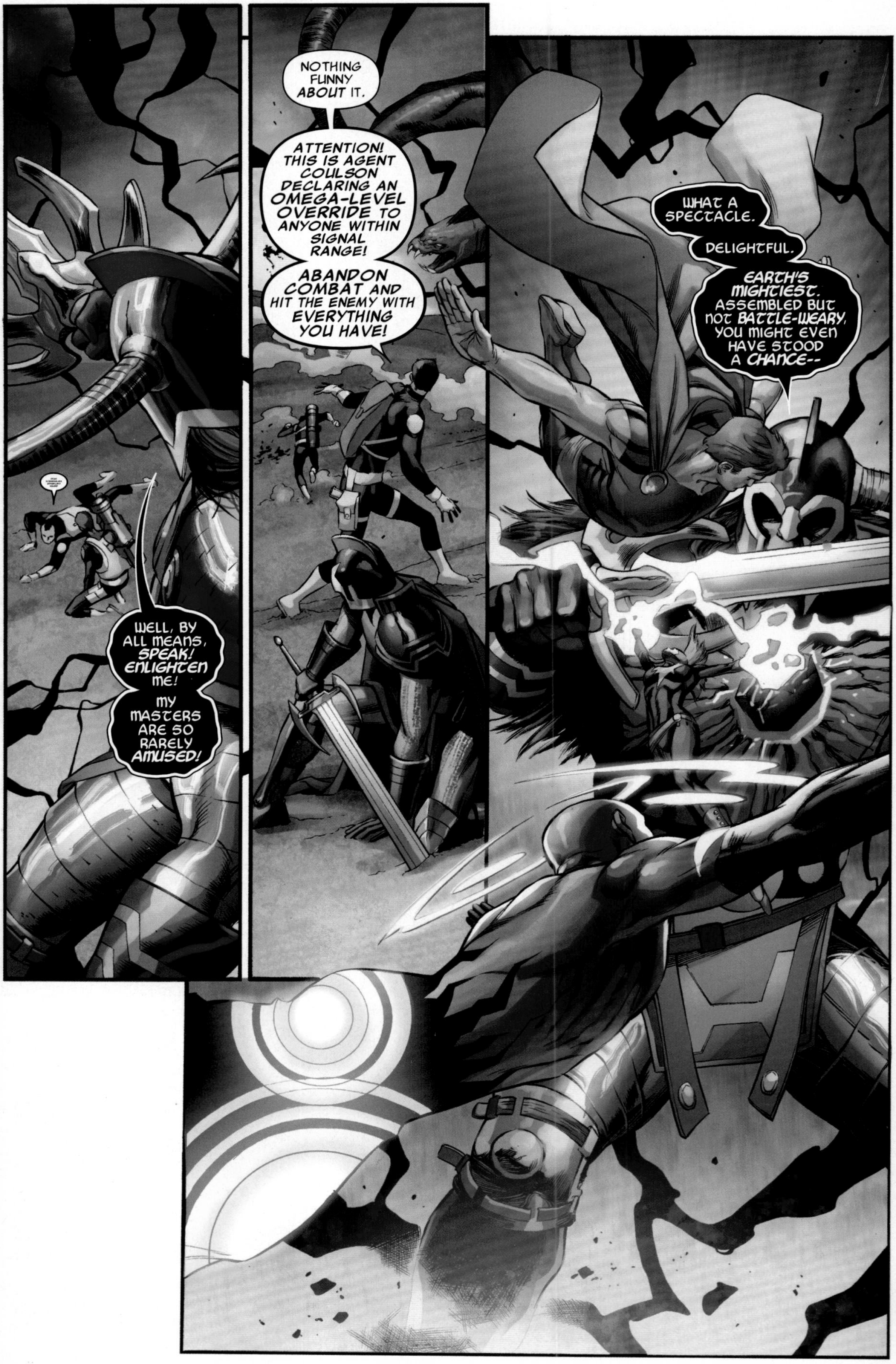
WELL, BY ALL MEANS, SPEAK! ENLIGHTEN ME!
MY MASTERS ARE SO RARELY AMUSED!
NOTHING FUNNY ABOUT IT.
ATTENTION! THIS IS AGENT COULSON DECLARING AN OMEGA-LEVEL OVERRIDE TO ANYONE WITHIN SIGNAL RANGE!
ABANDON COMBAT AND HIT THE ENEMY WITH EVERYTHING YOU HAVE!
WHAT A SPECTACLE.
DELIGHTFUL.
EARTH'S MIGHTIEST. ASSEMBLED BUT NOT BATTLE-WEARY, YOU MIGHT EVEN HAVE STOOD A CHANCE--

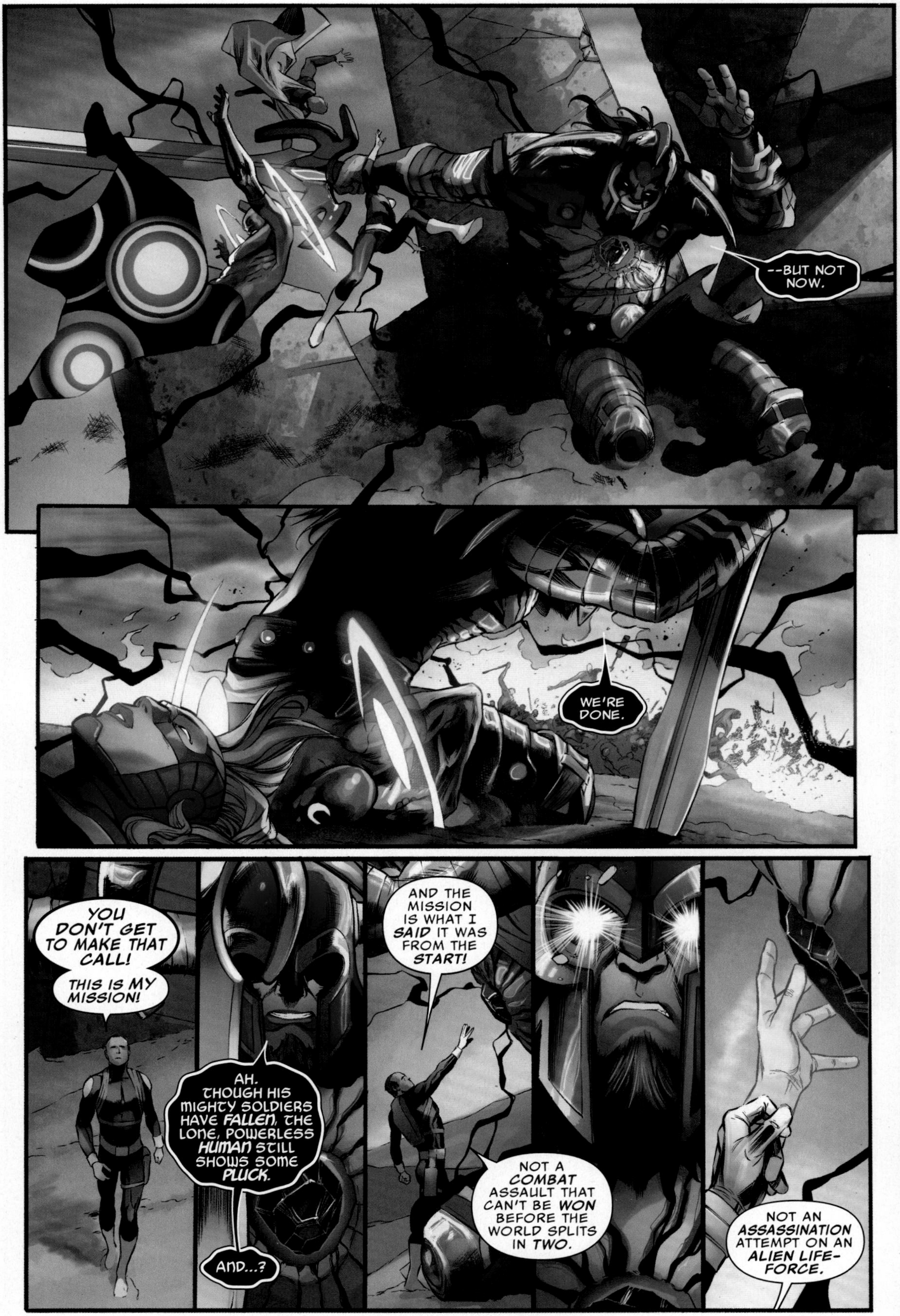
--BUT NOT NOW.
WE'RE DONE.
YOU DON'T GET TO MAKE THAT CALL!
THIS IS MY MISSION!
AH. THOUGH HIS MIGHTY SOLDIERS HAVE FALLEN, THE LONE, POWERLESS HUMAN STILL SHOWS SOME PLUCK.
AND...?
AND THE MISSION IS WHAT I SAID IT WAS FROM THE START!
NOT A COMBAT ASSAULT THAT CAN'T BE WON BEFORE THE WORLD SPLITS IN TWO.
NOT AN ASSASSINATION ATTEMPT ON AN ALIEN LIFE-FORCE.

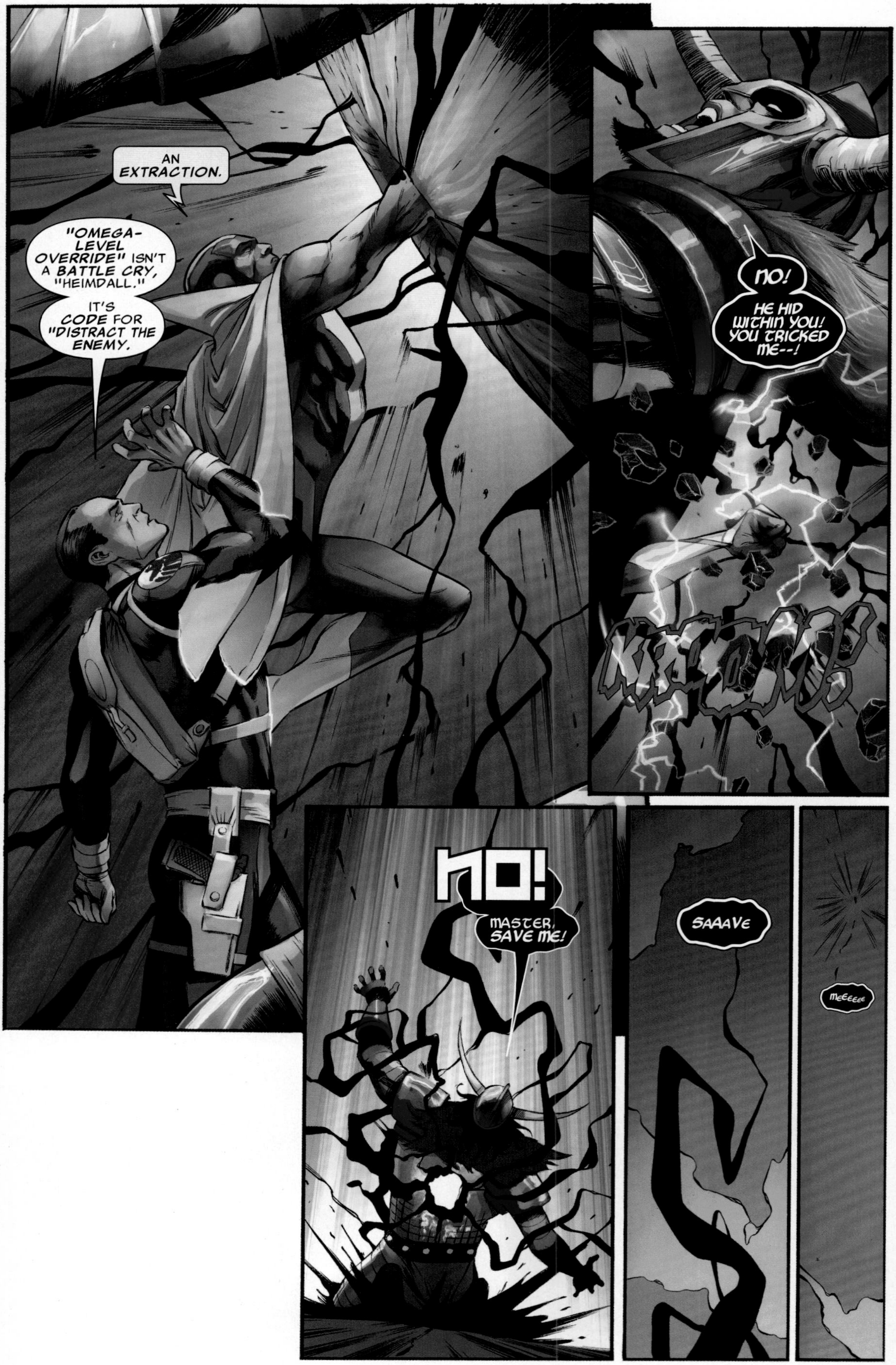
AN EXTRACTION.
"OMEGA-LEVEL OVERRIDE" ISN'T A BATTLE CRY, "HEIMDALL."
IT'S CODE FOR "DISTRACT THE ENEMY.
NO!
HE HID WITHIN YOU! YOU TRICKED ME--!
NO!
MASTER, SAVE ME!
SAAAVE
MEEEEEE

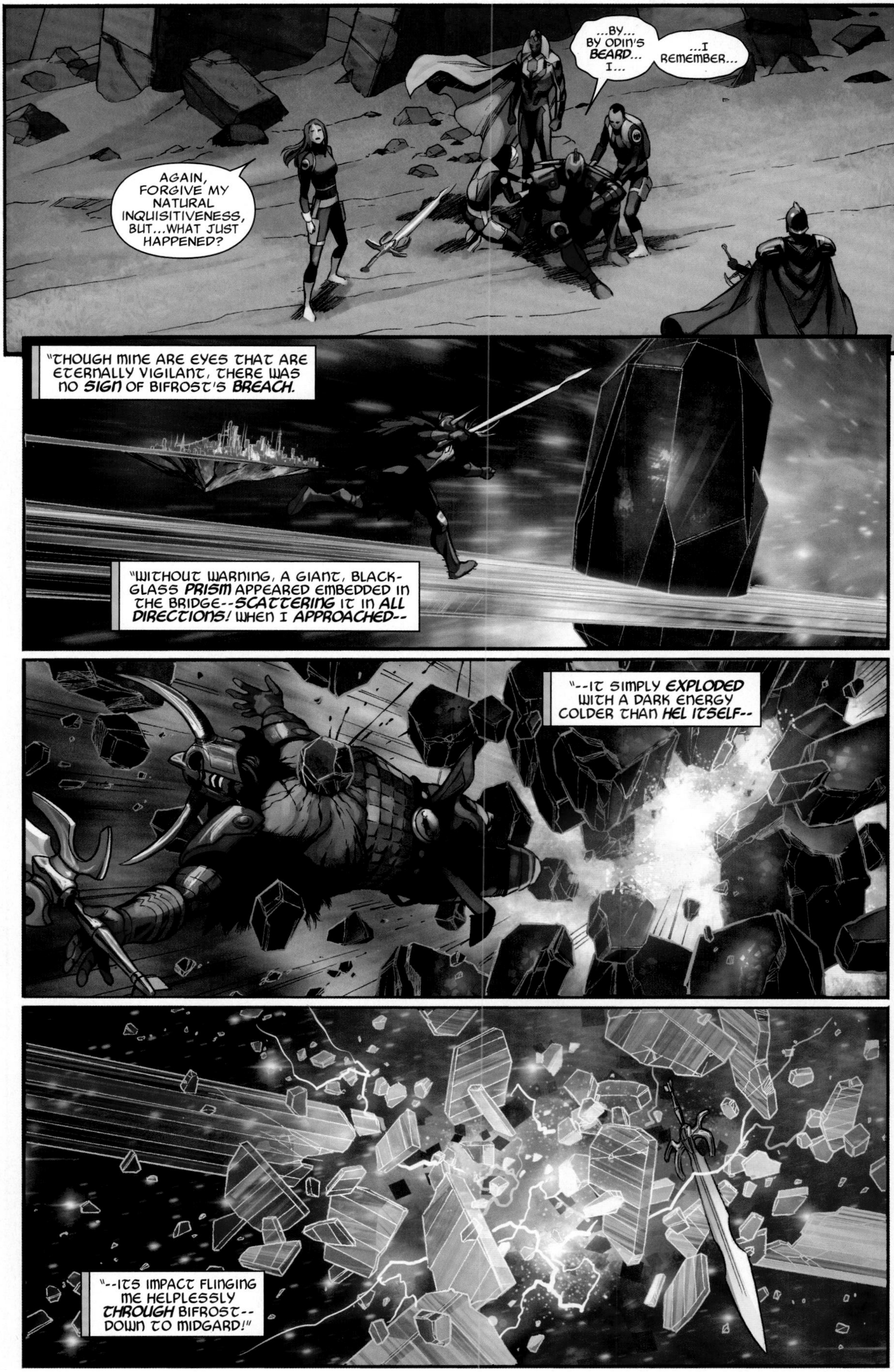
AGAIN, FORGIVE MY NATURAL INQUISITIVENESS, BUT...WHAT JUST HAPPENED?
...BY... BY ODIN'S BEARD... I...
...I REMEMBER...
"THOUGH MINE ARE EYES THAT ARE ETERNALLY VIGILANT, THERE WAS NO SIGN OF BIFROST'S BREACH.
"WITHOUT WARNING, A GIANT, BLACK-GLASS PRISM APPEARED EMBEDDED IN THE BRIDGE--SCATTERING IT IN ALL DIRECTIONS! WHEN I APPROACHED--
"--IT SIMPLY EXPLODED WITH A DARK ENERGY COLDER THAN HEL ITSELF--
"--ITS IMPACT FLINGING ME HELPLESSLY THROUGH BIFROST--DOWN TO MIDGARD!"

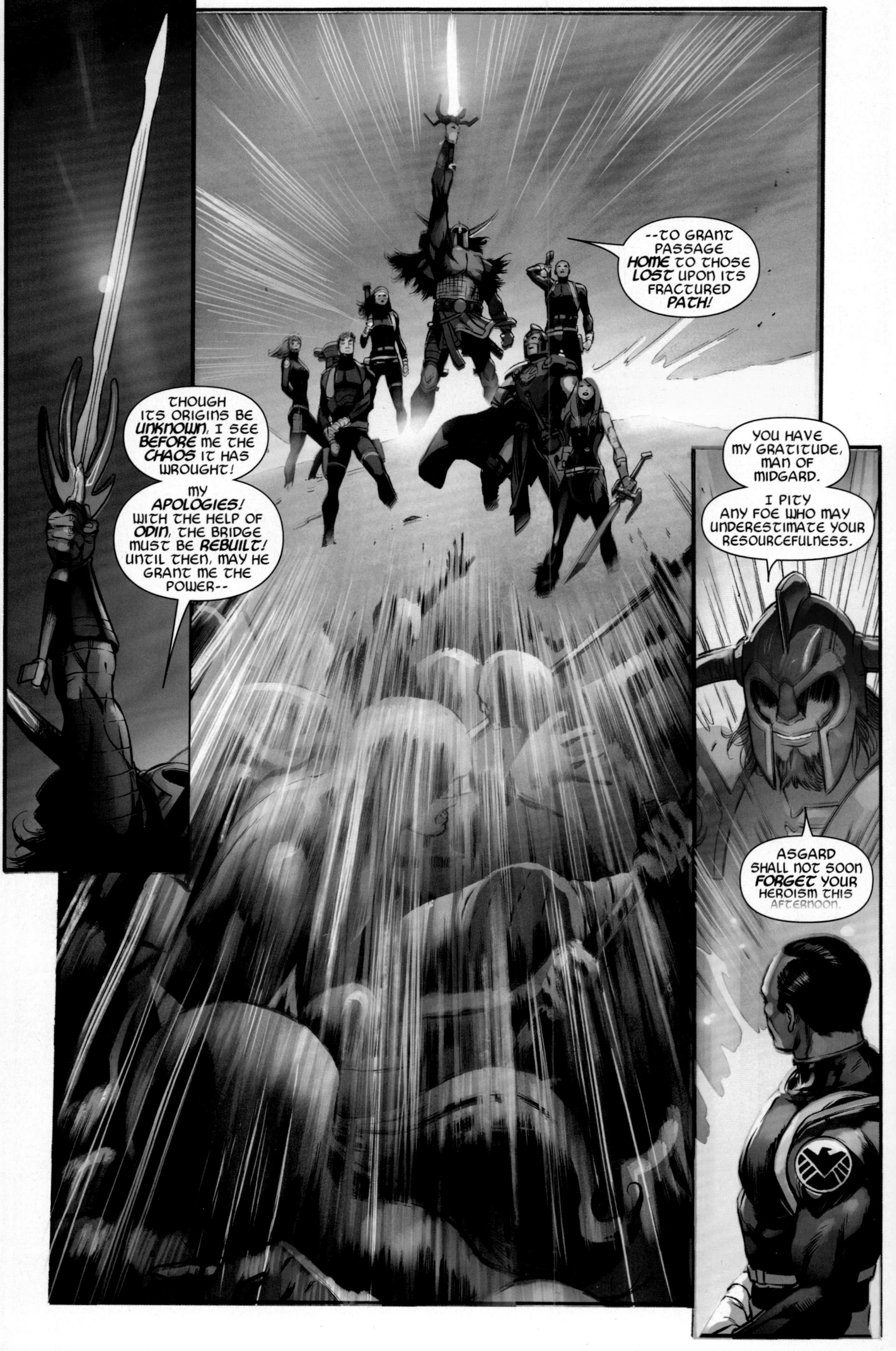
THOUGH ITS ORIGINS BE UNKNOWN, I SEE BEFORE ME THE CHAOS IT HAS WROUGHT!
MY APOLOGIES! WITH THE HELP OF ODIN, THE BRIDGE MUST BE REBUILT! UNTIL THEN, MAY HE GRANT ME THE POWER--
--TO GRANT PASSAGE HOME TO THOSE LOST UPON ITS FRACTURED PATH!
YOU HAVE MY GRATITUDE, MAN OF MIDGARD.
I PITY ANY FOE WHO MAY UNDERESTIMATE YOUR RESOURCEFULNESS.
ASGARD SHALL NOT SOON FORGET YOUR HEROISM THIS AFTERNOON.

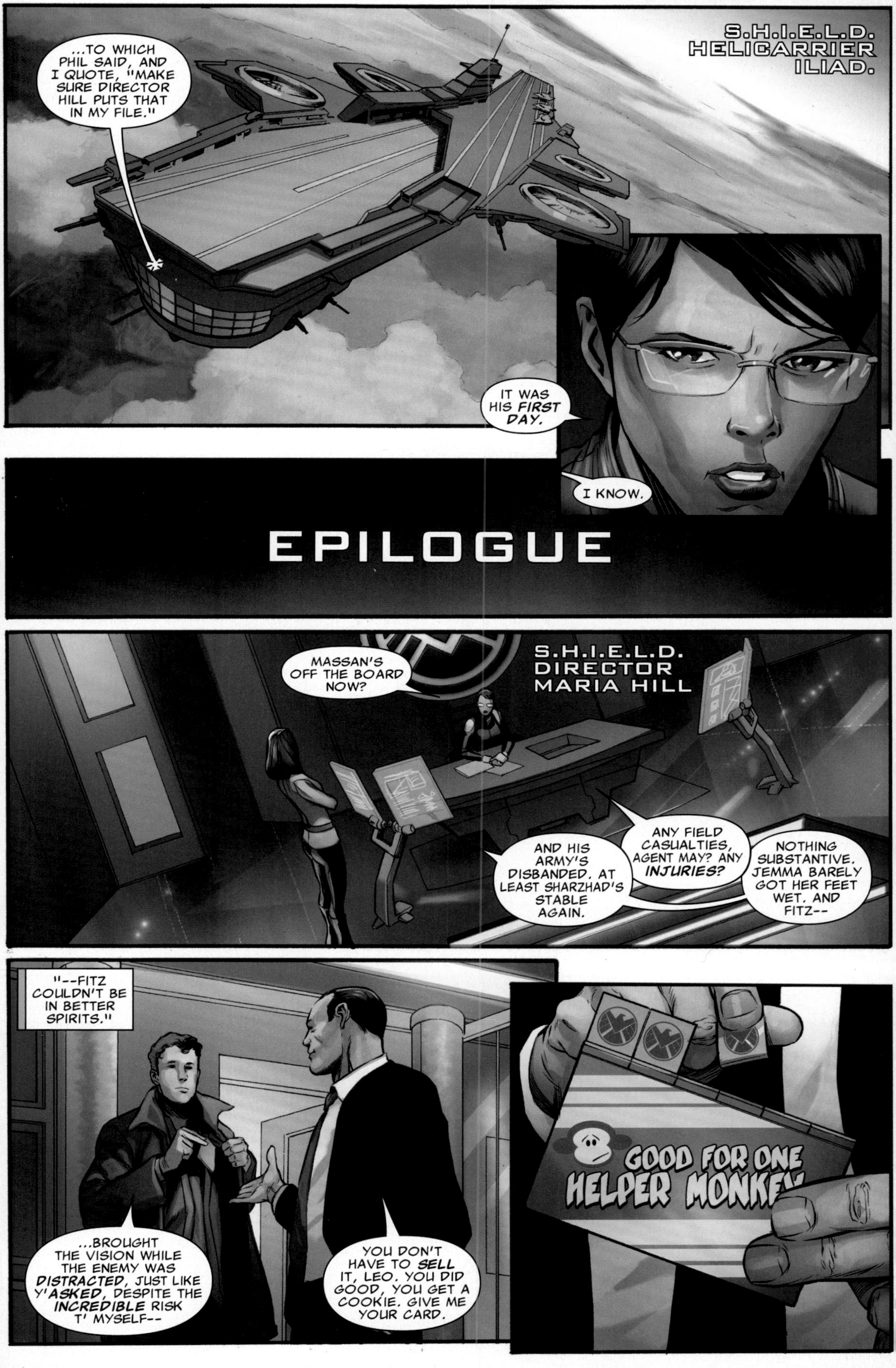
S.H.I.E.L.D. HELICARRIER ILIAD.
...TO WHICH PHIL SAID, AND I QUOTE, "MAKE SURE DIRECTOR HILL PUTS THAT IN MY FILE."
IT WAS HIS FIRST DAY.
I KNOW.
EPILOGUE
MASSAN'S OFF THE BOARD NOW?
S.H.I.E.L.D. DIRECTOR MARIA HILL
AND HIS ARMY'S DISBANDED. AT LEAST SHARZHAD'S STABLE AGAIN.
ANY FIELD CASUALTIES, AGENT MAY? ANY INJURIES?
NOTHING SUBSTANTIVE. JEMMA BARELY GOT HER FEET WET. AND FITZ--
"--FITZ COULDN'T BE IN BETTER SPIRITS."
...BROUGHT THE VISION WHILE THE ENEMY WAS DISTRACTED, JUST LIKE Y'ASKED, DESPITE THE INCREDIBLE RISK T' MYSELF--
YOU DON'T HAVE TO SELL IT, LEO. YOU DID GOOD, YOU GET A COOKIE. GIVE ME YOUR CARD.
GOOD FOR ONE HELPER MONKEY

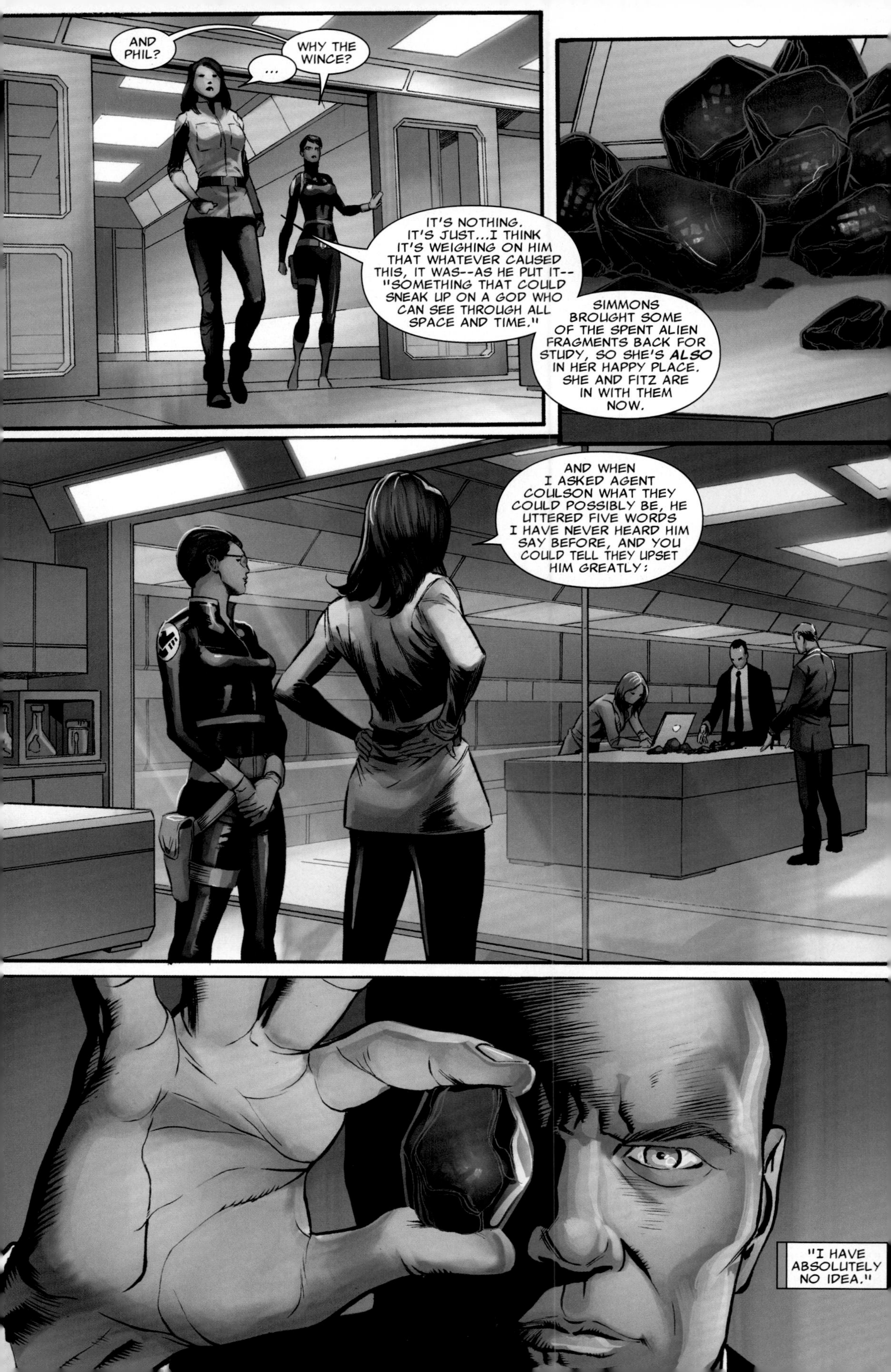
AND PHIL?
...
WHY THE WINCE?
IT'S NOTHING. IT'S JUST...I THINK IT'S WEIGHING ON HIM THAT WHATEVER CAUSED THIS, IT WAS--AS HE PUT IT--"SOMETHING THAT COULD SNEAK UP ON A GOD WHO CAN SEE THROUGH ALL SPACE AND TIME."
SIMMONS BROUGHT SOME OF THE SPENT ALIEN FRAGMENTS BACK FOR STUDY, SO SHE'S ALSO IN HER HAPPY PLACE. SHE AND FITZ ARE IN WITH THEM NOW.
AND WHEN I ASKED AGENT COULSON WHAT THEY COULD POSSIBLY BE, HE UTTERED FIVE WORDS I HAVE NEVER HEARD HIM SAY BEFORE, AND YOU COULD TELL THEY UPSET HIM GREATLY:
"I HAVE ABSOLUTELY NO IDEA."

2.

ACTIVE MISSION:

THE ANIMATOR

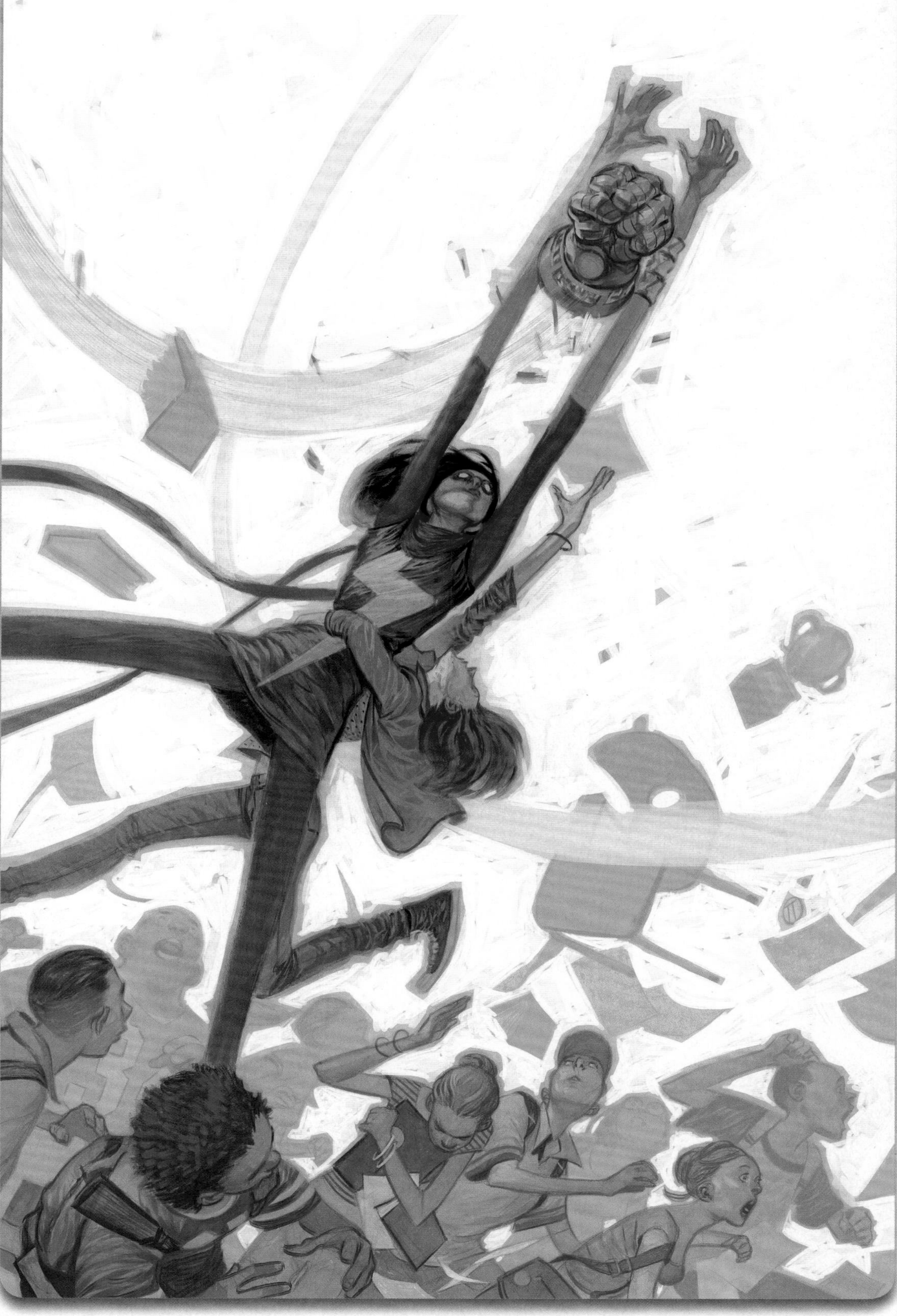

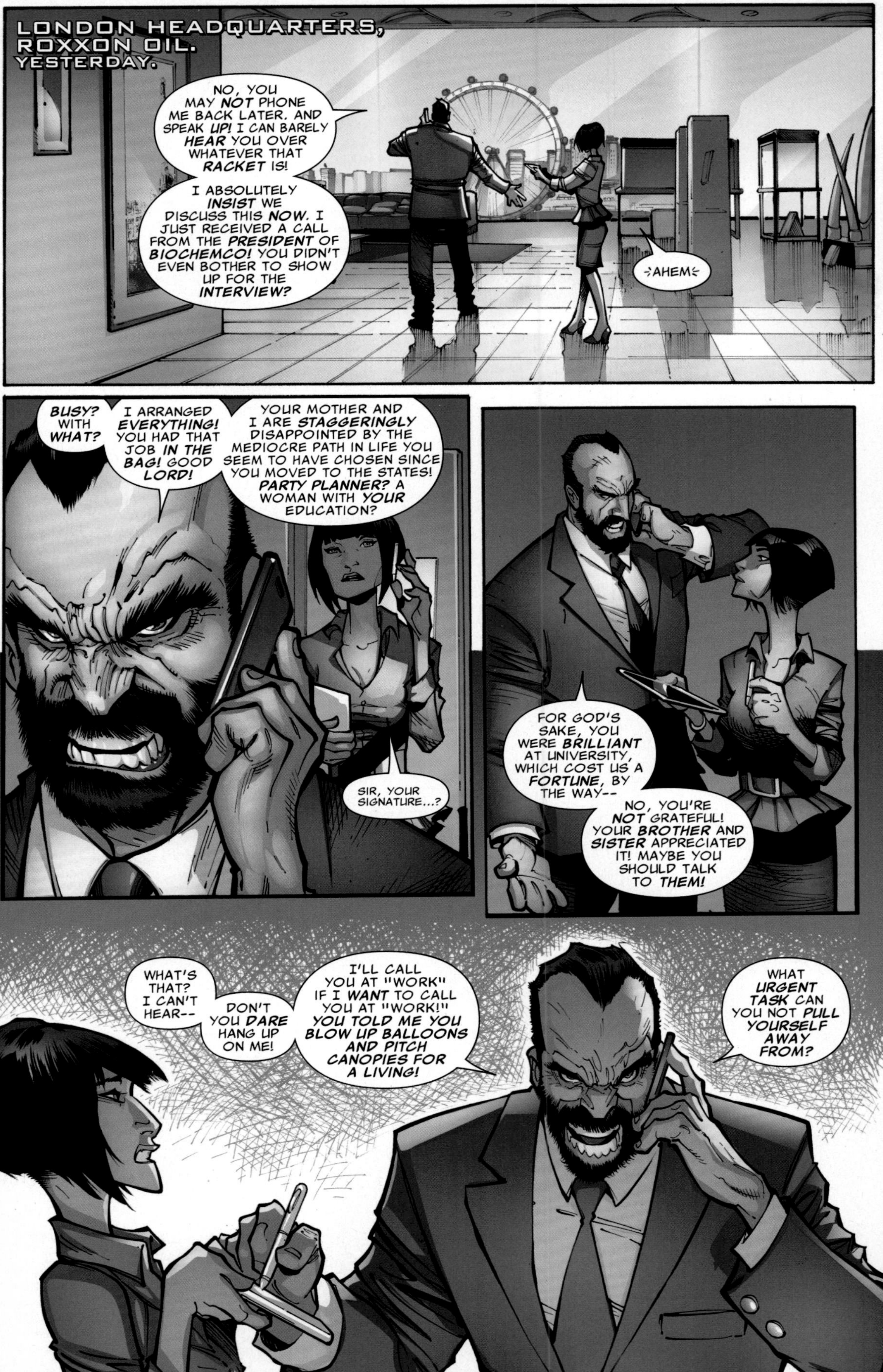
LONDON HEADQUARTERS, ROXXON OIL. YESTERDAY.
NO, YOU MAY NOT PHONE ME BACK LATER. AND SPEAK UP! I CAN BARELY HEAR YOU OVER WHATEVER THAT RACKET IS!
I ABSOLUTELY INSIST WE DISCUSS THIS NOW. I JUST RECEIVED A CALL FROM THE PRESIDENT OF BIOCHEMCO! YOU DIDN'T EVEN BOTHER TO SHOW UP FOR THE INTERVIEW?
AHEM
BUSY? WITH WHAT?
I ARRANGED EVERYTHING! YOU HAD THAT JOB IN THE BAG! GOOD LORD!
YOUR MOTHER AND I ARE STAGGERINGLY DISAPPOINTED BY THE MEDIOCRE PATH IN LIFE YOU SEEM TO HAVE CHOSEN SINCE YOU MOVED TO THE STATES! PARTY PLANNER? A WOMAN WITH YOUR EDUCATION?
SIR, YOUR SIGNATURE...?
FOR GOD'S SAKE, YOU WERE BRILLIANT AT UNIVERSITY, WHICH COST US A FORTUNE, BY THE WAY--
NO, YOU'RE NOT GRATEFUL! YOUR BROTHER AND SISTER APPRECIATED IT! MAYBE YOU SHOULD TALK TO THEM!
WHAT'S THAT? I CAN'T HEAR--
DON'T YOU DARE HANG UP ON ME!
I'LL CALL YOU AT "WORK" IF I WANT TO CALL YOU AT "WORK!" YOU TOLD ME YOU BLOW UP BALLOONS AND PITCH CANOPIES FOR A LIVING!
WHAT URGENT TASK CAN YOU NOT PULL YOURSELF AWAY FROM?

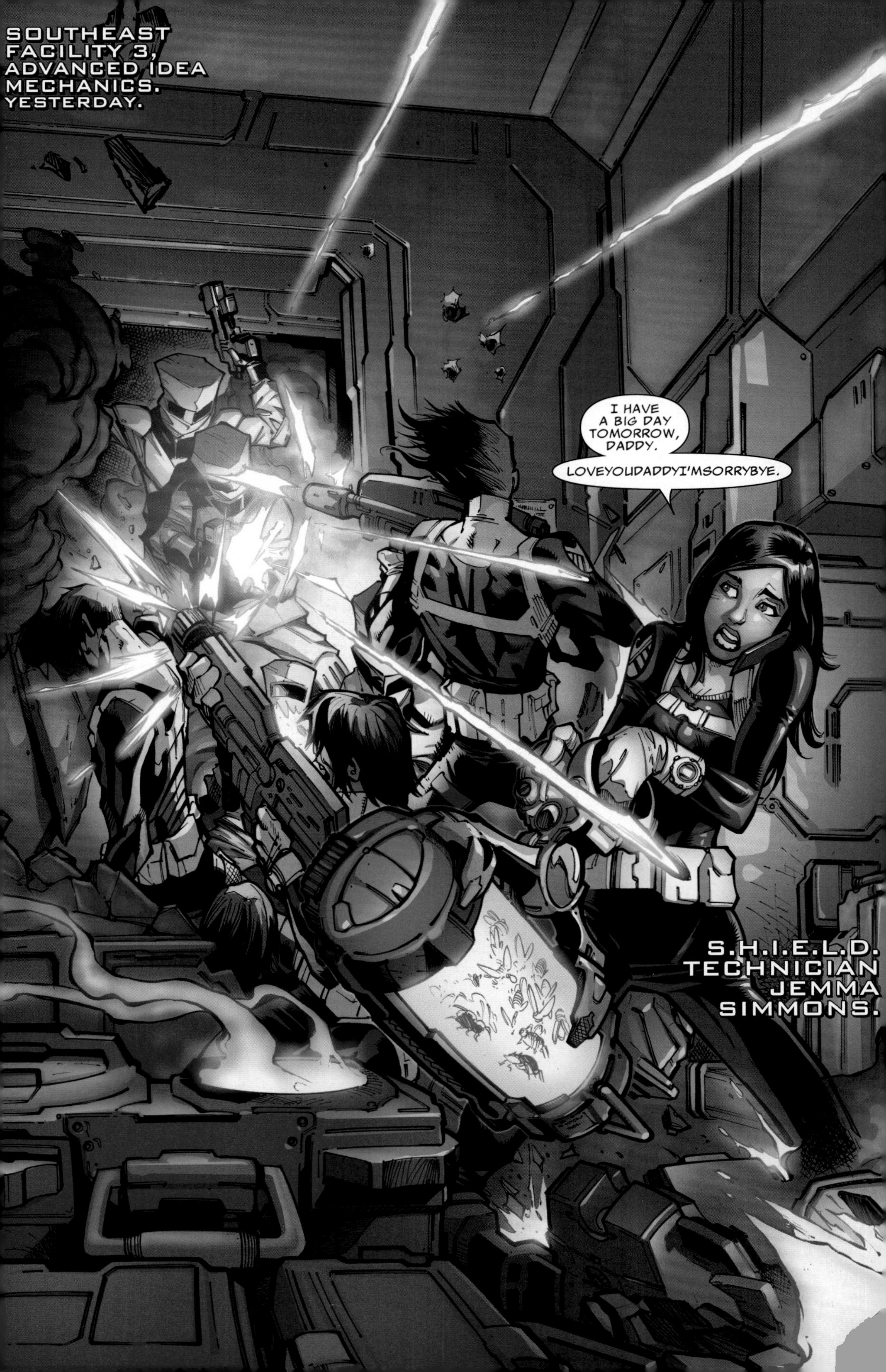
SOUTHEAST FACILITY 3, ADVANCED IDEA MECHANICS. YESTERDAY.
I HAVE A BIG DAY TOMORROW, DADDY.
LOVEYOUDADDYI'MSORRYBYE.
S.H.I.E.L.D. TECHNICIAN JEMMA SIMMONS.

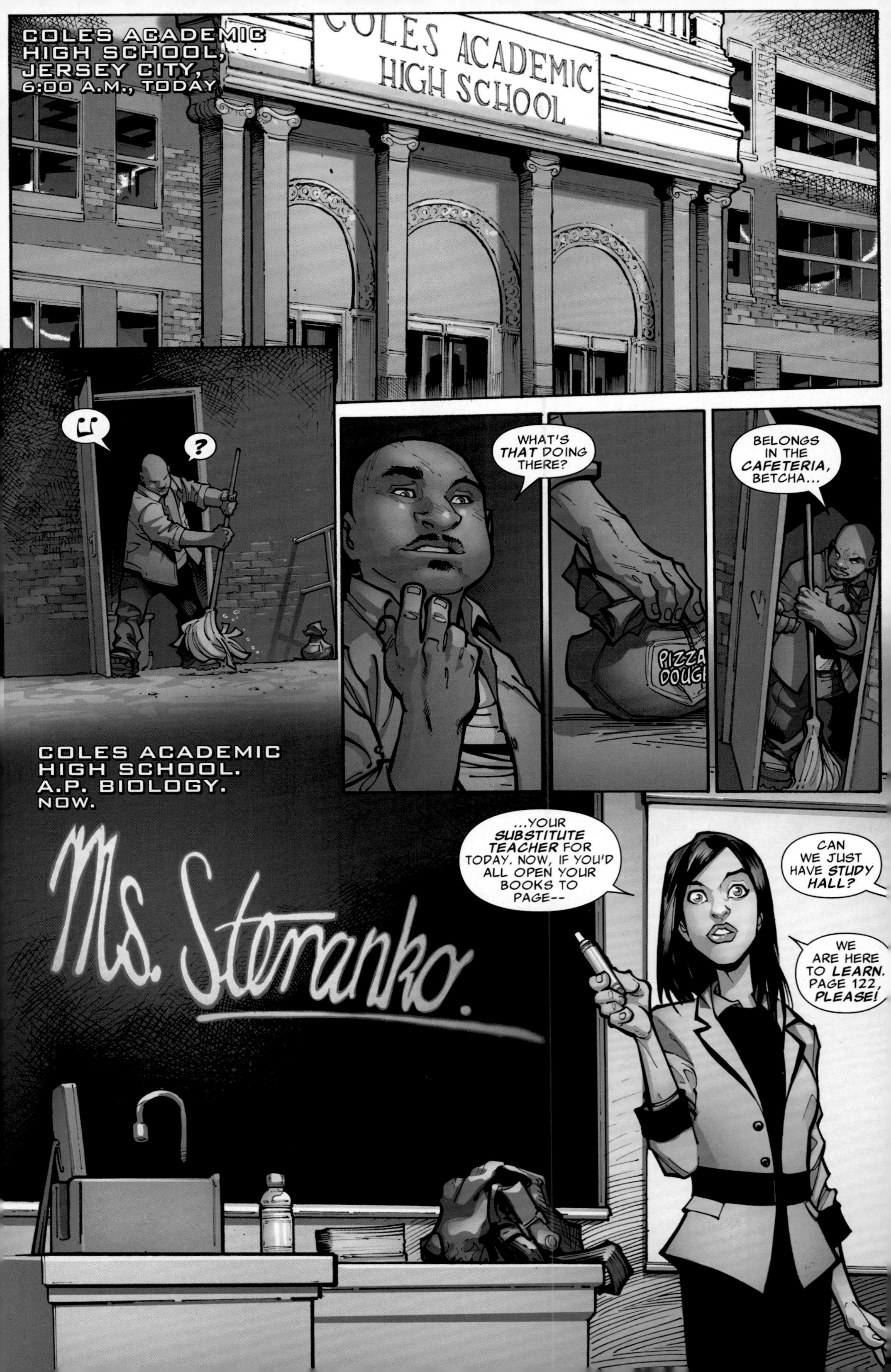
COLES ACADEMIC HIGH SCHOOL, JERSEY CITY, 6:00 A.M., TODAY
COLES ACADEMIC HIGH SCHOOL
?
WHAT'S THAT DOING THERE?
PIZZA DOUGH
BELONGS IN THE CAFETERIA, BETCHA...
COLES ACADEMIC HIGH SCHOOL. A.P. BIOLOGY. NOW.
Ms. Stenanko.
...YOUR SUBSTITUTE TEACHER FOR TODAY. NOW, IF YOU'D ALL OPEN YOUR BOOKS TO PAGE--
CAN WE JUST HAVE STUDY HALL?
WE ARE HERE TO LEARN. PAGE 122, PLEASE!

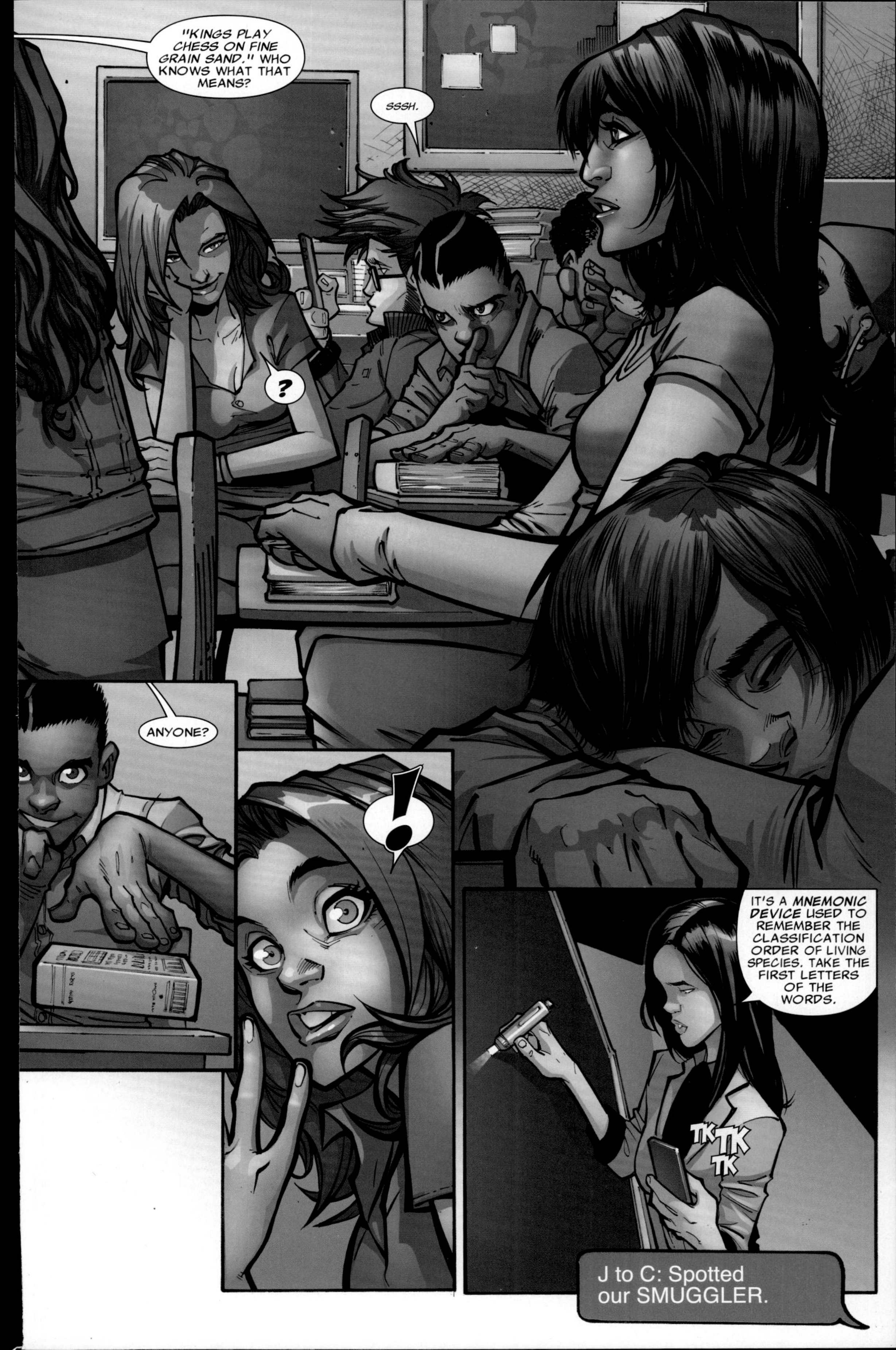
"KINGS PLAY CHESS ON FINE GRAIN SAND." WHO KNOWS WHAT THAT MEANS?
SSSH.
?
ANYONE?
!
IT'S A MNEMONIC DEVICE USED TO REMEMBER THE CLASSIFICATION ORDER OF LIVING SPECIES. TAKE THE FIRST LETTERS OF THE WORDS.
TK TK TK
J to C: Spotted our SMUGGLER.

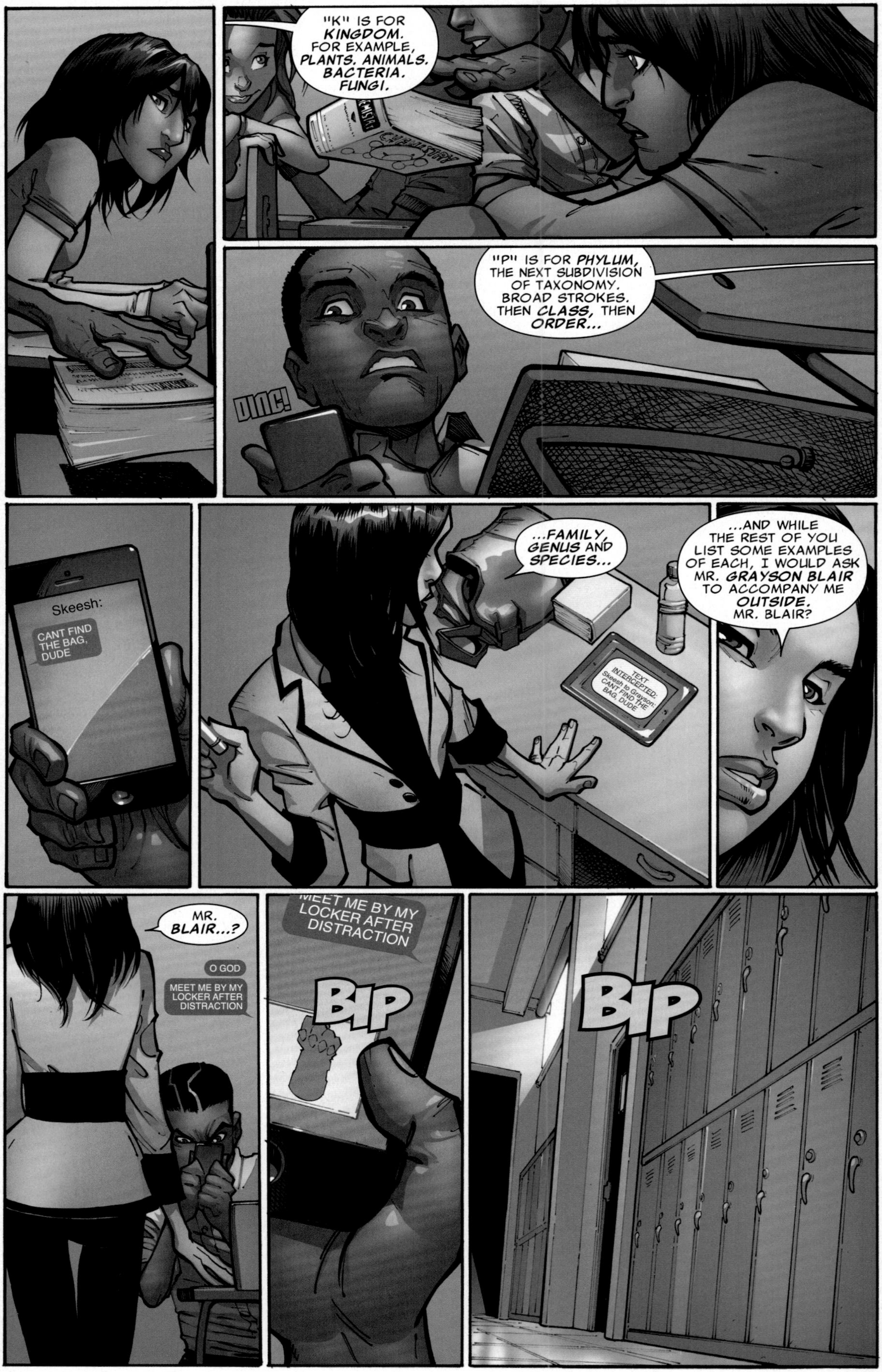
"K" IS FOR KINGDOM. FOR EXAMPLE, PLANTS. ANIMALS. BACTERIA. FUNGI.
"P" IS FOR PHYLUM, THE NEXT SUBDIVISION OF TAXONOMY. BROAD STROKES. THEN CLASS, THEN ORDER...
DING!
Skeesh:
CANT FIND THE BAG, DUDE
...FAMILY, GENUS AND SPECIES...
TEXT INTERCEPTED: Skeesh to Grayson: CANT FIND THE BAG, DUDE
...AND WHILE THE REST OF YOU LIST SOME EXAMPLES OF EACH, I WOULD ASK MR. GRAYSON BLAIR TO ACCOMPANY ME OUTSIDE. MR. BLAIR?
MR. BLAIR...?
O GOD
MEET ME BY MY LOCKER AFTER DISTRACTION
MEET ME BY MY LOCKER AFTER DISTRACTION
BIP
BIP

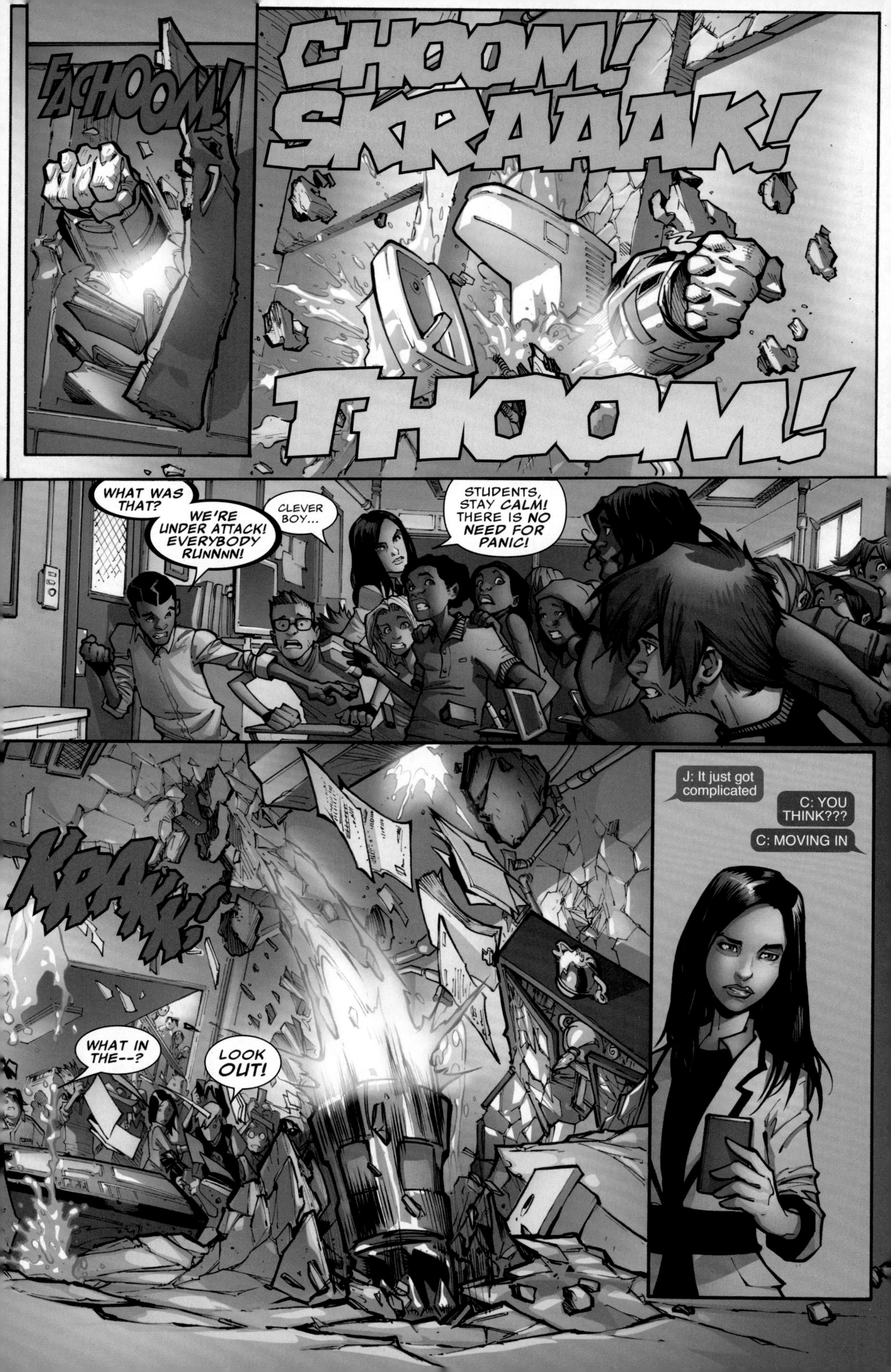
FACHOOM!
CHOOM!
SKRAAAK!
THOOM!
WHAT WAS THAT?
WE'RE UNDER ATTACK! EVERYBODY RUNNNNN!
CLEVER BOY...
STUDENTS, STAY CALM! THERE IS NO NEED FOR PANIC!
KRAKK!
WHAT IN THE--?
LOOK OUT!
J: It just got complicated
C: YOU THINK???
C: MOVING IN

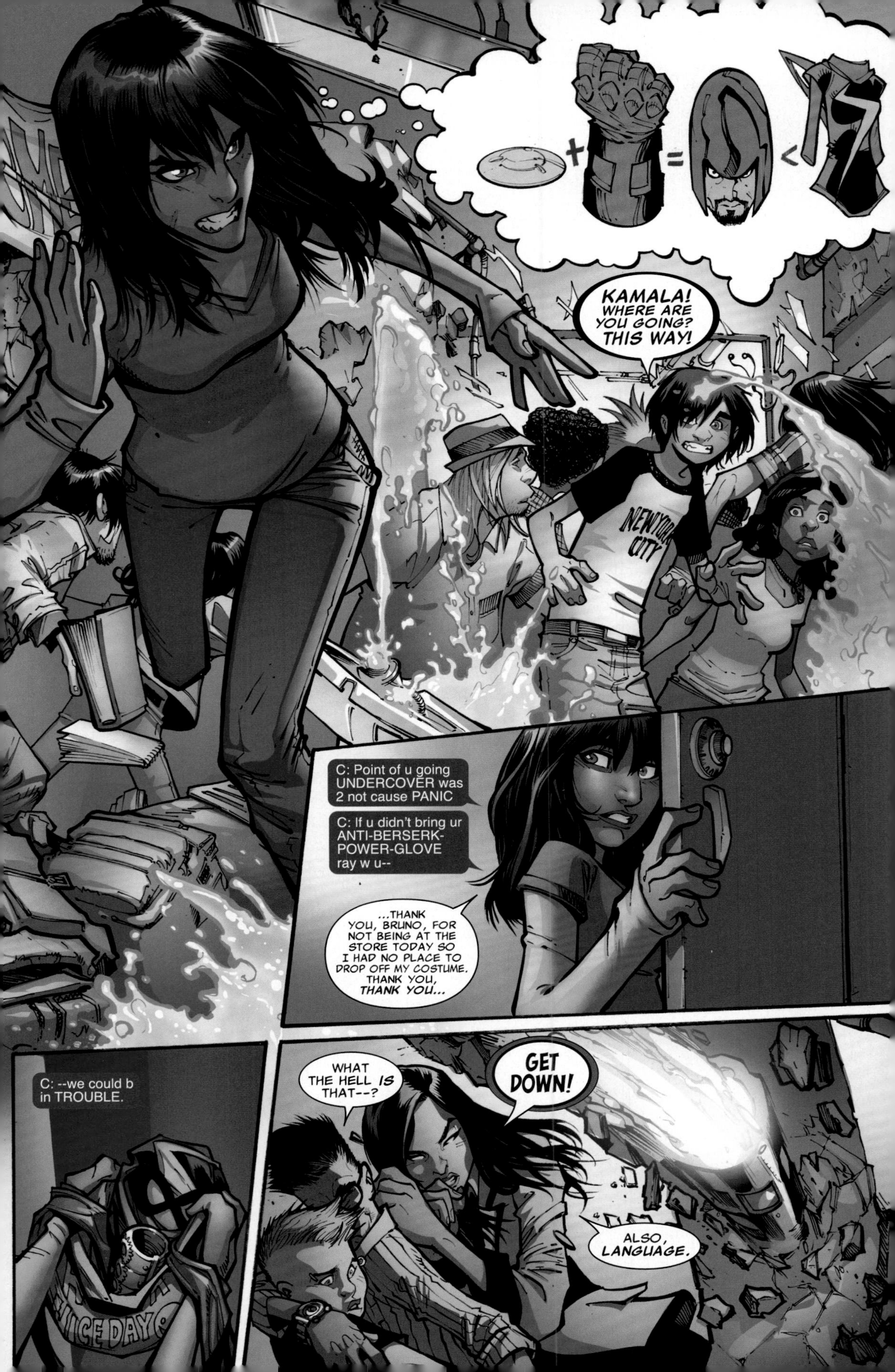
KAMALA! WHERE ARE YOU GOING? THIS WAY!
C: Point of u going UNDERCOVER was 2 not cause PANIC
C: If u didn't bring ur ANTI-BERSERK-POWER-GLOVE ray w u--
...THANK YOU, BRUNO, FOR NOT BEING AT THE STORE TODAY SO I HAD NO PLACE TO DROP OFF MY COSTUME. THANK YOU, THANK YOU...
C: --we could b in TROUBLE.
WHAT THE HELL IS THAT--?
GET DOWN!
ALSO, LANGUAGE.

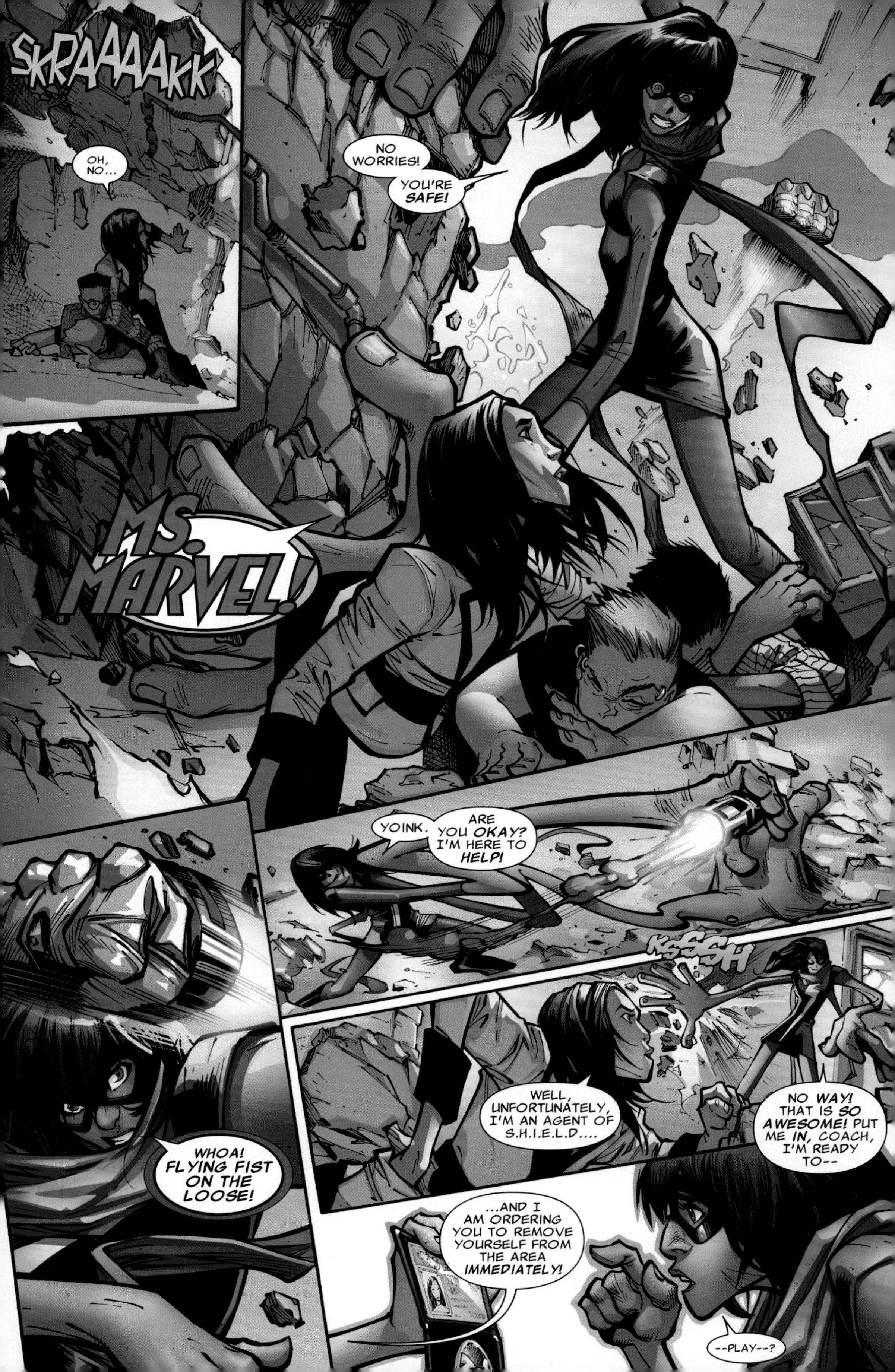
SKRAAAAAKK
OH, NO...
NO WORRIES!
YOU'RE SAFE!
MS. MARVEL!
YOINK.
ARE YOU OKAY? I'M HERE TO HELP!
WHOA! FLYING FIST ON THE LOOSE!
KSSSH
WELL, UNFORTUNATELY, I'M AN AGENT OF S.H.I.E.L.D....
NO WAY! THAT IS SO AWESOME! PUT ME IN, COACH, I'M READY TO--
...AND I AM ORDERING YOU TO REMOVE YOURSELF FROM THE AREA IMMEDIATELY!
--PLAY--?

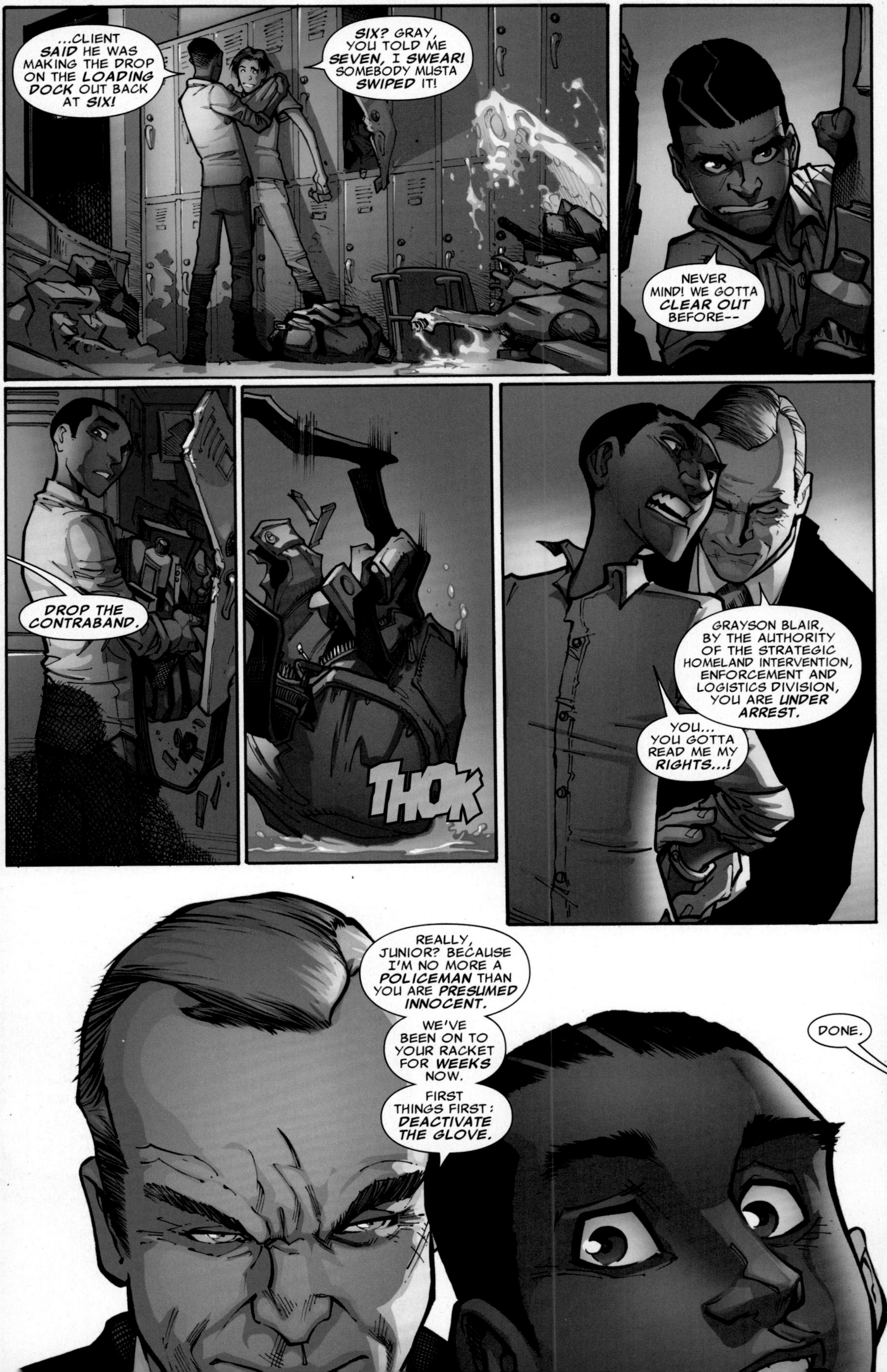
...CLIENT SAID HE WAS MAKING THE DROP ON THE LOADING DOCK OUT BACK AT SIX!
SIX? GRAY, YOU TOLD ME SEVEN, I SWEAR! SOMEBODY MUSTA SWIPED IT!
NEVER MIND! WE GOTTA CLEAR OUT BEFORE--
DROP THE CONTRABAND.
THOK
GRAYSON BLAIR, BY THE AUTHORITY OF THE STRATEGIC HOMELAND INTERVENTION, ENFORCEMENT AND LOGISTICS DIVISION, YOU ARE UNDER ARREST.
YOU... YOU GOTTA READ ME MY RIGHTS...!
REALLY, JUNIOR? BECAUSE I'M NO MORE A POLICEMAN THAN YOU ARE PRESUMED INNOCENT.
WE'VE BEEN ON TO YOUR RACKET FOR WEEKS NOW.
FIRST THINGS FIRST: DEACTIVATE THE GLOVE.
DONE.

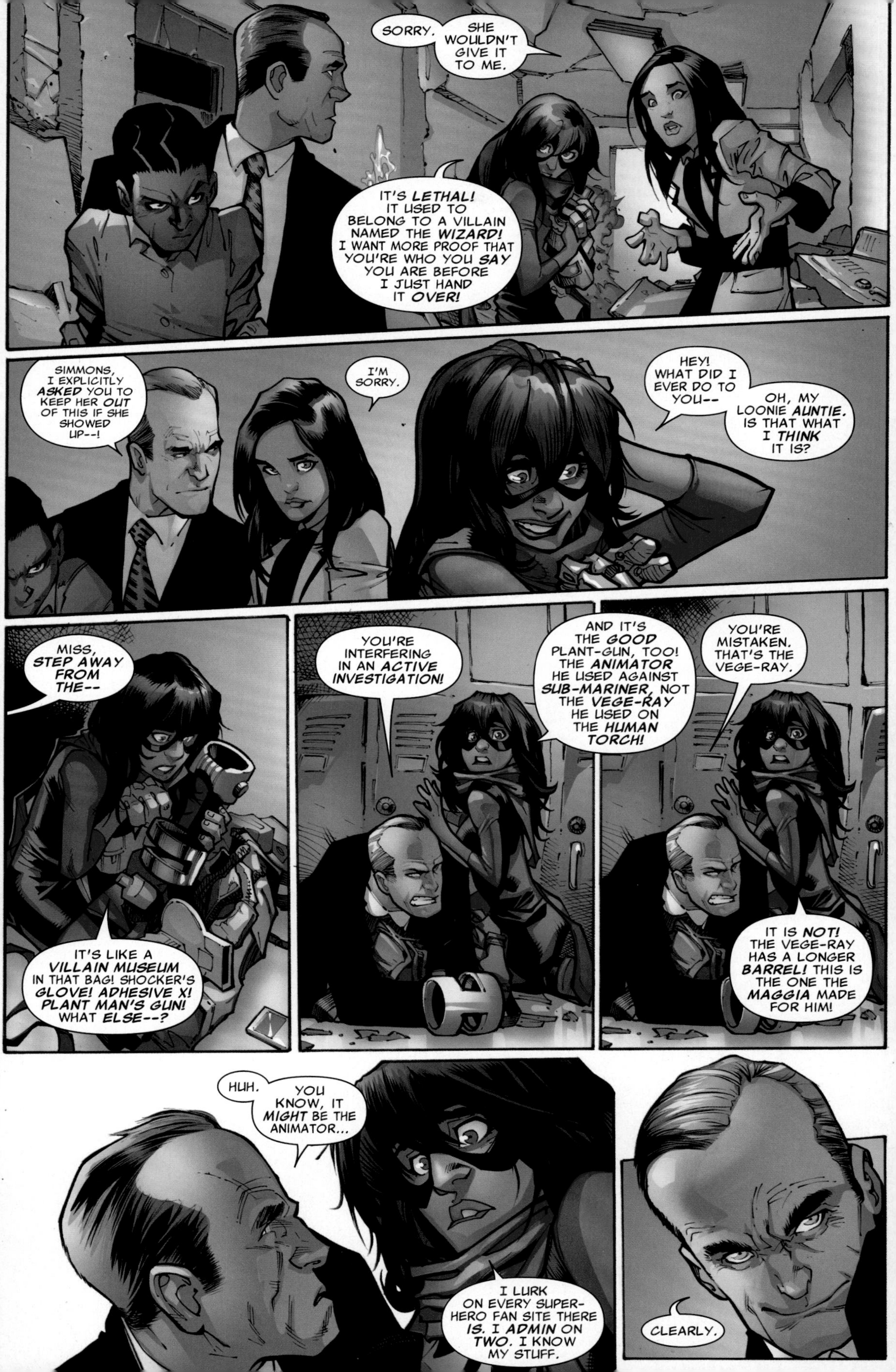

SORRY.
SHE WOULDN'T GIVE IT TO ME.
IT'S LETHAL! IT USED TO BELONG TO A VILLAIN NAMED THE WIZARD! I WANT MORE PROOF THAT YOU'RE WHO YOU SAY YOU ARE BEFORE I JUST HAND IT OVER!
SIMMONS, I EXPLICITLY ASKED YOU TO KEEP HER OUT OF THIS IF SHE SHOWED UP--!
I'M SORRY.
HEY! WHAT DID I EVER DO TO YOU--
OH, MY LOONIE AUNTIE. IS THAT WHAT I THINK IT IS?
MISS, STEP AWAY FROM THE--
IT'S LIKE A VILLAIN MUSEUM IN THAT BAG! SHOCKER'S GLOVE! ADHESIVE X! PLANT MAN'S GUN! WHAT ELSE--?
YOU'RE INTERFERING IN AN ACTIVE INVESTIGATION!
AND IT'S THE GOOD PLANT-GUN, TOO! THE ANIMATOR HE USED AGAINST SUB-MARINER, NOT THE VEGE-RAY HE USED ON THE HUMAN TORCH!
YOU'RE MISTAKEN. THAT'S THE VEGE-RAY.
IT IS NOT! THE VEGE-RAY HAS A LONGER BARREL! THIS IS THE ONE THE MAGGIA MADE FOR HIM!
HUH.
YOU KNOW, IT MIGHT BE THE ANIMATOR...
I LURK ON EVERY SUPER-HERO FAN SITE THERE IS. I ADMIN ON TWO. I KNOW MY STUFF.
CLEARLY.

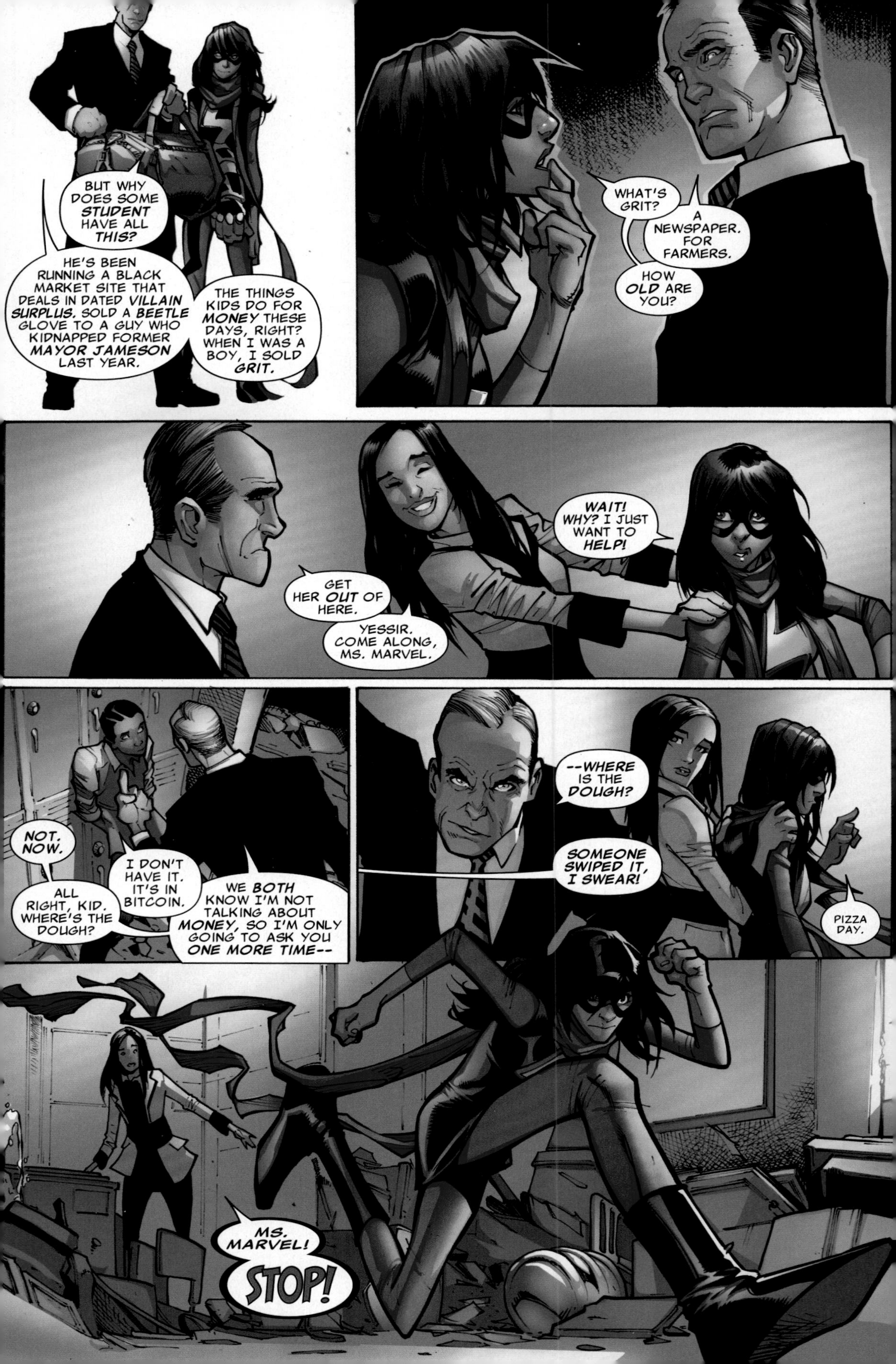
BUT WHY DOES SOME STUDENT HAVE ALL THIS?
HE'S BEEN RUNNING A BLACK MARKET SITE THAT DEALS IN DATED VILLAIN SURPLUS. SOLD A BEETLE GLOVE TO A GUY WHO KIDNAPPED FORMER MAYOR JAMESON LAST YEAR.
THE THINGS KIDS DO FOR MONEY THESE DAYS, RIGHT? WHEN I WAS A BOY, I SOLD GRIT.
WHAT'S GRIT?
A NEWSPAPER. FOR FARMERS.
HOW OLD ARE YOU?
WAIT! WHY? I JUST WANT TO HELP!
GET HER OUT OF HERE.
YESSIR. COME ALONG, MS. MARVEL.
NOT. NOW.
ALL RIGHT, KID. WHERE'S THE DOUGH?
I DON'T HAVE IT. IT'S IN BITCOIN.
WE BOTH KNOW I'M NOT TALKING ABOUT MONEY, SO I'M ONLY GOING TO ASK YOU ONE MORE TIME--
--WHERE IS THE DOUGH?
SOMEONE SWIPED IT, I SWEAR!
PIZZA DAY.
MS. MARVEL!
STOP!

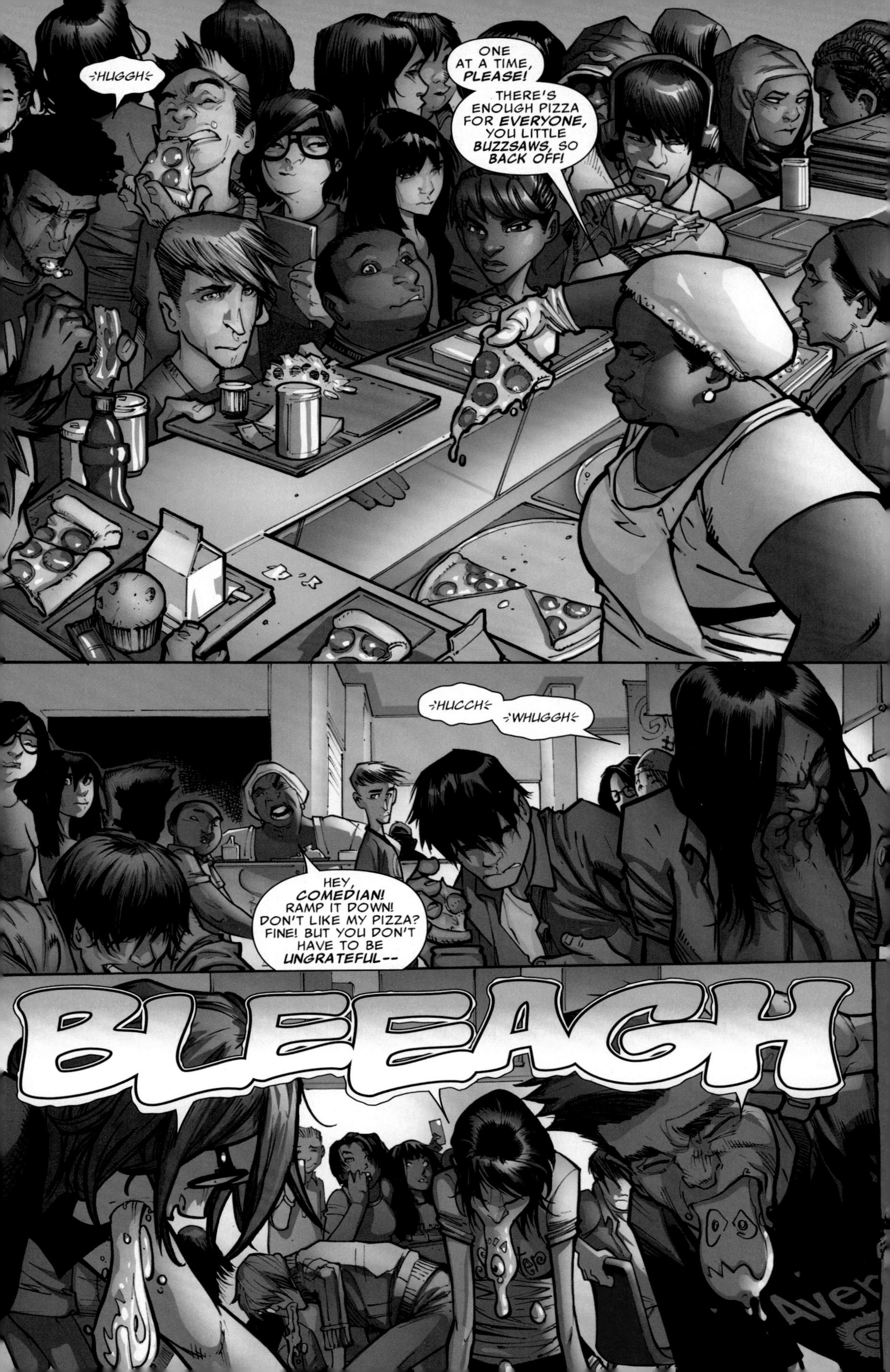
HUGGH
ONE AT A TIME, PLEASE!
THERE'S ENOUGH PIZZA FOR EVERYONE, YOU LITTLE BUZZSAWS, SO BACK OFF!
HUCCH
WHUGGH
HEY, COMEDIAN! RAMP IT DOWN! DON'T LIKE MY PIZZA? FINE! BUT YOU DON'T HAVE TO BE UNGRATEFUL--
BLEEACH

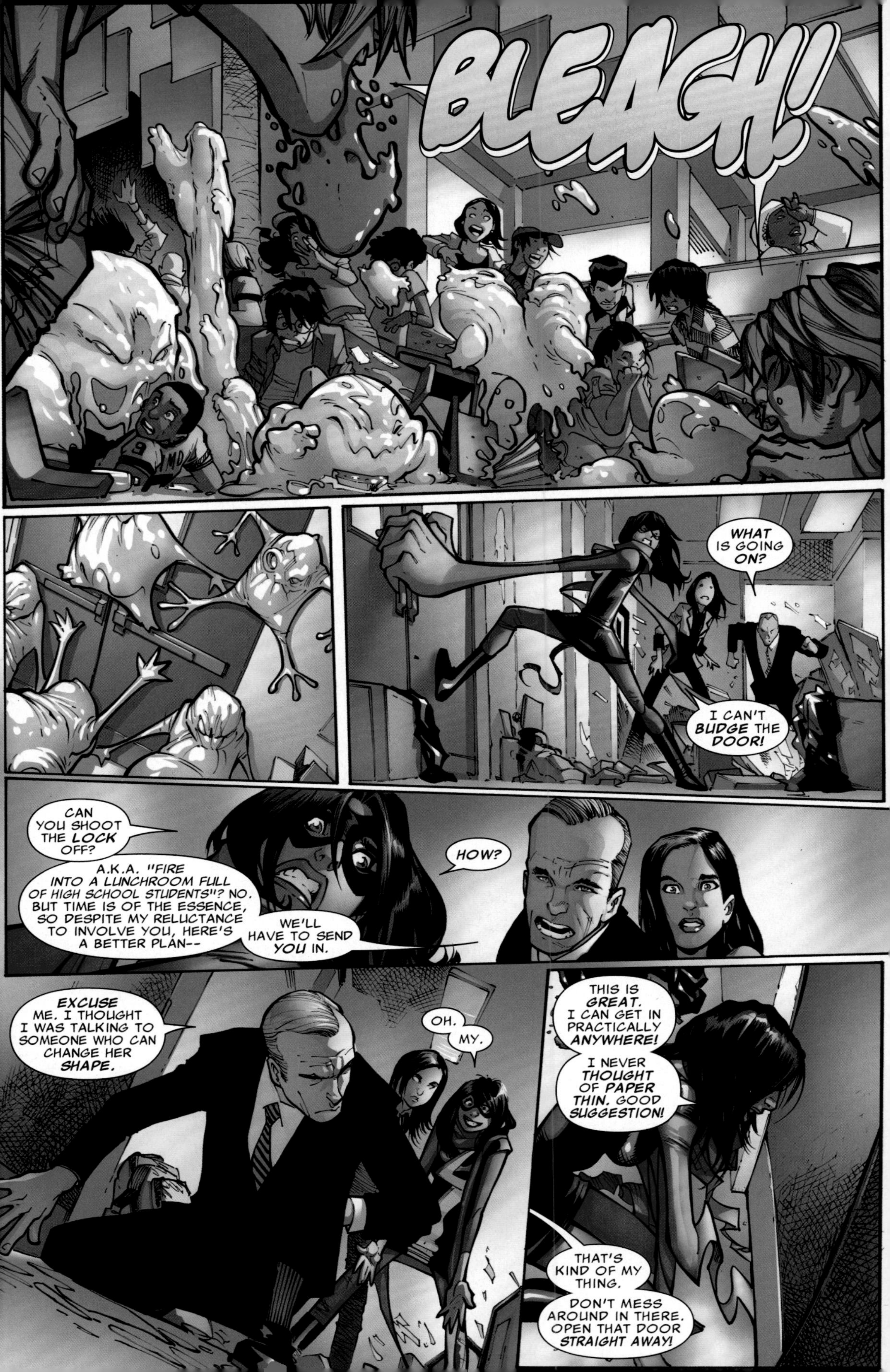

BLEACH!
WHAT IS GOING ON?
I CAN'T BUDGE THE DOOR!
CAN YOU SHOOT THE LOCK OFF?
A.K.A. "FIRE INTO A LUNCHROOM FULL OF HIGH SCHOOL STUDENTS"? NO. BUT TIME IS OF THE ESSENCE, SO DESPITE MY RELUCTANCE TO INVOLVE YOU, HERE'S A BETTER PLAN--
HOW?
WE'LL HAVE TO SEND YOU IN.
EXCUSE ME. I THOUGHT I WAS TALKING TO SOMEONE WHO CAN CHANGE HER SHAPE.
OH.
MY.
THIS IS GREAT. I CAN GET IN PRACTICALLY ANYWHERE!
I NEVER THOUGHT OF PAPER THIN. GOOD SUGGESTION!
THAT'S KIND OF MY THING.
DON'T MESS AROUND IN THERE. OPEN THAT DOOR STRAIGHT AWAY!

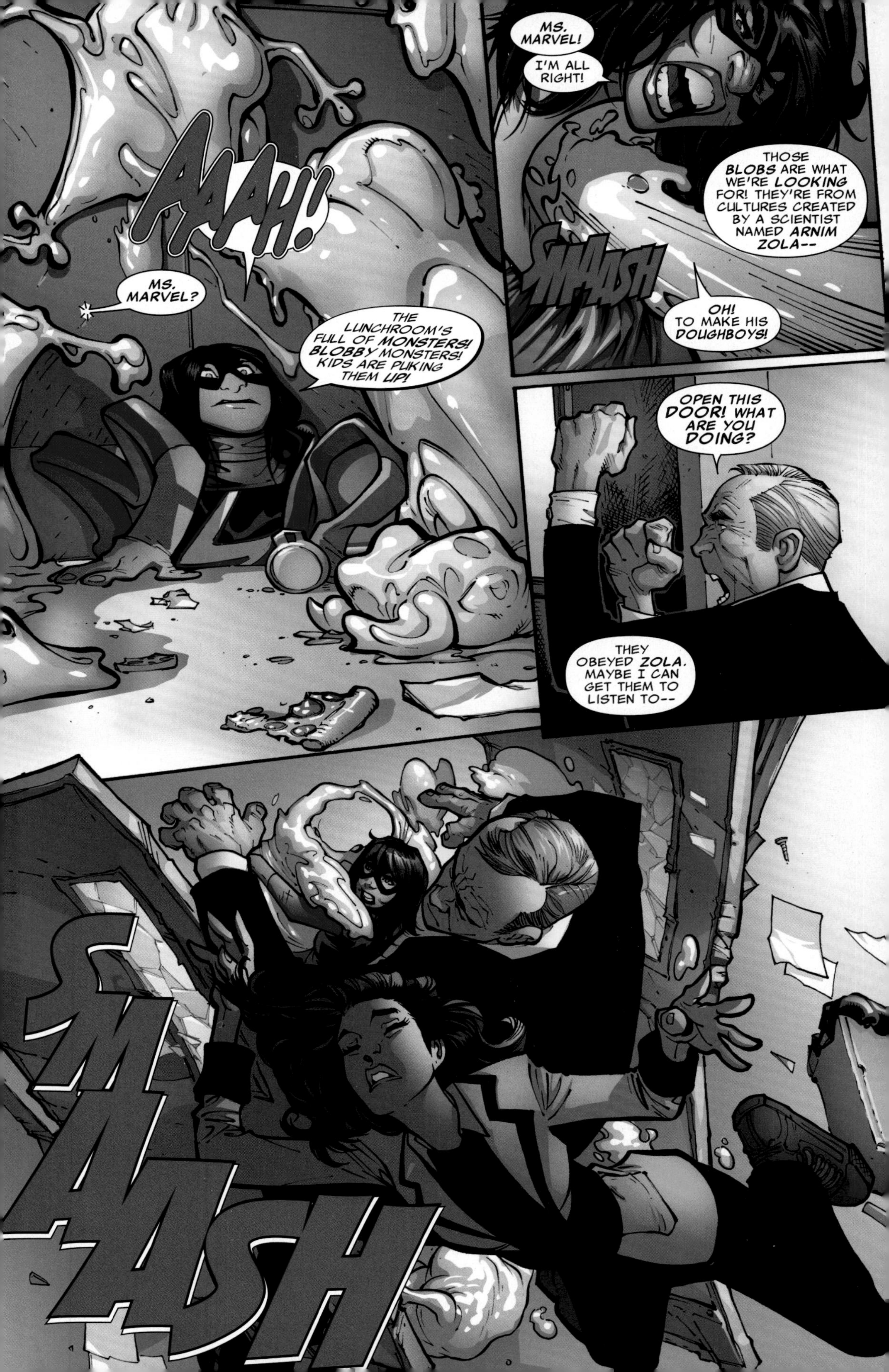
AAAH!
MS. MARVEL?
THE LUNCHROOM'S FULL OF MONSTERS! BLOBBY MONSTERS! KIDS ARE PUKING THEM UP!
MS. MARVEL!
I'M ALL RIGHT!
THOSE BLOBS ARE WHAT WE'RE LOOKING FOR! THEY'RE FROM CULTURES CREATED BY A SCIENTIST NAMED ARNIM ZOLA--
SMAASH
OH! TO MAKE HIS DOUGHBOYS!
OPEN THIS DOOR! WHAT ARE YOU DOING?
THEY OBEYED ZOLA. MAYBE I CAN GET THEM TO LISTEN TO--
SMAASH

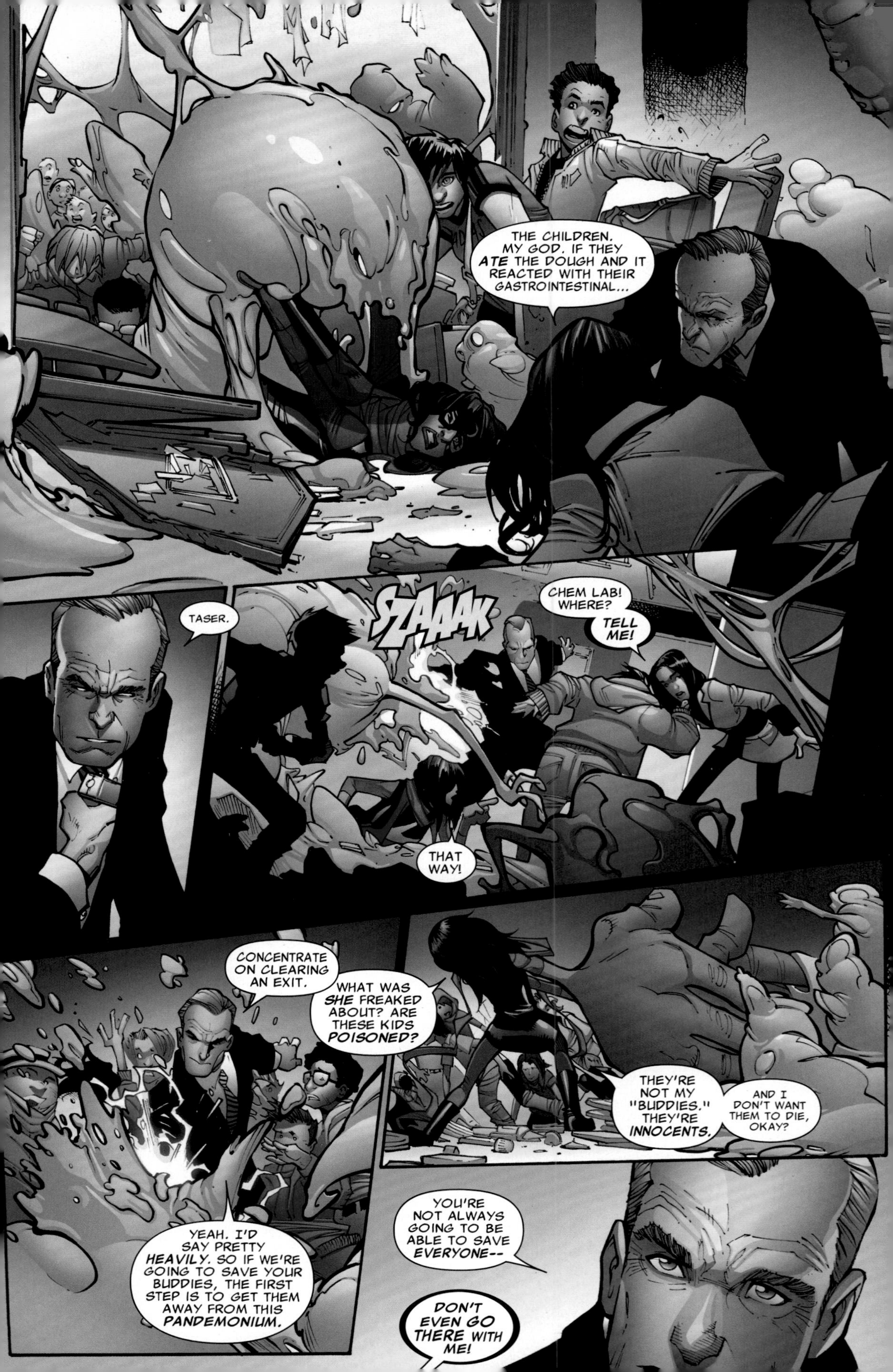

THE CHILDREN. MY GOD. IF THEY ATE THE DOUGH AND IT REACTED WITH THEIR GASTROINTESTINAL...
TASER.
SZAAAK
CHEM LAB! WHERE? TELL ME!
THAT WAY!
CONCENTRATE ON CLEARING AN EXIT.
WHAT WAS SHE FREAKED ABOUT? ARE THESE KIDS POISONED?
YEAH. I'D SAY PRETTY HEAVILY. SO IF WE'RE GOING TO SAVE YOUR BUDDIES, THE FIRST STEP IS TO GET THEM AWAY FROM THIS PANDEMONIUM.
THEY'RE NOT MY "BUDDIES." THEY'RE INNOCENTS.
AND I DON'T WANT THEM TO DIE, OKAY?
YOU'RE NOT ALWAYS GOING TO BE ABLE TO SAVE EVERYONE--
DON'T EVEN GO THERE WITH ME!

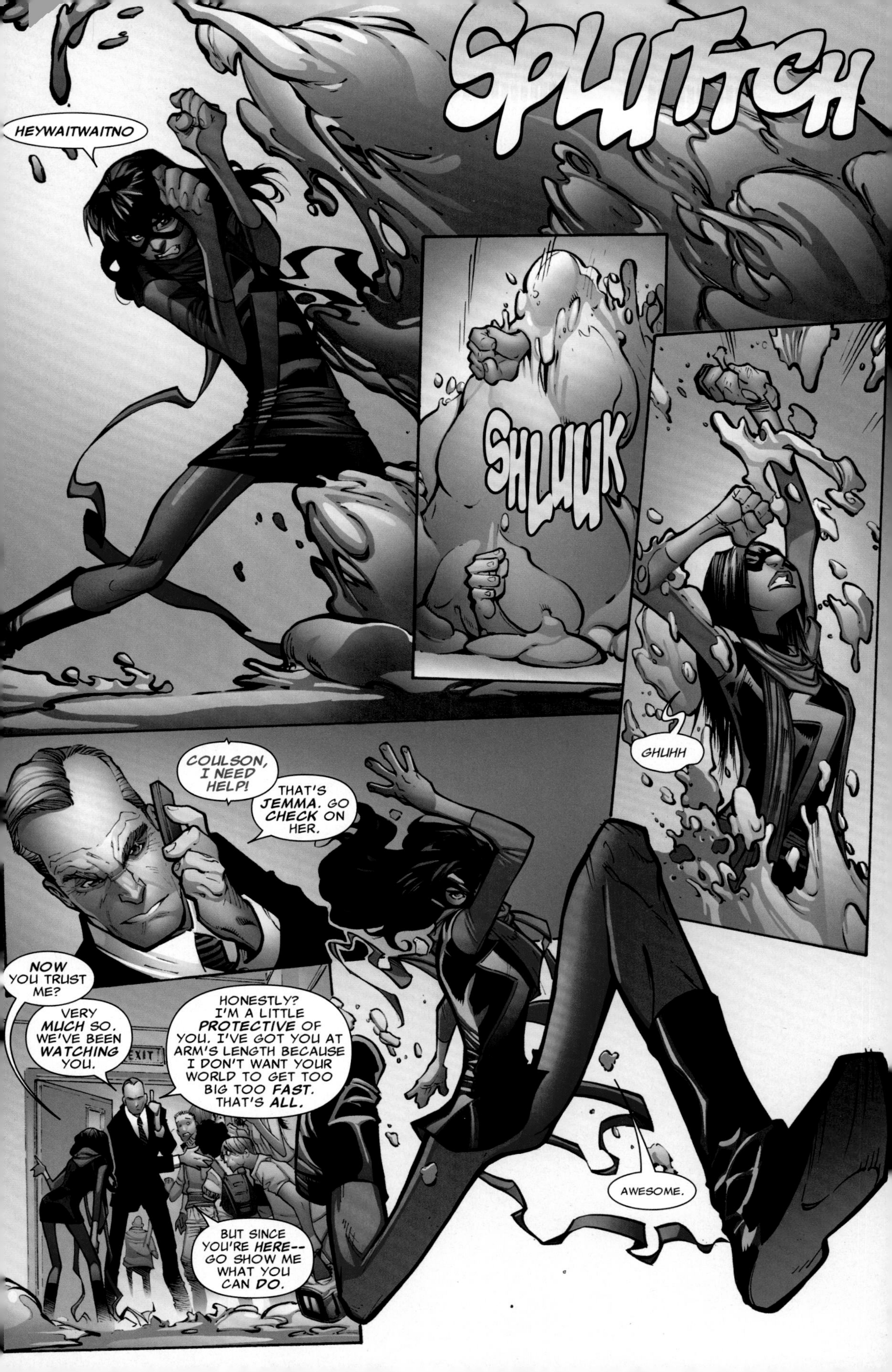
SPLUTCH
HEYWAITWAITNO
SHLUUK
GHUHH
COULSON, I NEED HELP!
THAT'S JEMMA. GO CHECK ON HER.
NOW YOU TRUST ME?
VERY MUCH SO. WE'VE BEEN WATCHING YOU.
HONESTLY? I'M A LITTLE PROTECTIVE OF YOU. I'VE GOT YOU AT ARM'S LENGTH BECAUSE I DON'T WANT YOUR WORLD TO GET TOO BIG TOO FAST. THAT'S ALL.
EXIT
BUT SINCE YOU'RE HERE-- GO SHOW ME WHAT YOU CAN DO.
AWESOME.

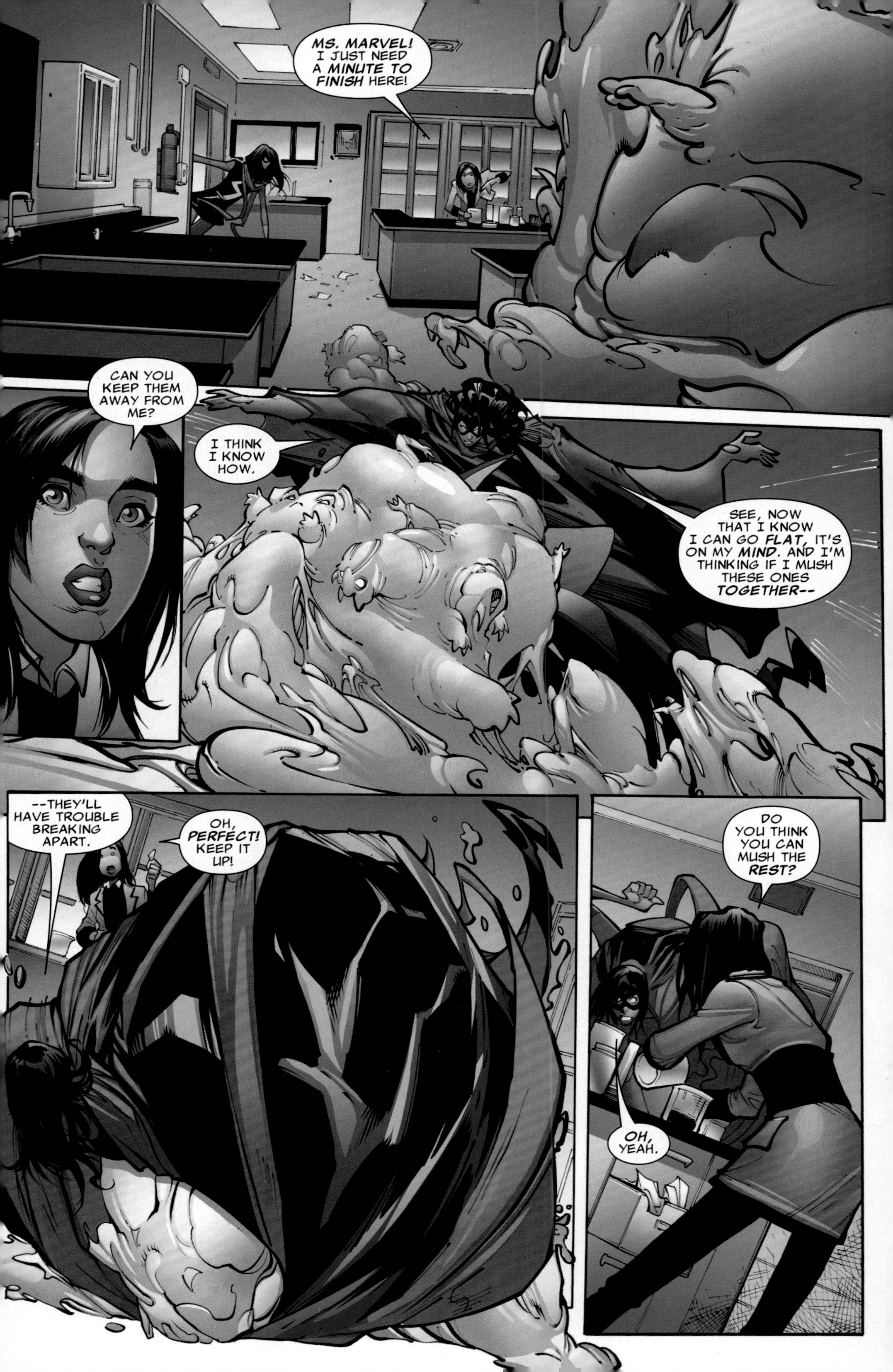
MS. MARVEL! I JUST NEED A MINUTE TO FINISH HERE!
CAN YOU KEEP THEM AWAY FROM ME?
I THINK I KNOW HOW.
SEE, NOW THAT I KNOW I CAN GO FLAT, IT'S ON MY MIND. AND I'M THINKING IF I MUSH THESE ONES TOGETHER--
--THEY'LL HAVE TROUBLE BREAKING APART.
OH, PERFECT! KEEP IT UP!
DO YOU THINK YOU CAN MUSH THE REST?
OH, YEAH.

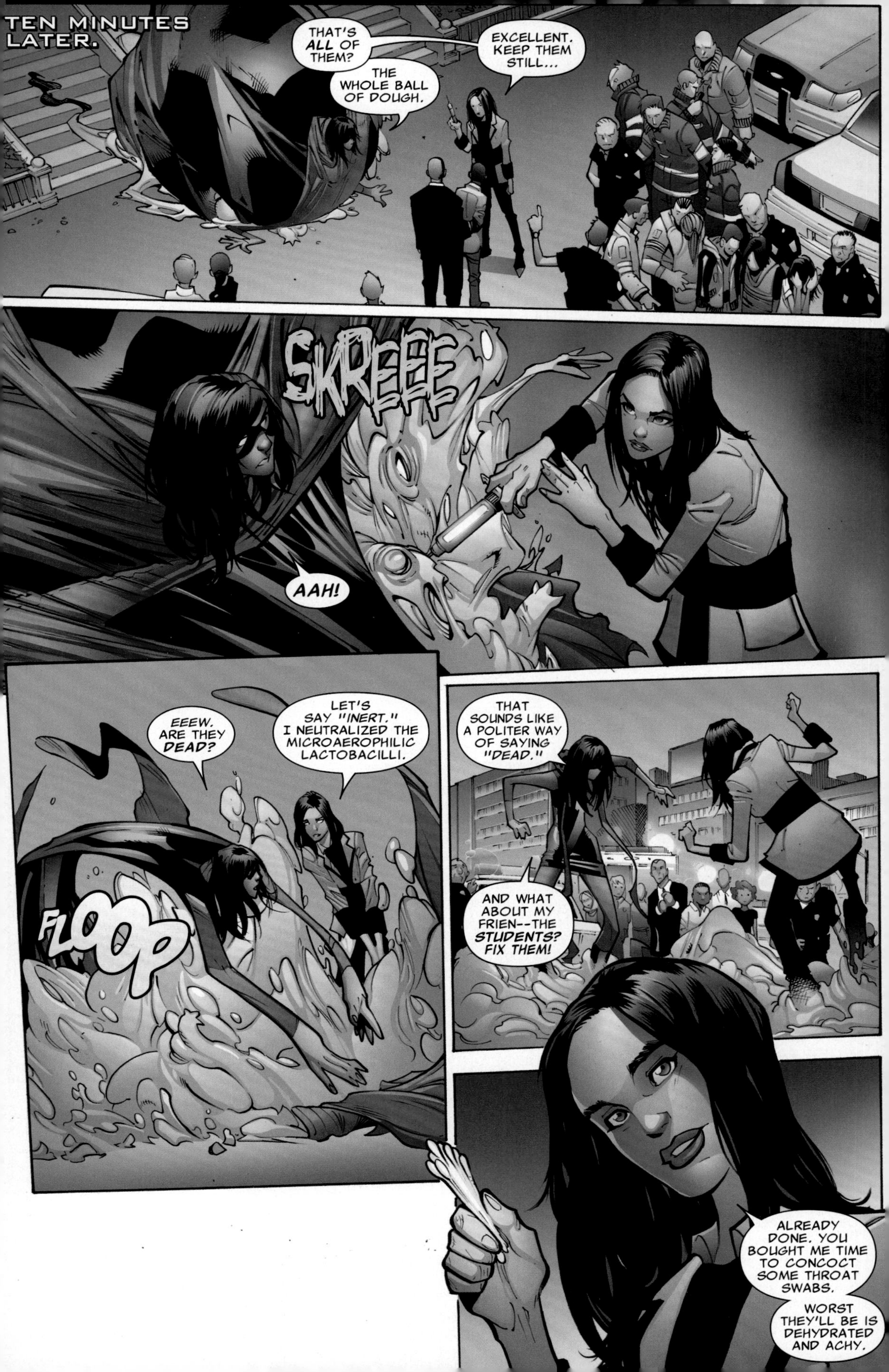
TEN MINUTES LATER.
THAT'S ALL OF THEM?
THE WHOLE BALL OF DOUGH.
EXCELLENT. KEEP THEM STILL...
SKREEEE
AAH!
EEEW. ARE THEY DEAD?
LET'S SAY "INERT." I NEUTRALIZED THE MICROAEROPHILIC LACTOBACILLI.
FLOOP
THAT SOUNDS LIKE A POLITER WAY OF SAYING "DEAD."
AND WHAT ABOUT MY FRIEN--THE STUDENTS? FIX THEM!
ALREADY DONE. YOU BOUGHT ME TIME TO CONCOCT SOME THROAT SWABS.
WORST THEY'LL BE IS DEHYDRATED AND ACHY.

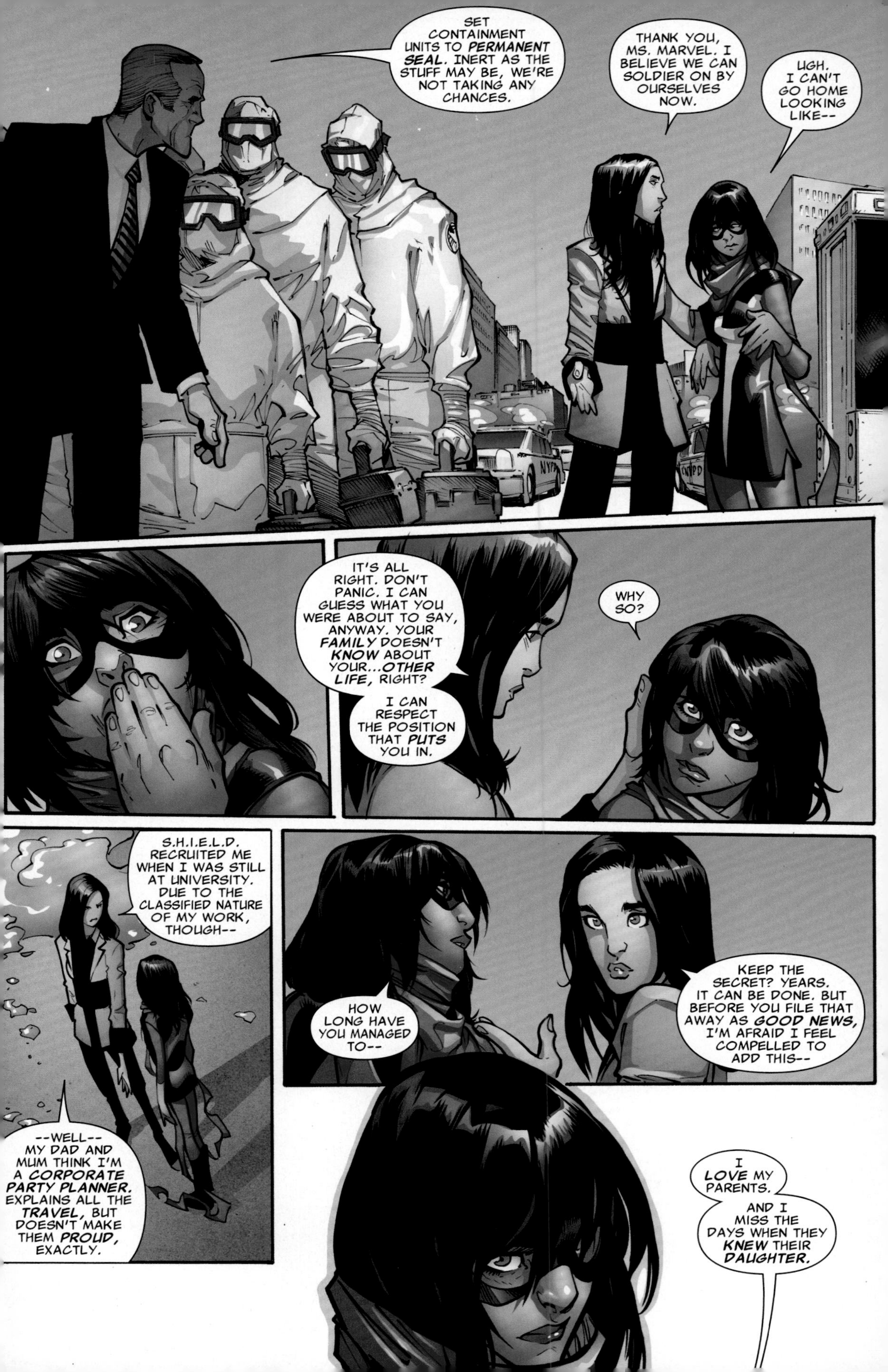
SET CONTAINMENT UNITS TO PERMANENT SEAL. INERT AS THE STUFF MAY BE, WE'RE NOT TAKING ANY CHANCES.
THANK YOU, MS. MARVEL. I BELIEVE WE CAN SOLDIER ON BY OURSELVES NOW.
UGH. I CAN'T GO HOME LOOKING LIKE--
IT'S ALL RIGHT. DON'T PANIC. I CAN GUESS WHAT YOU WERE ABOUT TO SAY, ANYWAY. YOUR FAMILY DOESN'T KNOW ABOUT YOUR...OTHER LIFE, RIGHT?
I CAN RESPECT THE POSITION THAT PUTS YOU IN.
WHY SO?
S.H.I.E.L.D. RECRUITED ME WHEN I WAS STILL AT UNIVERSITY. DUE TO THE CLASSIFIED NATURE OF MY WORK, THOUGH--
--WELL-- MY DAD AND MUM THINK I'M A CORPORATE PARTY PLANNER. EXPLAINS ALL THE TRAVEL, BUT DOESN'T MAKE THEM PROUD, EXACTLY.
HOW LONG HAVE YOU MANAGED TO--
KEEP THE SECRET? YEARS. IT CAN BE DONE. BUT BEFORE YOU FILE THAT AWAY AS GOOD NEWS, I'M AFRAID I FEEL COMPELLED TO ADD THIS--
I LOVE MY PARENTS.
AND I MISS THE DAYS WHEN THEY KNEW THEIR DAUGHTER.

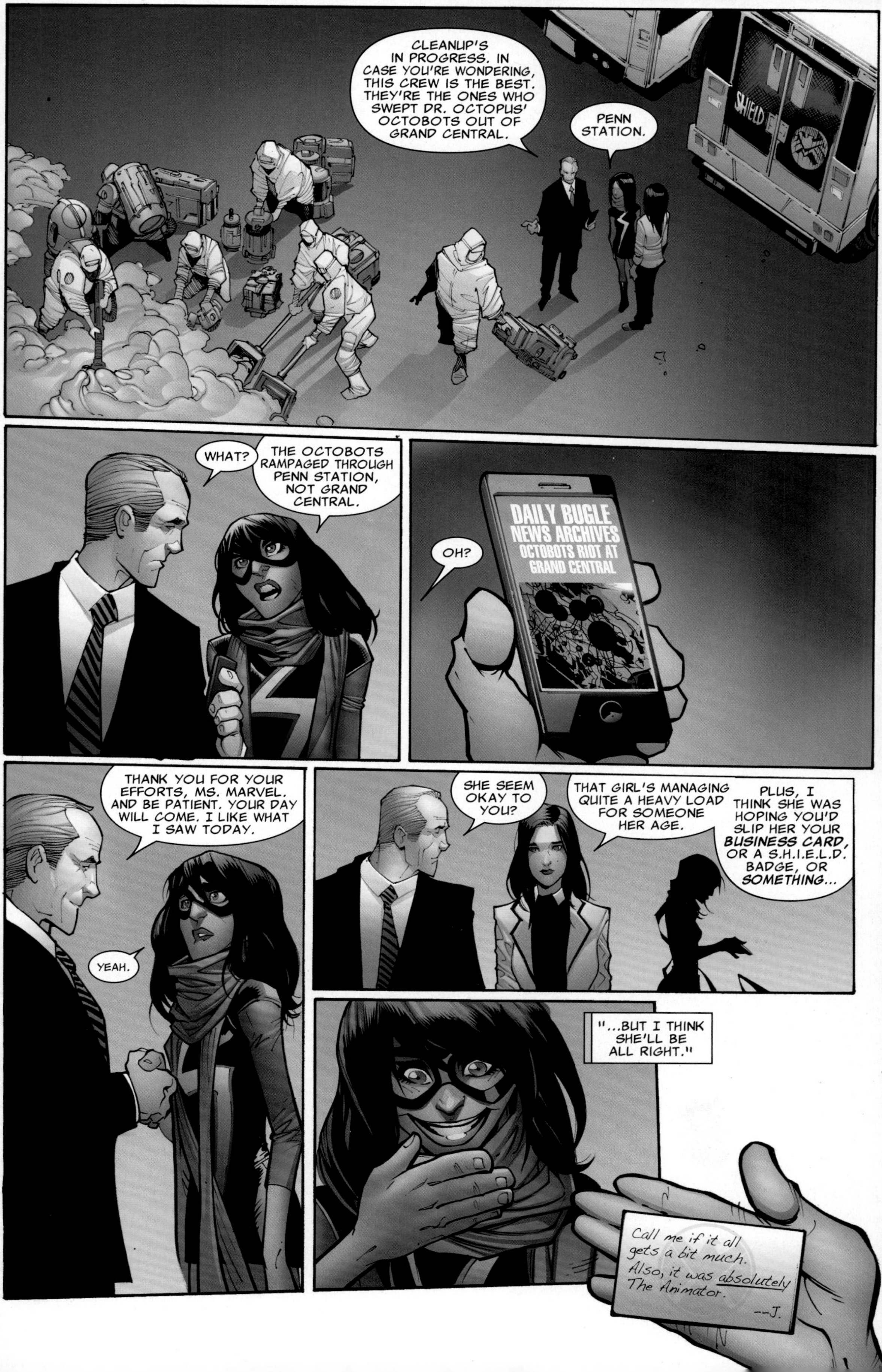
CLEANUP'S IN PROGRESS. IN CASE YOU'RE WONDERING, THIS CREW IS THE BEST. THEY'RE THE ONES WHO SWEPT DR. OCTOPUS' OCTOBOTS OUT OF GRAND CENTRAL.
PENN STATION.
SHIELD
WHAT?
THE OCTOBOTS RAMPAGED THROUGH PENN STATION, NOT GRAND CENTRAL.
OH?
DAILY BUGLE NEWS ARCHIVES OCTOBOTS RIOT AT GRAND CENTRAL
THANK YOU FOR YOUR EFFORTS, MS. MARVEL. AND BE PATIENT. YOUR DAY WILL COME. I LIKE WHAT I SAW TODAY.
YEAH.
SHE SEEM OKAY TO YOU?
THAT GIRL'S MANAGING QUITE A HEAVY LOAD FOR SOMEONE HER AGE.
PLUS, I THINK SHE WAS HOPING YOU'D SLIP HER YOUR BUSINESS CARD, OR A S.H.I.E.L.D. BADGE, OR SOMETHING...
"...BUT I THINK SHE'LL BE ALL RIGHT."
Call me if it all gets a bit much. Also, it was absolutely The Animator. --J.

3. ACTIVE MISSION: HOME INVASION

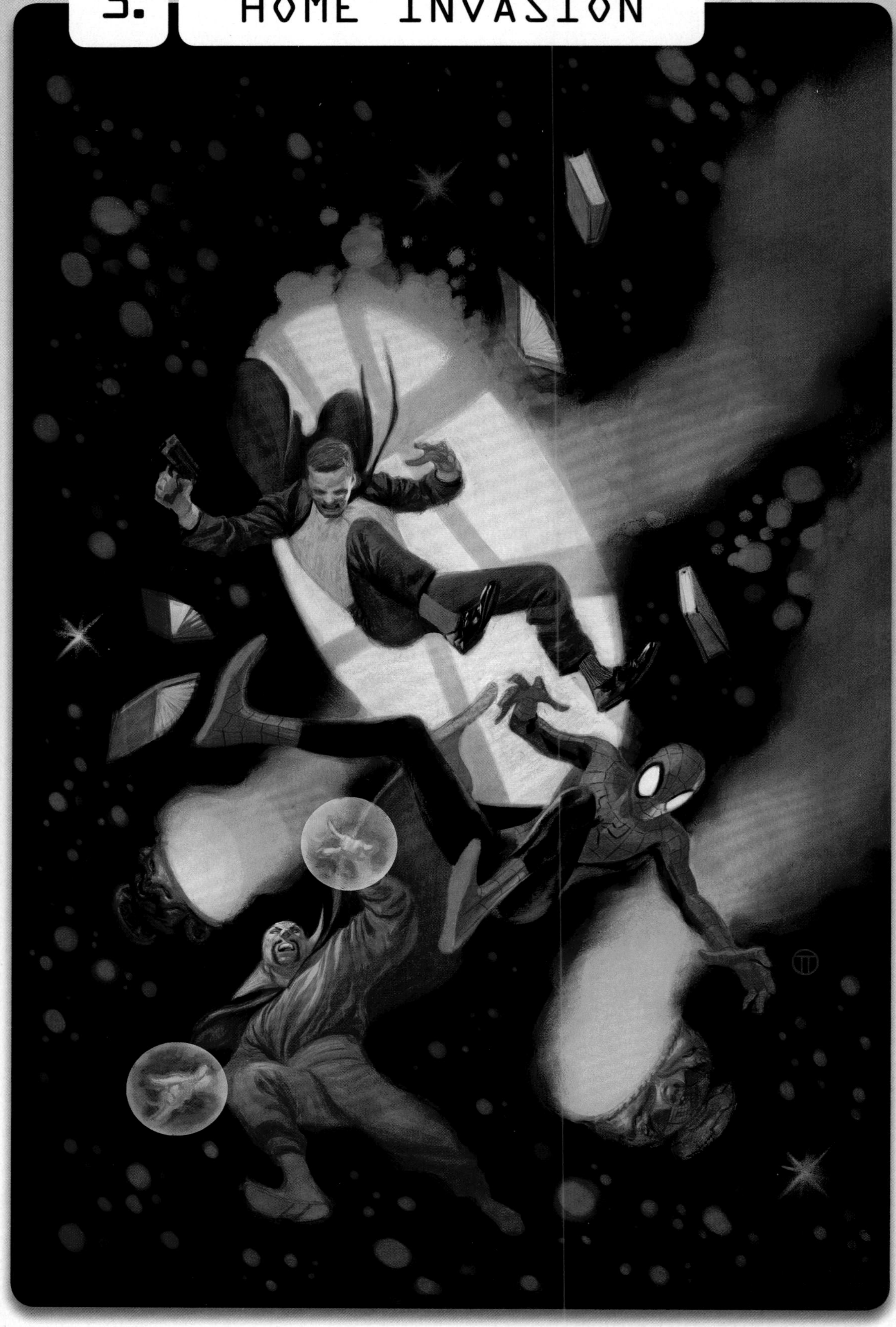

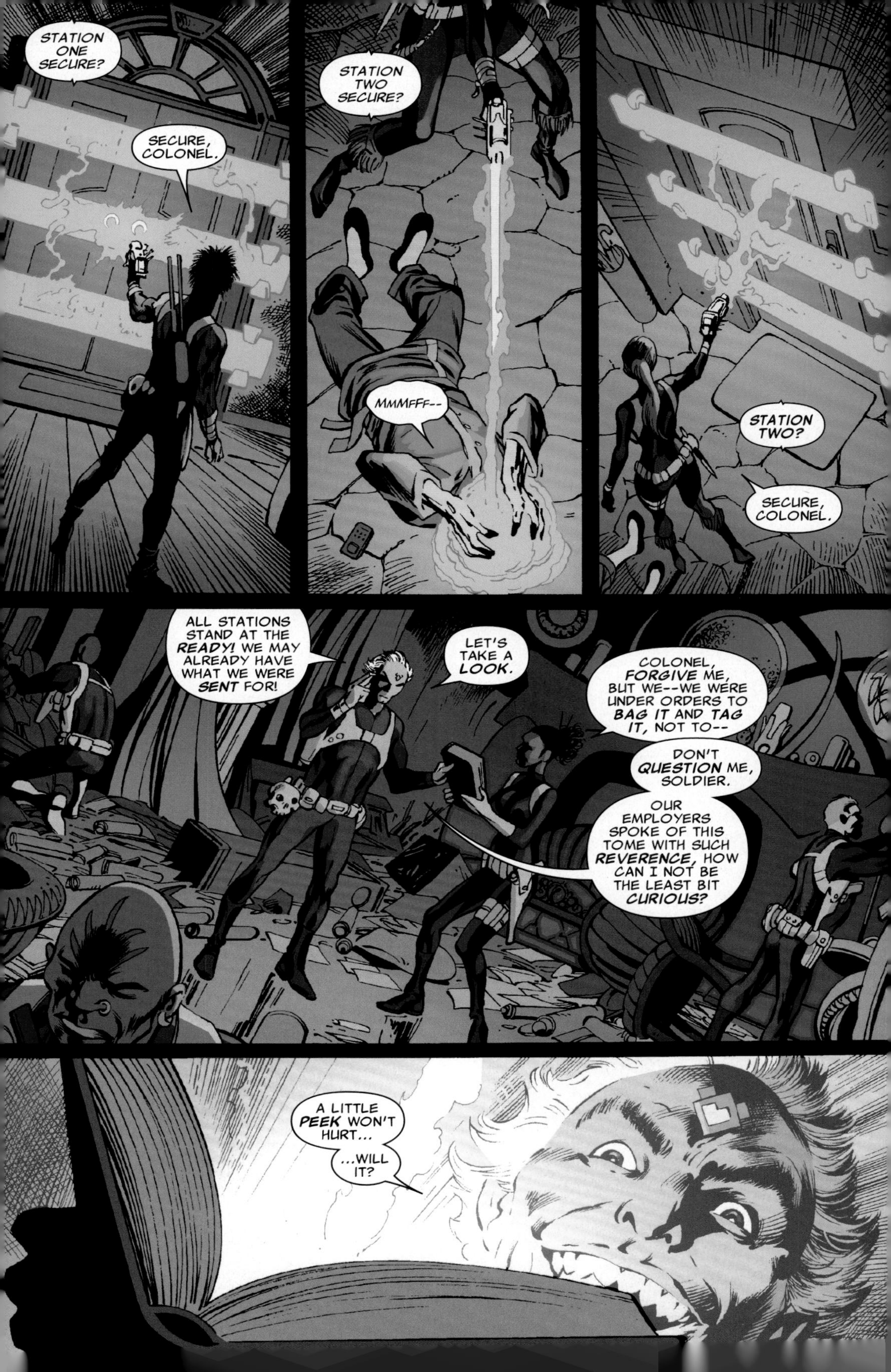

STATION ONE SECURE?
SECURE, COLONEL.
STATION TWO SECURE?
MMMFFF--
STATION TWO?
SECURE, COLONEL.
ALL STATIONS STAND AT THE READY! WE MAY ALREADY HAVE WHAT WE WERE SENT FOR!
LET'S TAKE A LOOK.
COLONEL, FORGIVE ME, BUT WE--WE WERE UNDER ORDERS TO BAG IT AND TAG IT, NOT TO--
DON'T QUESTION ME, SOLDIER.
OUR EMPLOYERS SPOKE OF THIS TOME WITH SUCH REVERENCE, HOW CAN I NOT BE THE LEAST BIT CURIOUS?
A LITTLE PEEK WON'T HURT...
...WILL IT?

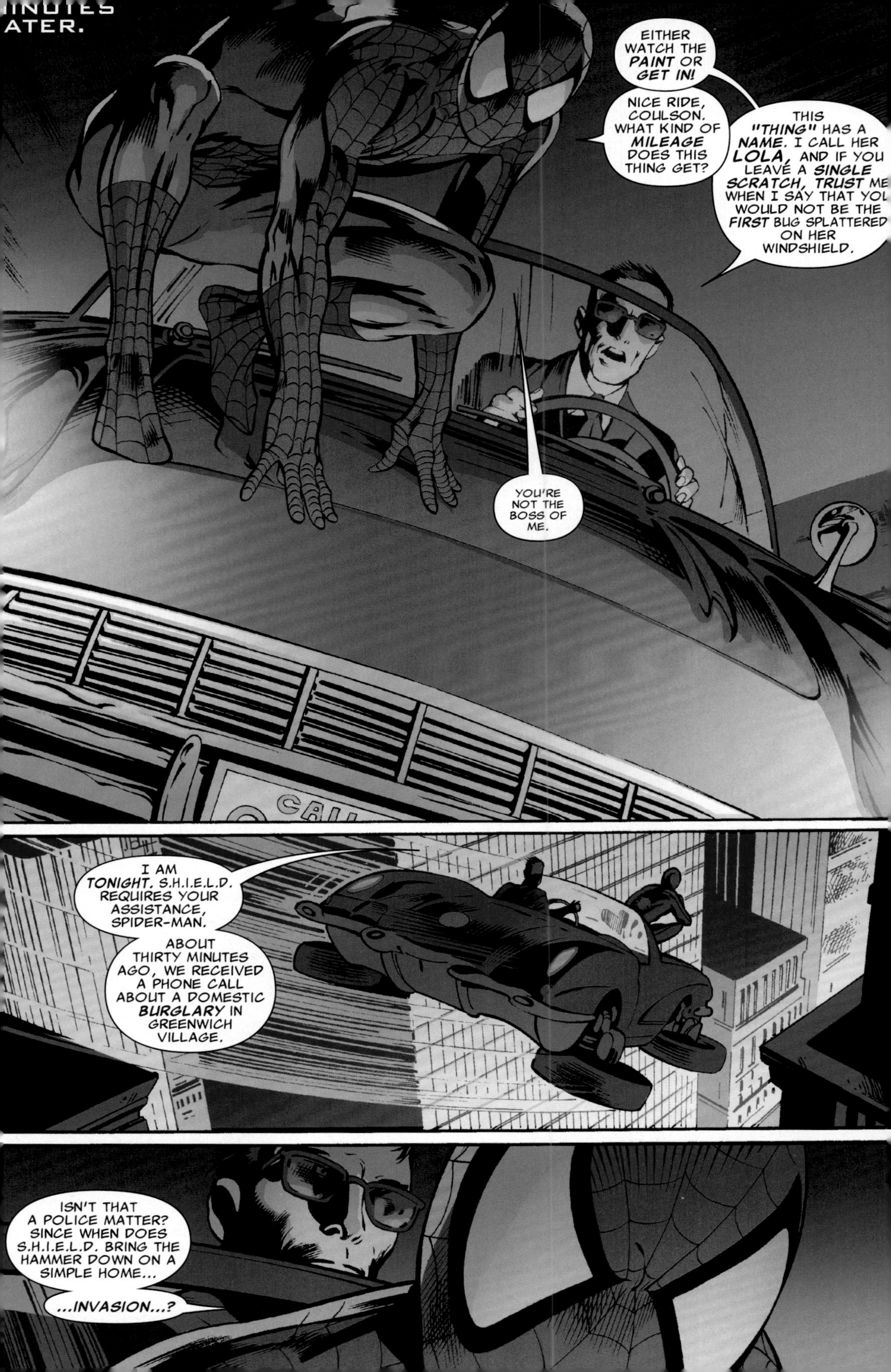
EITHER WATCH THE PAINT OR GET IN!
NICE RIDE, COULSON. WHAT KIND OF MILEAGE DOES THIS THING GET?
THIS "THING" HAS A NAME. I CALL HER LOLA, AND IF YOU LEAVE A SINGLE SCRATCH, TRUST ME WHEN I SAY THAT YOU WOULD NOT BE THE FIRST BUG SPLATTERED ON HER WINDSHIELD.
YOU'RE NOT THE BOSS OF ME.
I AM TONIGHT. S.H.I.E.L.D. REQUIRES YOUR ASSISTANCE, SPIDER-MAN.
ABOUT THIRTY MINUTES AGO, WE RECEIVED A PHONE CALL ABOUT A DOMESTIC BURGLARY IN GREENWICH VILLAGE.
ISN'T THAT A POLICE MATTER? SINCE WHEN DOES S.H.I.E.L.D. BRING THE HAMMER DOWN ON A SIMPLE HOME...
...INVASION...?

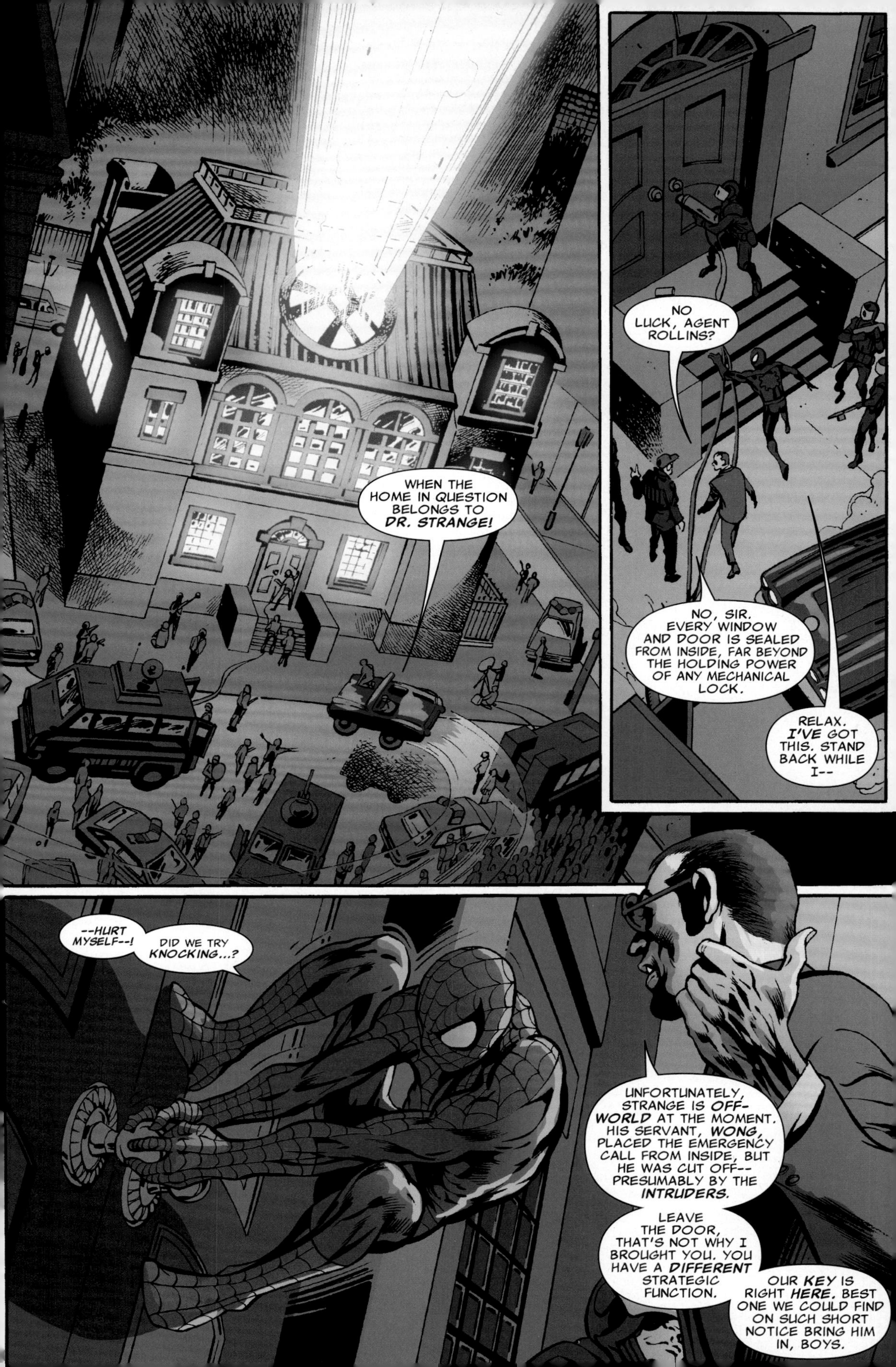
WHEN THE HOME IN QUESTION BELONGS TO DR. STRANGE!
NO LUCK, AGENT ROLLINS?
NO, SIR. EVERY WINDOW AND DOOR IS SEALED FROM INSIDE, FAR BEYOND THE HOLDING POWER OF ANY MECHANICAL LOCK.
RELAX. I'VE GOT THIS. STAND BACK WHILE I--
--HURT MYSELF--!
DID WE TRY KNOCKING...?
UNFORTUNATELY, STRANGE IS OFF-WORLD AT THE MOMENT. HIS SERVANT, WONG, PLACED THE EMERGENCY CALL FROM INSIDE, BUT HE WAS CUT OFF--PRESUMABLY BY THE INTRUDERS.
LEAVE THE DOOR, THAT'S NOT WHY I BROUGHT YOU. YOU HAVE A DIFFERENT STRATEGIC FUNCTION.
OUR KEY IS RIGHT HERE. BEST ONE WE COULD FIND ON SUCH SHORT NOTICE BRING HIM IN, BOYS.

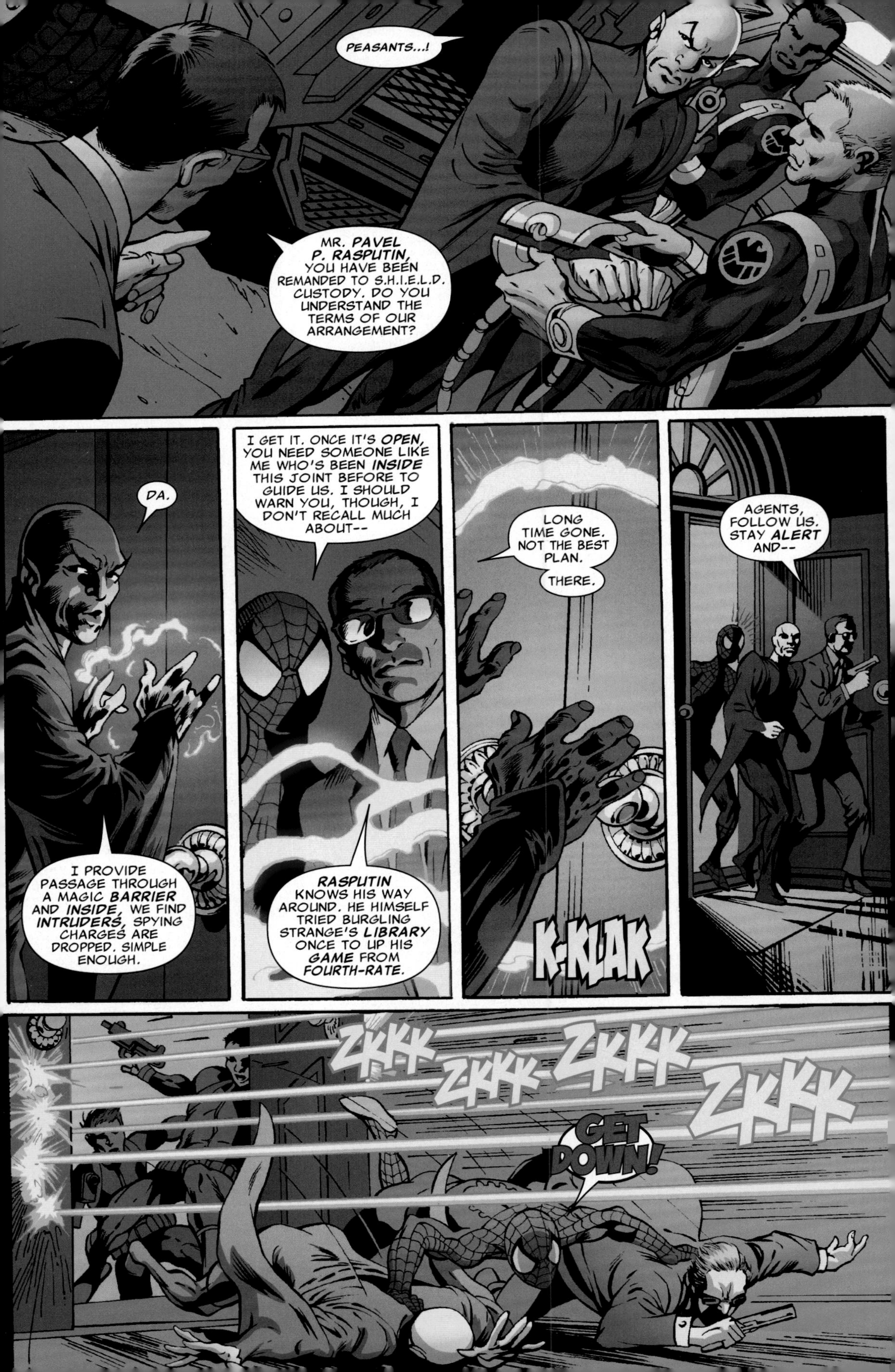
PEASANTS...!
MR. PAVEL P. RASPUTIN, YOU HAVE BEEN REMANDED TO S.H.I.E.L.D. CUSTODY. DO YOU UNDERSTAND THE TERMS OF OUR ARRANGEMENT?
DA.
I PROVIDE PASSAGE THROUGH A MAGIC BARRIER AND INSIDE, WE FIND INTRUDERS, SPYING CHARGES ARE DROPPED. SIMPLE ENOUGH.
I GET IT. ONCE IT'S OPEN, YOU NEED SOMEONE LIKE ME WHO'S BEEN INSIDE THIS JOINT BEFORE TO GUIDE US. I SHOULD WARN YOU, THOUGH, I DON'T RECALL MUCH ABOUT--
RASPUTIN KNOWS HIS WAY AROUND. HE HIMSELF TRIED BURGLING STRANGE'S LIBRARY ONCE TO UP HIS GAME FROM FOURTH-RATE.
LONG TIME GONE. NOT THE BEST PLAN.
THERE.
K-KLAK
AGENTS, FOLLOW US. STAY ALERT AND--
ZKKK ZKKK ZKKK ZKKK
GET DOWN!

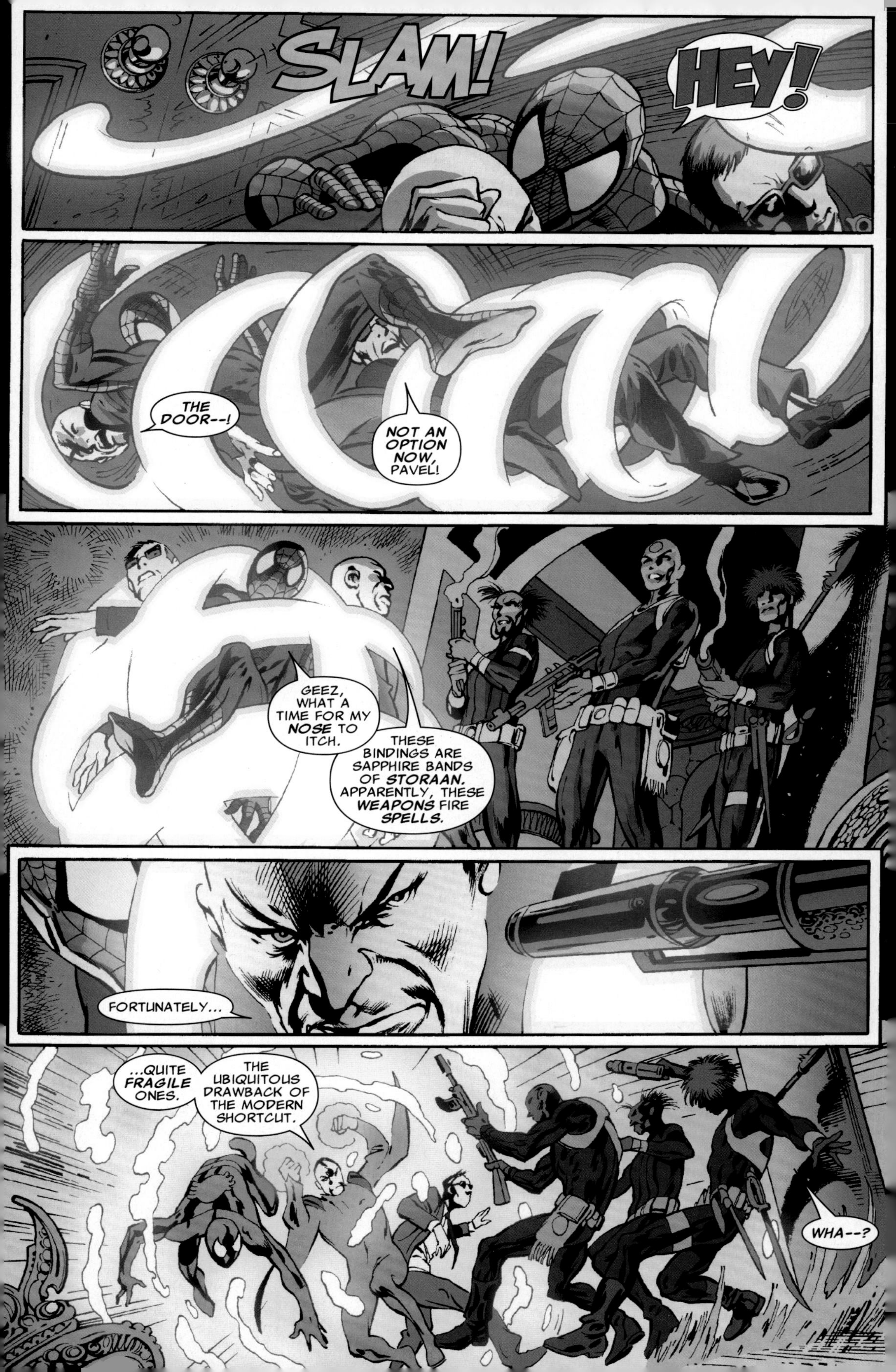
SLAM!
HEY!
THE DOOR--!
NOT AN OPTION NOW, PAVEL!
GEEZ, WHAT A TIME FOR MY NOSE TO ITCH.
THESE BINDINGS ARE SAPPHIRE BANDS OF STORAAN. APPARENTLY, THESE WEAPONS FIRE SPELLS.
FORTUNATELY...
...QUITE FRAGILE ONES.
THE UBIQUITOUS DRAWBACK OF THE MODERN SHORTCUT.
WHA--?

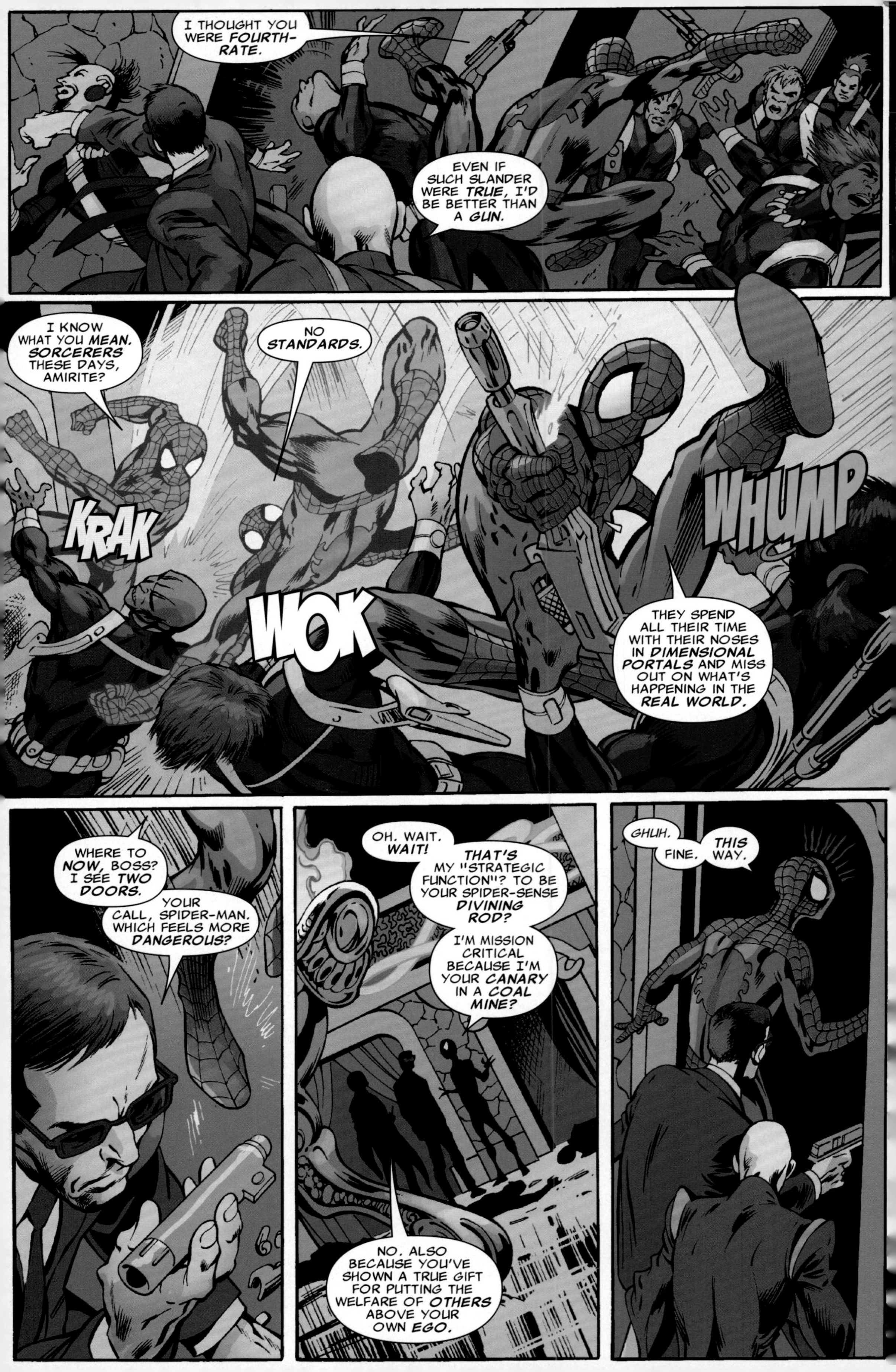
I THOUGHT YOU WERE FOURTH-RATE.
EVEN IF SUCH SLANDER WERE TRUE, I'D BE BETTER THAN A GUN.
I KNOW WHAT YOU MEAN. SORCERERS THESE DAYS, AMIRITE?
NO STANDARDS.
KRAK
WOK
WHUMP
THEY SPEND ALL THEIR TIME WITH THEIR NOSES IN DIMENSIONAL PORTALS AND MISS OUT ON WHAT'S HAPPENING IN THE REAL WORLD.
WHERE TO NOW, BOSS? I SEE TWO DOORS.
YOUR CALL, SPIDER-MAN. WHICH FEELS MORE DANGEROUS?
OH. WAIT. WAIT!
THAT'S MY "STRATEGIC FUNCTION"? TO BE YOUR SPIDER-SENSE DIVINING ROD?
I'M MISSION CRITICAL BECAUSE I'M YOUR CANARY IN A COAL MINE?
NO. ALSO BECAUSE YOU'VE SHOWN A TRUE GIFT FOR PUTTING THE WELFARE OF OTHERS ABOVE YOUR OWN EGO.
GHUH.
FINE.
THIS WAY.

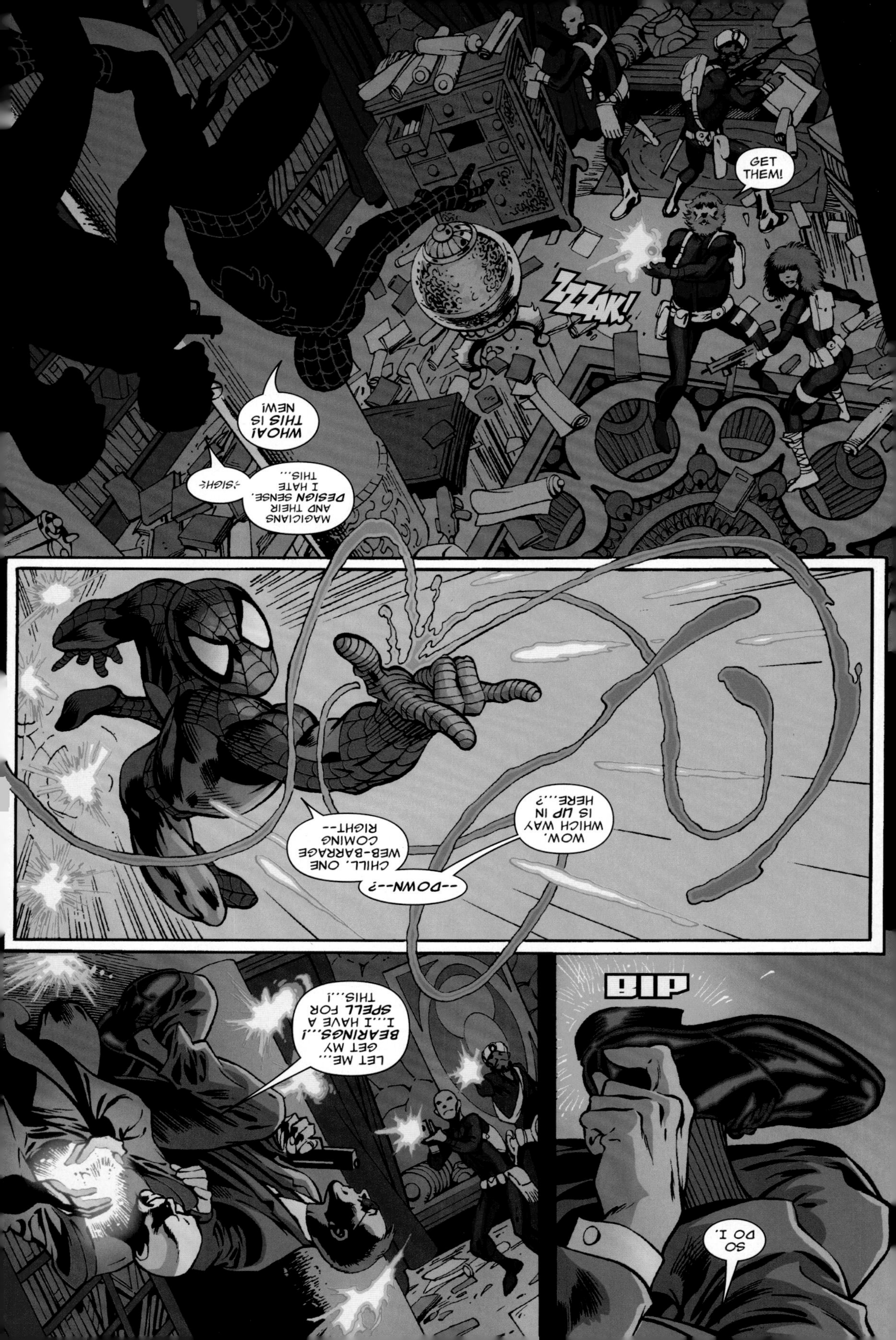

GET THEM!
ZZZAK!
WHOA! THIS IS NEW!
MAGICIANS AND THEIR DESIGN SENSE. I HATE THIS...
SIGH
WOW. WHICH WAY IS UP IN HERE...?
--DOWN--?
CHILL, ONE WEB-BARRAGE COMING RIGHT--
LET ME... GET MY BEARINGS...! I... I HAVE A SPELL FOR THIS...!
BIP
SO DO I.

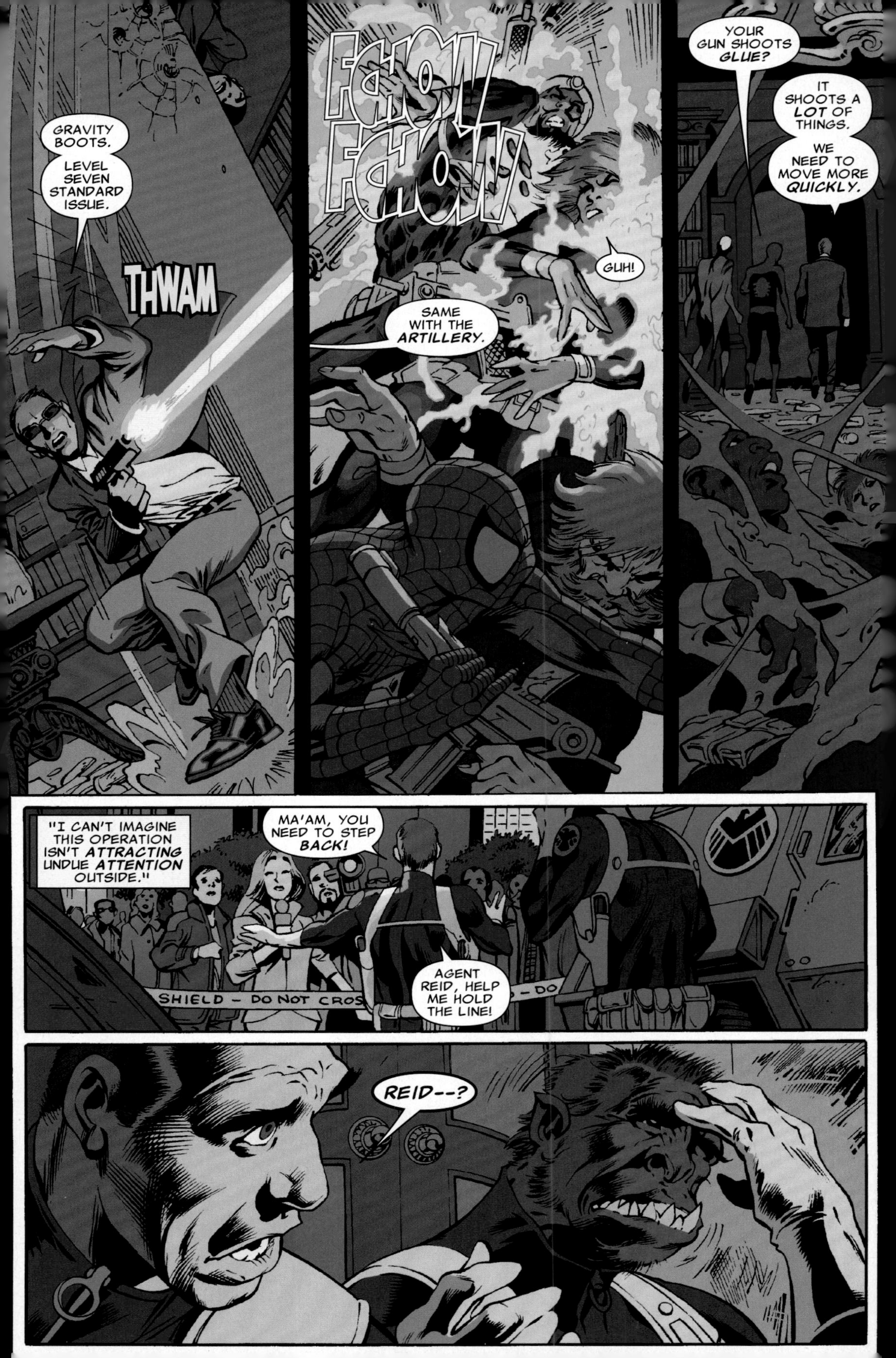
GRAVITY BOOTS.
LEVEL SEVEN STANDARD ISSUE.
THWAM
FCHOW FCHOW
GUH!
SAME WITH THE ARTILLERY.
YOUR GUN SHOOTS GLUE?
IT SHOOTS A LOT OF THINGS.
WE NEED TO MOVE MORE QUICKLY.
"I CAN'T IMAGINE THIS OPERATION ISN'T ATTRACTING UNDUE ATTENTION OUTSIDE."
MA'AM, YOU NEED TO STEP BACK!
AGENT REID, HELP ME HOLD THE LINE!
SHIELD - DO NOT CROS
- DO
REID--?

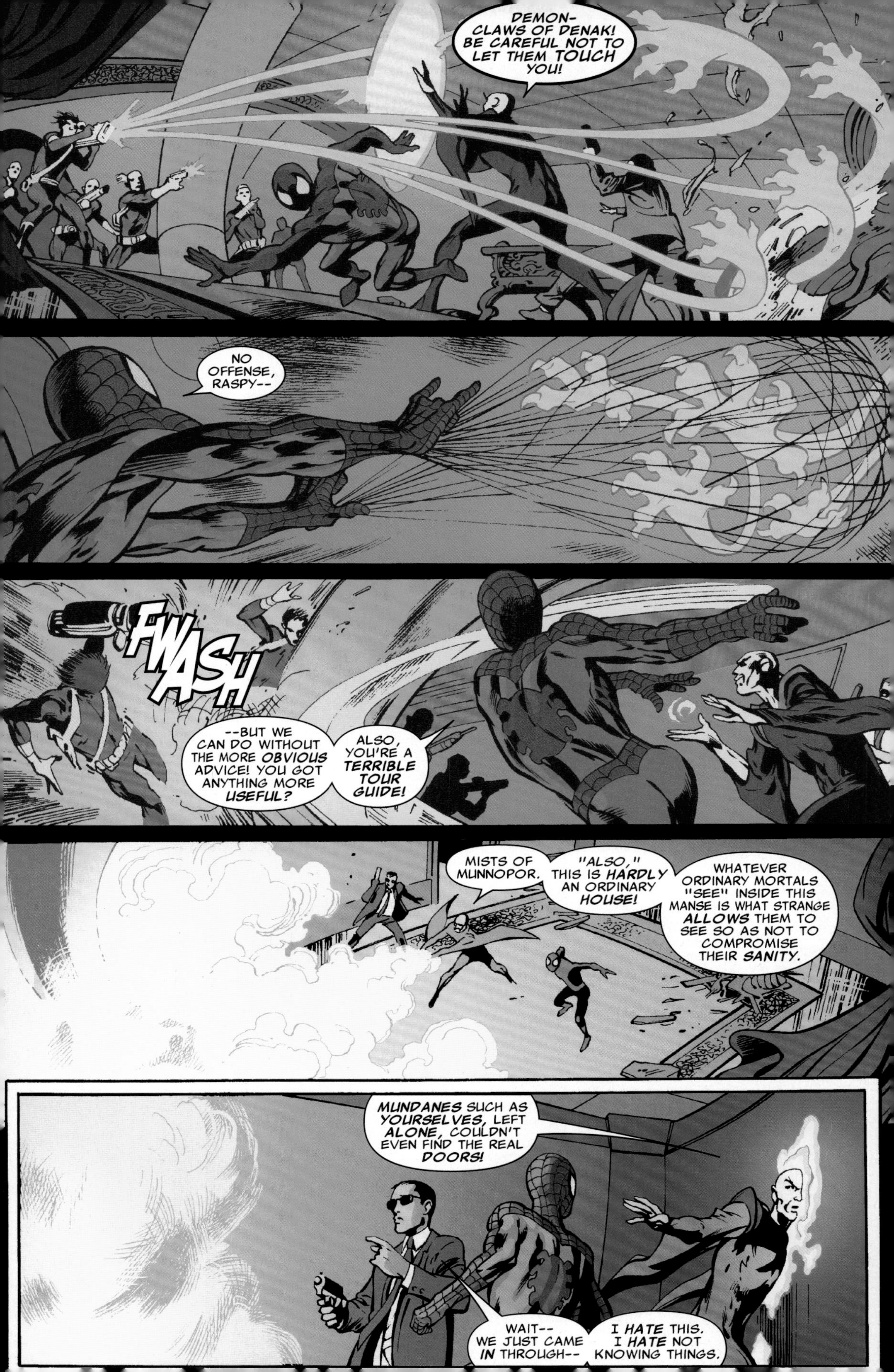
DEMON-CLAWS OF DENAK! BE CAREFUL NOT TO LET THEM TOUCH YOU!
NO OFFENSE, RASPY--
FWASH
--BUT WE CAN DO WITHOUT THE MORE OBVIOUS ADVICE! YOU GOT ANYTHING MORE USEFUL?
ALSO, YOU'RE A TERRIBLE TOUR GUIDE!
MISTS OF MUNNOPOR.
"ALSO," THIS IS HARDLY AN ORDINARY HOUSE!
WHATEVER ORDINARY MORTALS "SEE" INSIDE THIS MANSE IS WHAT STRANGE ALLOWS THEM TO SEE SO AS NOT TO COMPROMISE THEIR SANITY.
MUNDANES SUCH AS YOURSELVES, LEFT ALONE, COULDN'T EVEN FIND THE REAL DOORS!
WAIT-- WE JUST CAME IN THROUGH--
I HATE THIS. I HATE NOT KNOWING THINGS.

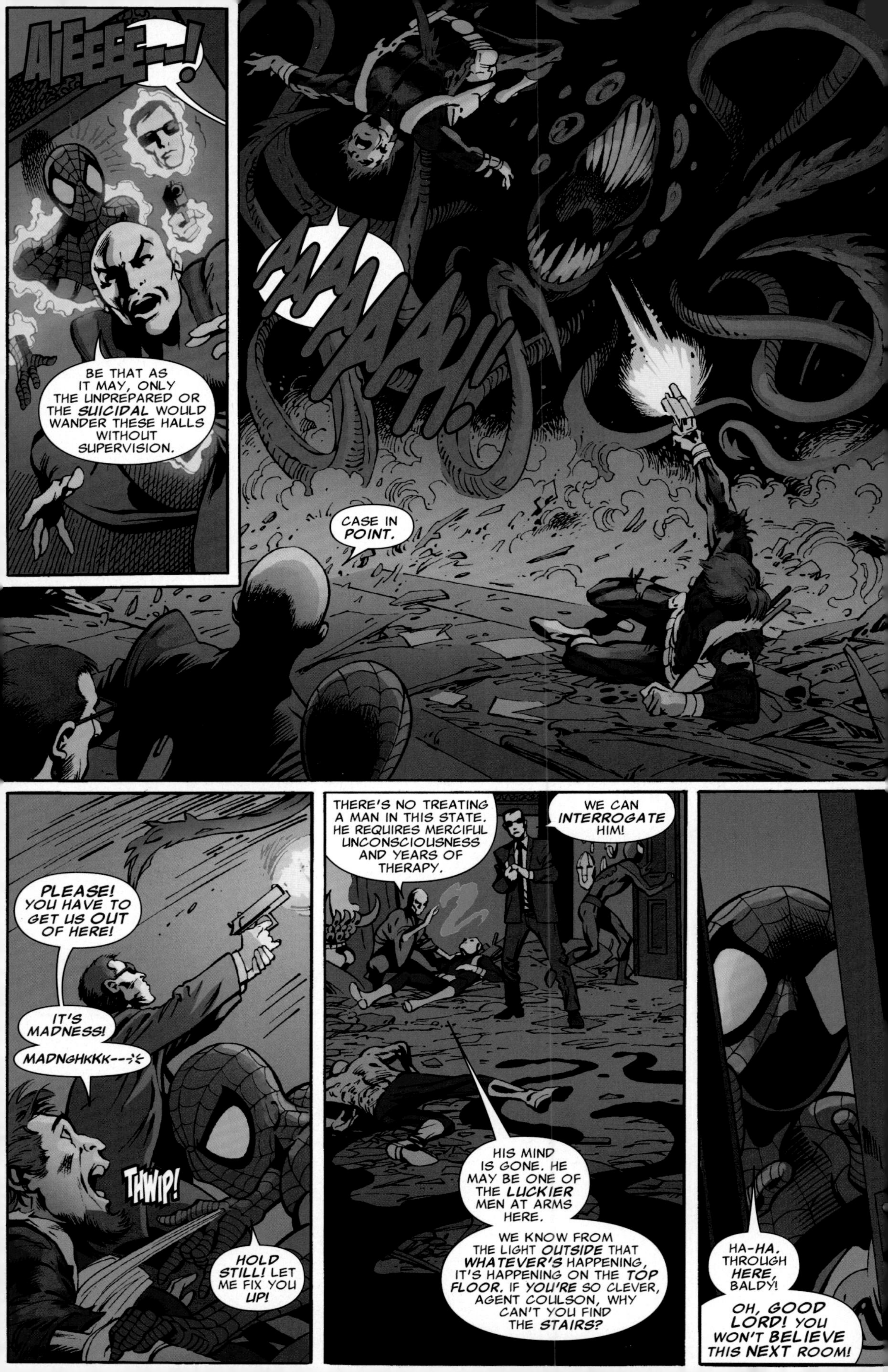
AIEEEEE--!
BE THAT AS IT MAY, ONLY THE UNPREPARED OR THE SUICIDAL WOULD WANDER THESE HALLS WITHOUT SUPERVISION.
AAAAAAAH!
CASE IN POINT.
PLEASE! YOU HAVE TO GET US OUT OF HERE!
IT'S MADNESS!
MADNGHKKK--
THWIP!
HOLD STILL! LET ME FIX YOU UP!
THERE'S NO TREATING A MAN IN THIS STATE. HE REQUIRES MERCIFUL UNCONSCIOUSNESS AND YEARS OF THERAPY.
WE CAN INTERROGATE HIM!
HIS MIND IS GONE. HE MAY BE ONE OF THE LUCKIER MEN AT ARMS HERE.
WE KNOW FROM THE LIGHT OUTSIDE THAT WHATEVER'S HAPPENING, IT'S HAPPENING ON THE TOP FLOOR. IF YOU'RE SO CLEVER, AGENT COULSON, WHY CAN'T YOU FIND THE STAIRS?
HA-HA. THROUGH HERE, BALDY!
OH, GOOD LORD! YOU WON'T BELIEVE THIS NEXT ROOM!

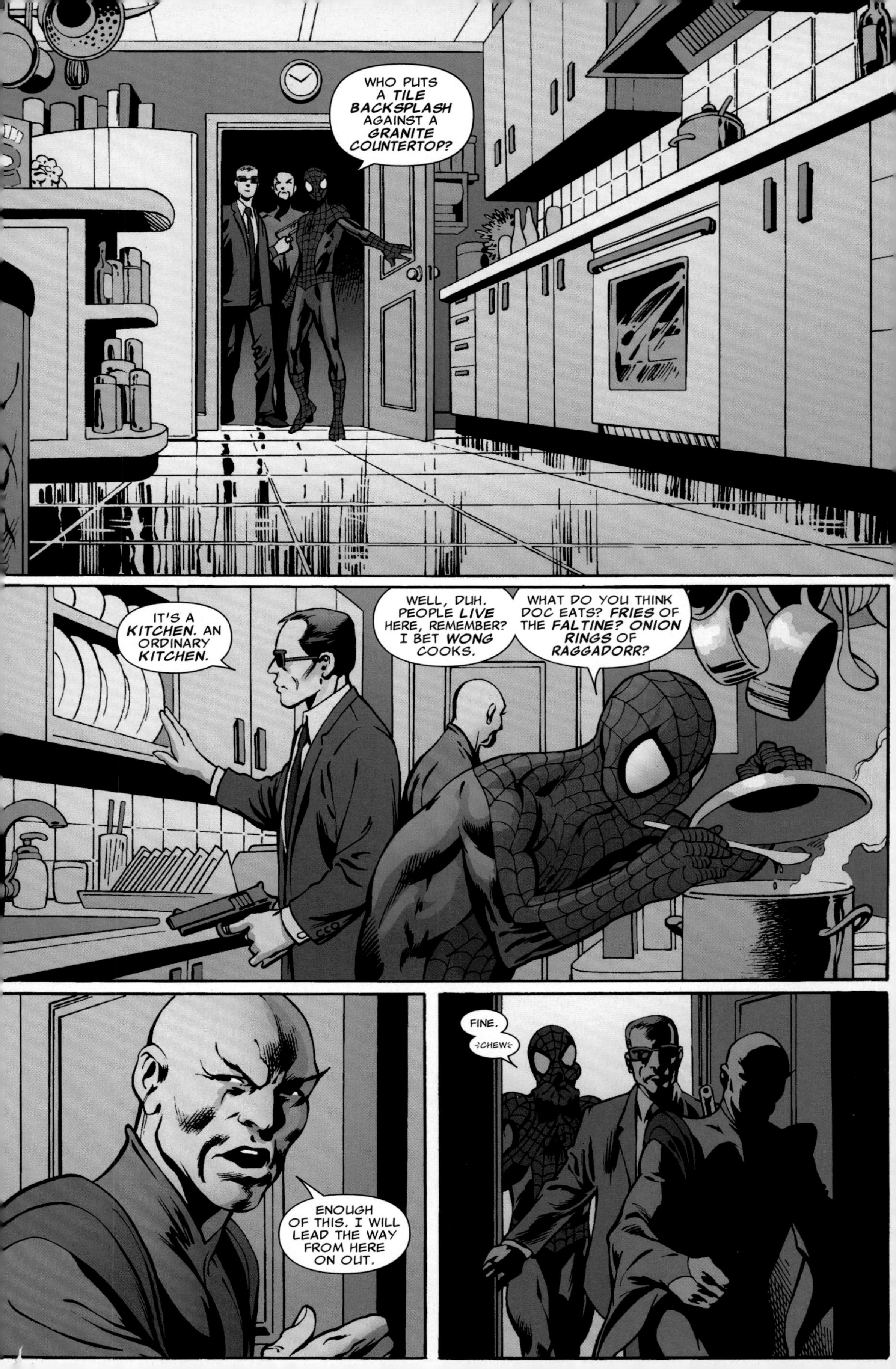
WHO PUTS A TILE BACKSPLASH AGAINST A GRANITE COUNTERTOP?
IT'S A KITCHEN. AN ORDINARY KITCHEN.
WELL, DUH. PEOPLE LIVE HERE, REMEMBER? I BET WONG COOKS.
WHAT DO YOU THINK DOC EATS? FRIES OF THE FALTINE? ONION RINGS OF RAGGADORR?
ENOUGH OF THIS. I WILL LEAD THE WAY FROM HERE ON OUT.
FINE.
CHEW

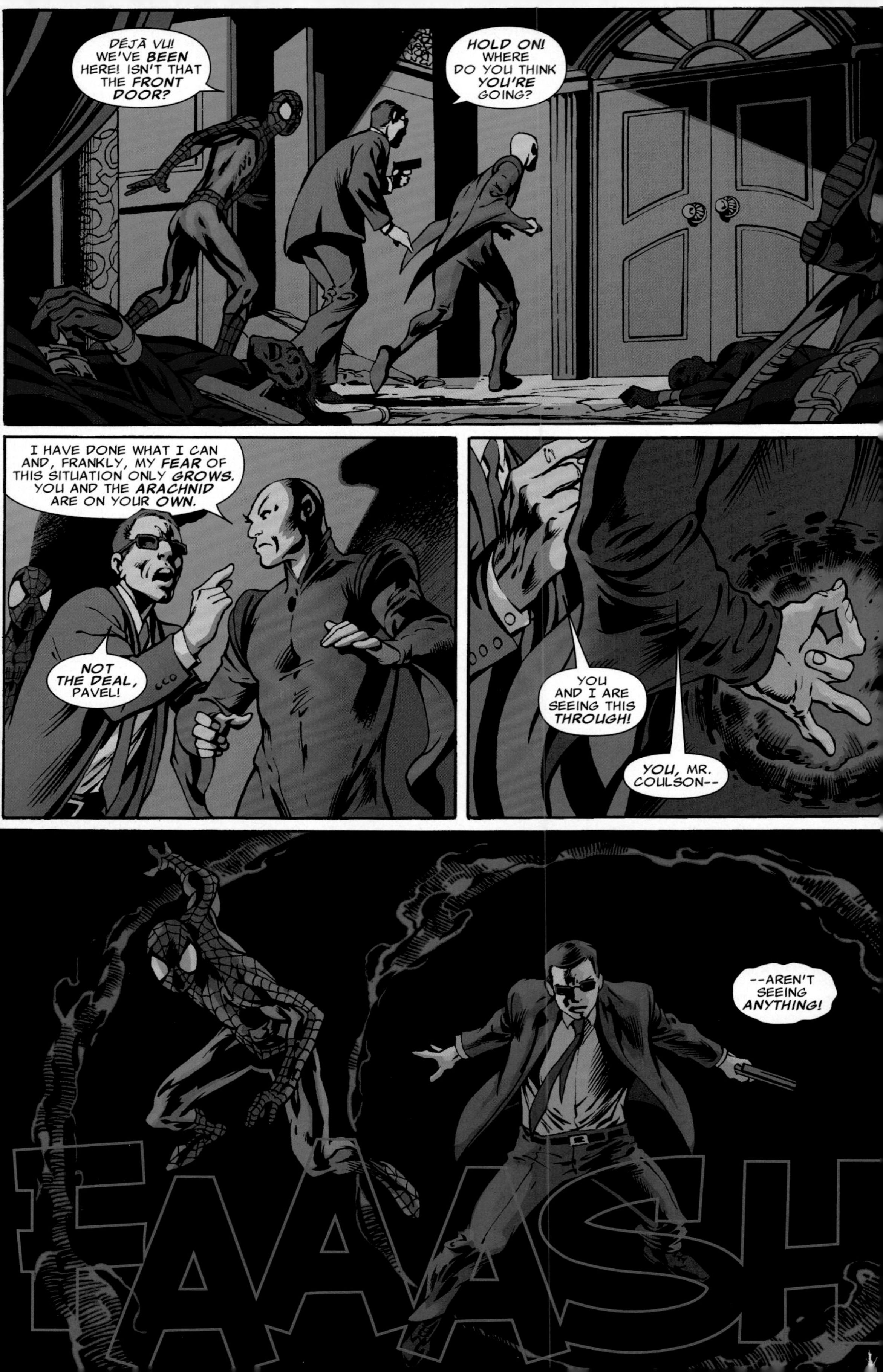
DÉJÀ VU! WE'VE BEEN HERE! ISN'T THAT THE FRONT DOOR?
HOLD ON! WHERE DO YOU THINK YOU'RE GOING?
I HAVE DONE WHAT I CAN AND, FRANKLY, MY FEAR OF THIS SITUATION ONLY GROWS. YOU AND THE ARACHNID ARE ON YOUR OWN.
NOT THE DEAL, PAVEL!
YOU AND I ARE SEEING THIS THROUGH!
YOU, MR. COULSON--
--AREN'T SEEING ANYTHING!
FAAASH!

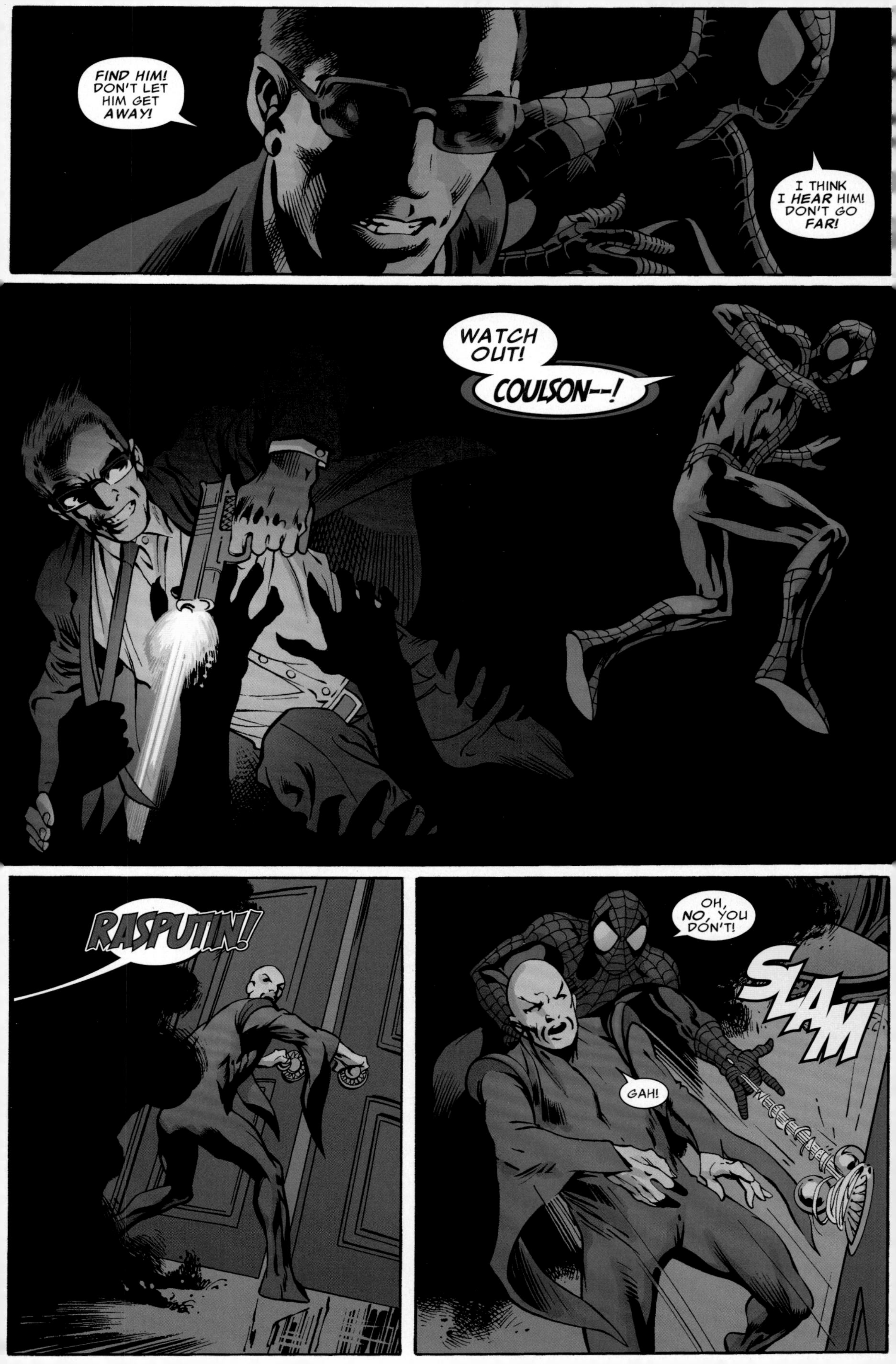
FIND HIM! DON'T LET HIM GET AWAY!
I THINK I HEAR HIM! DON'T GO FAR!
WATCH OUT!
COULSON--!
RASPUTIN!
OH, NO, YOU DON'T!
SLAM
GAH!

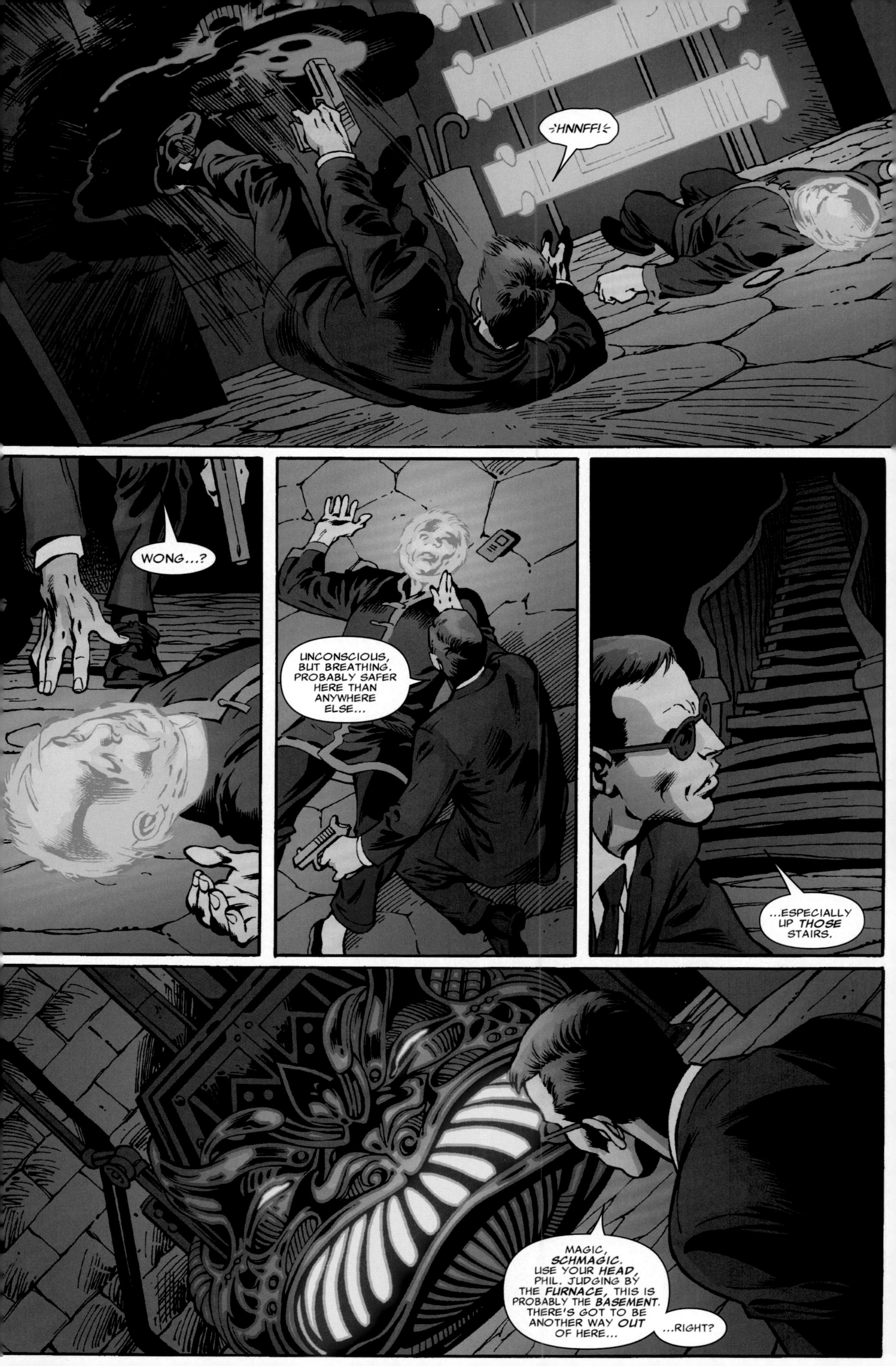
HNNFF!
WONG...?
UNCONSCIOUS, BUT BREATHING. PROBABLY SAFER HERE THAN ANYWHERE ELSE...
...ESPECIALLY UP THOSE STAIRS.
MAGIC, SCHMAGIC. USE YOUR HEAD, PHIL. JUDGING BY THE FURNACE, THIS IS PROBABLY THE BASEMENT. THERE'S GOT TO BE ANOTHER WAY OUT OF HERE...
...RIGHT?

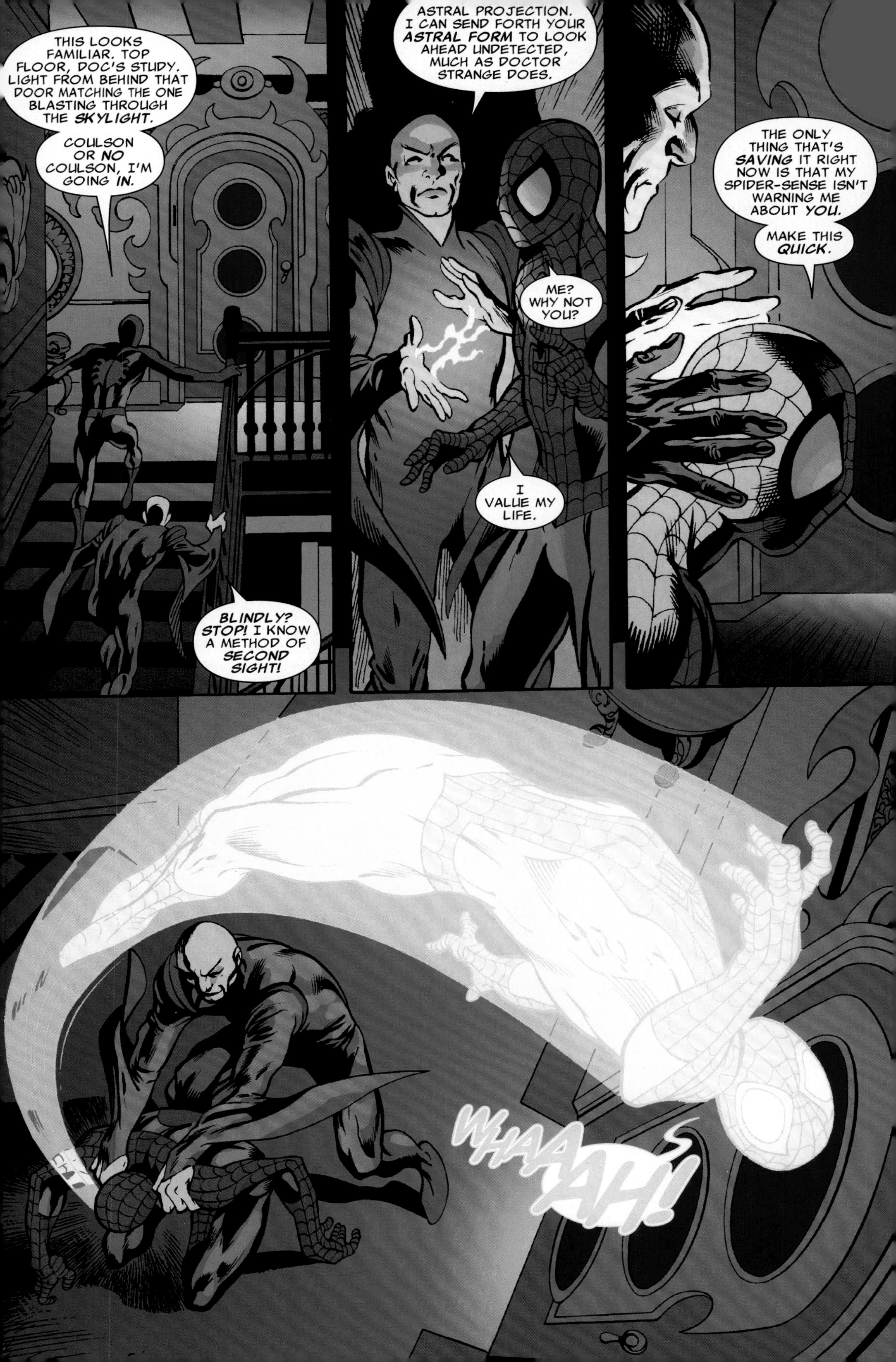

THIS LOOKS FAMILIAR. TOP FLOOR, DOC'S STUDY. LIGHT FROM BEHIND THAT DOOR MATCHING THE ONE BLASTING THROUGH THE SKYLIGHT.
COULSON OR NO COULSON, I'M GOING IN.
BLINDLY? STOP! I KNOW A METHOD OF SECOND SIGHT!
ASTRAL PROJECTION. I CAN SEND FORTH YOUR ASTRAL FORM TO LOOK AHEAD UNDETECTED, MUCH AS DOCTOR STRANGE DOES.
ME? WHY NOT YOU?
I VALUE MY LIFE.
THE ONLY THING THAT'S SAVING IT RIGHT NOW IS THAT MY SPIDER-SENSE ISN'T WARNING ME ABOUT YOU.
MAKE THIS QUICK.
WHAAAAH!

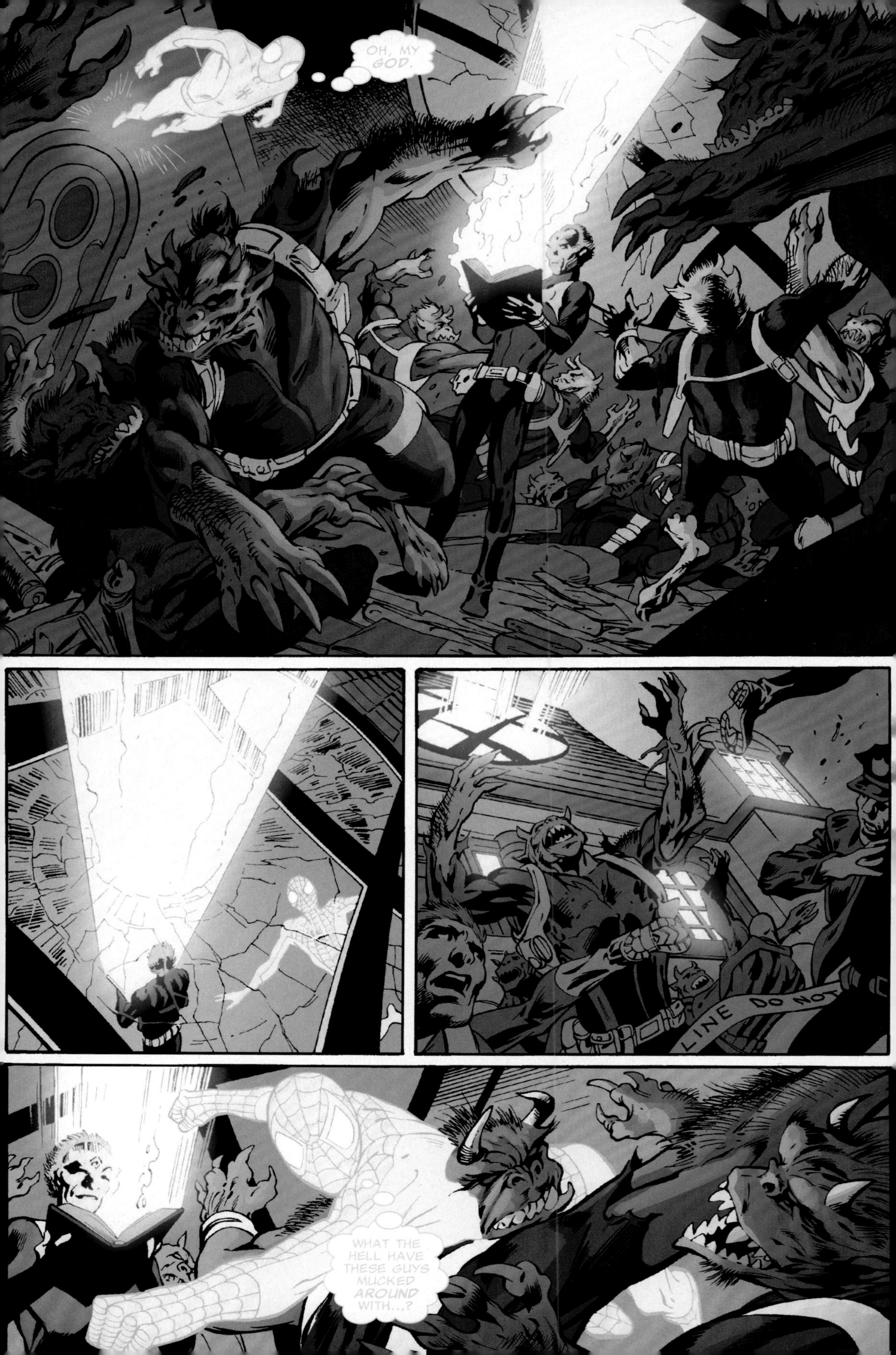
OH, MY GOD.
LINE DO NOT
WHAT THE HELL HAVE THESE GUYS MUCKED AROUND WITH...?

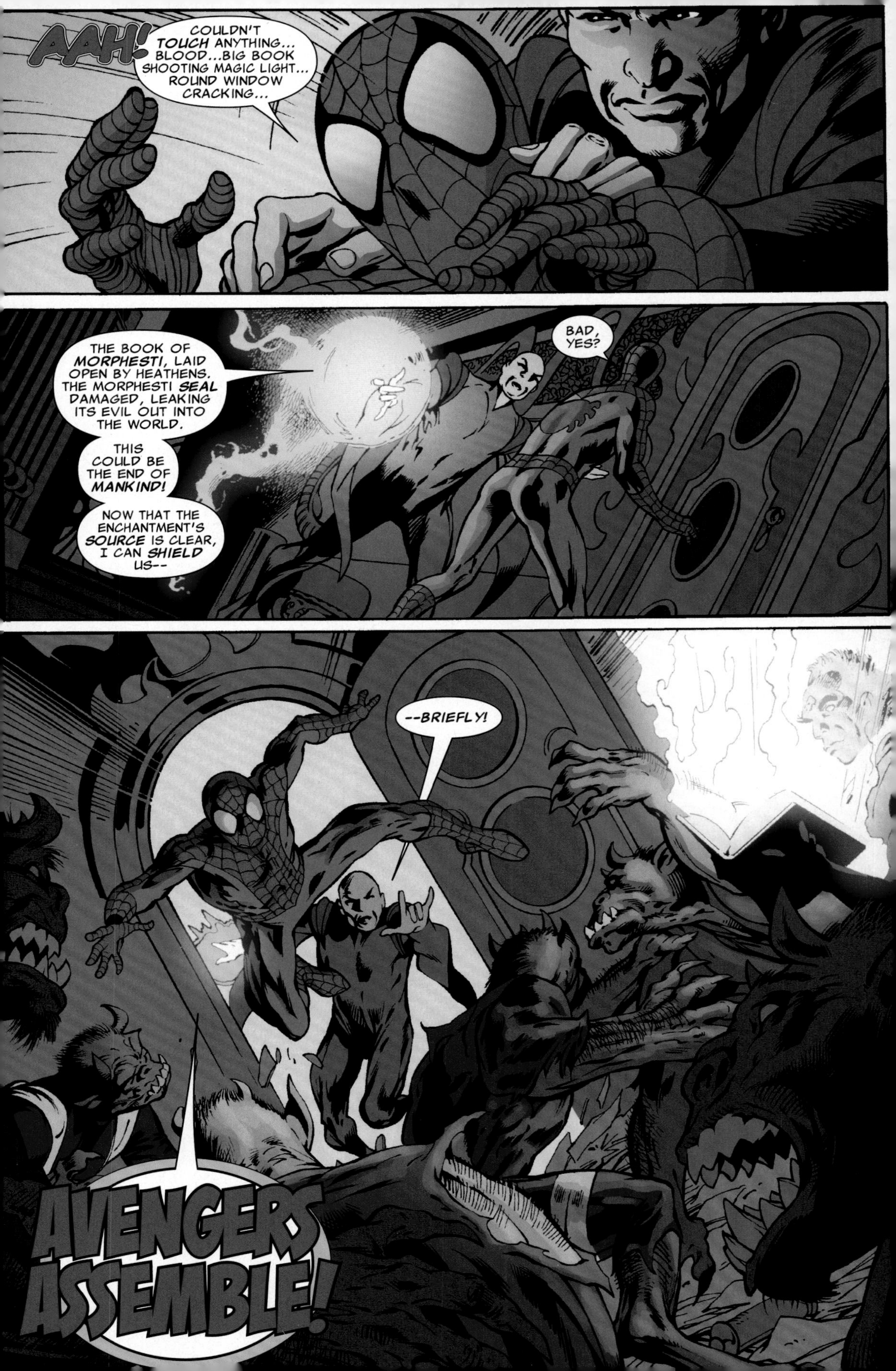
AAH!
COULDN'T TOUCH ANYTHING... BLOOD...BIG BOOK SHOOTING MAGIC LIGHT... ROUND WINDOW CRACKING...
THE BOOK OF MORPHESTI, LAID OPEN BY HEATHENS. THE MORPHESTI SEAL DAMAGED, LEAKING ITS EVIL OUT INTO THE WORLD.
BAD, YES?
THIS COULD BE THE END OF MANKIND!
NOW THAT THE ENCHANTMENT'S SOURCE IS CLEAR, I CAN SHIELD US--
--BRIEFLY!
AVENGERS ASSEMBLE!

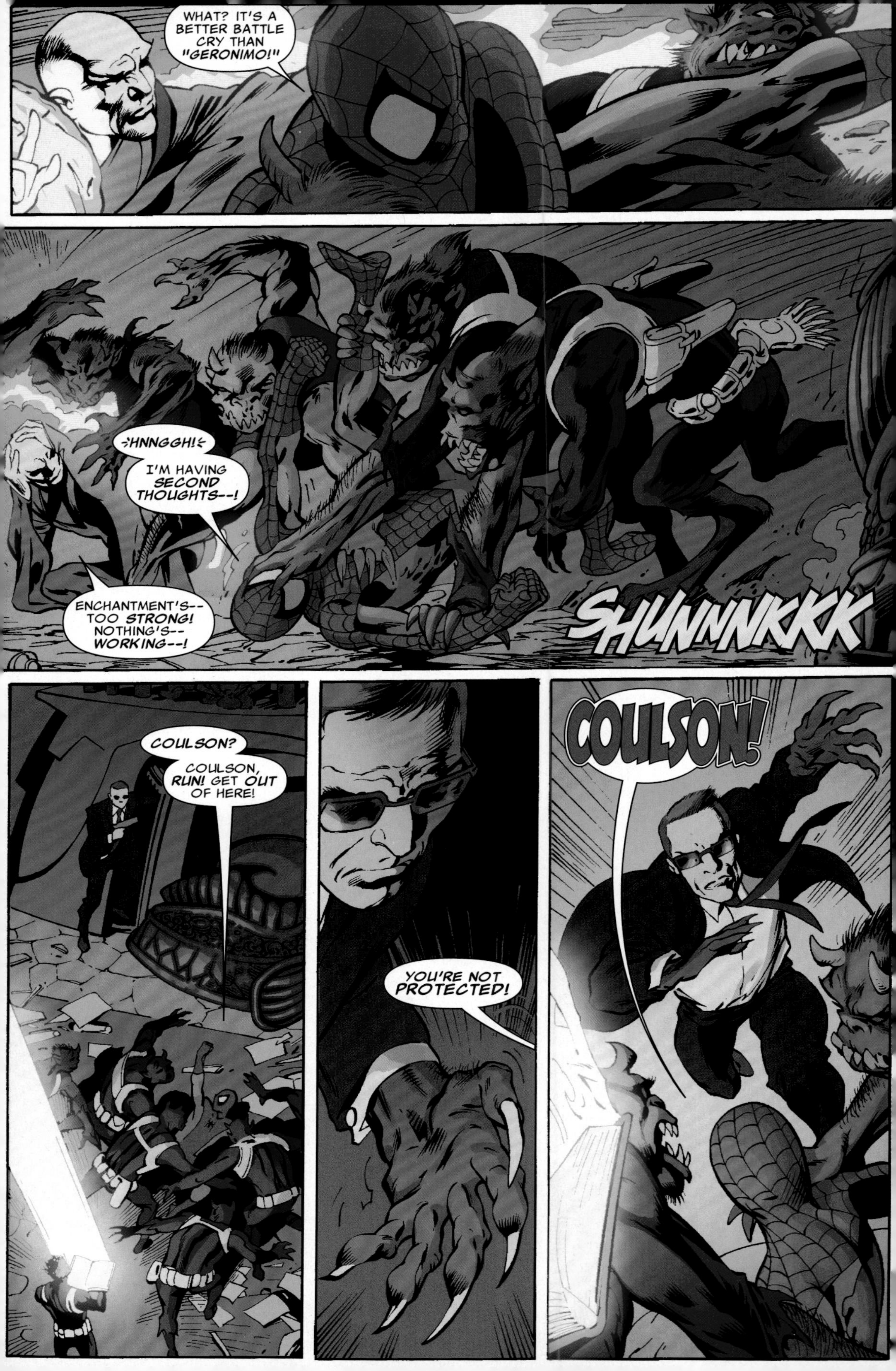
WHAT? IT'S A BETTER BATTLE CRY THAN "GERONIMO!"
HNNGGH! I'M HAVING SECOND THOUGHTS--!
ENCHANTMENT'S-- TOO STRONG! NOTHING'S-- WORKING--!
SHUNNNKKK
COULSON?
COULSON, RUN! GET OUT OF HERE!
YOU'RE NOT PROTECTED!
COULSON!

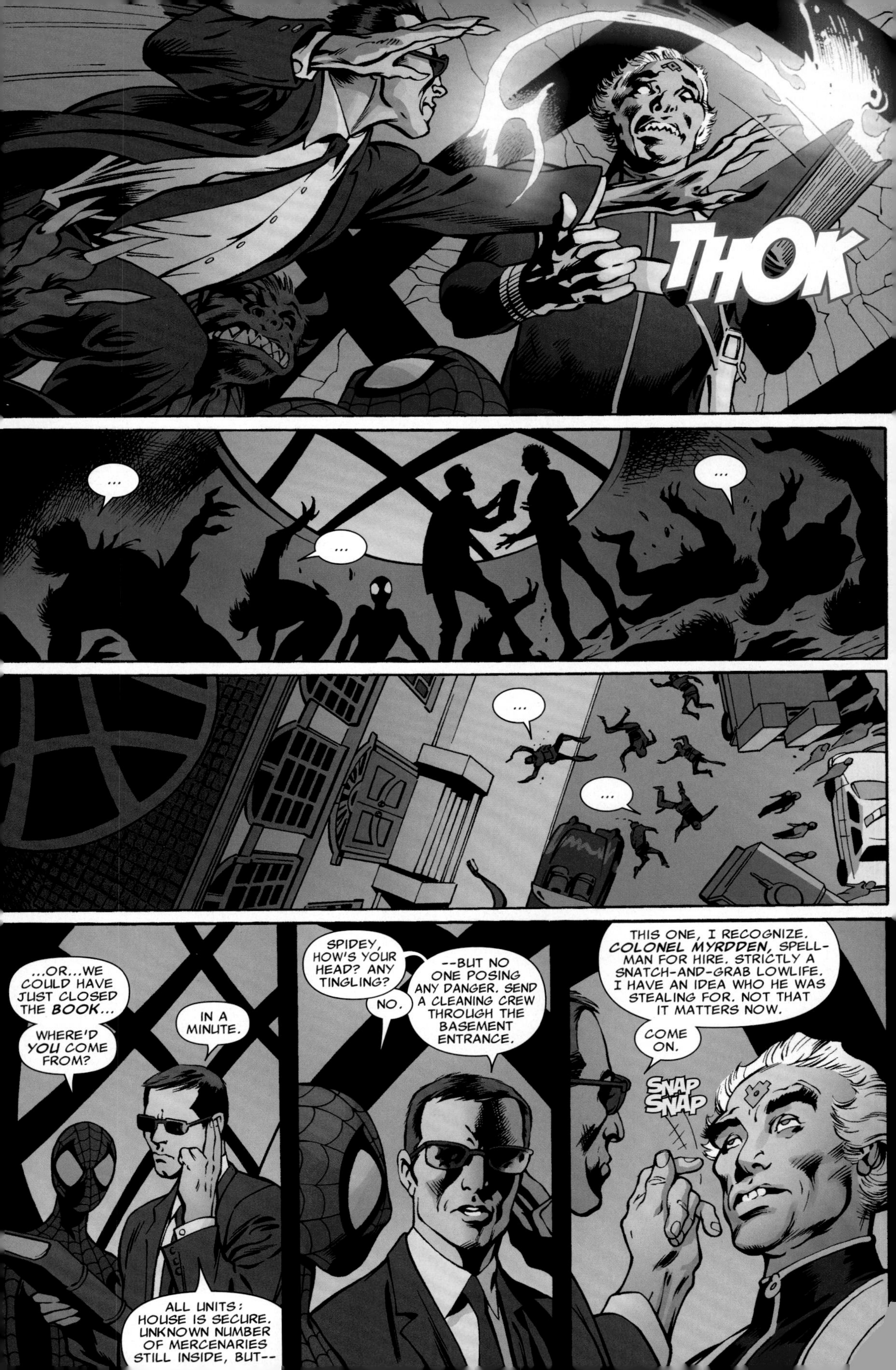
THOK
...
...
...
...
...
...OR...WE COULD HAVE JUST CLOSED THE BOOK...
WHERE'D YOU COME FROM?
IN A MINUTE.
ALL UNITS: HOUSE IS SECURE. UNKNOWN NUMBER OF MERCENARIES STILL INSIDE, BUT--
SPIDEY, HOW'S YOUR HEAD? ANY TINGLING?
NO.
--BUT NO ONE POSING ANY DANGER. SEND A CLEANING CREW THROUGH THE BASEMENT ENTRANCE.
THIS ONE, I RECOGNIZE. COLONEL MYRDDEN, SPELLMAN FOR HIRE. STRICTLY A SNATCH-AND-GRAB LOWLIFE. I HAVE AN IDEA WHO HE WAS STEALING FOR. NOT THAT IT MATTERS NOW.
COME ON.
SNAP SNAP

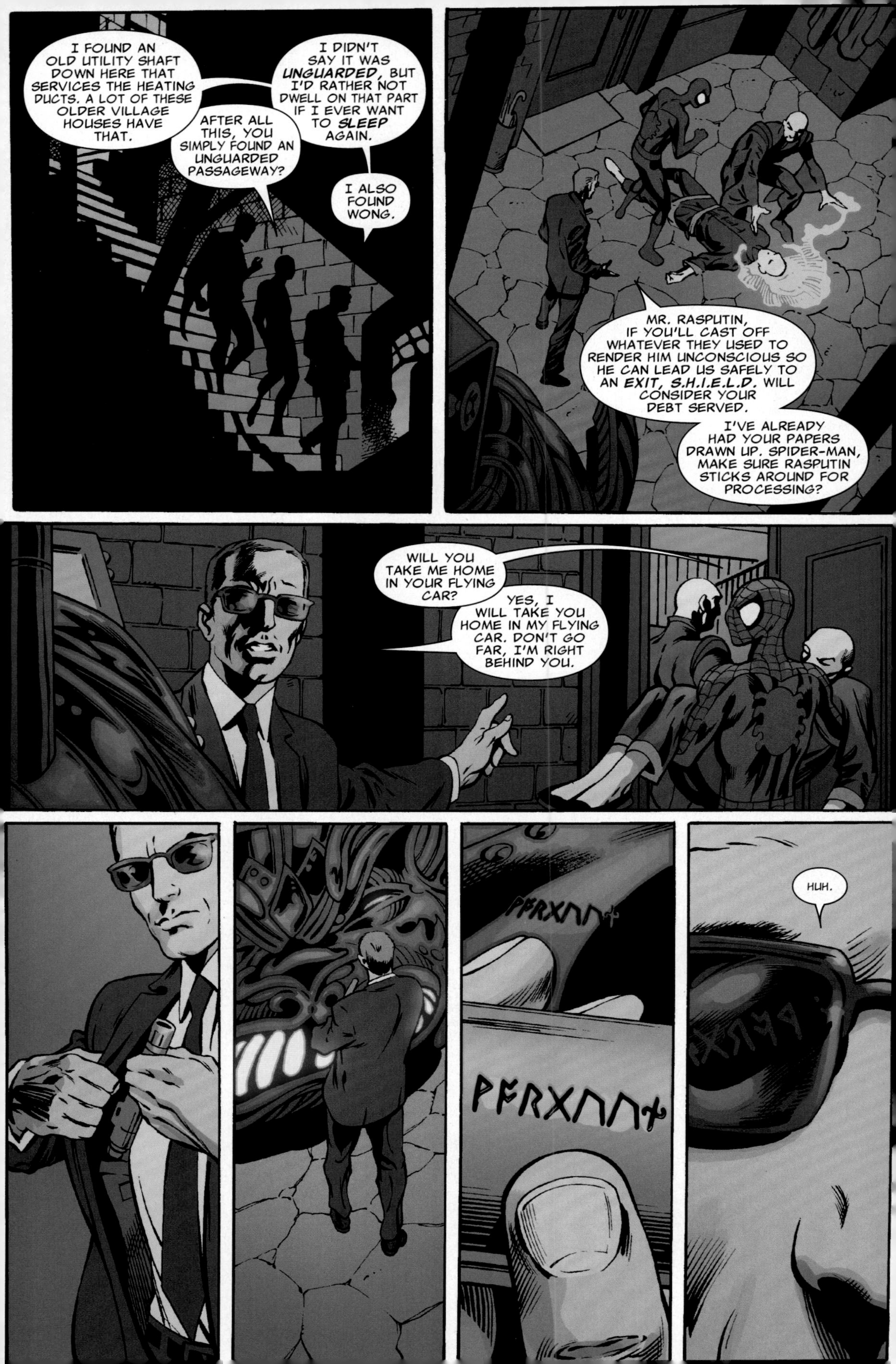
I FOUND AN OLD UTILITY SHAFT DOWN HERE THAT SERVICES THE HEATING DUCTS. A LOT OF THESE OLDER VILLAGE HOUSES HAVE THAT.
AFTER ALL THIS, YOU SIMPLY FOUND AN UNGUARDED PASSAGEWAY?
I DIDN'T SAY IT WAS UNGUARDED, BUT I'D RATHER NOT DWELL ON THAT PART IF I EVER WANT TO SLEEP AGAIN.
I ALSO FOUND WONG.
MR. RASPUTIN, IF YOU'LL CAST OFF WHATEVER THEY USED TO RENDER HIM UNCONSCIOUS SO HE CAN LEAD US SAFELY TO AN EXIT, S.H.I.E.L.D. WILL CONSIDER YOUR DEBT SERVED.
I'VE ALREADY HAD YOUR PAPERS DRAWN UP. SPIDER-MAN, MAKE SURE RASPUTIN STICKS AROUND FOR PROCESSING?
WILL YOU TAKE ME HOME IN YOUR FLYING CAR?
YES, I WILL TAKE YOU HOME IN MY FLYING CAR. DON'T GO FAR, I'M RIGHT BEHIND YOU.
HUH.

4.

ACTIVE MISSION:

FUEL

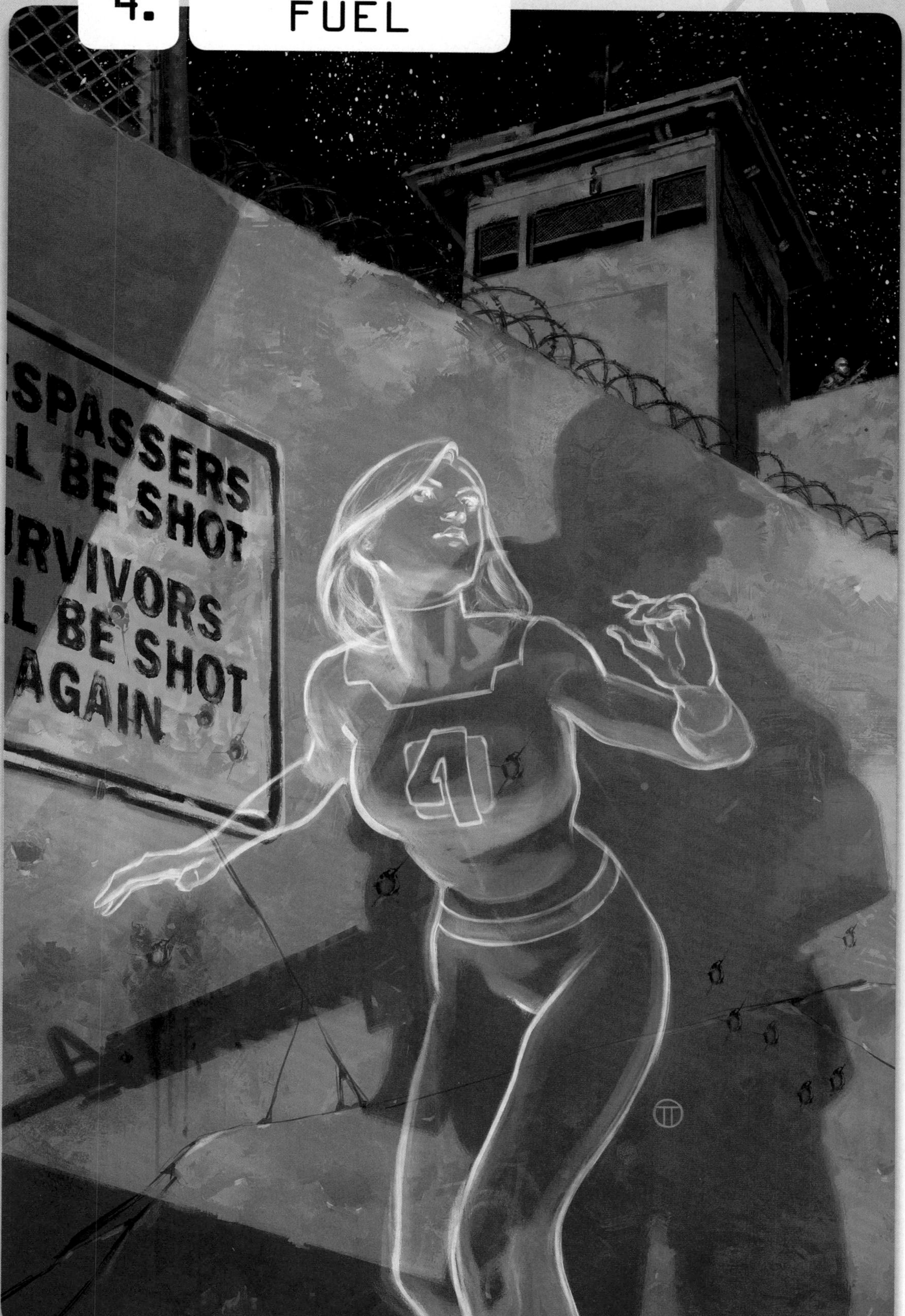

ESPASSERS
LL BE SHOT
URVIVORS
LL BE SHOT
AGAIN

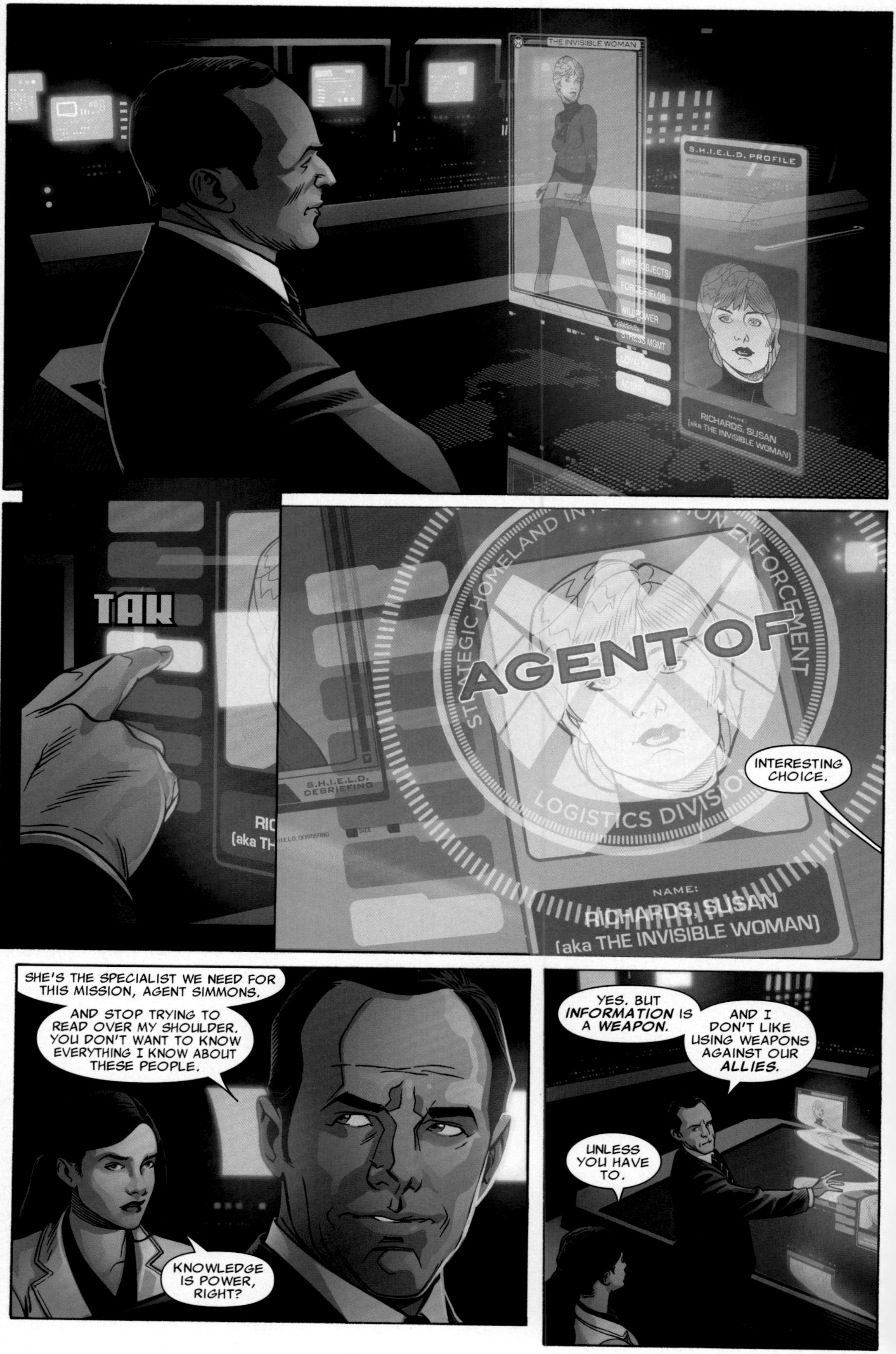
THE INVISIBLE WOMAN
S.H.I.E.L.D. PROFILE
INVIS (SELF)
INVIS (OBJECTS)
FORCE FIELDS
WILLPOWER
STRESS MGMT
LOYALTY
NAME:
RICHARDS, SUSAN
(aka THE INVISIBLE WOMAN)
TAK
S.H.I.E.L.D. DEBRIEFING
STRATEGIC HOMELAND INTERVENTION ENFORCEMENT
LOGISTICS DIVISION
AGENT OF
INTERESTING CHOICE.
NAME:
RICHARDS, SUSAN
(aka THE INVISIBLE WOMAN)
SHE'S THE SPECIALIST WE NEED FOR THIS MISSION, AGENT SIMMONS.
AND STOP TRYING TO READ OVER MY SHOULDER. YOU DON'T WANT TO KNOW EVERYTHING I KNOW ABOUT THESE PEOPLE.
KNOWLEDGE IS POWER, RIGHT?
YES. BUT *INFORMATION* IS A *WEAPON*.
AND I DON'T LIKE USING WEAPONS AGAINST OUR *ALLIES*.
UNLESS YOU HAVE TO.

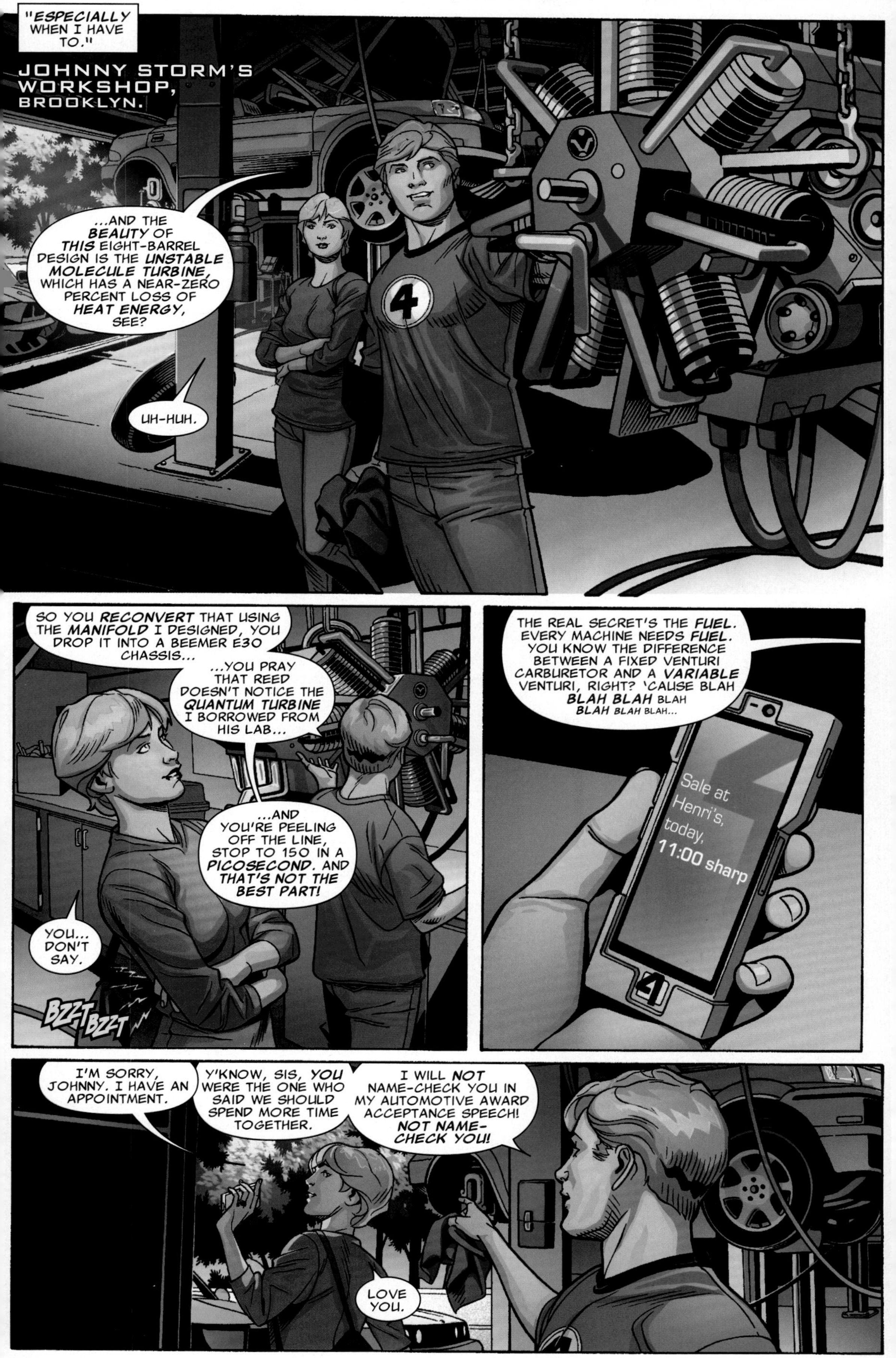
"ESPECIALLY WHEN I HAVE TO."
JOHNNY STORM'S WORKSHOP, BROOKLYN.
...AND THE BEAUTY OF THIS EIGHT-BARREL DESIGN IS THE UNSTABLE MOLECULE TURBINE, WHICH HAS A NEAR-ZERO PERCENT LOSS OF HEAT ENERGY, SEE?
UH-HUH.
SO YOU RECONVERT THAT USING THE MANIFOLD I DESIGNED, YOU DROP IT INTO A BEEMER E30 CHASSIS...
...YOU PRAY THAT REED DOESN'T NOTICE THE QUANTUM TURBINE I BORROWED FROM HIS LAB...
...AND YOU'RE PEELING OFF THE LINE, STOP TO 150 IN A PICOSECOND. AND THAT'S NOT THE BEST PART!
YOU... DON'T SAY.
BZZT BZZT
THE REAL SECRET'S THE FUEL. EVERY MACHINE NEEDS FUEL. YOU KNOW THE DIFFERENCE BETWEEN A FIXED VENTURI CARBURETOR AND A VARIABLE VENTURI, RIGHT? 'CAUSE BLAH BLAH BLAH BLAH BLAH BLAH BLAH...
Sale at Henri's, today, 11:00 sharp
I'M SORRY, JOHNNY. I HAVE AN APPOINTMENT.
Y'KNOW, SIS, YOU WERE THE ONE WHO SAID WE SHOULD SPEND MORE TIME TOGETHER.
I WILL NOT NAME-CHECK YOU IN MY AUTOMOTIVE AWARD ACCEPTANCE SPEECH! NOT NAME-CHECK YOU!
LOVE YOU.

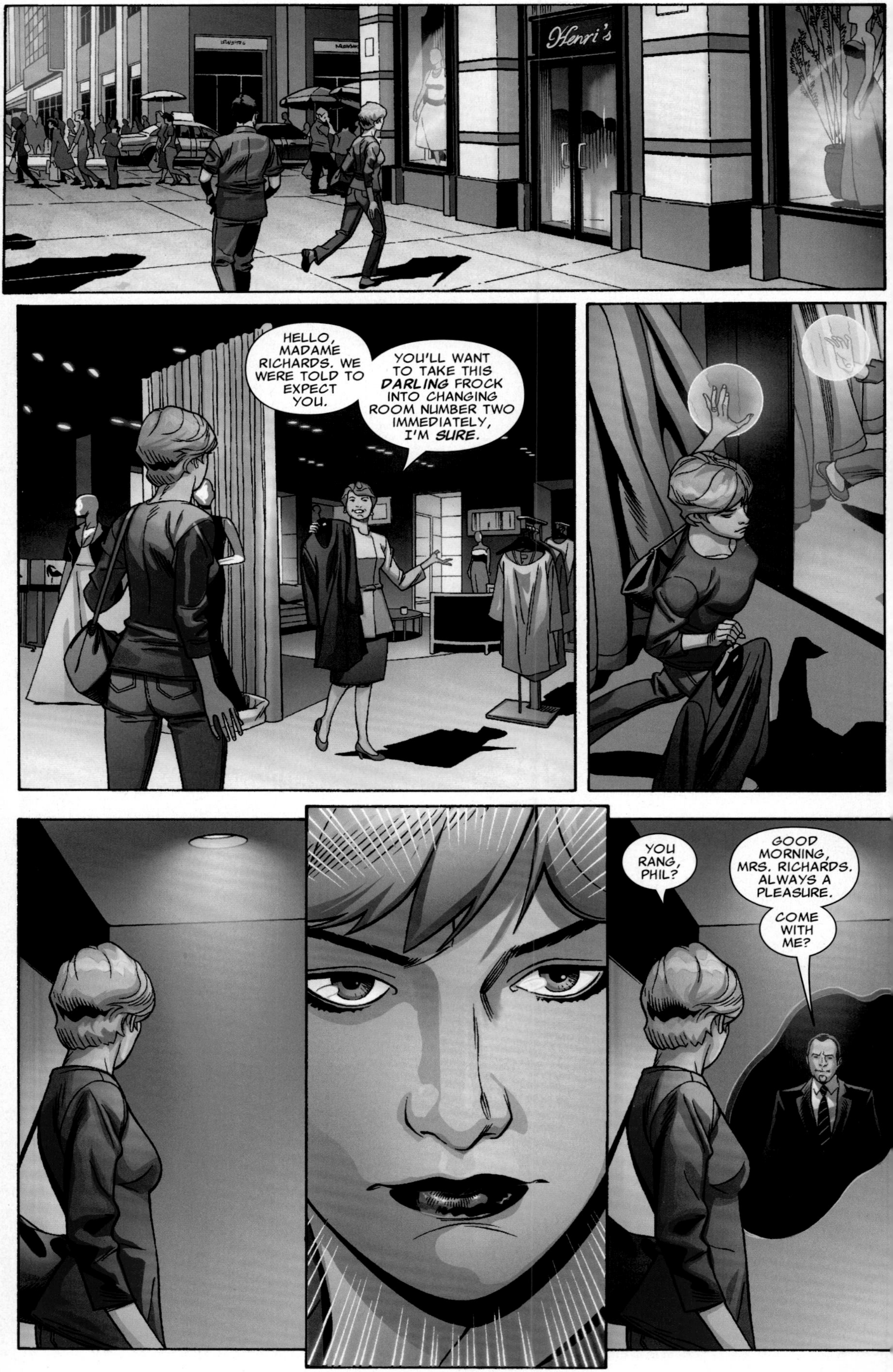
Henri's
HELLO, MADAME RICHARDS. WE WERE TOLD TO EXPECT YOU.
YOU'LL WANT TO TAKE THIS DARLING FROCK INTO CHANGING ROOM NUMBER TWO IMMEDIATELY, I'M SURE.
YOU RANG, PHIL?
GOOD MORNING, MRS. RICHARDS. ALWAYS A PLEASURE.
COME WITH ME?

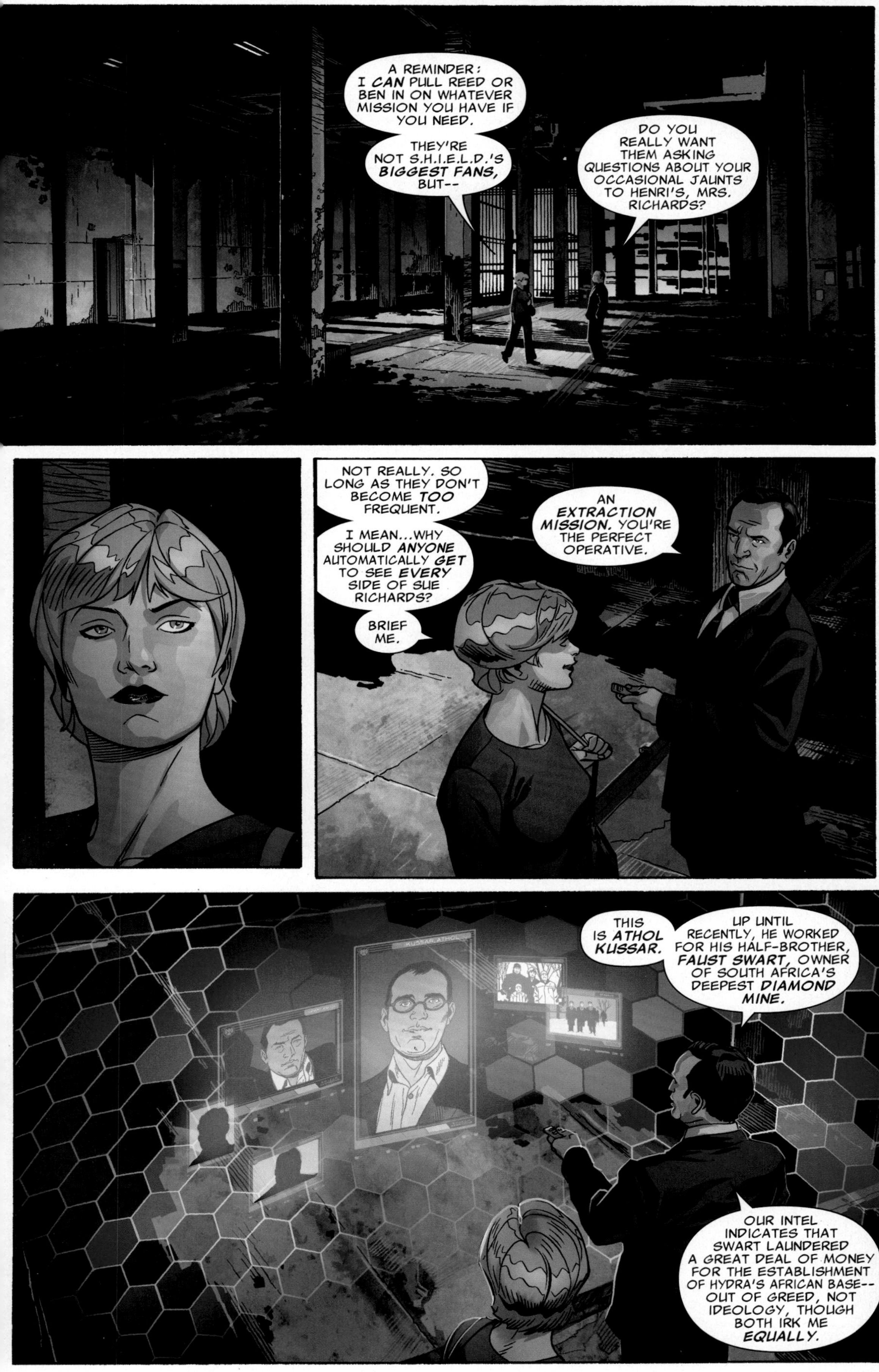
A REMINDER: I CAN PULL REED OR BEN IN ON WHATEVER MISSION YOU HAVE IF YOU NEED.
THEY'RE NOT S.H.I.E.L.D.'S BIGGEST FANS, BUT--
DO YOU REALLY WANT THEM ASKING QUESTIONS ABOUT YOUR OCCASIONAL JAUNTS TO HENRI'S, MRS. RICHARDS?
NOT REALLY. SO LONG AS THEY DON'T BECOME TOO FREQUENT.
I MEAN...WHY SHOULD ANYONE AUTOMATICALLY GET TO SEE EVERY SIDE OF SUE RICHARDS?
BRIEF ME.
AN EXTRACTION MISSION. YOU'RE THE PERFECT OPERATIVE.
THIS IS ATHOL KUSSAR.
UP UNTIL RECENTLY, HE WORKED FOR HIS HALF-BROTHER, FAUST SWART, OWNER OF SOUTH AFRICA'S DEEPEST DIAMOND MINE.
OUR INTEL INDICATES THAT SWART LAUNDERED A GREAT DEAL OF MONEY FOR THE ESTABLISHMENT OF HYDRA'S AFRICAN BASE--OUT OF GREED, NOT IDEOLOGY, THOUGH BOTH IRK ME EQUALLY.

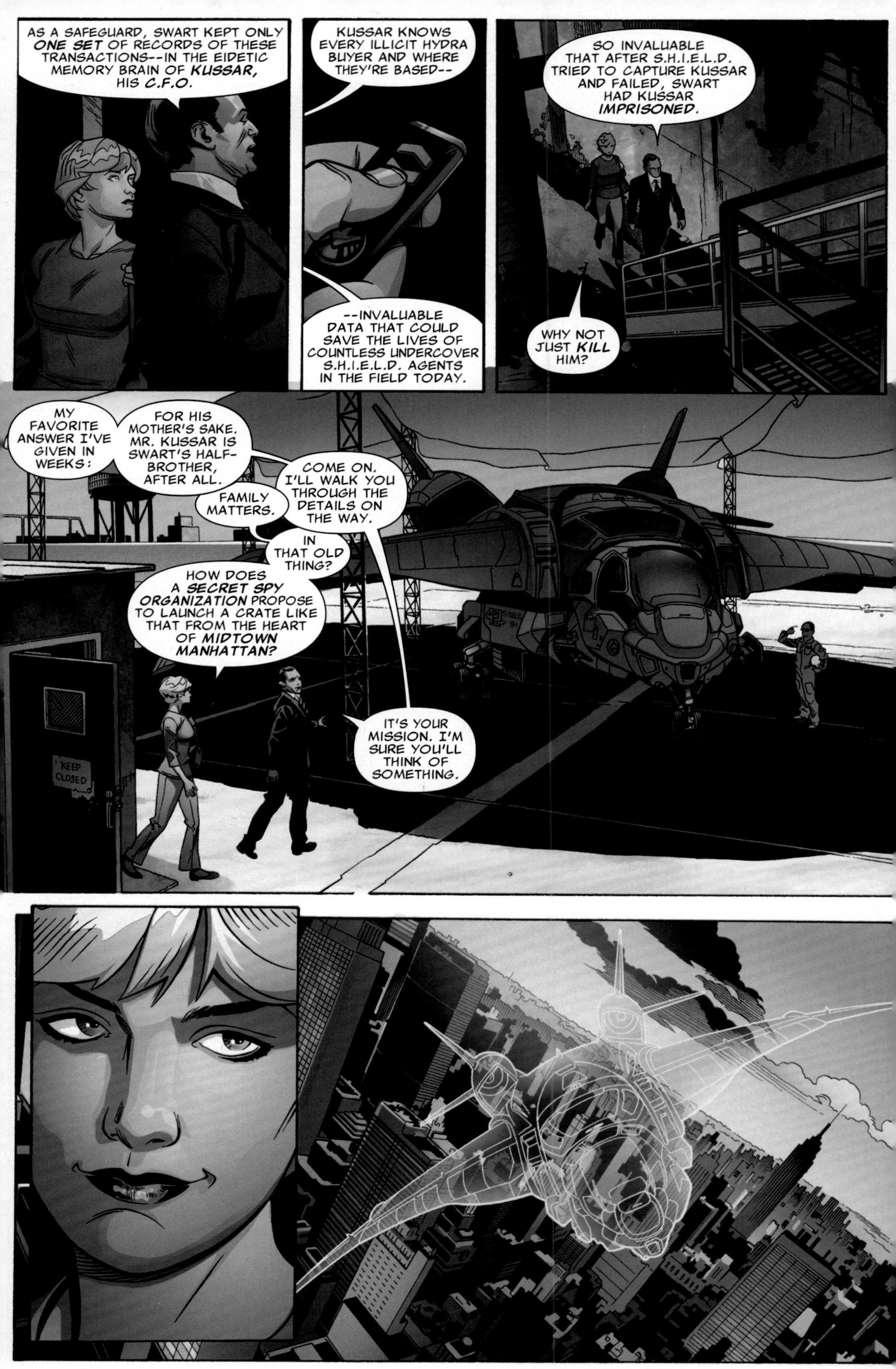
AS A SAFEGUARD, SWART KEPT ONLY ONE SET OF RECORDS OF THESE TRANSACTIONS--IN THE EIDETIC MEMORY BRAIN OF KUSSAR, HIS C.F.O.
KUSSAR KNOWS EVERY ILLICIT HYDRA BUYER AND WHERE THEY'RE BASED--
--INVALUABLE DATA THAT COULD SAVE THE LIVES OF COUNTLESS UNDERCOVER S.H.I.E.L.D. AGENTS IN THE FIELD TODAY.
SO INVALUABLE THAT AFTER S.H.I.E.L.D. TRIED TO CAPTURE KUSSAR AND FAILED, SWART HAD KUSSAR IMPRISONED.
WHY NOT JUST KILL HIM?
FOR HIS MOTHER'S SAKE. MR. KUSSAR IS SWART'S HALF-BROTHER, AFTER ALL.
MY FAVORITE ANSWER I'VE GIVEN IN WEEKS:
FAMILY MATTERS.
COME ON. I'LL WALK YOU THROUGH THE DETAILS ON THE WAY.
IN THAT OLD THING?
HOW DOES A SECRET SPY ORGANIZATION PROPOSE TO LAUNCH A CRATE LIKE THAT FROM THE HEART OF MIDTOWN MANHATTAN?
IT'S YOUR MISSION. I'M SURE YOU'LL THINK OF SOMETHING.
KEEP CLOSED

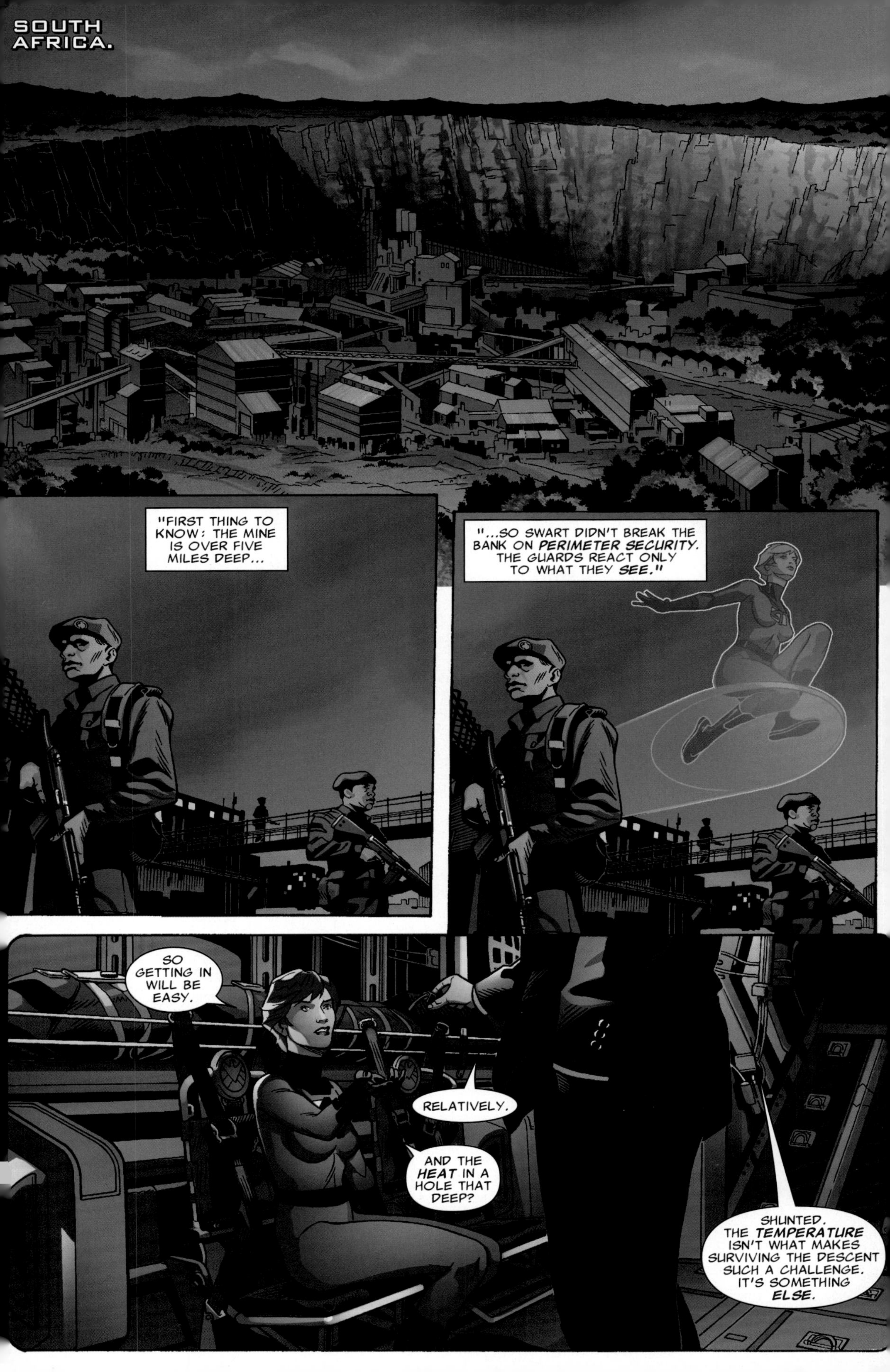
SOUTH AFRICA.
"FIRST THING TO KNOW: THE MINE IS OVER FIVE MILES DEEP...
"...SO SWART DIDN'T BREAK THE BANK ON PERIMETER SECURITY. THE GUARDS REACT ONLY TO WHAT THEY SEE."
SO GETTING IN WILL BE EASY.
RELATIVELY.
AND THE HEAT IN A HOLE THAT DEEP?
SHUNTED. THE TEMPERATURE ISN'T WHAT MAKES SURVIVING THE DESCENT SUCH A CHALLENGE. IT'S SOMETHING ELSE.

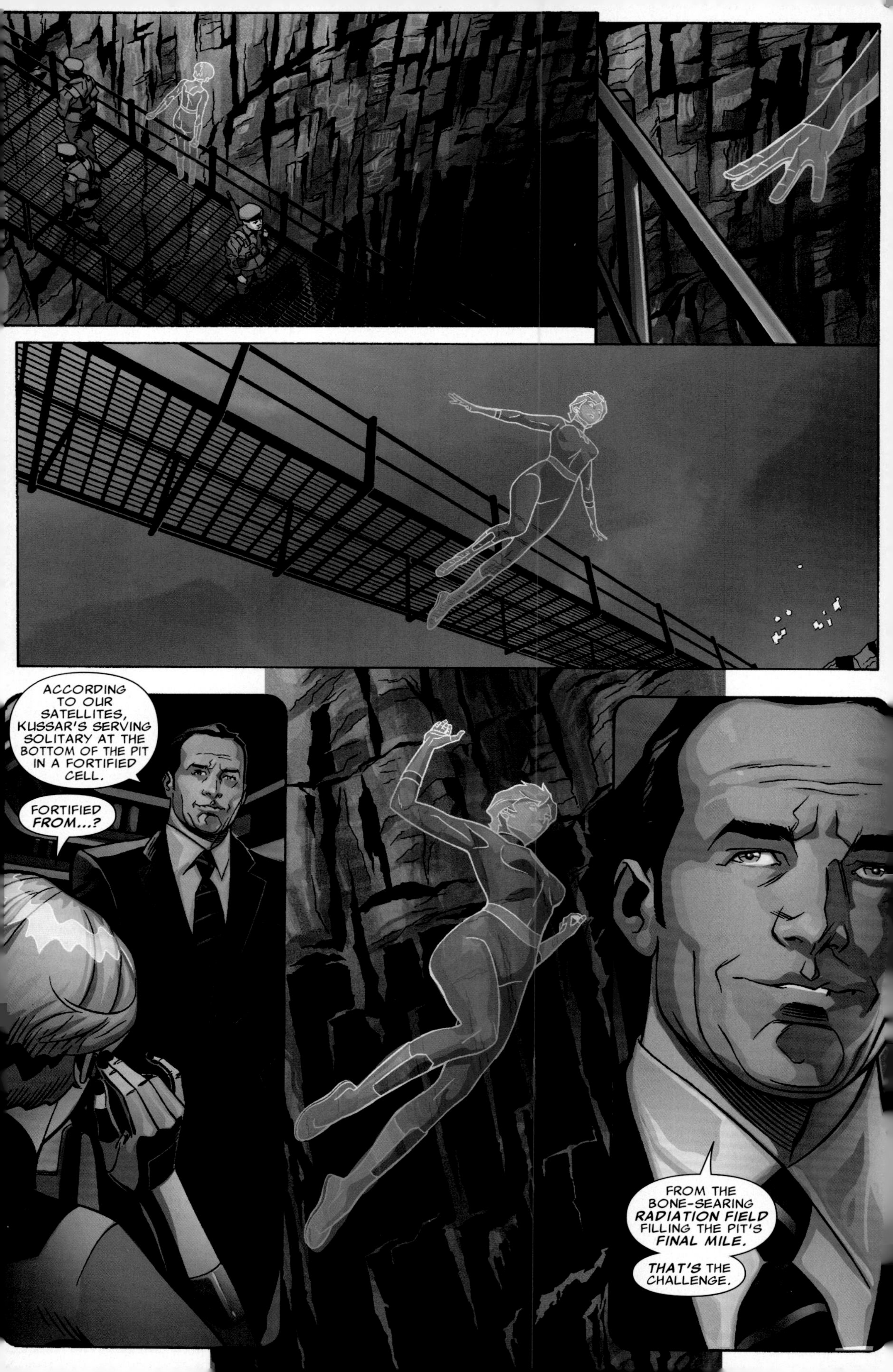
ACCORDING TO OUR SATELLITES, KUSSAR'S SERVING SOLITARY AT THE BOTTOM OF THE PIT IN A FORTIFIED CELL.
FORTIFIED FROM...?
FROM THE BONE-SEARING RADIATION FIELD FILLING THE PIT'S FINAL MILE.
THAT'S THE CHALLENGE.

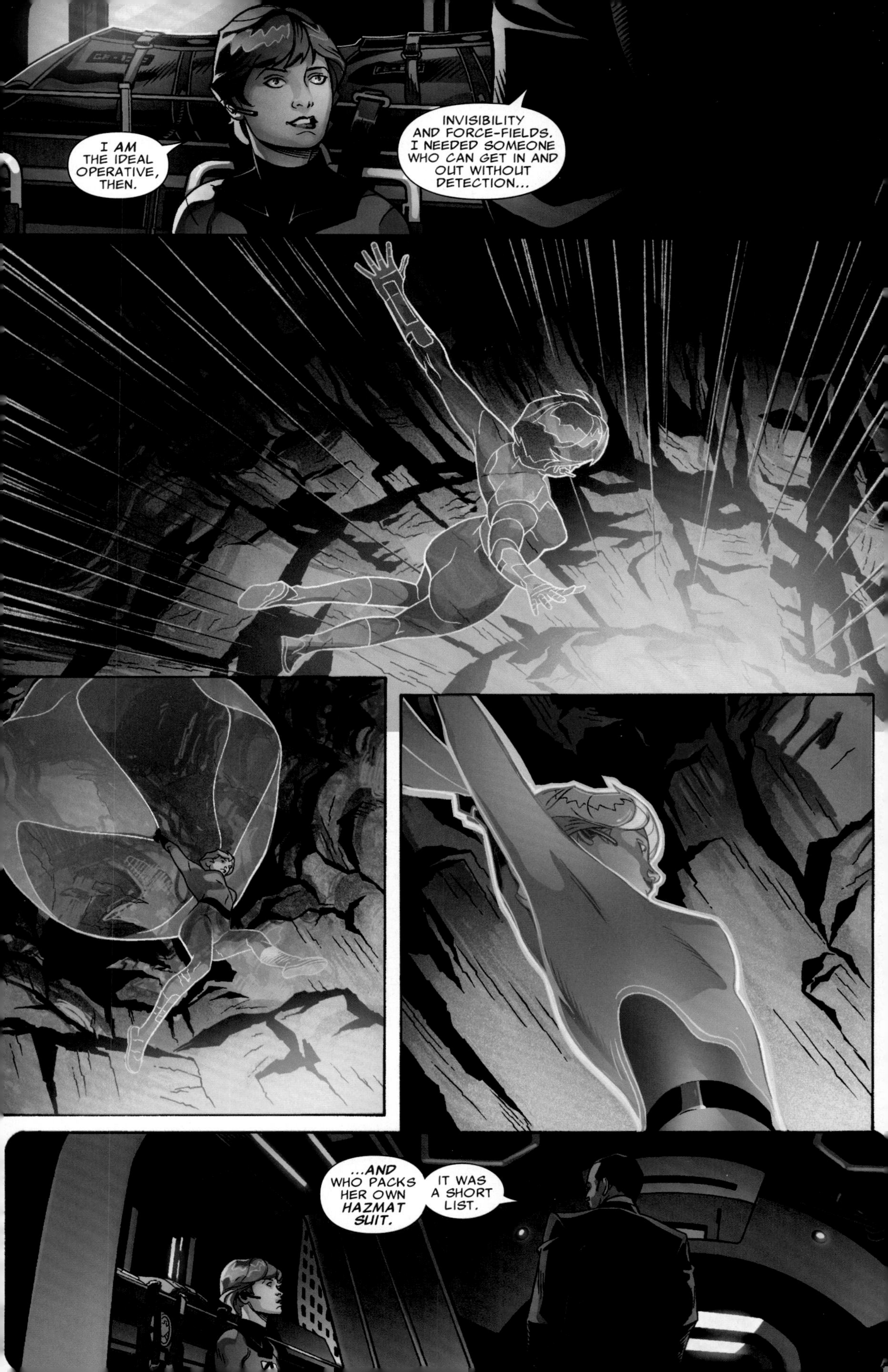
INVISIBILITY AND FORCE-FIELDS. I NEEDED SOMEONE WHO CAN GET IN AND OUT WITHOUT DETECTION...
I AM THE IDEAL OPERATIVE, THEN.
...AND WHO PACKS HER OWN HAZMAT SUIT.
IT WAS A SHORT LIST.

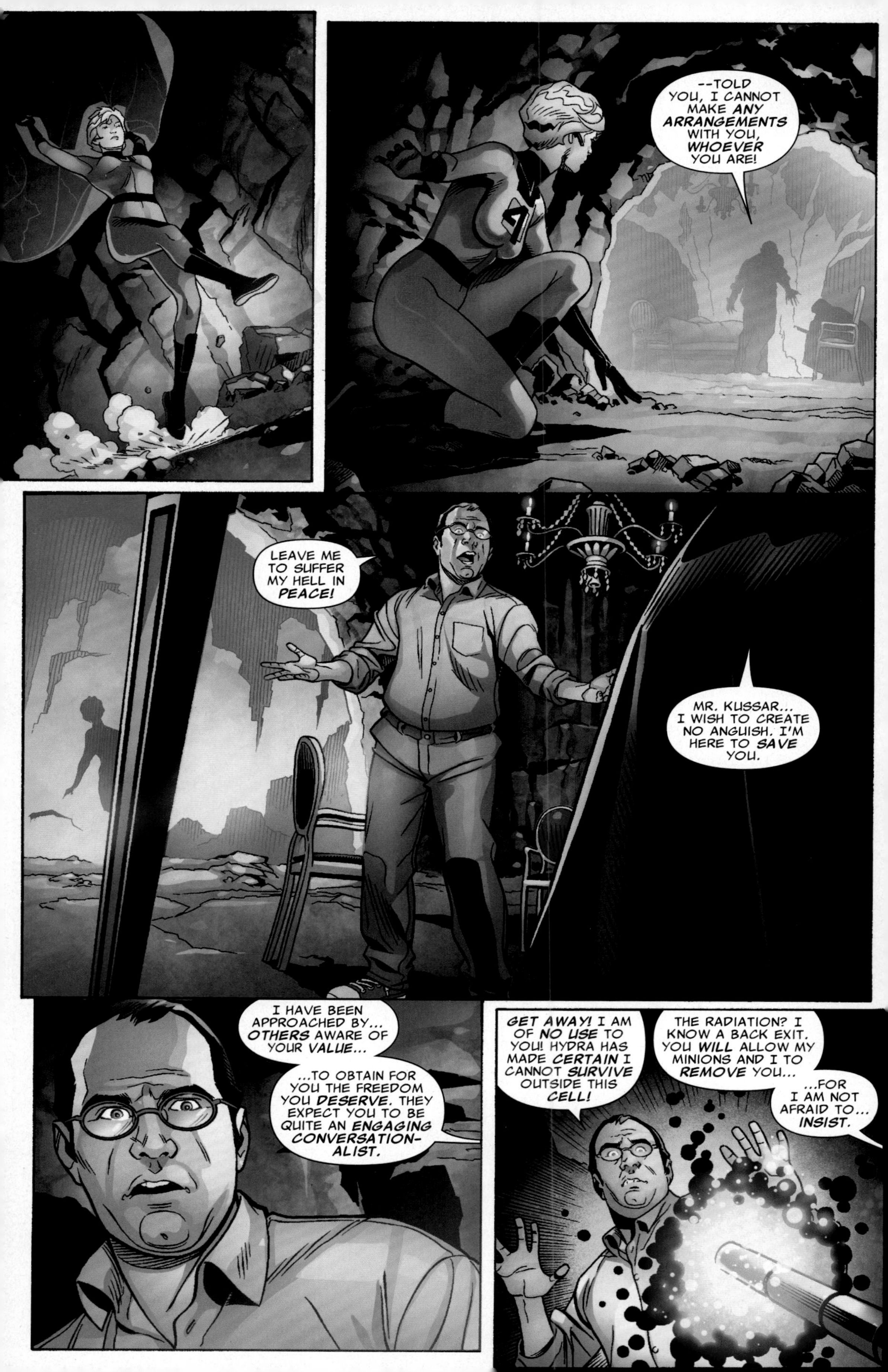
--TOLD YOU, I CANNOT MAKE ANY ARRANGEMENTS WITH YOU, WHOEVER YOU ARE!
LEAVE ME TO SUFFER MY HELL IN PEACE!
MR. KUSSAR... I WISH TO CREATE NO ANGUISH. I'M HERE TO SAVE YOU.
I HAVE BEEN APPROACHED BY... OTHERS AWARE OF YOUR VALUE...
...TO OBTAIN FOR YOU THE FREEDOM YOU DESERVE. THEY EXPECT YOU TO BE QUITE AN ENGAGING CONVERSATION-ALIST.
GET AWAY! I AM OF NO USE TO YOU! HYDRA HAS MADE CERTAIN I CANNOT SURVIVE OUTSIDE THIS CELL!
THE RADIATION? I KNOW A BACK EXIT. YOU WILL ALLOW MY MINIONS AND I TO REMOVE YOU...
...FOR I AM NOT AFRAID TO... INSIST.

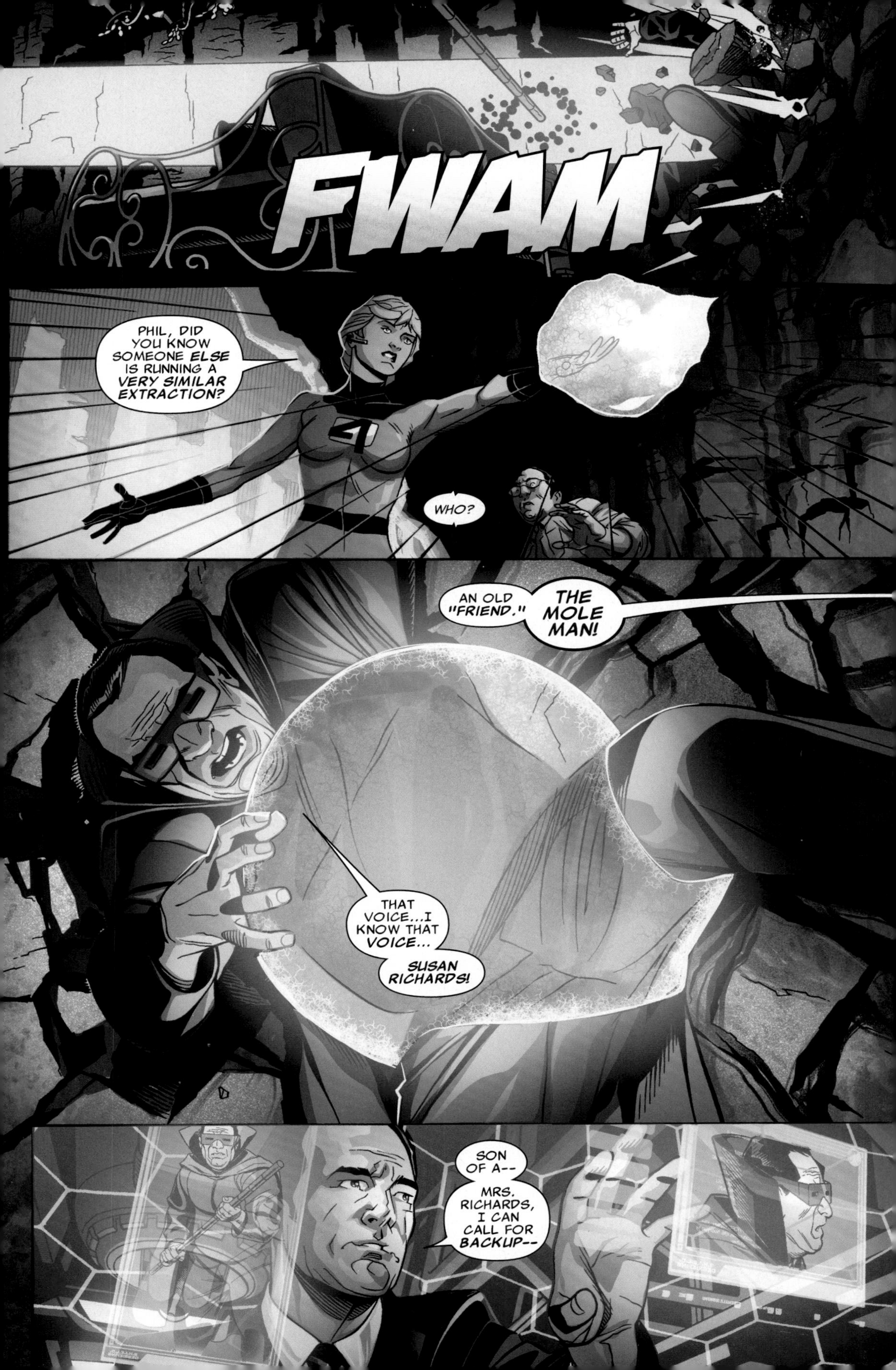
FWAM
PHIL, DID YOU KNOW SOMEONE ELSE IS RUNNING A VERY SIMILAR EXTRACTION?
WHO?
AN OLD "FRIEND."
THE MOLE MAN!
THAT VOICE...I KNOW THAT VOICE...
SUSAN RICHARDS!
SON OF A--
MRS. RICHARDS, I CAN CALL FOR BACKUP--

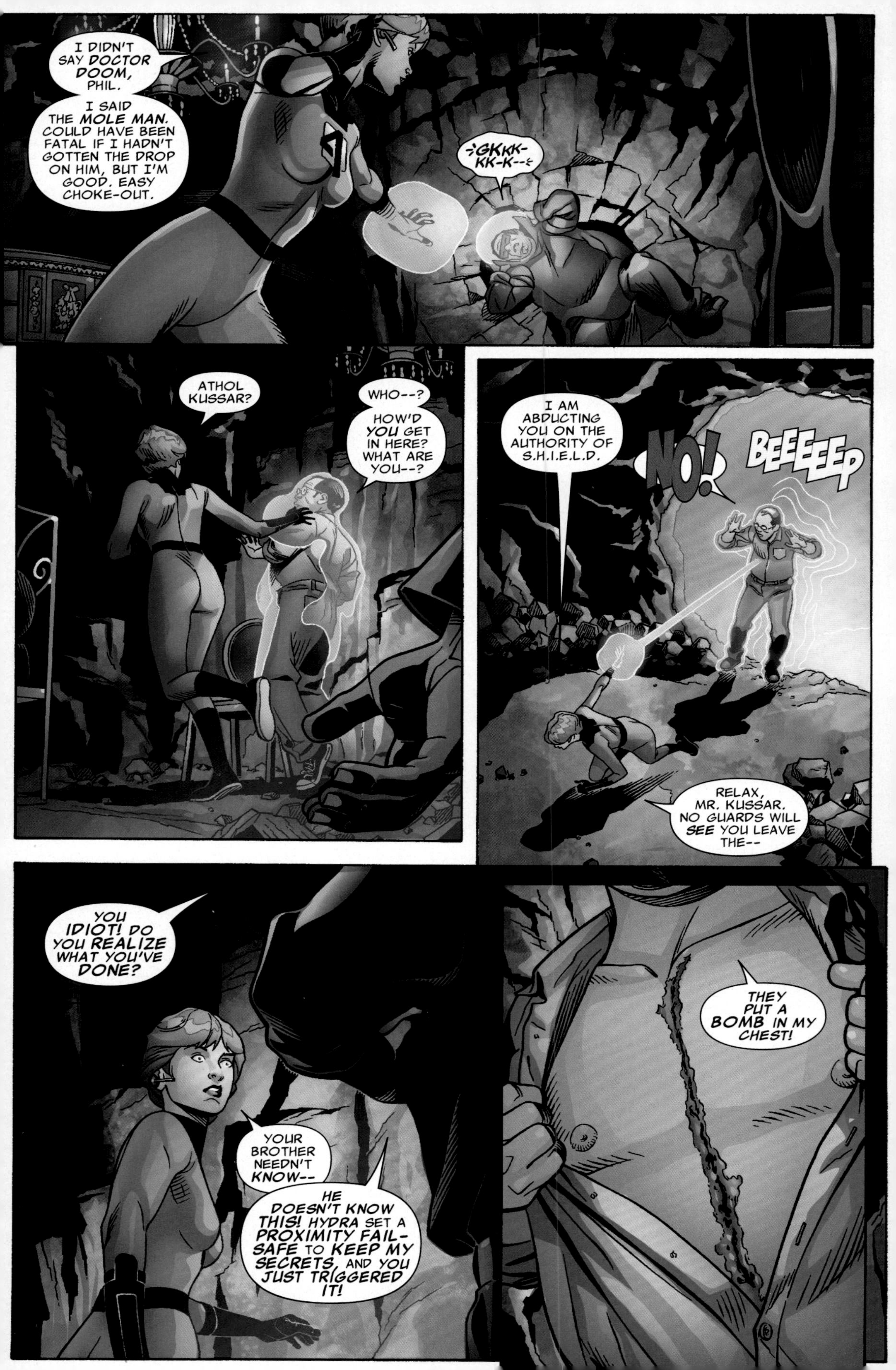
I DIDN'T SAY DOCTOR DOOM, PHIL.
I SAID THE MOLE MAN. COULD HAVE BEEN FATAL IF I HADN'T GOTTEN THE DROP ON HIM, BUT I'M GOOD. EASY CHOKE-OUT.
GKKK-KK-K--
ATHOL KUSSAR?
WHO--?
HOW'D YOU GET IN HERE? WHAT ARE YOU--?
I AM ABDUCTING YOU ON THE AUTHORITY OF S.H.I.E.L.D.
NO!
BEEEEEP
RELAX, MR. KUSSAR. NO GUARDS WILL SEE YOU LEAVE THE--
YOU IDIOT! DO YOU REALIZE WHAT YOU'VE DONE?
THEY PUT A BOMB IN MY CHEST!
YOUR BROTHER NEEDN'T KNOW--
HE DOESN'T KNOW THIS! HYDRA SET A PROXIMITY FAIL-SAFE TO KEEP MY SECRETS, AND YOU JUST TRIGGERED IT!

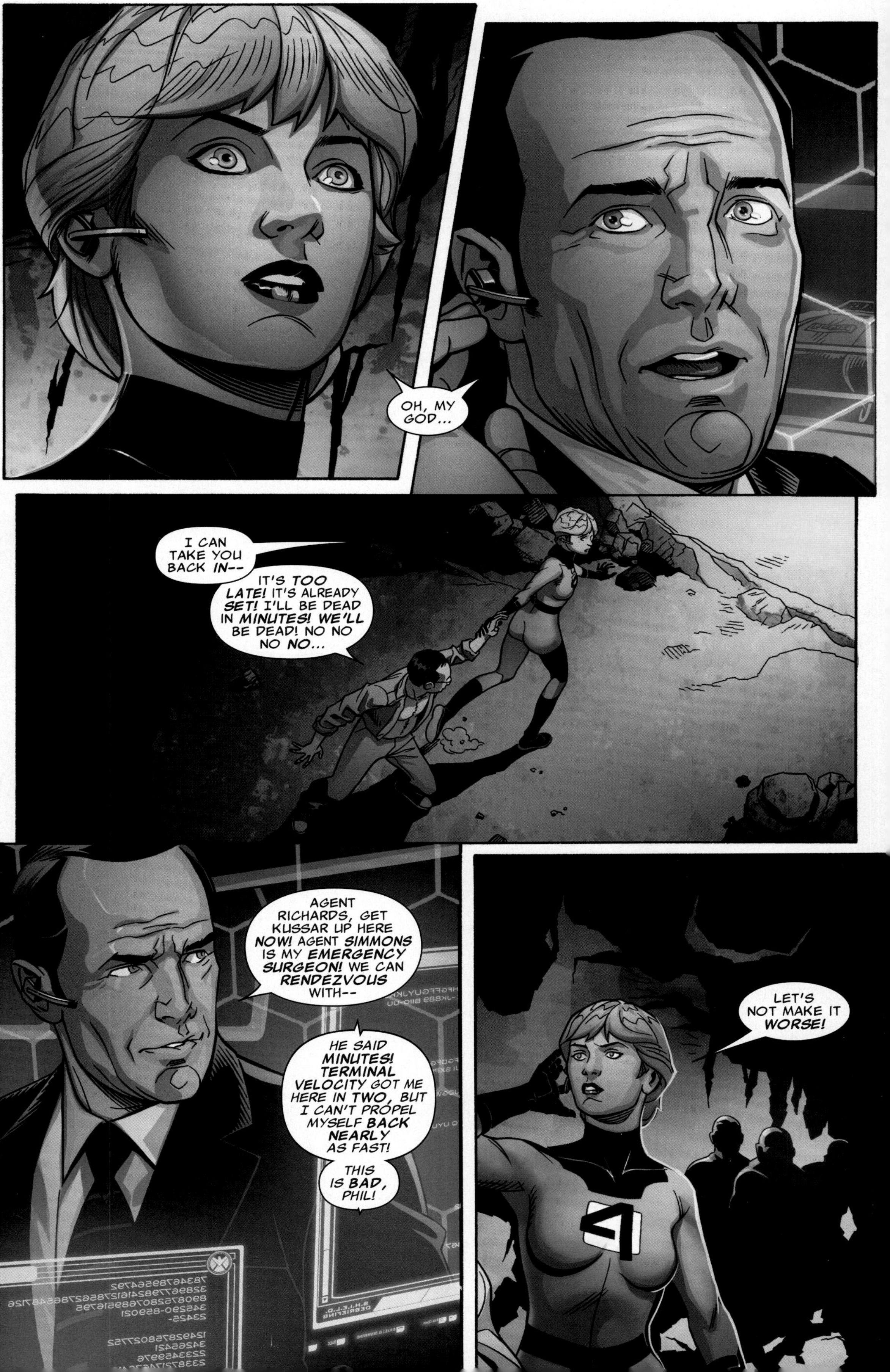
OH, MY GOD...
I CAN TAKE YOU BACK IN--
IT'S TOO LATE! IT'S ALREADY SET! I'LL BE DEAD IN MINUTES! WE'LL BE DEAD! NO NO NO NO...
AGENT RICHARDS, GET KUSSAR UP HERE NOW! AGENT SIMMONS IS MY EMERGENCY SURGEON! WE CAN RENDEZVOUS WITH--
HE SAID MINUTES! TERMINAL VELOCITY GOT ME HERE IN TWO, BUT I CAN'T PROPEL MYSELF BACK NEARLY AS FAST!
THIS IS BAD, PHIL!
LET'S NOT MAKE IT WORSE!

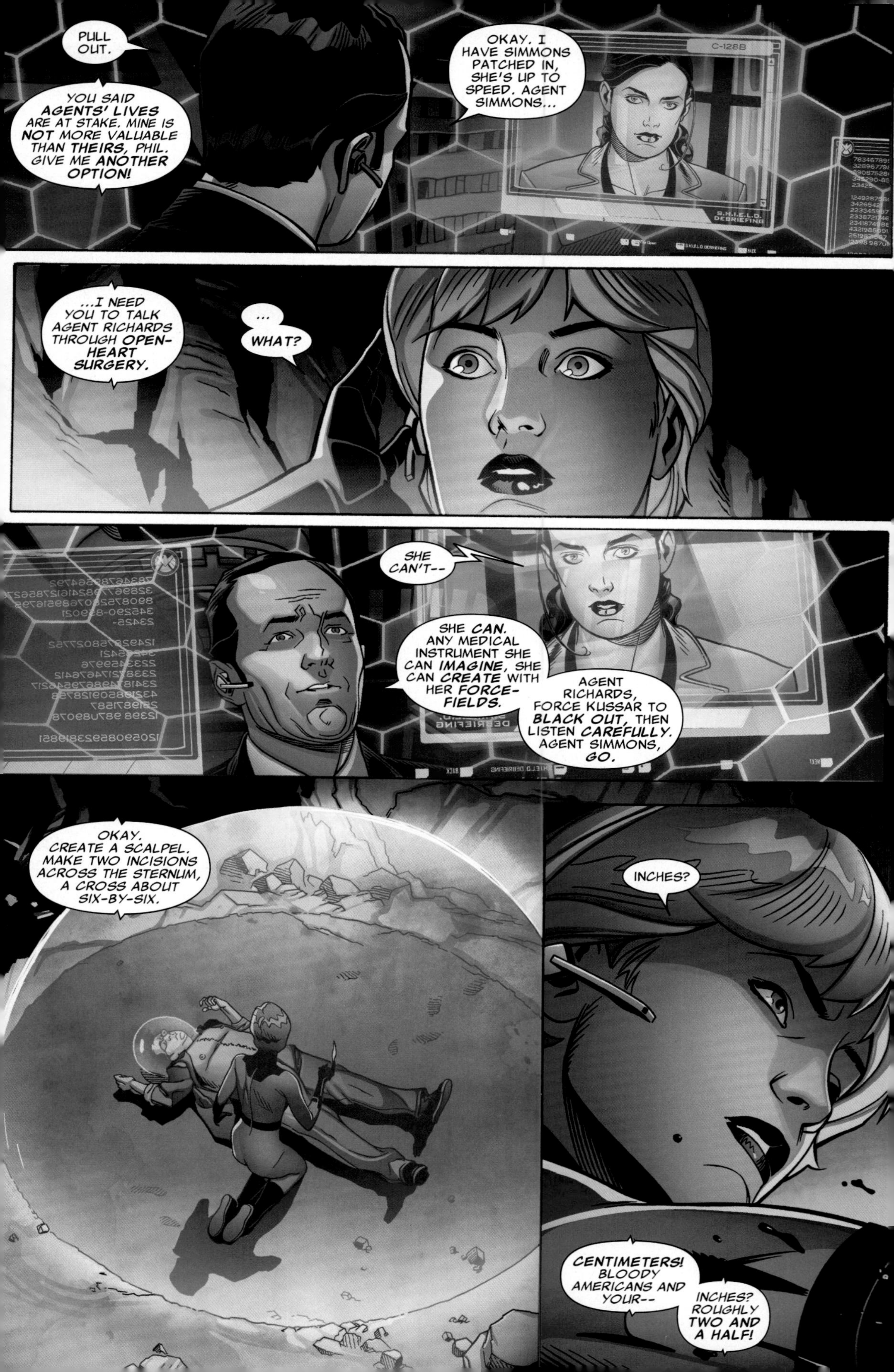
PULL OUT.
YOU SAID AGENTS' LIVES ARE AT STAKE. MINE IS NOT MORE VALUABLE THAN THEIRS, PHIL. GIVE ME ANOTHER OPTION!
OKAY. I HAVE SIMMONS PATCHED IN, SHE'S UP TO SPEED. AGENT SIMMONS...
C-128B
S.H.I.E.L.D. DEBRIEFING
...I NEED YOU TO TALK AGENT RICHARDS THROUGH OPEN-HEART SURGERY.
... WHAT?
SHE CAN'T--
SHE CAN. ANY MEDICAL INSTRUMENT SHE CAN IMAGINE, SHE CAN CREATE WITH HER FORCE-FIELDS.
AGENT RICHARDS, FORCE KUSSAR TO BLACK OUT, THEN LISTEN CAREFULLY. AGENT SIMMONS, GO.
OKAY. CREATE A SCALPEL. MAKE TWO INCISIONS ACROSS THE STERNUM, A CROSS ABOUT SIX-BY-SIX.
INCHES?
CENTIMETERS! BLOODY AMERICANS AND YOUR--
INCHES? ROUGHLY TWO AND A HALF!

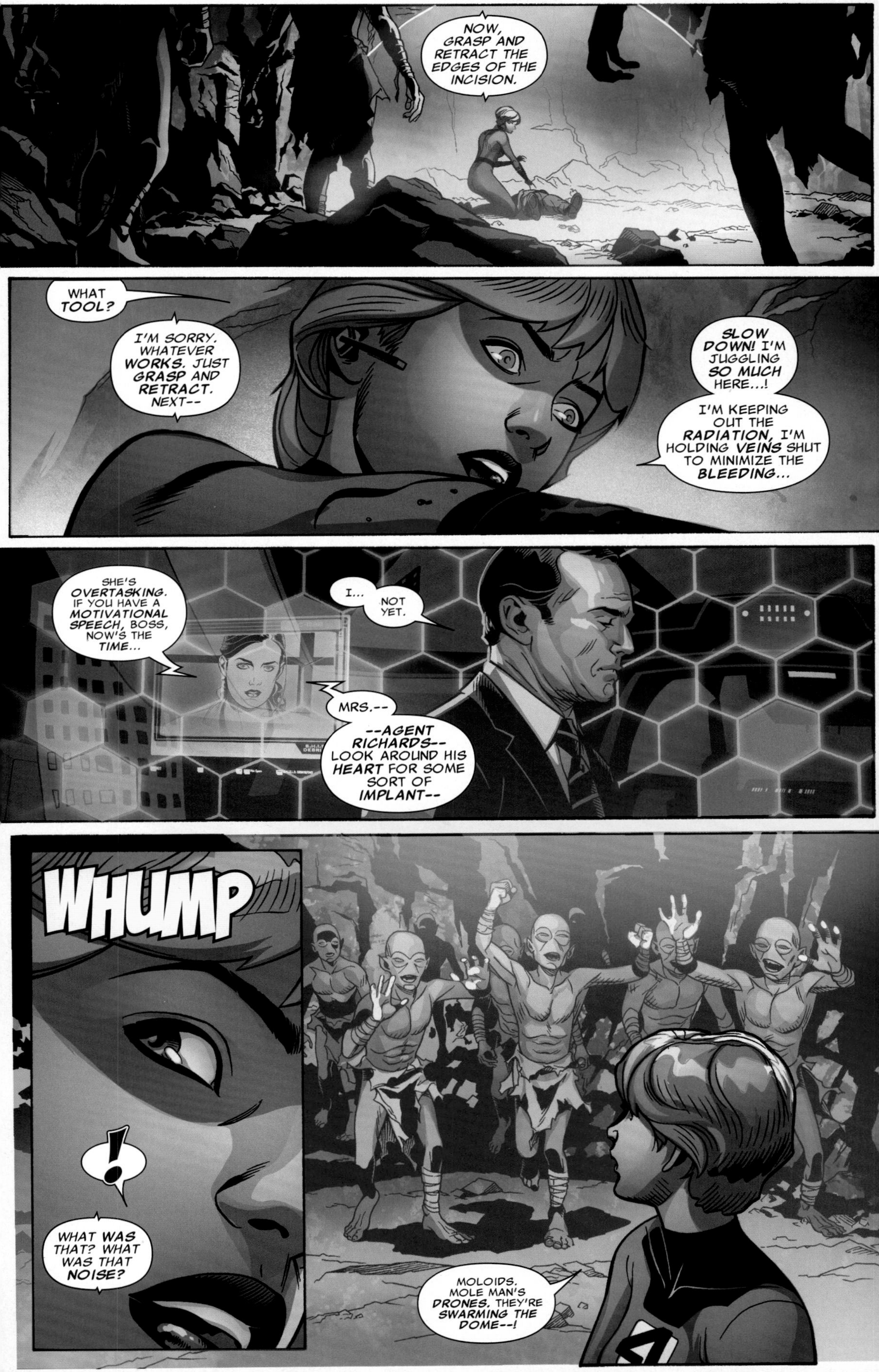

NOW, GRASP AND RETRACT THE EDGES OF THE INCISION.
WHAT TOOL?
I'M SORRY. WHATEVER WORKS. JUST GRASP AND RETRACT. NEXT--
SLOW DOWN! I'M JUGGLING SO MUCH HERE...!
I'M KEEPING OUT THE RADIATION, I'M HOLDING VEINS SHUT TO MINIMIZE THE BLEEDING...
SHE'S OVERTASKING. IF YOU HAVE A MOTIVATIONAL SPEECH, BOSS, NOW'S THE TIME...
I... NOT YET.
MRS.--
--AGENT RICHARDS-- LOOK AROUND HIS HEART FOR SOME SORT OF IMPLANT--
WHUMP
!
WHAT WAS THAT? WHAT WAS THAT NOISE?
MOLOIDS. MOLE MAN'S DRONES. THEY'RE SWARMING THE DOME--!

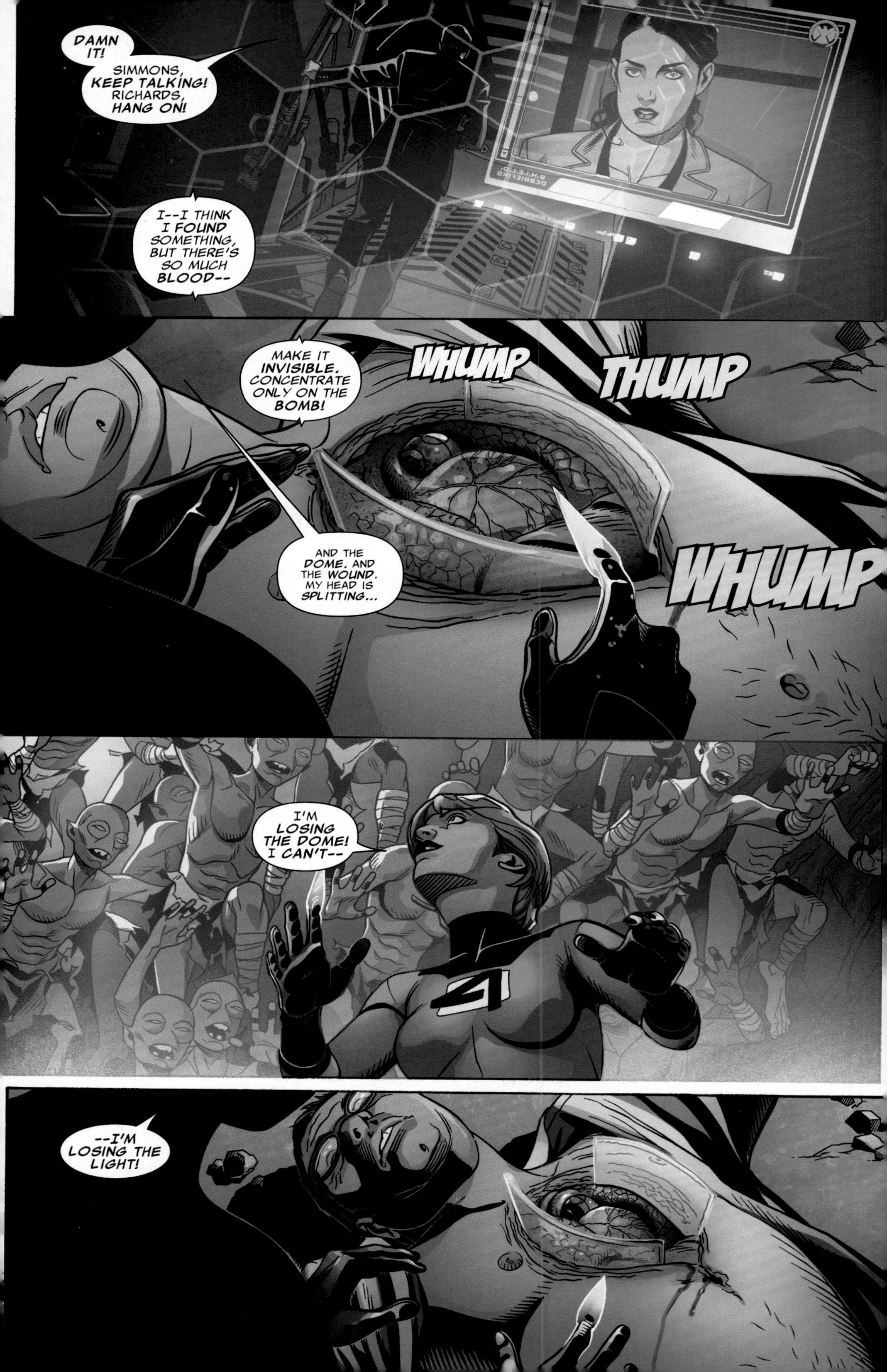
DAMN IT! SIMMONS, KEEP TALKING! RICHARDS, HANG ON!
I--I THINK I FOUND SOMETHING, BUT THERE'S SO MUCH BLOOD--
S.H.I.E.L.D. DEBRIEFING
MAKE IT INVISIBLE. CONCENTRATE ONLY ON THE BOMB!
WHUMP
THUMP
AND THE DOME. AND THE WOUND. MY HEAD IS SPLITTING...
WHUMP
I'M LOSING THE DOME! I CAN'T--
--I'M LOSING THE LIGHT!

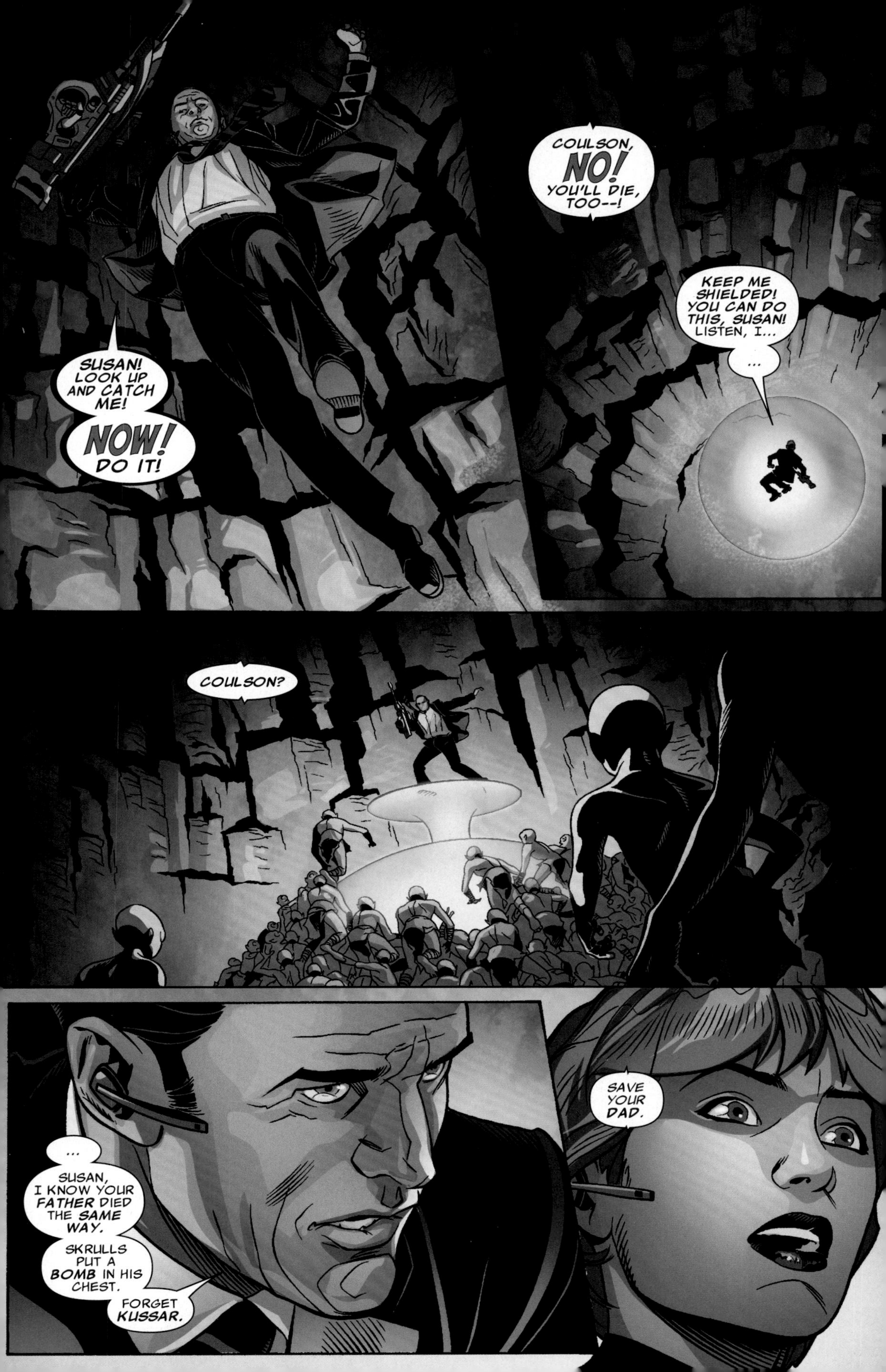
SUSAN! LOOK UP AND CATCH ME!
NOW! DO IT!
COULSON, NO! YOU'LL DIE, TOO--!
KEEP ME SHIELDED! YOU CAN DO THIS, SUSAN! LISTEN, I...
...
COULSON?
...
SUSAN, I KNOW YOUR FATHER DIED THE SAME WAY.
SKRULLS PUT A BOMB IN HIS CHEST.
FORGET KUSSAR.
SAVE YOUR DAD.

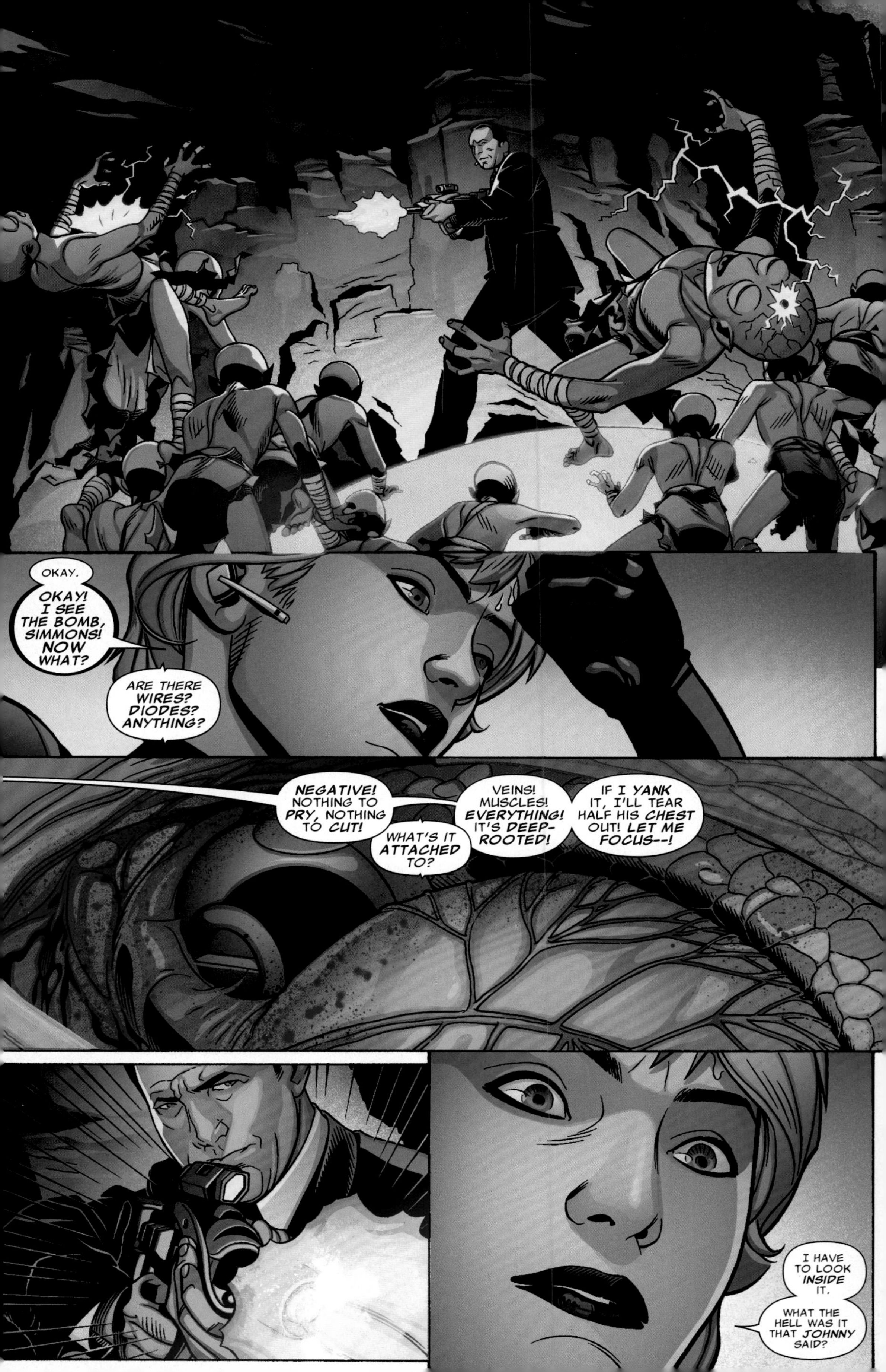
OKAY.
OKAY! I SEE THE BOMB, SIMMONS! NOW WHAT?
ARE THERE WIRES? DIODES? ANYTHING?
NEGATIVE! NOTHING TO PRY, NOTHING TO CUT!
WHAT'S IT ATTACHED TO?
VEINS! MUSCLES! EVERYTHING! IT'S DEEP-ROOTED!
IF I YANK IT, I'LL TEAR HALF HIS CHEST OUT! LET ME FOCUS--!
I HAVE TO LOOK INSIDE IT.
WHAT THE HELL WAS IT THAT JOHNNY SAID?

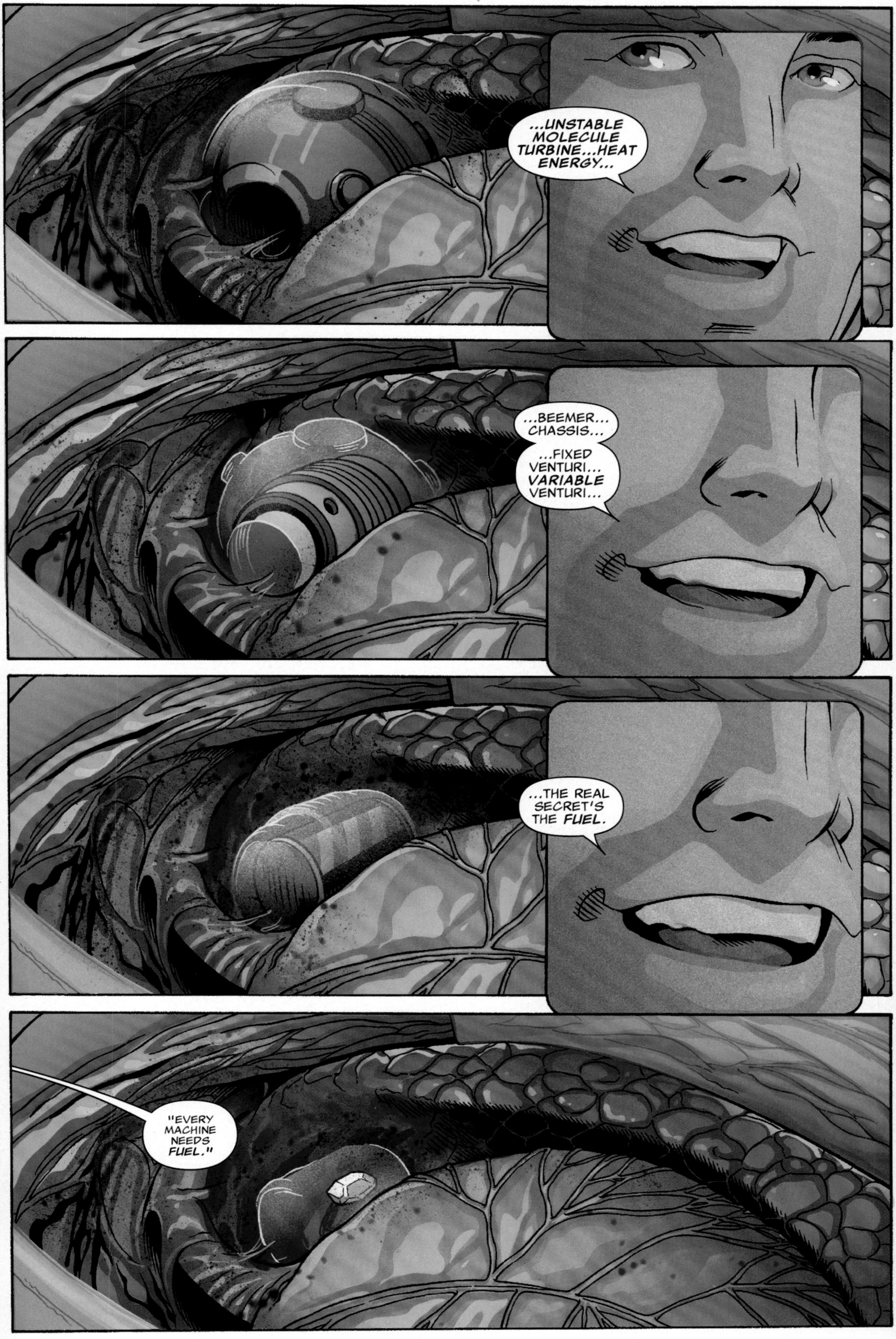
...UNSTABLE MOLECULE TURBINE...HEAT ENERGY...
...BEEMER... CHASSIS...
...FIXED VENTURI... VARIABLE VENTURI...
...THE REAL SECRET'S THE FUEL.
"EVERY MACHINE NEEDS FUEL."

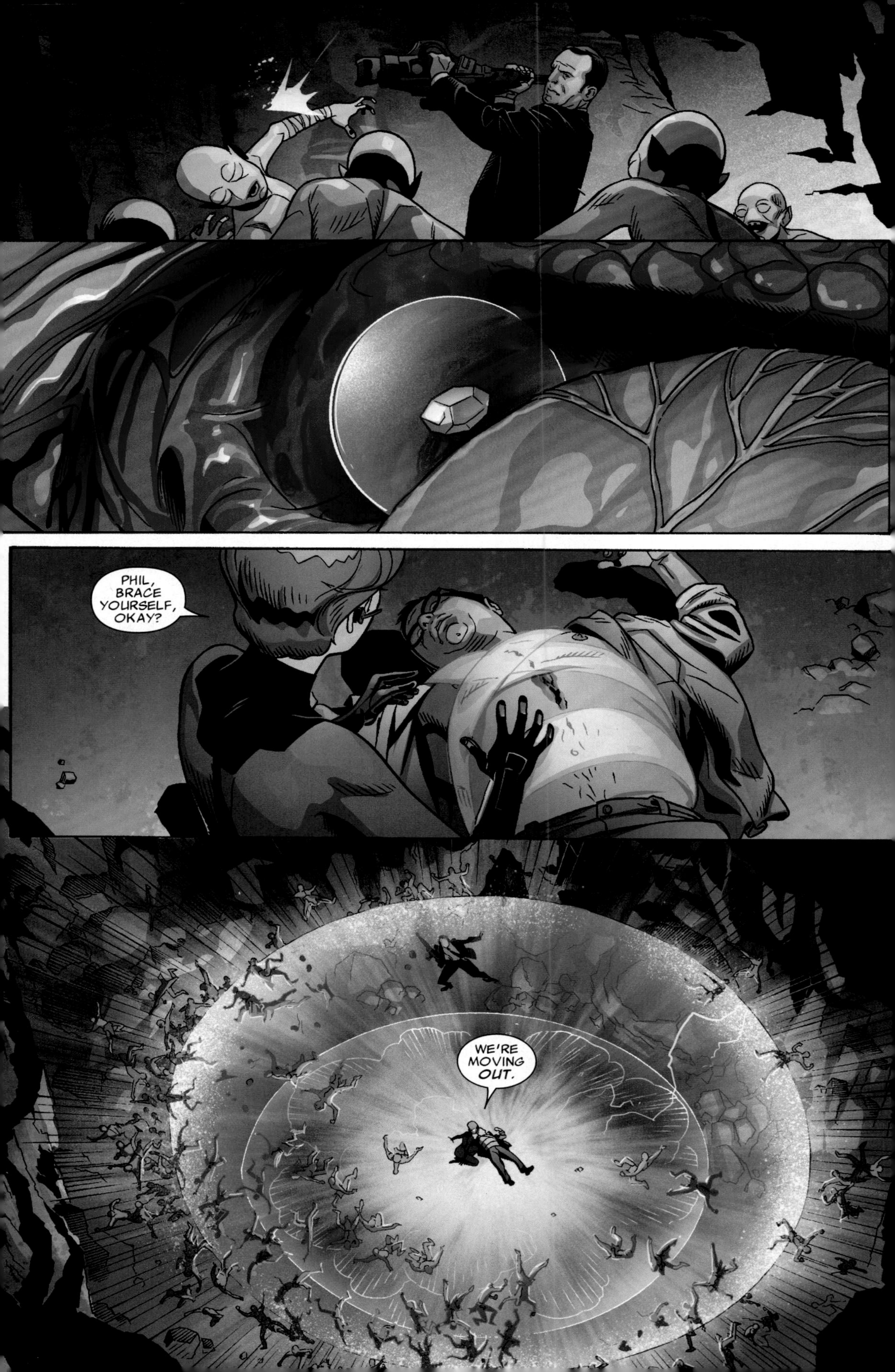
PHIL, BRACE YOURSELF, OKAY?
WE'RE MOVING OUT.

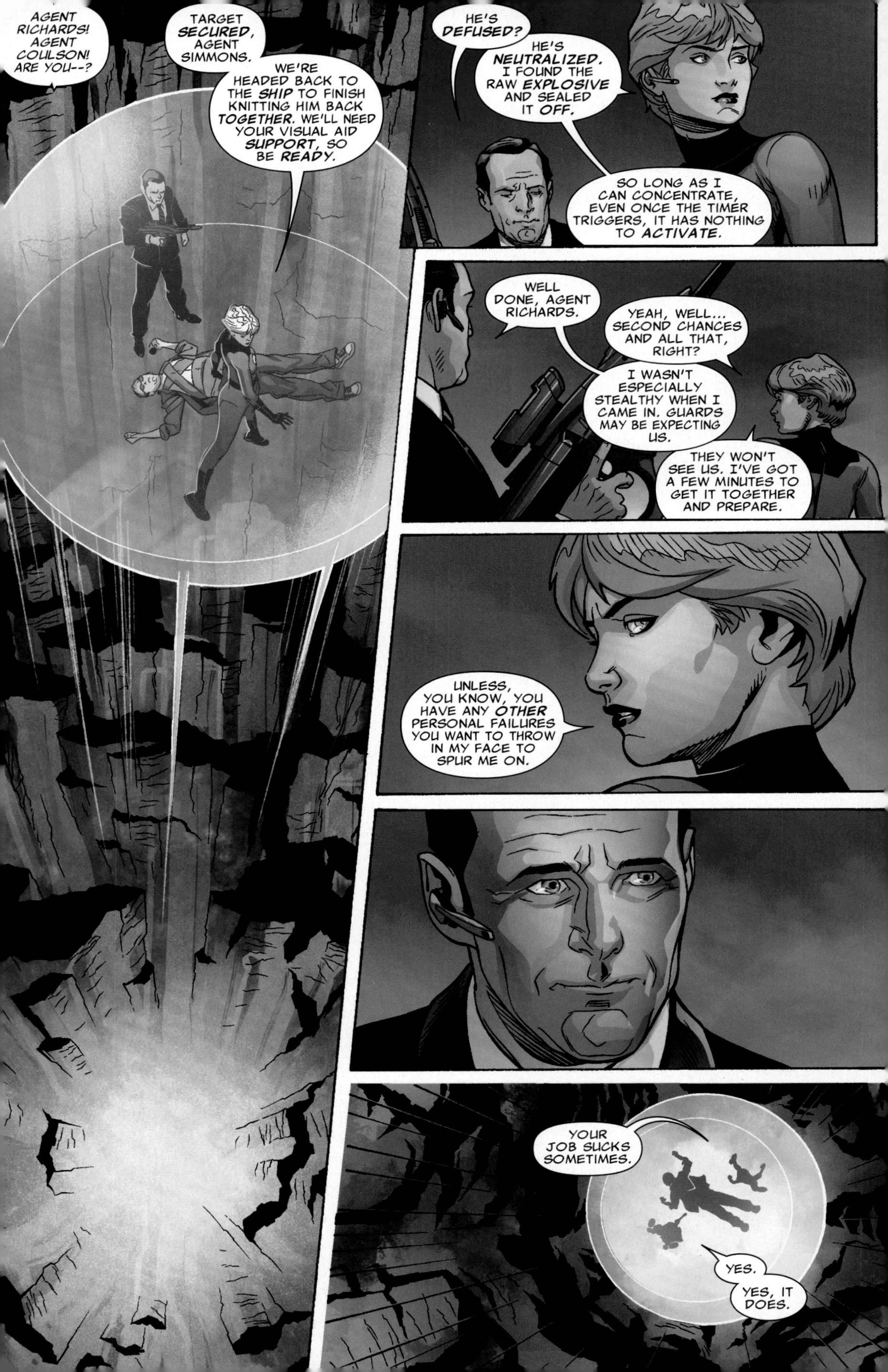
AGENT RICHARDS! AGENT COULSON! ARE YOU--?
TARGET SECURED, AGENT SIMMONS.
WE'RE HEADED BACK TO THE SHIP TO FINISH KNITTING HIM BACK TOGETHER. WE'LL NEED YOUR VISUAL AID SUPPORT, SO BE READY.
HE'S DEFUSED?
HE'S NEUTRALIZED. I FOUND THE RAW EXPLOSIVE AND SEALED IT OFF.
SO LONG AS I CAN CONCENTRATE, EVEN ONCE THE TIMER TRIGGERS, IT HAS NOTHING TO ACTIVATE.
WELL DONE, AGENT RICHARDS.
YEAH, WELL... SECOND CHANCES AND ALL THAT, RIGHT?
I WASN'T ESPECIALLY STEALTHY WHEN I CAME IN. GUARDS MAY BE EXPECTING US.
THEY WON'T SEE US. I'VE GOT A FEW MINUTES TO GET IT TOGETHER AND PREPARE.
UNLESS, YOU KNOW, YOU HAVE ANY OTHER PERSONAL FAILURES YOU WANT TO THROW IN MY FACE TO SPUR ME ON.
YOUR JOB SUCKS SOMETIMES.
YES.
YES, IT DOES.

5. ACTIVE MISSION:

MAGIC BULLETS

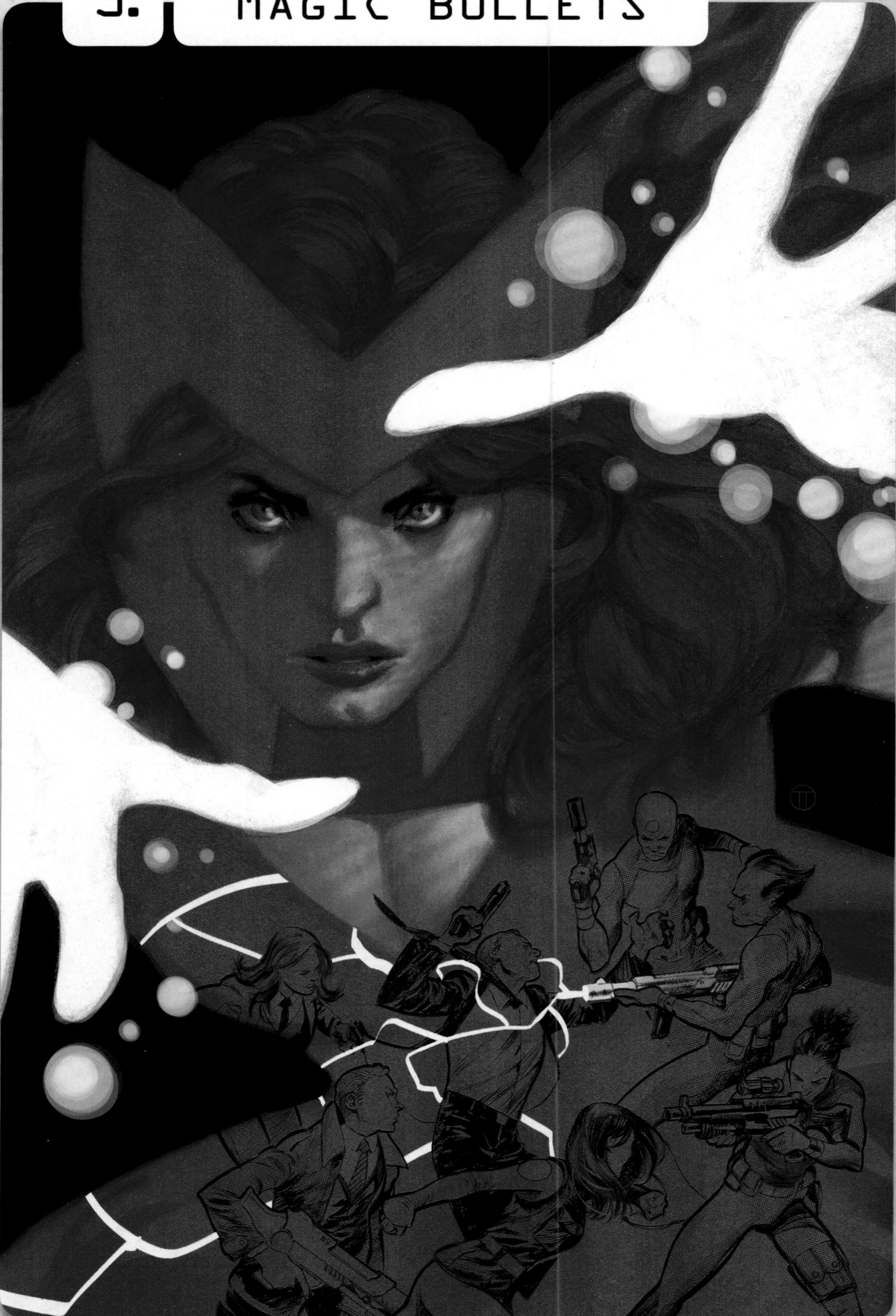

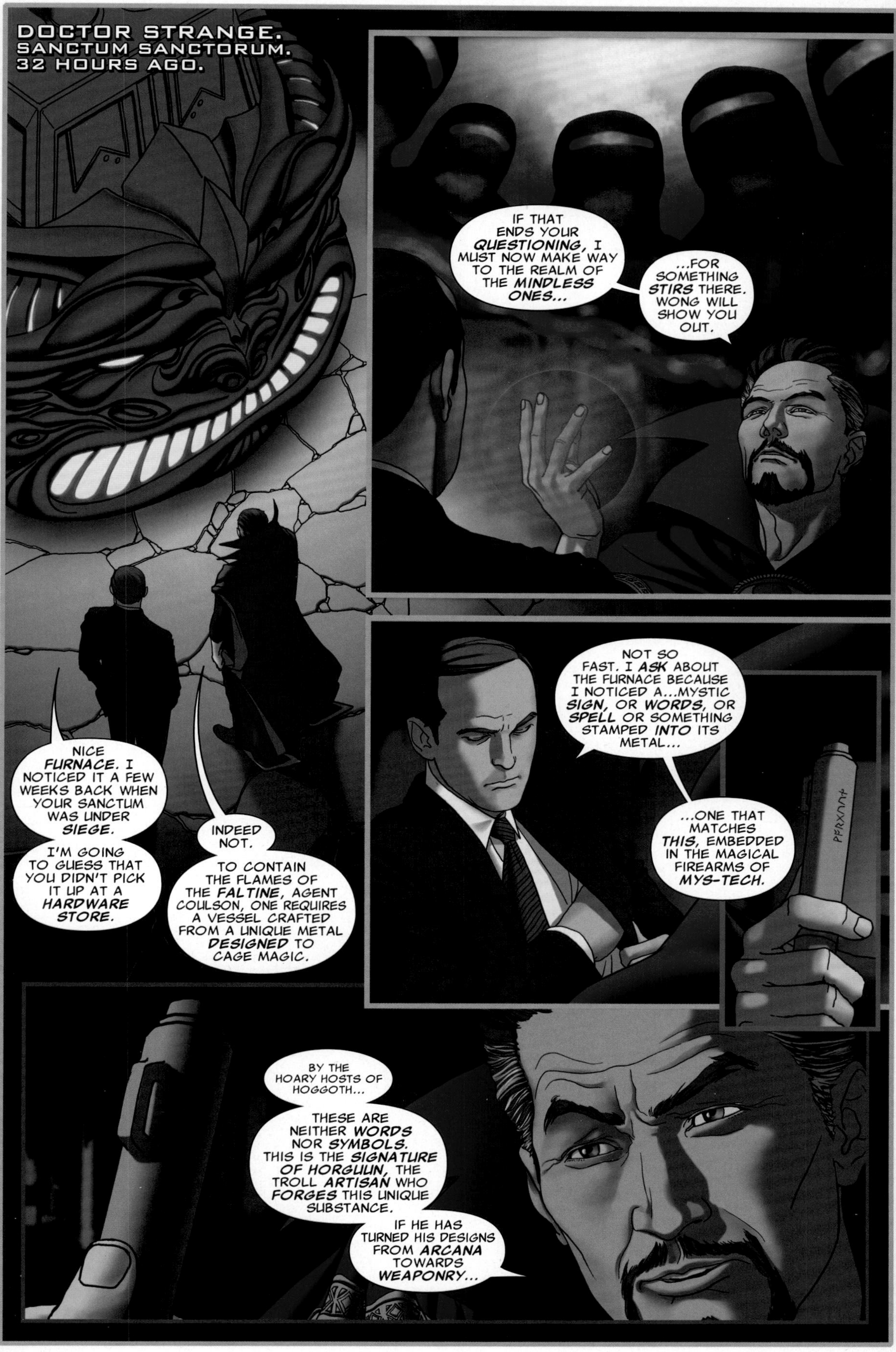
DOCTOR STRANGE.
SANCTUM SANCTORUM.
32 HOURS AGO.
NICE FURNACE. I NOTICED IT A FEW WEEKS BACK WHEN YOUR SANCTUM WAS UNDER SIEGE.
I'M GOING TO GUESS THAT YOU DIDN'T PICK IT UP AT A HARDWARE STORE.
INDEED NOT.
TO CONTAIN THE FLAMES OF THE FALTINE, AGENT COULSON, ONE REQUIRES A VESSEL CRAFTED FROM A UNIQUE METAL DESIGNED TO CAGE MAGIC.
IF THAT ENDS YOUR QUESTIONING, I MUST NOW MAKE WAY TO THE REALM OF THE MINDLESS ONES...
...FOR SOMETHING STIRS THERE. WONG WILL SHOW YOU OUT.
NOT SO FAST. I ASK ABOUT THE FURNACE BECAUSE I NOTICED A...MYSTIC SIGN, OR WORDS, OR SPELL OR SOMETHING STAMPED INTO ITS METAL...
...ONE THAT MATCHES THIS, EMBEDDED IN THE MAGICAL FIREARMS OF MYS-TECH.
BY THE HOARY HOSTS OF HOGGOTH...
THESE ARE NEITHER WORDS NOR SYMBOLS. THIS IS THE SIGNATURE OF HORGULIN, THE TROLL ARTISAN WHO FORGES THIS UNIQUE SUBSTANCE.
IF HE HAS TURNED HIS DESIGNS FROM ARCANA TOWARDS WEAPONRY...

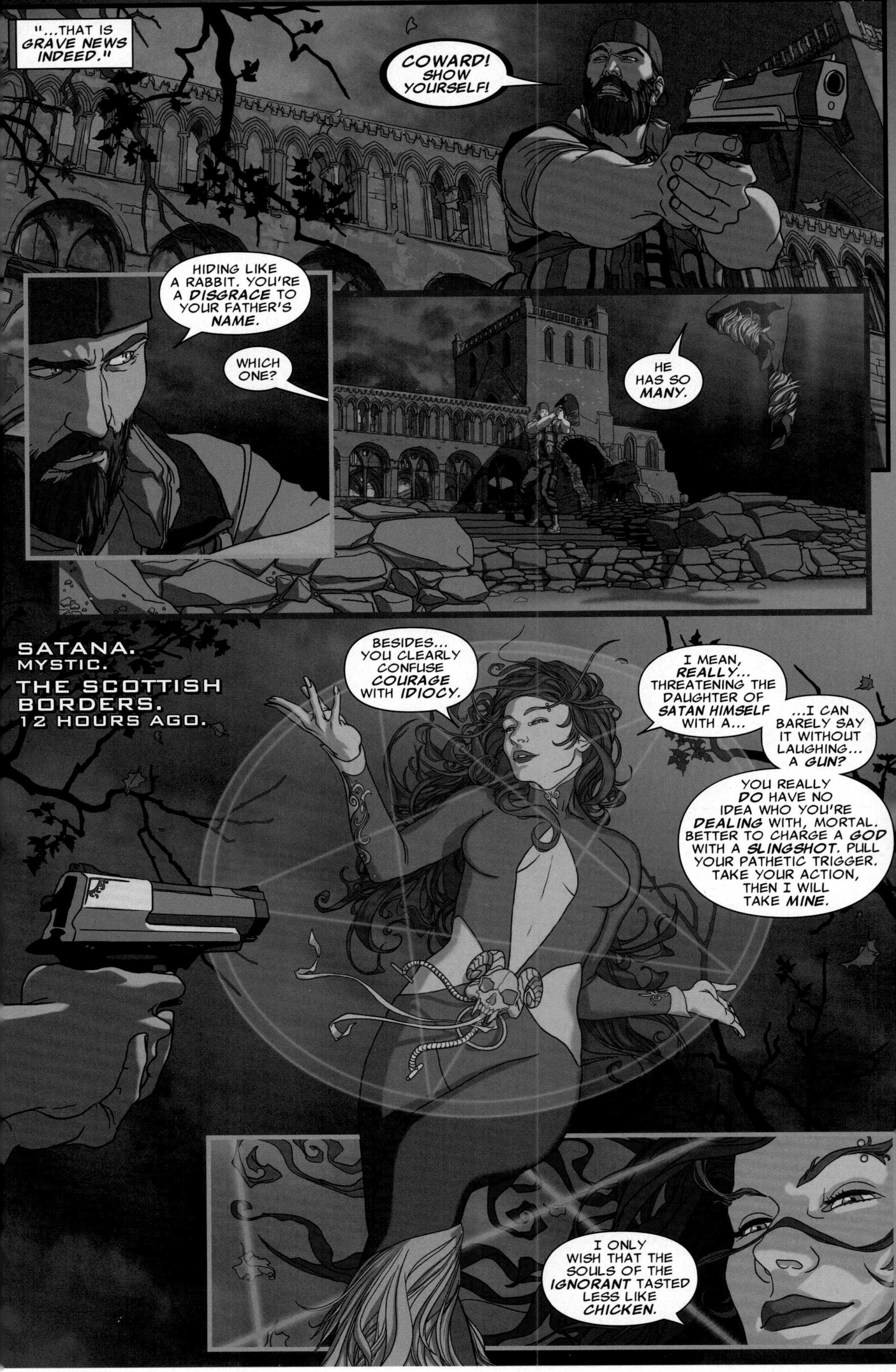
"...THAT IS GRAVE NEWS INDEED."
COWARD! SHOW YOURSELF!
HIDING LIKE A RABBIT. YOU'RE A DISGRACE TO YOUR FATHER'S NAME.
WHICH ONE?
HE HAS SO MANY.
SATANA. MYSTIC.
THE SCOTTISH BORDERS. 12 HOURS AGO.
BESIDES... YOU CLEARLY CONFUSE COURAGE WITH IDIOCY.
I MEAN, REALLY... THREATENING THE DAUGHTER OF SATAN HIMSELF WITH A...
...I CAN BARELY SAY IT WITHOUT LAUGHING... A GUN?
YOU REALLY DO HAVE NO IDEA WHO YOU'RE DEALING WITH, MORTAL. BETTER TO CHARGE A GOD WITH A SLINGSHOT. PULL YOUR PATHETIC TRIGGER. TAKE YOUR ACTION, THEN I WILL TAKE MINE.
I ONLY WISH THAT THE SOULS OF THE IGNORANT TASTED LESS LIKE CHICKEN.

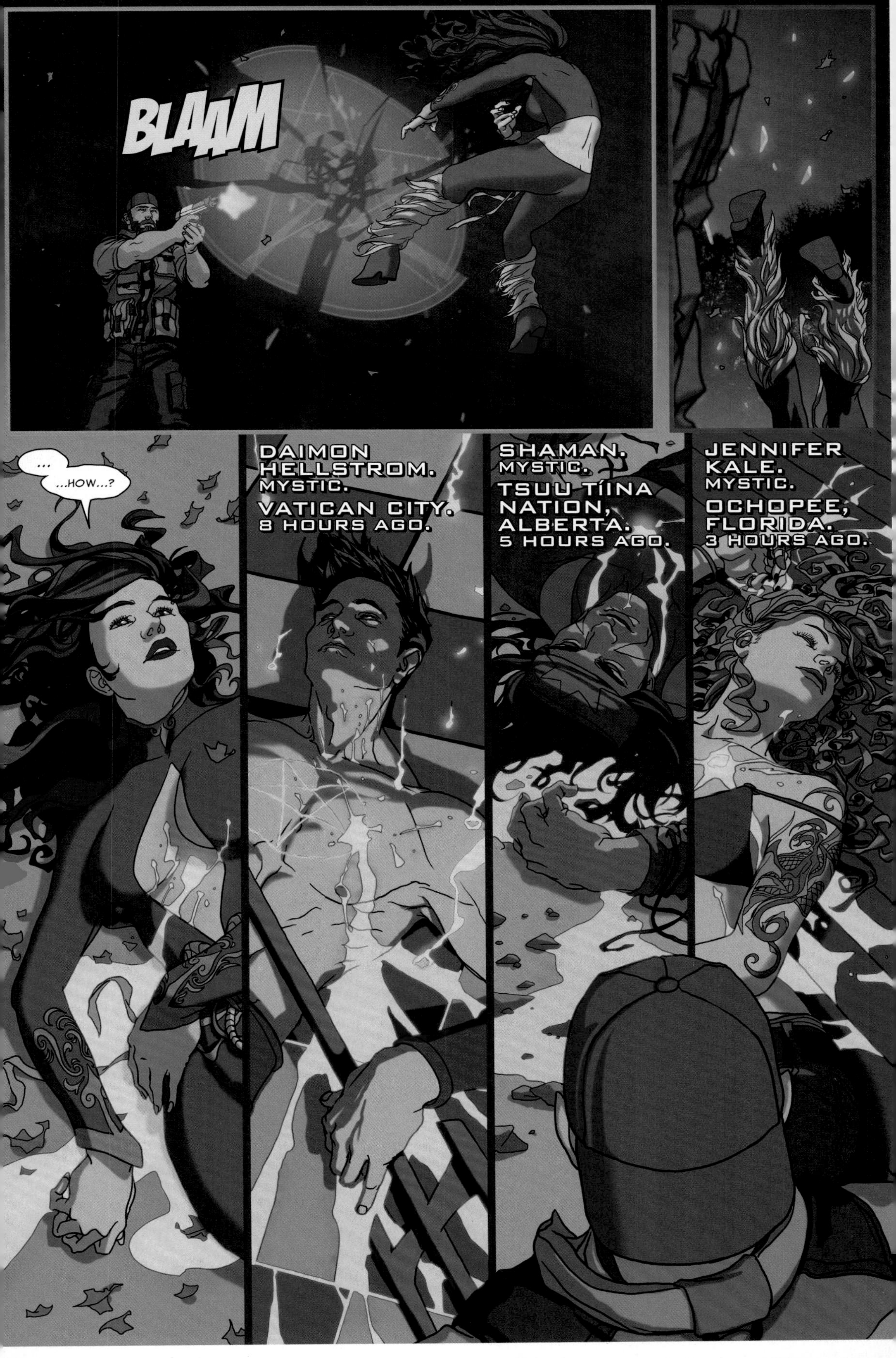
BLAAM
...
...HOW...?
DAIMON HELLSTROM. MYSTIC.
VATICAN CITY. 8 HOURS AGO.
SHAMAN. MYSTIC.
TSUU TÍINA NATION, ALBERTA. 5 HOURS AGO.
JENNIFER KALE. MYSTIC.
OCHOPEE, FLORIDA. 3 HOURS AGO.

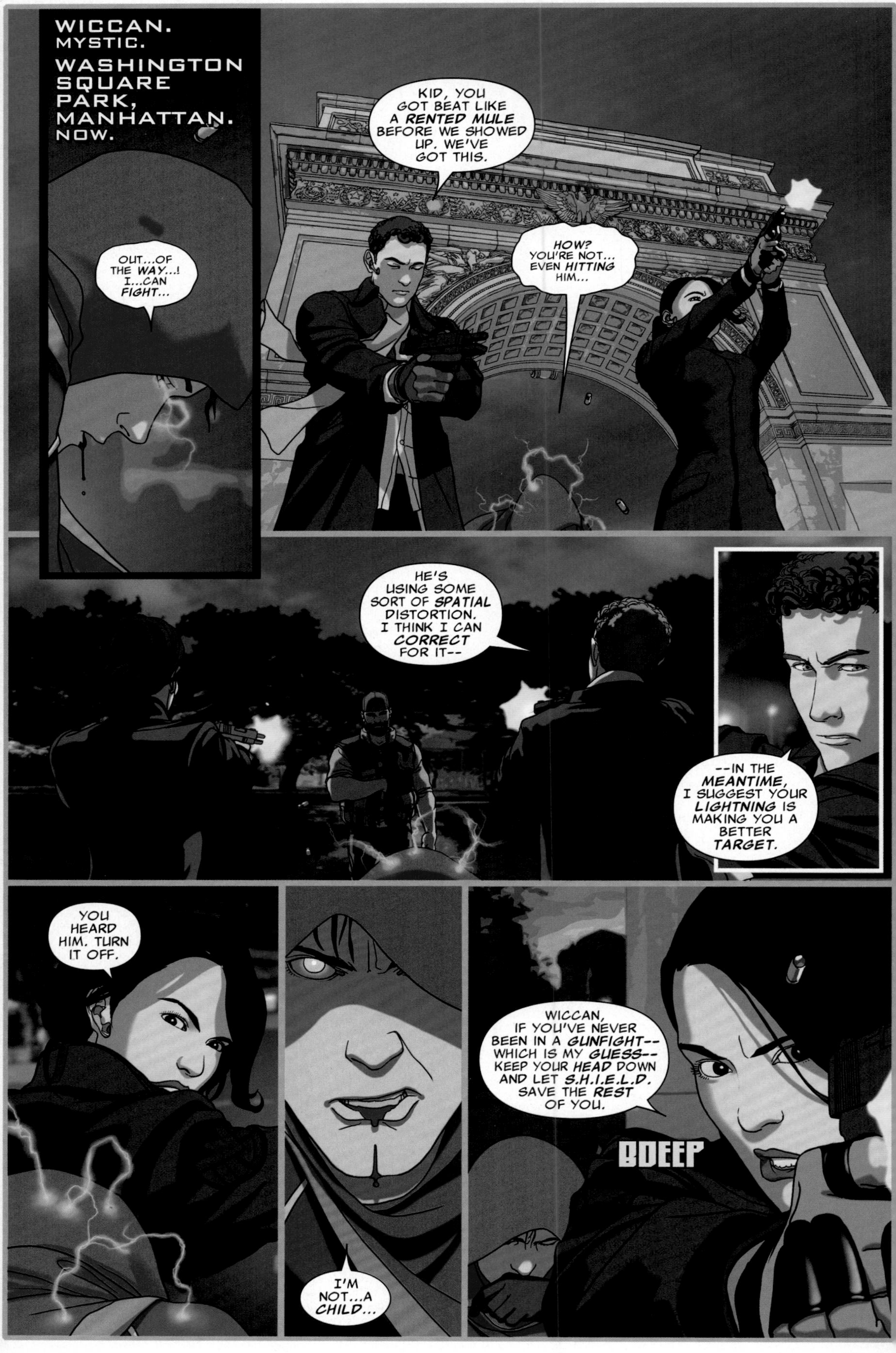
WICCAN. MYSTIC.
WASHINGTON SQUARE PARK, MANHATTAN. NOW.
KID, YOU GOT BEAT LIKE A RENTED MULE BEFORE WE SHOWED UP. WE'VE GOT THIS.
OUT...OF THE WAY...! I...CAN FIGHT...
HOW? YOU'RE NOT... EVEN HITTING HIM...
HE'S USING SOME SORT OF SPATIAL DISTORTION. I THINK I CAN CORRECT FOR IT--
--IN THE MEANTIME, I SUGGEST YOUR LIGHTNING IS MAKING YOU A BETTER TARGET.
YOU HEARD HIM. TURN IT OFF.
I'M NOT...A CHILD...
WICCAN, IF YOU'VE NEVER BEEN IN A GUNFIGHT-- WHICH IS MY GUESS-- KEEP YOUR HEAD DOWN AND LET S.H.I.E.L.D. SAVE THE REST OF YOU.
BDEEP

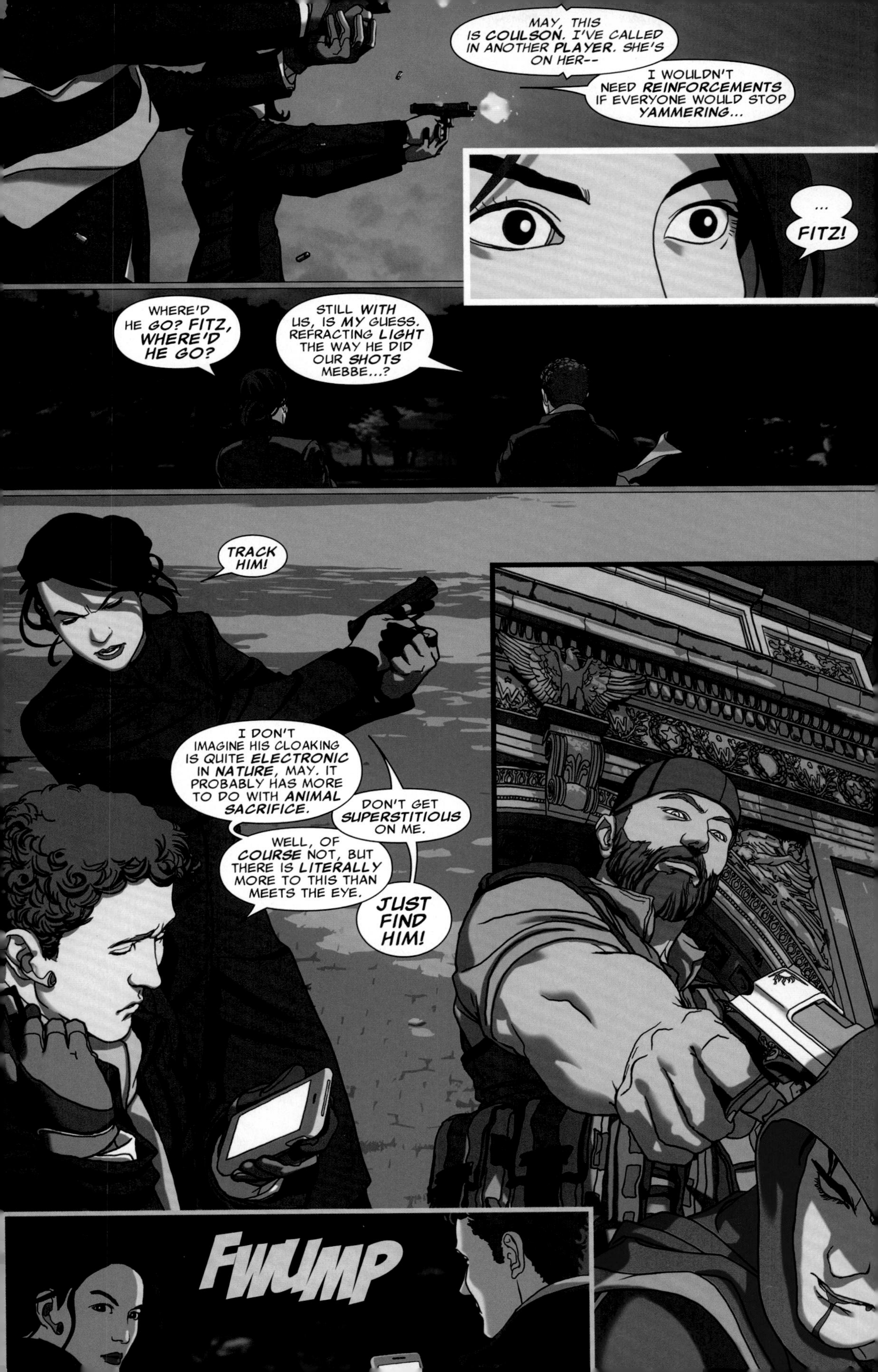
MAY, THIS IS COULSON. I'VE CALLED IN ANOTHER PLAYER. SHE'S ON HER--
I WOULDN'T NEED REINFORCEMENTS IF EVERYONE WOULD STOP YAMMERING...
... FITZ!
WHERE'D HE GO? FITZ, WHERE'D HE GO?
STILL WITH US, IS MY GUESS. REFRACTING LIGHT THE WAY HE DID OUR SHOTS MEBBE...?
TRACK HIM!
I DON'T IMAGINE HIS CLOAKING IS QUITE ELECTRONIC IN NATURE, MAY. IT PROBABLY HAS MORE TO DO WITH ANIMAL SACRIFICE.
DON'T GET SUPERSTITIOUS ON ME.
WELL, OF COURSE NOT, BUT THERE IS LITERALLY MORE TO THIS THAN MEETS THE EYE.
JUST FIND HIM!
FWUMP

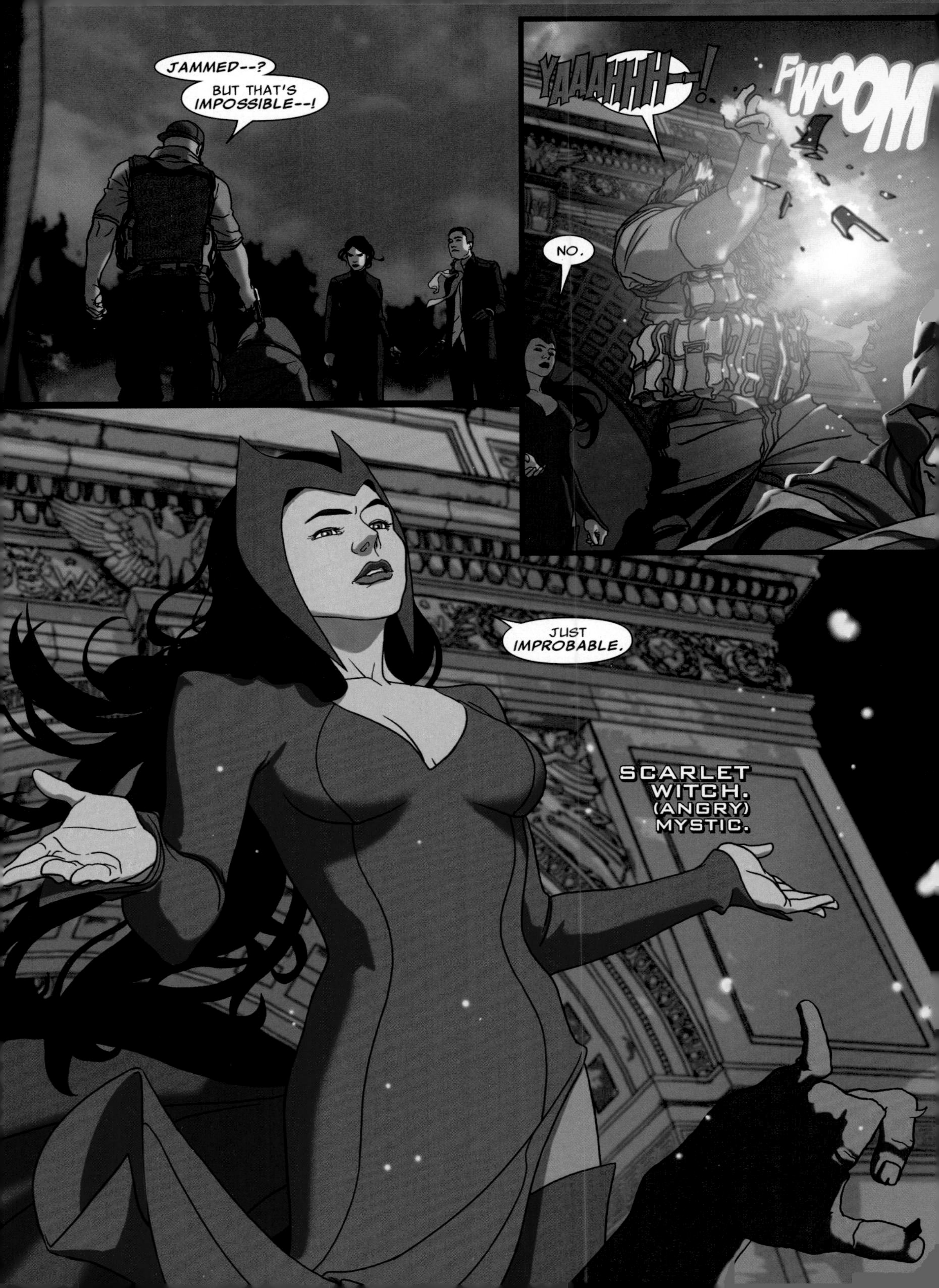
JAMMED--?
BUT THAT'S IMPOSSIBLE--!
YAAAHHH--!
FWOOM
NO.
JUST IMPROBABLE.
SCARLET WITCH. (ANGRY) MYSTIC.

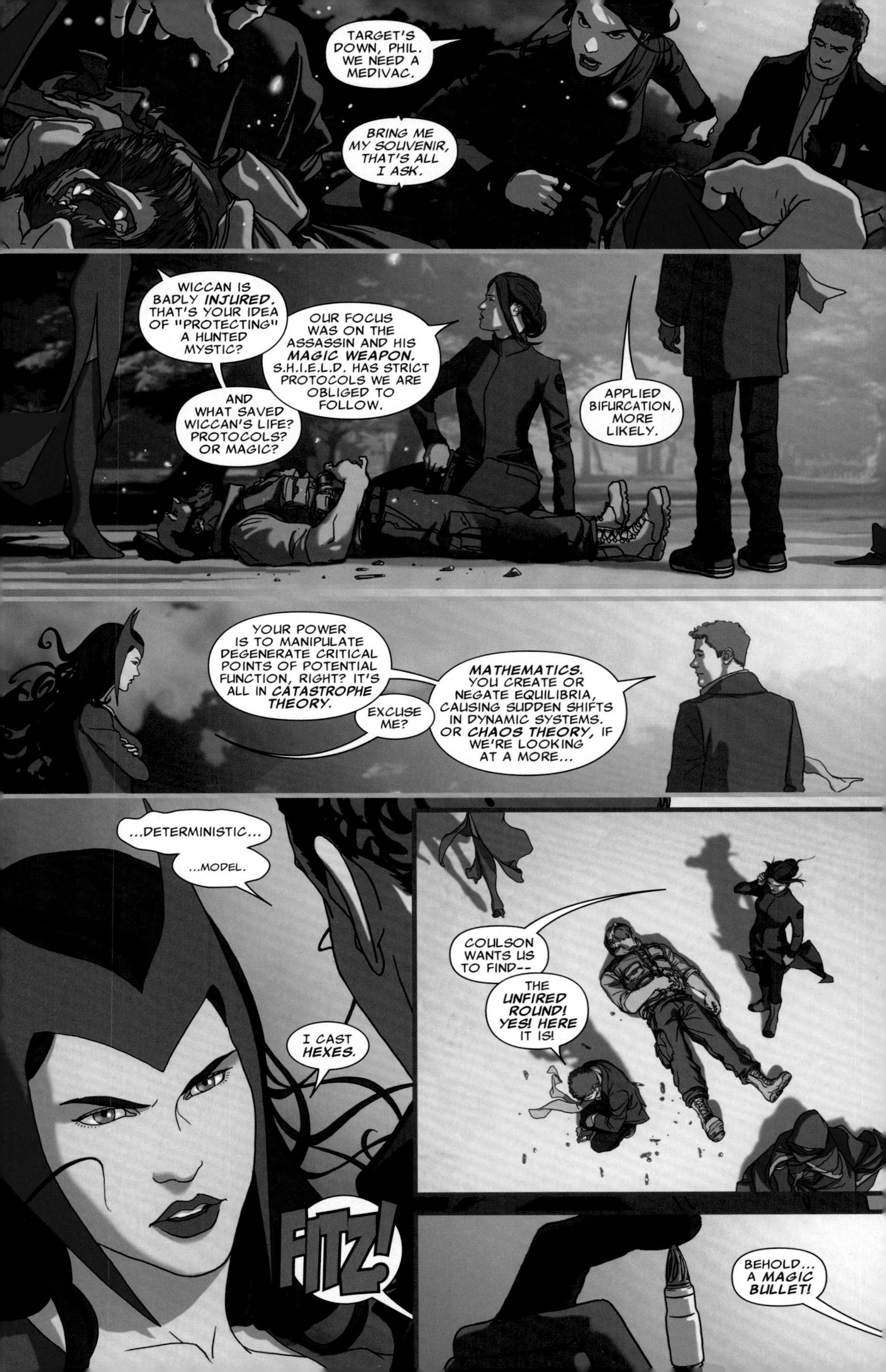
TARGET'S DOWN, PHIL. WE NEED A MEDIVAC.
BRING ME MY SOUVENIR, THAT'S ALL I ASK.
WICCAN IS BADLY INJURED. THAT'S YOUR IDEA OF "PROTECTING" A HUNTED MYSTIC?
OUR FOCUS WAS ON THE ASSASSIN AND HIS MAGIC WEAPON. S.H.I.E.L.D. HAS STRICT PROTOCOLS WE ARE OBLIGED TO FOLLOW.
AND WHAT SAVED WICCAN'S LIFE? PROTOCOLS? OR MAGIC?
APPLIED BIFURCATION, MORE LIKELY.
YOUR POWER IS TO MANIPULATE DEGENERATE CRITICAL POINTS OF POTENTIAL FUNCTION, RIGHT? IT'S ALL IN CATASTROPHE THEORY.
EXCUSE ME?
MATHEMATICS. YOU CREATE OR NEGATE EQUILIBRIA, CAUSING SUDDEN SHIFTS IN DYNAMIC SYSTEMS. OR CHAOS THEORY, IF WE'RE LOOKING AT A MORE...
...DETERMINISTIC...
...MODEL.
I CAST HEXES.
FITZ!
COULSON WANTS US TO FIND--
THE UNFIRED ROUND! YES! HERE IT IS!
BEHOLD... A MAGIC BULLET!

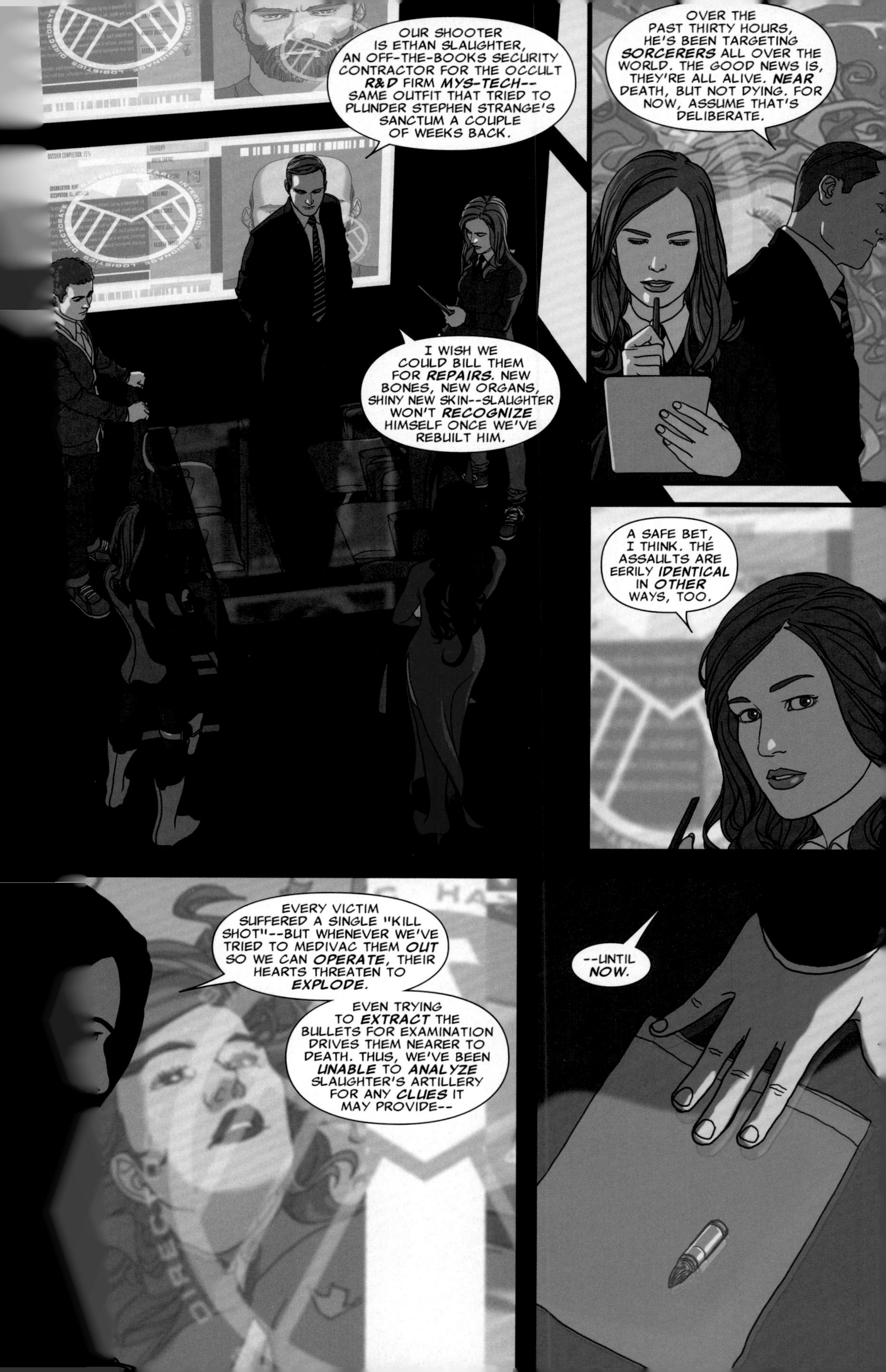
OUR SHOOTER IS ETHAN SLAUGHTER, AN OFF-THE-BOOKS SECURITY CONTRACTOR FOR THE OCCULT R&D FIRM MYS-TECH-- SAME OUTFIT THAT TRIED TO PLUNDER STEPHEN STRANGE'S SANCTUM A COUPLE OF WEEKS BACK.
I WISH WE COULD BILL THEM FOR REPAIRS. NEW BONES, NEW ORGANS, SHINY NEW SKIN--SLAUGHTER WON'T RECOGNIZE HIMSELF ONCE WE'VE REBUILT HIM.
OVER THE PAST THIRTY HOURS, HE'S BEEN TARGETING SORCERERS ALL OVER THE WORLD. THE GOOD NEWS IS, THEY'RE ALL ALIVE. NEAR DEATH, BUT NOT DYING. FOR NOW, ASSUME THAT'S DELIBERATE.
A SAFE BET, I THINK. THE ASSAULTS ARE EERILY IDENTICAL IN OTHER WAYS, TOO.
EVERY VICTIM SUFFERED A SINGLE "KILL SHOT"--BUT WHENEVER WE'VE TRIED TO MEDIVAC THEM OUT SO WE CAN OPERATE, THEIR HEARTS THREATEN TO EXPLODE.
EVEN TRYING TO EXTRACT THE BULLETS FOR EXAMINATION DRIVES THEM NEARER TO DEATH. THUS, WE'VE BEEN UNABLE TO ANALYZE SLAUGHTER'S ARTILLERY FOR ANY CLUES IT MAY PROVIDE--
--UNTIL NOW.

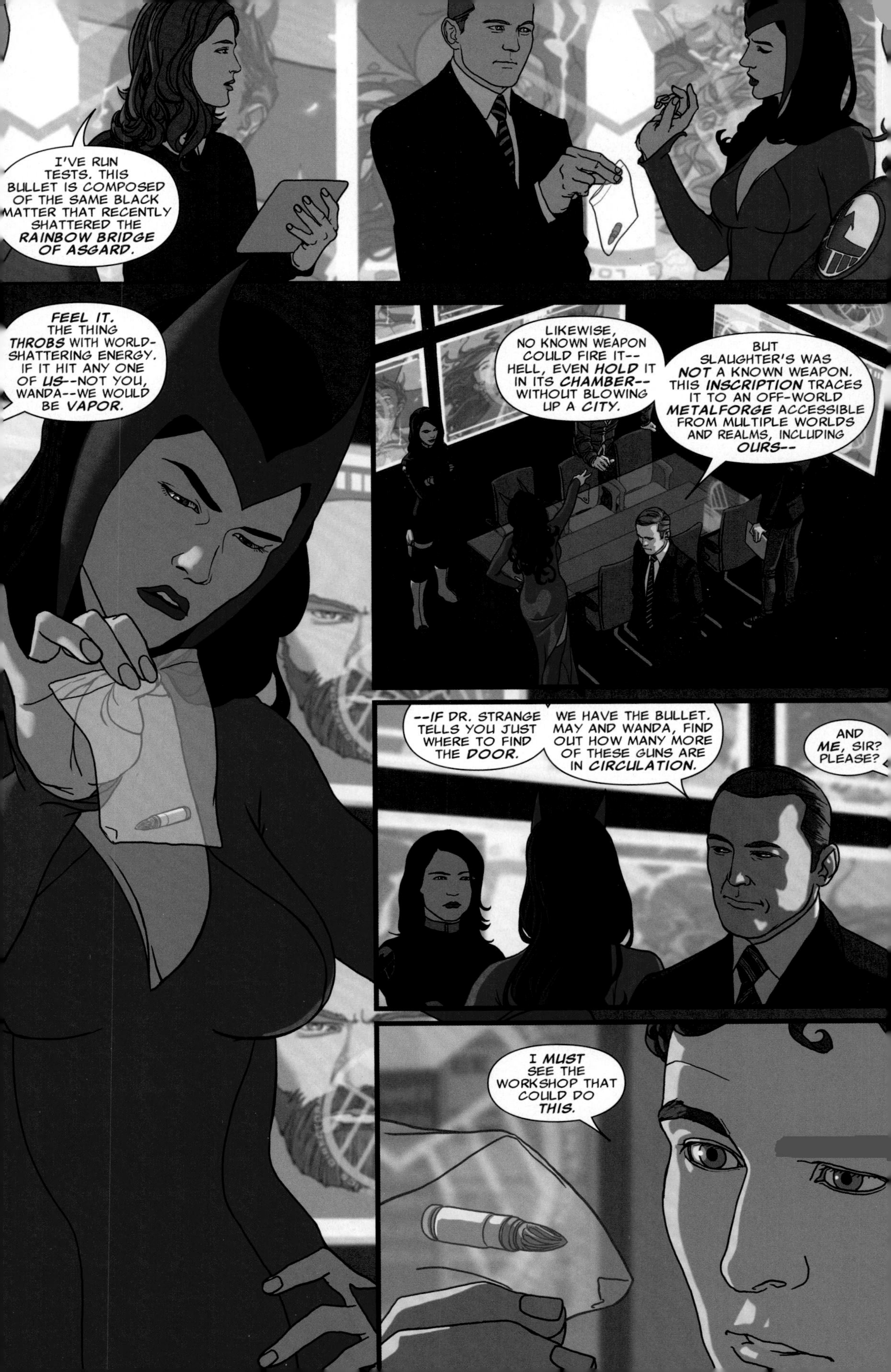
I'VE RUN TESTS. THIS BULLET IS COMPOSED OF THE SAME BLACK MATTER THAT RECENTLY SHATTERED THE RAINBOW BRIDGE OF ASGARD.
FEEL IT. THE THING THROBS WITH WORLD-SHATTERING ENERGY. IF IT HIT ANY ONE OF US--NOT YOU, WANDA--WE WOULD BE VAPOR.
LIKEWISE, NO KNOWN WEAPON COULD FIRE IT--HELL, EVEN HOLD IT IN ITS CHAMBER--WITHOUT BLOWING UP A CITY.
BUT SLAUGHTER'S WAS NOT A KNOWN WEAPON. THIS INSCRIPTION TRACES IT TO AN OFF-WORLD METALFORGE ACCESSIBLE FROM MULTIPLE WORLDS AND REALMS, INCLUDING OURS--
--IF DR. STRANGE TELLS YOU JUST WHERE TO FIND THE DOOR.
WE HAVE THE BULLET. MAY AND WANDA, FIND OUT HOW MANY MORE OF THESE GUNS ARE IN CIRCULATION.
AND ME, SIR? PLEASE?
I MUST SEE THE WORKSHOP THAT COULD DO THIS.

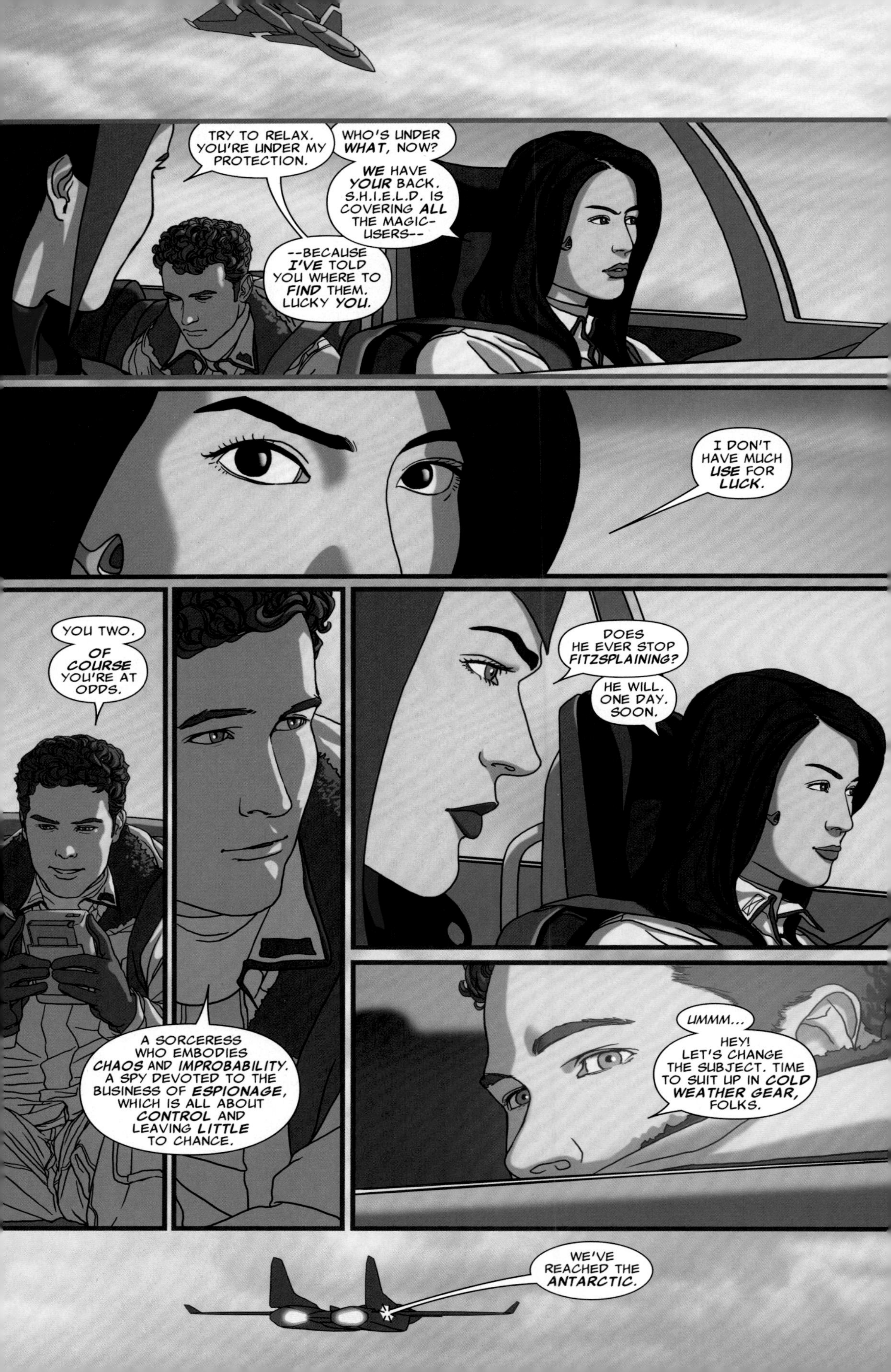
TRY TO RELAX. YOU'RE UNDER MY PROTECTION.
WHO'S UNDER WHAT, NOW?
WE HAVE YOUR BACK. S.H.I.E.L.D. IS COVERING ALL THE MAGIC-USERS--
--BECAUSE I'VE TOLD YOU WHERE TO FIND THEM. LUCKY YOU.
I DON'T HAVE MUCH USE FOR LUCK.
YOU TWO. OF COURSE YOU'RE AT ODDS.
A SORCERESS WHO EMBODIES CHAOS AND IMPROBABILITY. A SPY DEVOTED TO THE BUSINESS OF ESPIONAGE, WHICH IS ALL ABOUT CONTROL AND LEAVING LITTLE TO CHANCE.
DOES HE EVER STOP FITZSPLAINING?
HE WILL. ONE DAY. SOON.
UMMM...
HEY! LET'S CHANGE THE SUBJECT. TIME TO SUIT UP IN COLD WEATHER GEAR, FOLKS.
WE'VE REACHED THE ANTARCTIC.

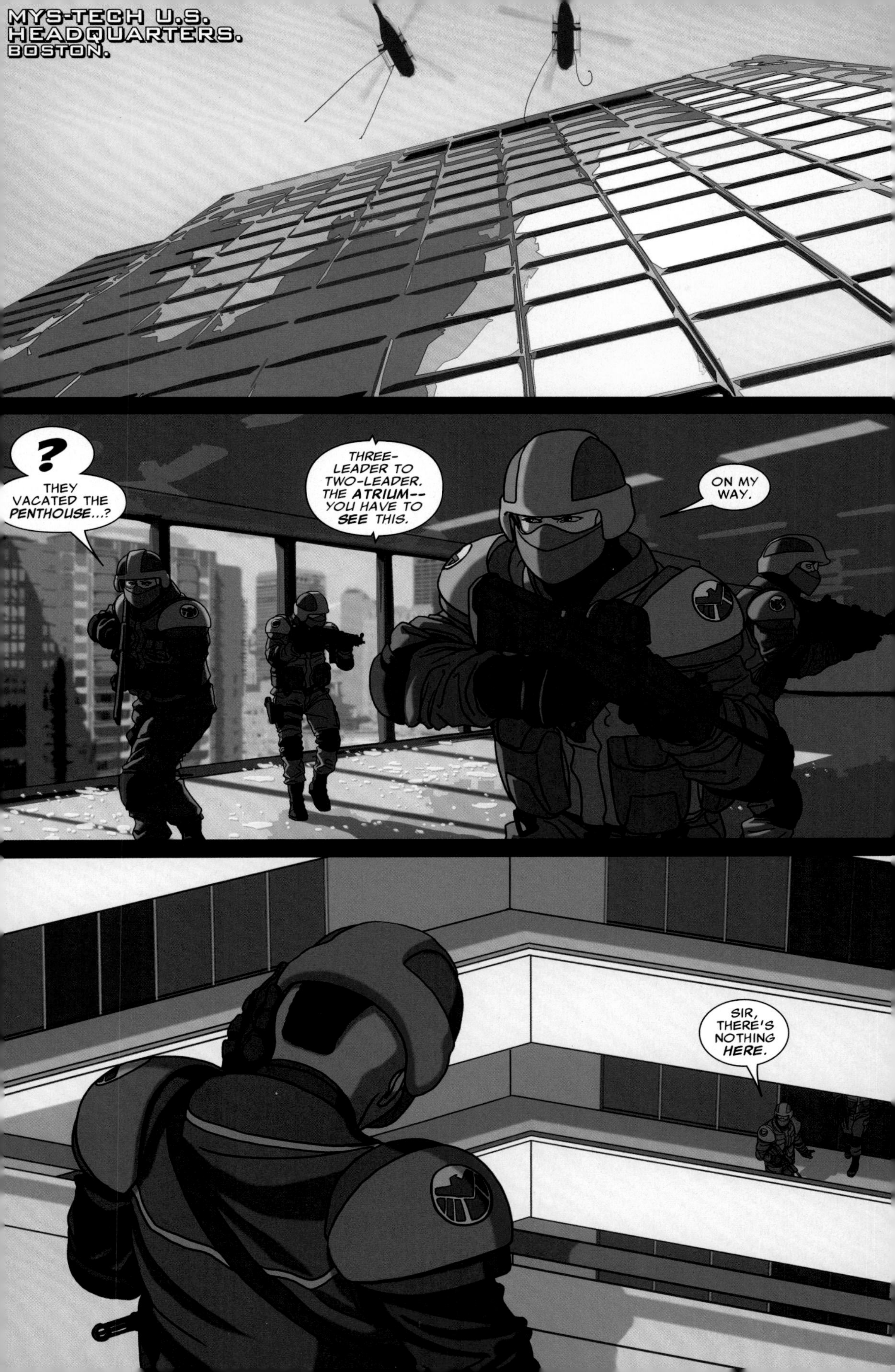
MYS-TECH U.S. HEADQUARTERS. BOSTON.
?
THEY VACATED THE PENTHOUSE...?
THREE-LEADER TO TWO-LEADER. THE ATRIUM-- YOU HAVE TO SEE THIS.
ON MY WAY.
SIR, THERE'S NOTHING HERE.

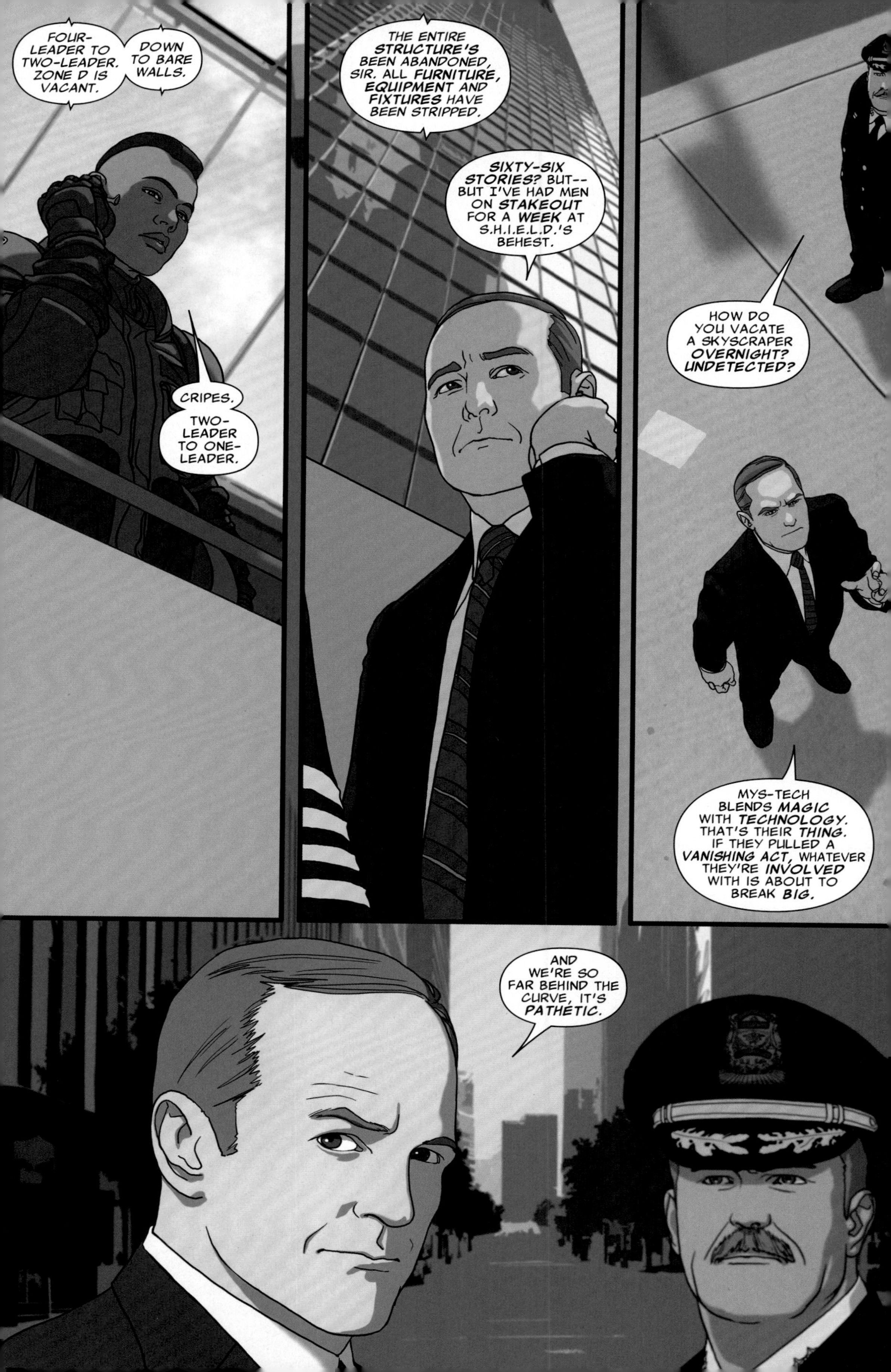
FOUR-LEADER TO TWO-LEADER. ZONE D IS VACANT.
DOWN TO BARE WALLS.
CRIPES.
TWO-LEADER TO ONE-LEADER.
THE ENTIRE STRUCTURE'S BEEN ABANDONED, SIR. ALL FURNITURE, EQUIPMENT AND FIXTURES HAVE BEEN STRIPPED.
SIXTY-SIX STORIES? BUT--BUT I'VE HAD MEN ON STAKEOUT FOR A WEEK AT S.H.I.E.L.D.'S BEHEST.
HOW DO YOU VACATE A SKYSCRAPER OVERNIGHT? UNDETECTED?
MYS-TECH BLENDS MAGIC WITH TECHNOLOGY. THAT'S THEIR THING. IF THEY PULLED A VANISHING ACT, WHATEVER THEY'RE INVOLVED WITH IS ABOUT TO BREAK BIG.
AND WE'RE SO FAR BEHIND THE CURVE, IT'S PATHETIC.

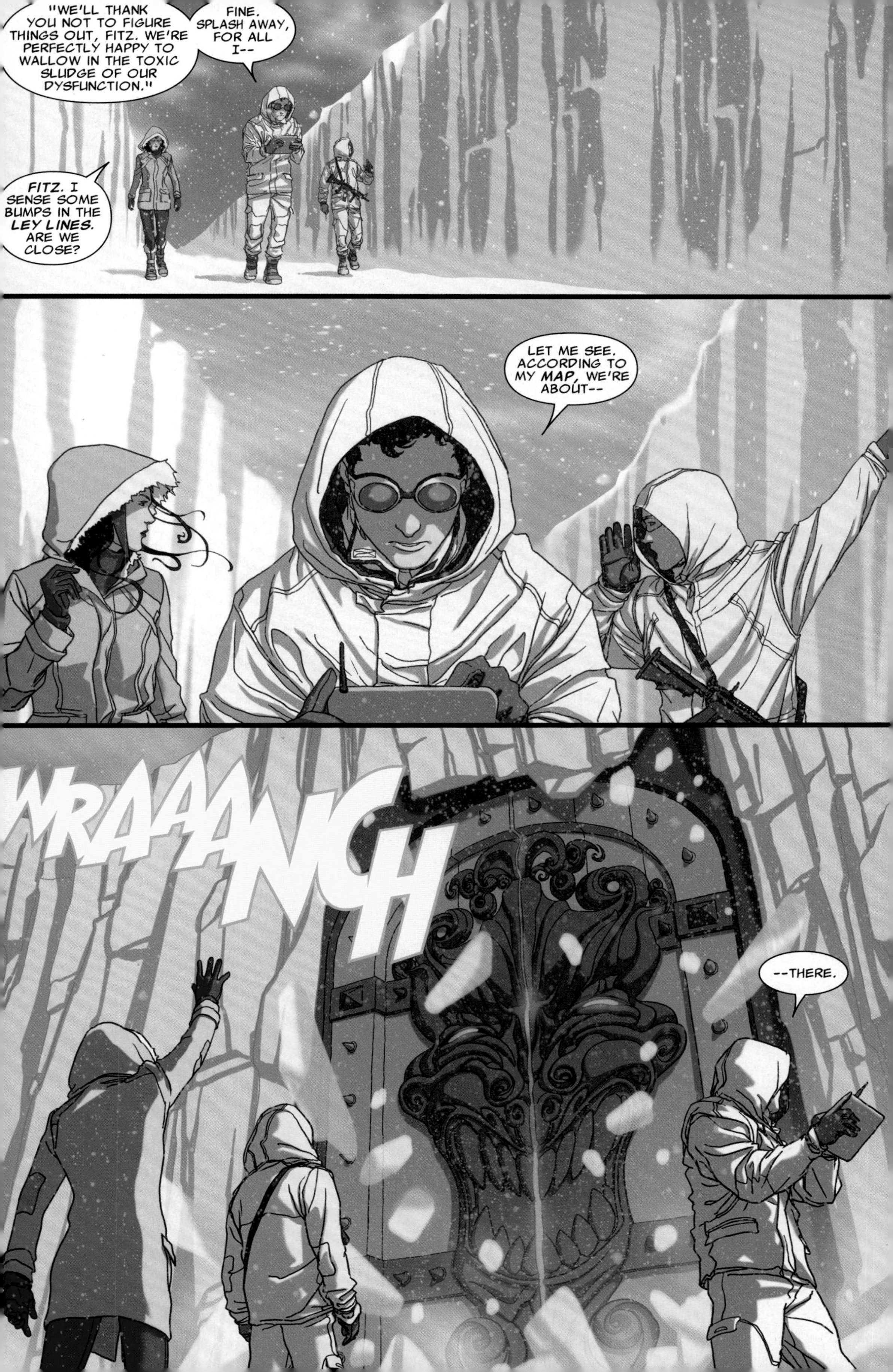
"WE'LL THANK YOU NOT TO FIGURE THINGS OUT, FITZ. WE'RE PERFECTLY HAPPY TO WALLOW IN THE TOXIC SLUDGE OF OUR DYSFUNCTION."
FINE. SPLASH AWAY, FOR ALL I--
FITZ. I SENSE SOME BUMPS IN THE LEY LINES. ARE WE CLOSE?
LET ME SEE. ACCORDING TO MY MAP, WE'RE ABOUT--
WRAAANCH
--THERE.

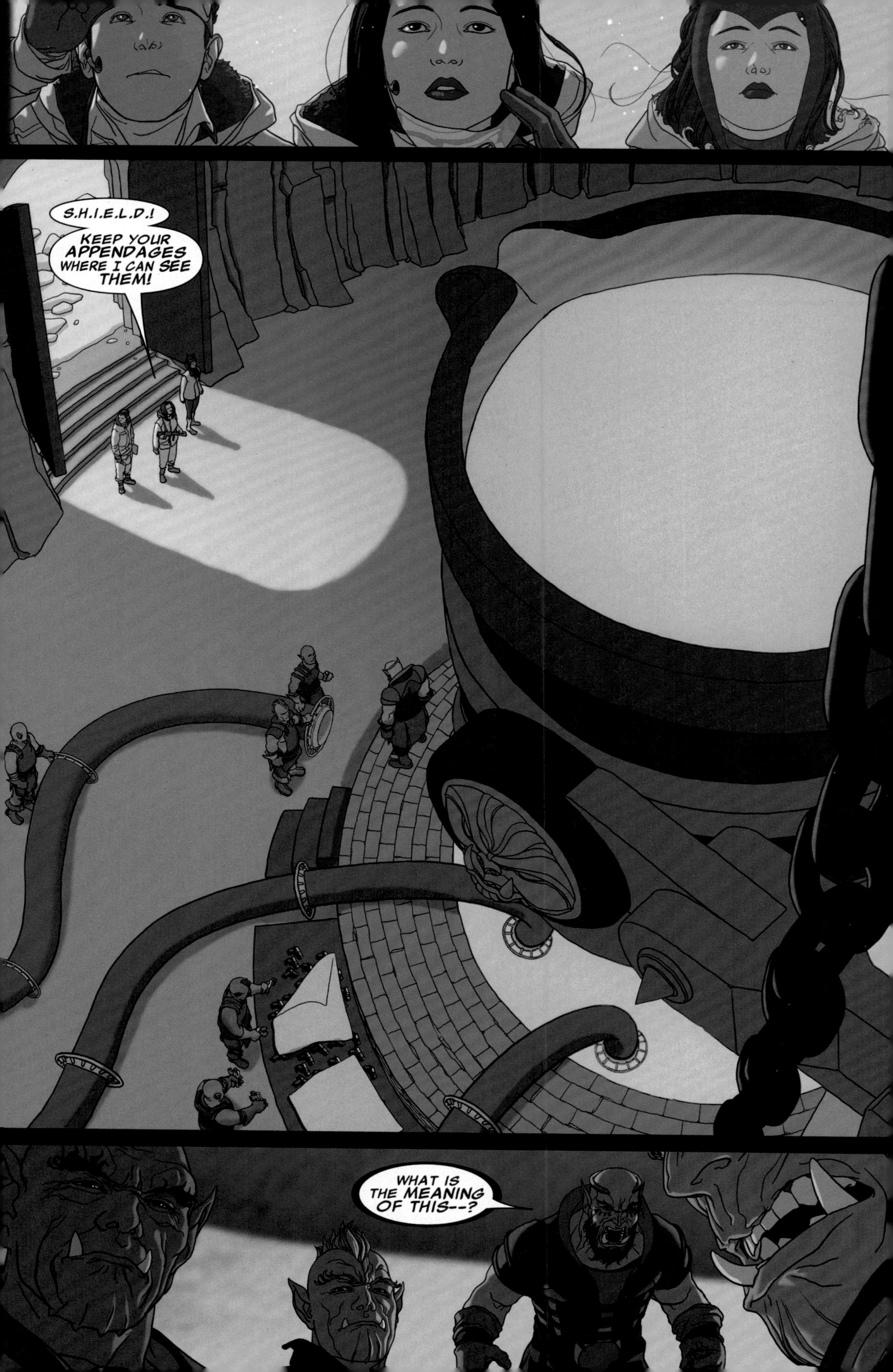
S.H.I.E.L.D.!
KEEP YOUR APPENDAGES WHERE I CAN SEE THEM!
WHAT IS THE MEANING OF THIS--?

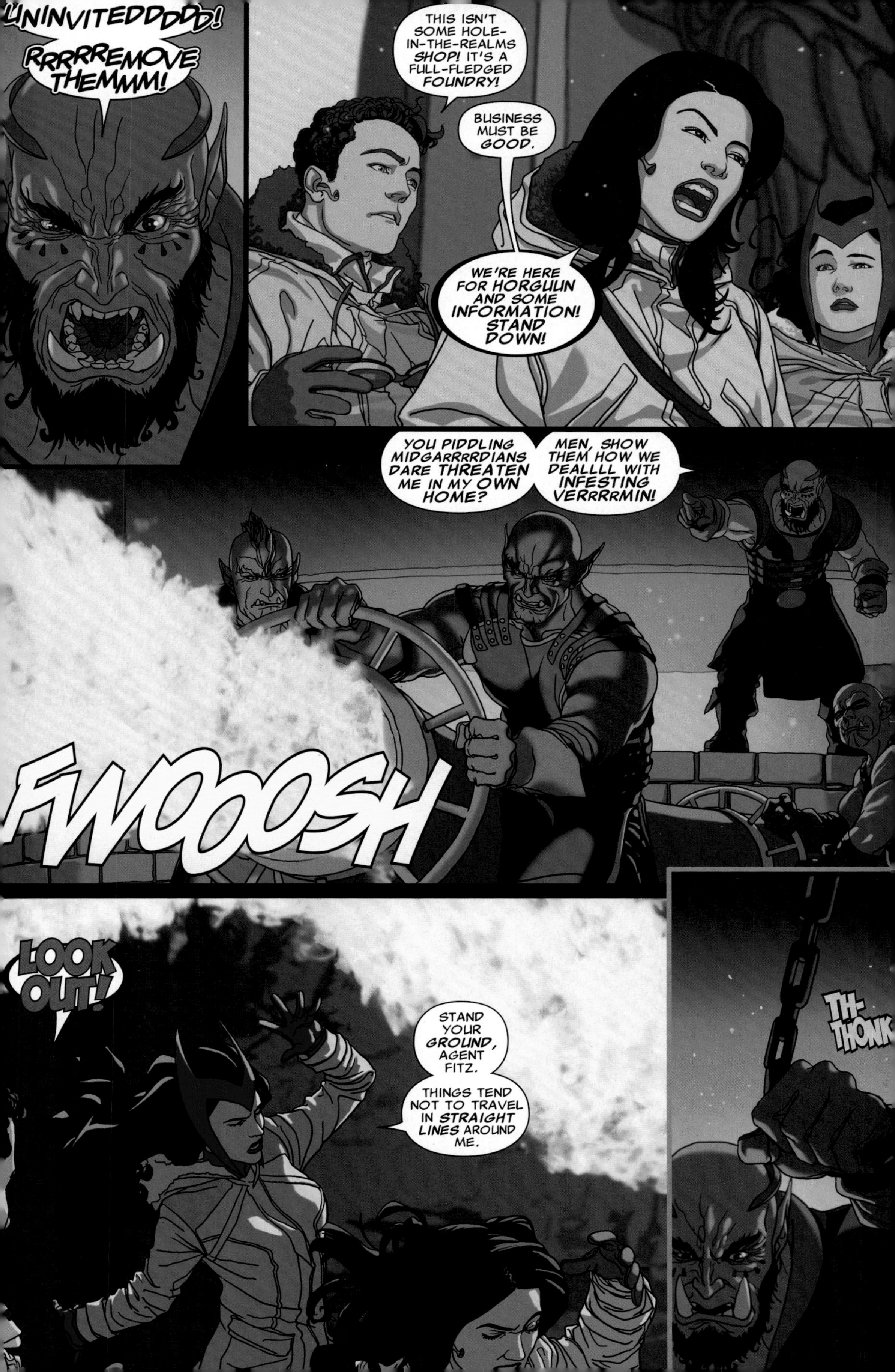
UNINVITEDDDDD!
RRRRREMOVE THEMMM!
THIS ISN'T SOME HOLE-IN-THE-REALMS SHOP! IT'S A FULL-FLEDGED FOUNDRY!
BUSINESS MUST BE GOOD.
WE'RE HERE FOR HORGULIN AND SOME INFORMATION! STAND DOWN!
YOU PIDDLING MIDGARRRRDIANS DARE THREATEN ME IN MY OWN HOME?
MEN, SHOW THEM HOW WE DEALLLL WITH INFESTING VERRRRMIN!
FWOOOSH
LOOK OUT!
STAND YOUR GROUND, AGENT FITZ.
THINGS TEND NOT TO TRAVEL IN STRAIGHT LINES AROUND ME.
TH-THONK

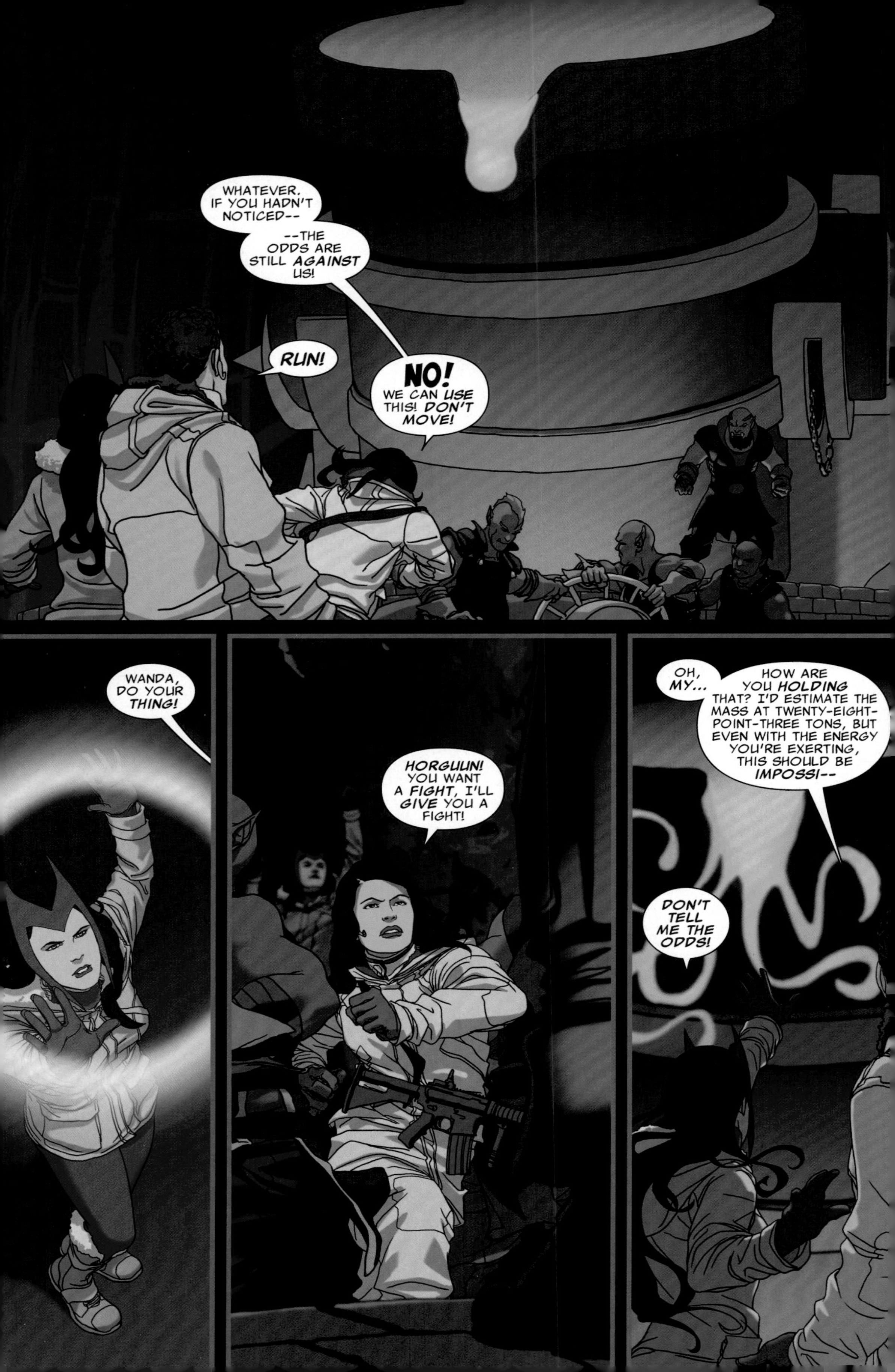
WHATEVER. IF YOU HADN'T NOTICED--
--THE ODDS ARE STILL AGAINST US!
RUN!
NO! WE CAN USE THIS! DON'T MOVE!
WANDA, DO YOUR THING!
HORGULIN! YOU WANT A FIGHT, I'LL GIVE YOU A FIGHT!
OH, MY...
HOW ARE YOU HOLDING THAT? I'D ESTIMATE THE MASS AT TWENTY-EIGHT-POINT-THREE TONS, BUT EVEN WITH THE ENERGY YOU'RE EXERTING, THIS SHOULD BE IMPOSSI--
DON'T TELL ME THE ODDS!

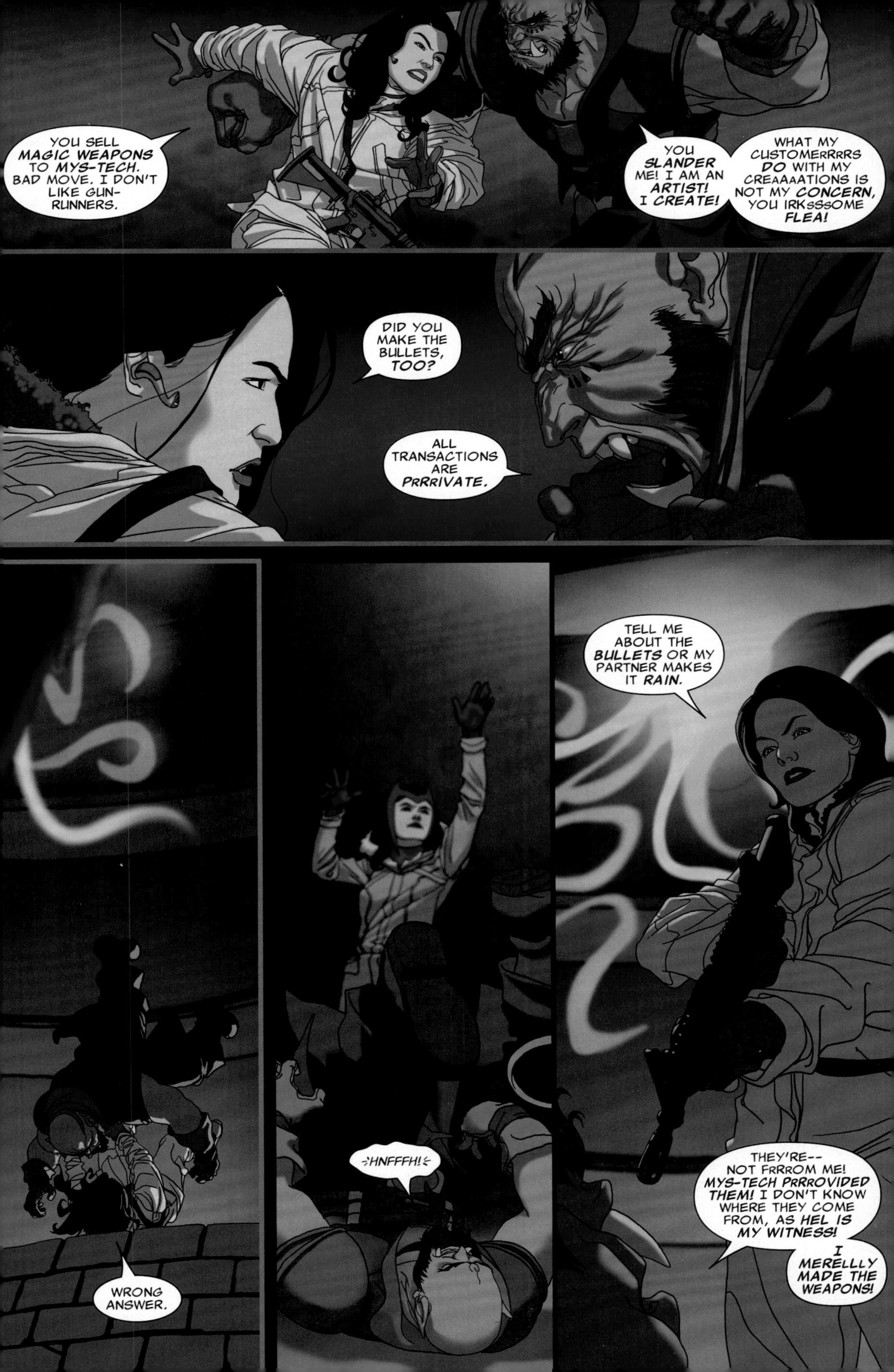
YOU SELL MAGIC WEAPONS TO MYS-TECH. BAD MOVE. I DON'T LIKE GUN-RUNNERS.
YOU SLANDER ME! I AM AN ARTIST! I CREATE!
WHAT MY CUSTOMERRRRS DO WITH MY CREAAAATIONS IS NOT MY CONCERN, YOU IRKSSSOME FLEA!
DID YOU MAKE THE BULLETS, TOO?
ALL TRANSACTIONS ARE PRRRIVATE.
WRONG ANSWER.
HNFFFH!
TELL ME ABOUT THE BULLETS OR MY PARTNER MAKES IT RAIN.
THEY'RE-- NOT FRRROM ME! MYS-TECH PRRROVIDED THEM! I DON'T KNOW WHERE THEY COME FROM, AS HEL IS MY WITNESS!
I MERELLLY MADE THE WEAPONS!

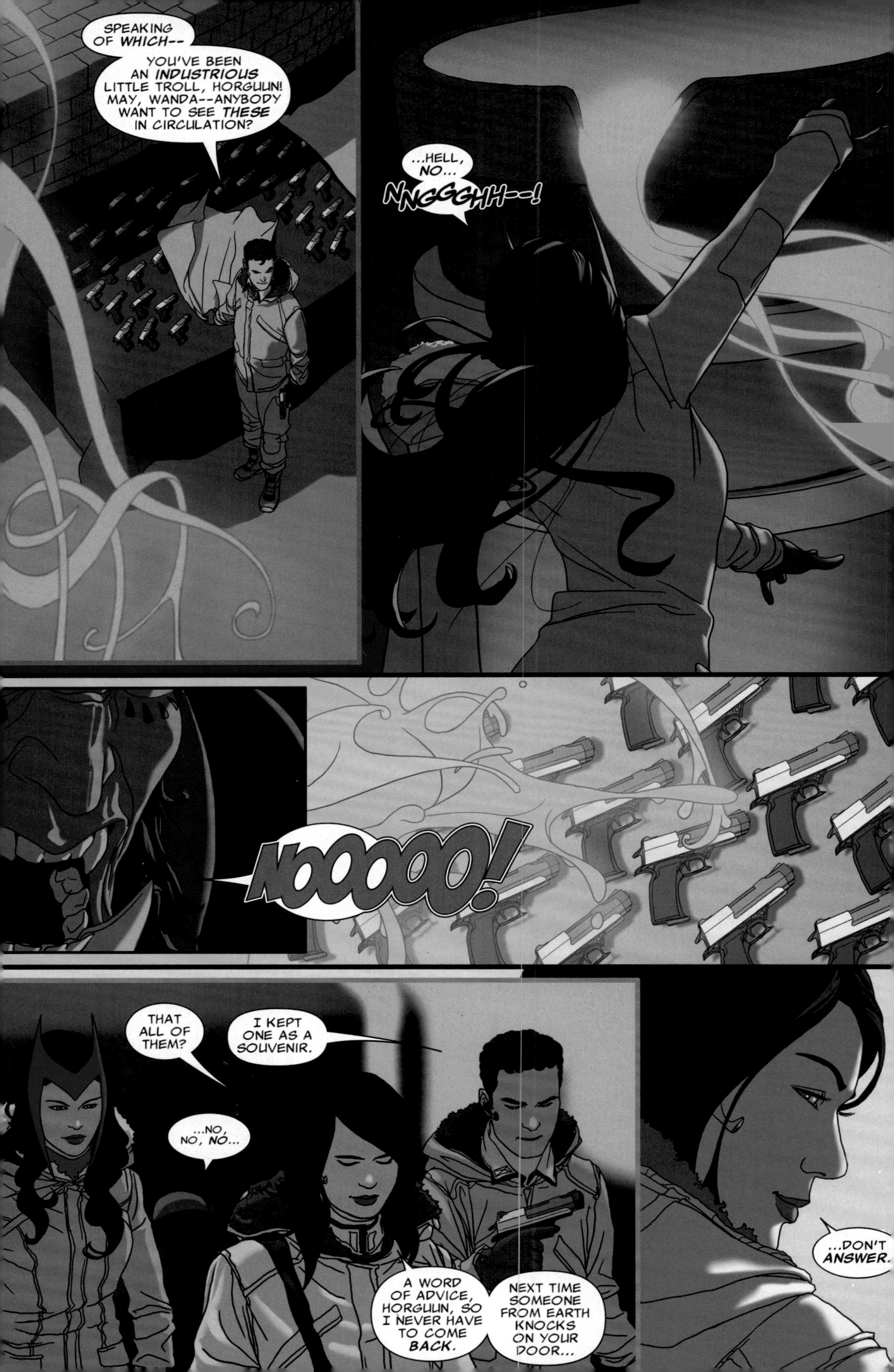
SPEAKING OF WHICH--
YOU'VE BEEN AN INDUSTRIOUS LITTLE TROLL, HORGULIN! MAY, WANDA--ANYBODY WANT TO SEE THESE IN CIRCULATION?
...HELL, NO...
NNGGGHH--!
NOOOOO!
THAT ALL OF THEM?
I KEPT ONE AS A SOUVENIR.
...NO, NO, NO...
A WORD OF ADVICE, HORGULIN, SO I NEVER HAVE TO COME BACK.
NEXT TIME SOMEONE FROM EARTH KNOCKS ON YOUR DOOR...
...DON'T ANSWER.

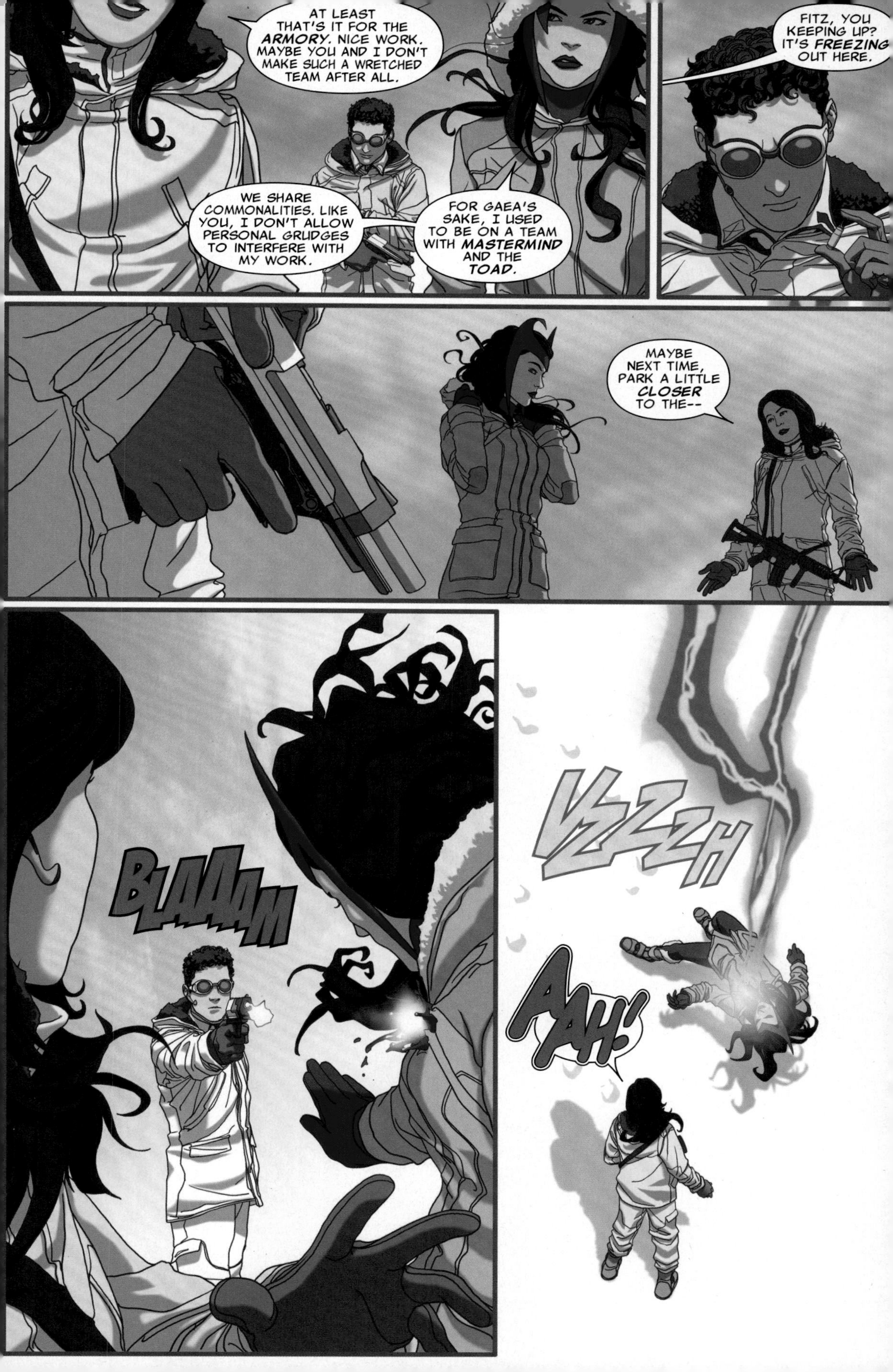
AT LEAST THAT'S IT FOR THE ARMORY. NICE WORK. MAYBE YOU AND I DON'T MAKE SUCH A WRETCHED TEAM AFTER ALL.
WE SHARE COMMONALITIES. LIKE YOU, I DON'T ALLOW PERSONAL GRUDGES TO INTERFERE WITH MY WORK.
FOR GAEA'S SAKE, I USED TO BE ON A TEAM WITH MASTERMIND AND THE TOAD.
FITZ, YOU KEEPING UP? IT'S FREEZING OUT HERE.
MAYBE NEXT TIME, PARK A LITTLE CLOSER TO THE--
BLAAAM
VSZZZH
AAH!

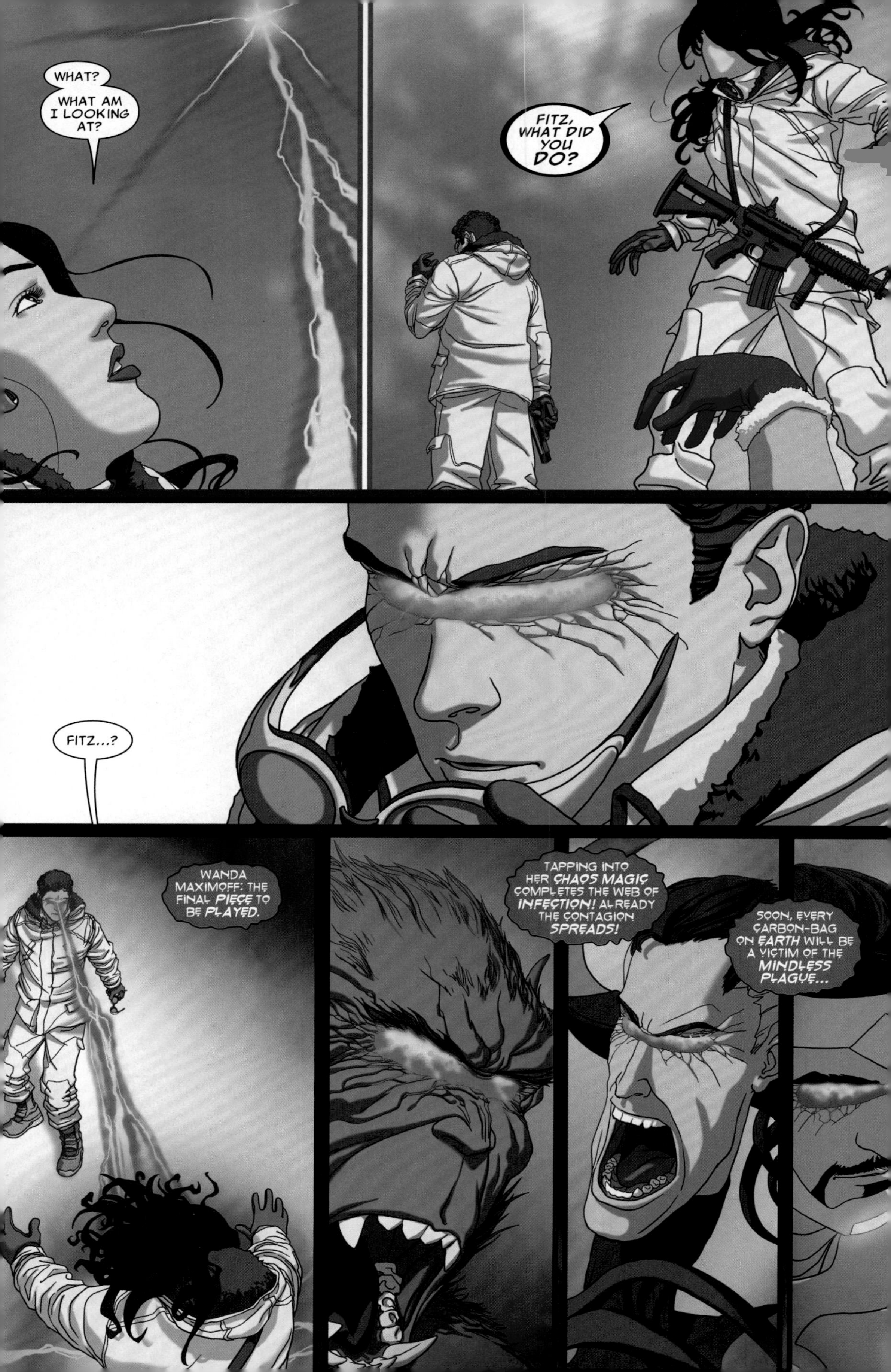
WHAT?
WHAT AM I LOOKING AT?
FITZ, WHAT DID YOU DO?
FITZ...?
WANDA MAXIMOFF: THE FINAL PIECE TO BE PLAYED.
TAPPING INTO HER CHAOS MAGIC COMPLETES THE WEB OF INFECTION! ALREADY THE CONTAGION SPREADS!
SOON, EVERY CARBON-BAG ON EARTH WILL BE A VICTIM OF THE MINDLESS PLAGUE...

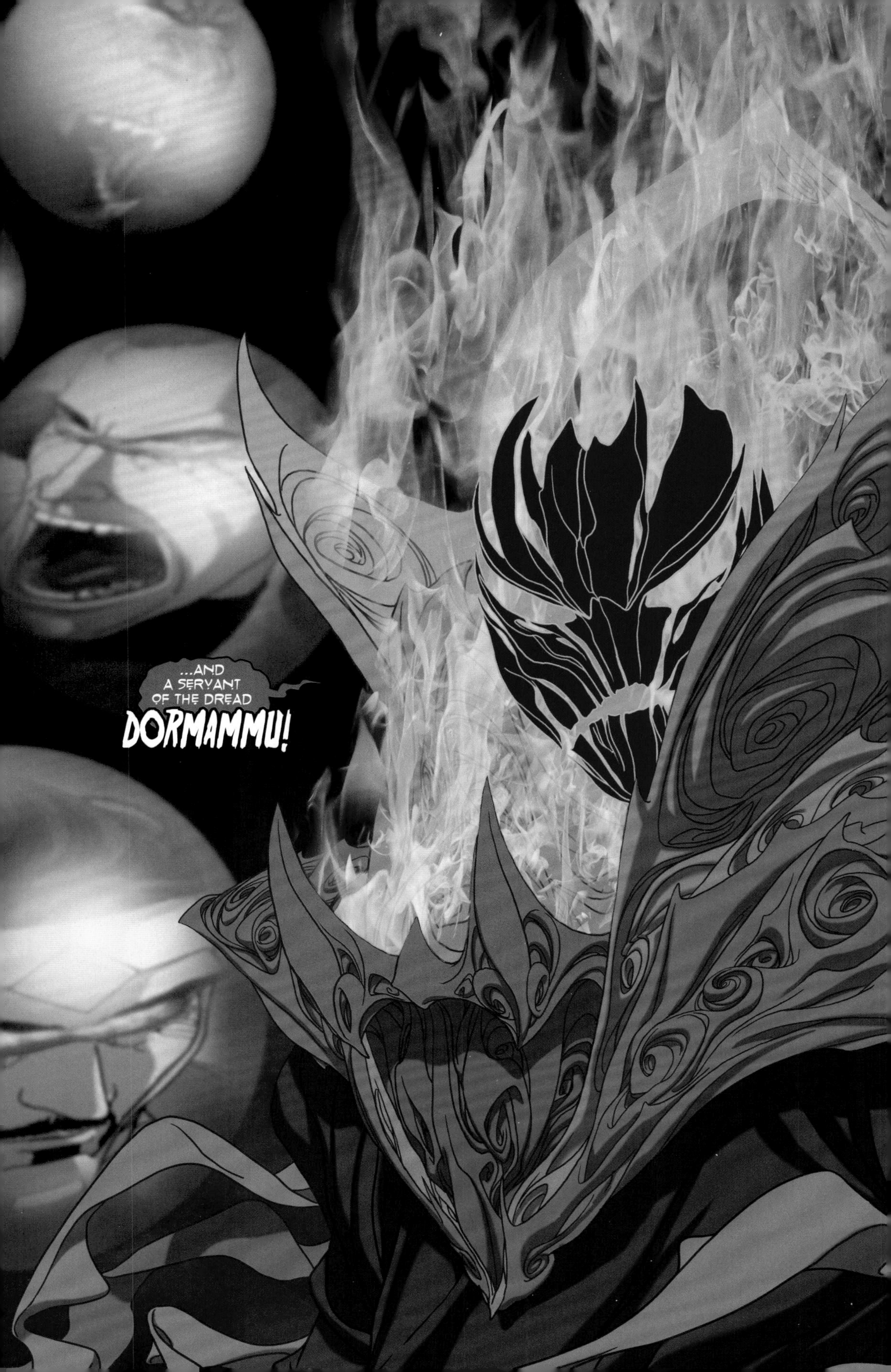
...AND A SERVANT OF THE DREAD DORMAMMU!

6. ACTIVE MISSION: DARK DIMENSIONS

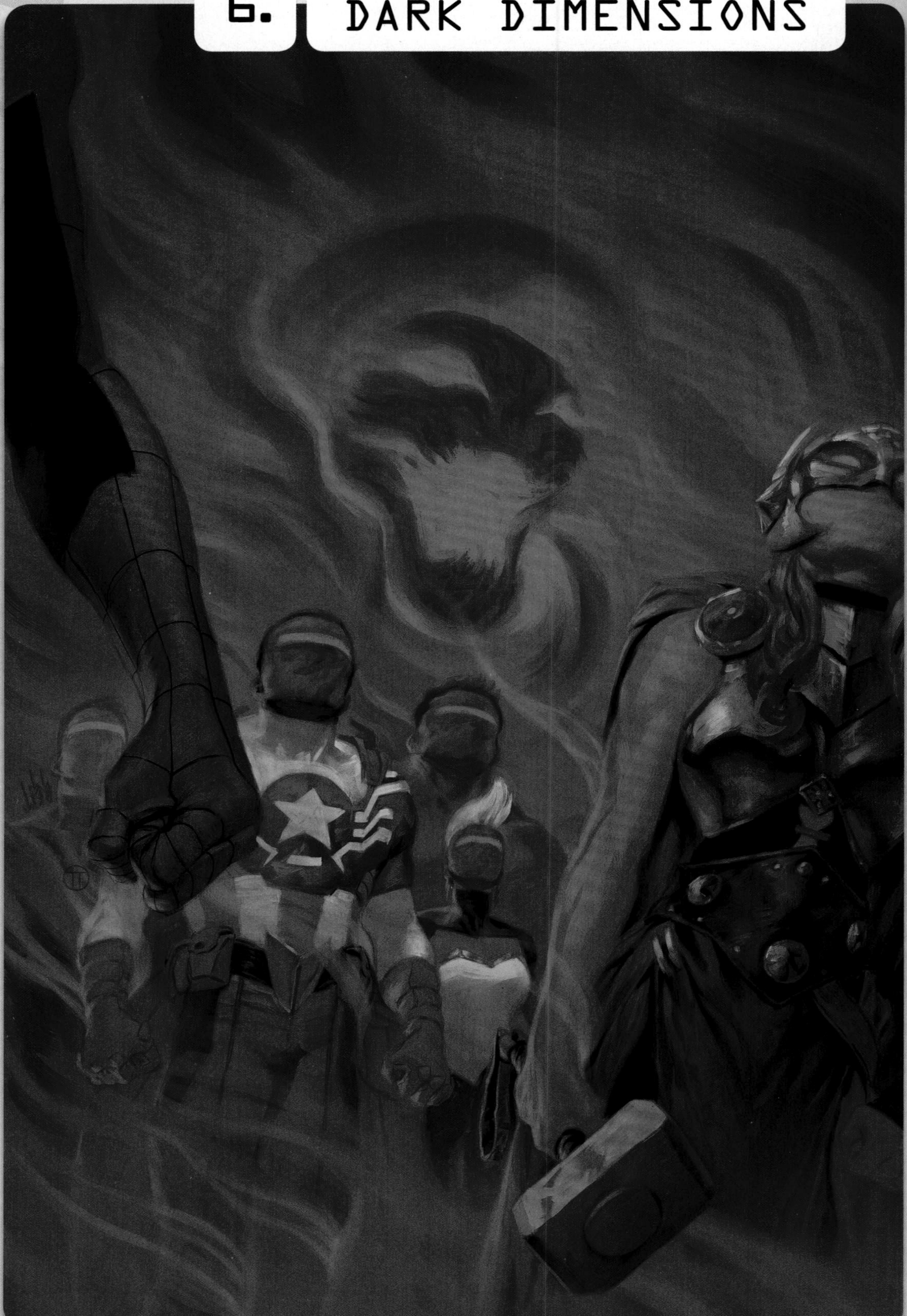

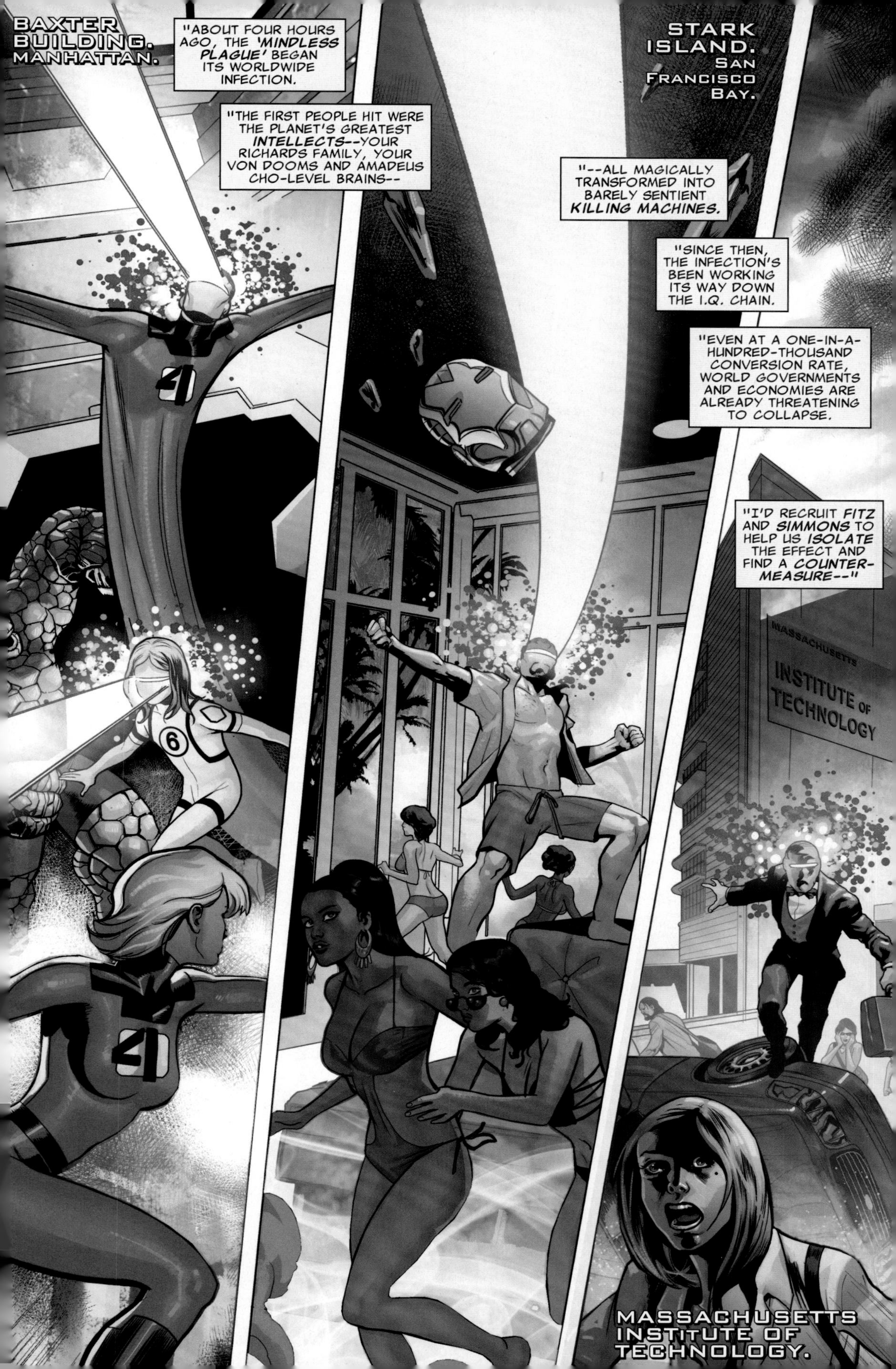
BAXTER BUILDING. MANHATTAN.
"ABOUT FOUR HOURS AGO, THE 'MINDLESS PLAGUE' BEGAN ITS WORLDWIDE INFECTION.
"THE FIRST PEOPLE HIT WERE THE PLANET'S GREATEST INTELLECTS--YOUR RICHARDS FAMILY, YOUR VON DOOMS AND AMADEUS CHO-LEVEL BRAINS--
STARK ISLAND. SAN FRANCISCO BAY.
"--ALL MAGICALLY TRANSFORMED INTO BARELY SENTIENT KILLING MACHINES.
"SINCE THEN, THE INFECTION'S BEEN WORKING ITS WAY DOWN THE I.Q. CHAIN.
"EVEN AT A ONE-IN-A-HUNDRED-THOUSAND CONVERSION RATE, WORLD GOVERNMENTS AND ECONOMIES ARE ALREADY THREATENING TO COLLAPSE.
"I'D RECRUIT FITZ AND SIMMONS TO HELP US ISOLATE THE EFFECT AND FIND A COUNTER-MEASURE--"
MASSACHUSETTS INSTITUTE OF TECHNOLOGY
MASSACHUSETTS INSTITUTE OF TECHNOLOGY.

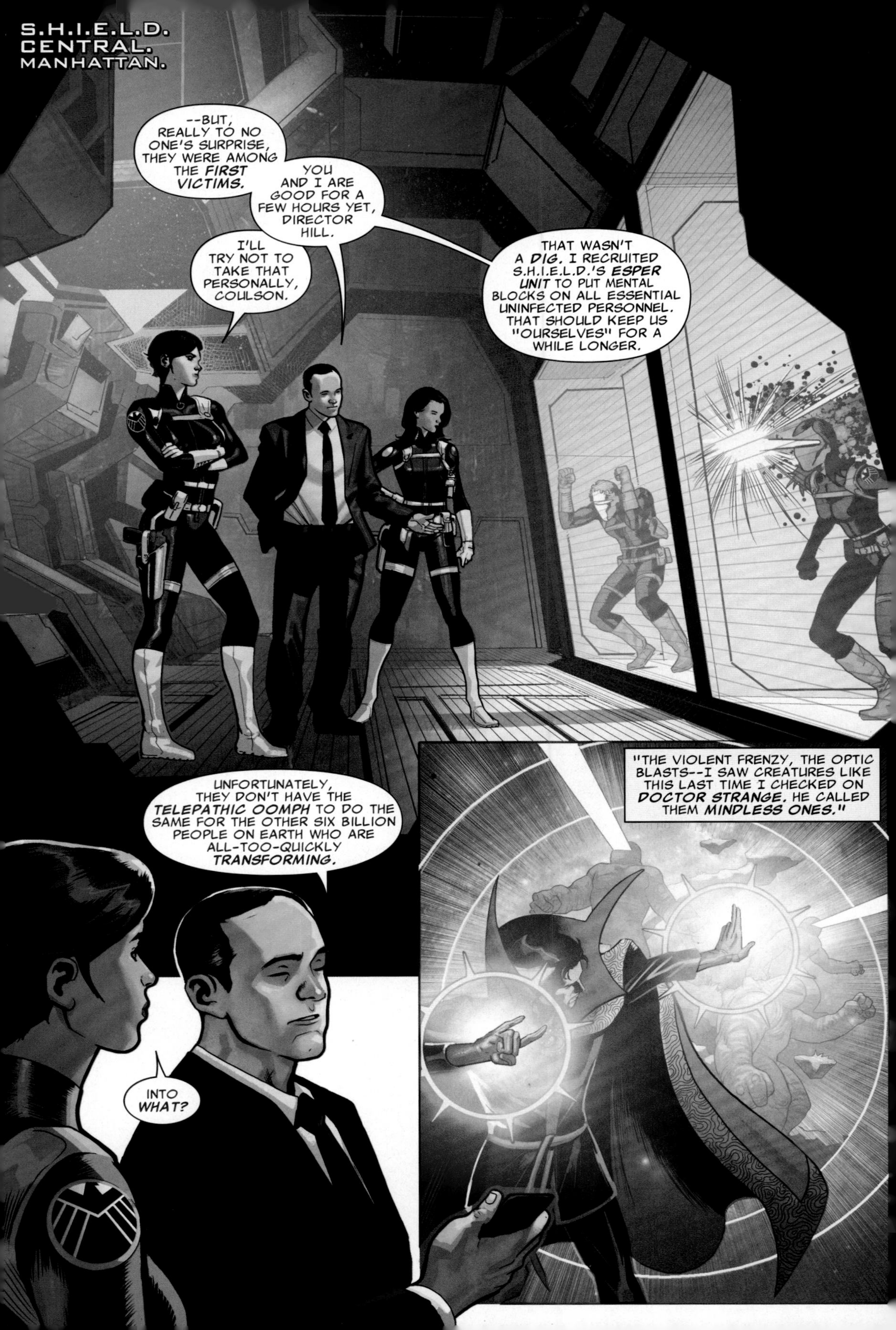
S.H.I.E.L.D. CENTRAL. MANHATTAN.
--BUT, REALLY TO NO ONE'S SURPRISE, THEY WERE AMONG THE FIRST VICTIMS.
YOU AND I ARE GOOD FOR A FEW HOURS YET, DIRECTOR HILL.
I'LL TRY NOT TO TAKE THAT PERSONALLY, COULSON.
THAT WASN'T A DIG. I RECRUITED S.H.I.E.L.D.'S ESPER UNIT TO PUT MENTAL BLOCKS ON ALL ESSENTIAL UNINFECTED PERSONNEL. THAT SHOULD KEEP US "OURSELVES" FOR A WHILE LONGER.
UNFORTUNATELY, THEY DON'T HAVE THE TELEPATHIC OOMPH TO DO THE SAME FOR THE OTHER SIX BILLION PEOPLE ON EARTH WHO ARE ALL-TOO-QUICKLY TRANSFORMING.
INTO WHAT?
"THE VIOLENT FRENZY, THE OPTIC BLASTS--I SAW CREATURES LIKE THIS LAST TIME I CHECKED ON DOCTOR STRANGE. HE CALLED THEM MINDLESS ONES."

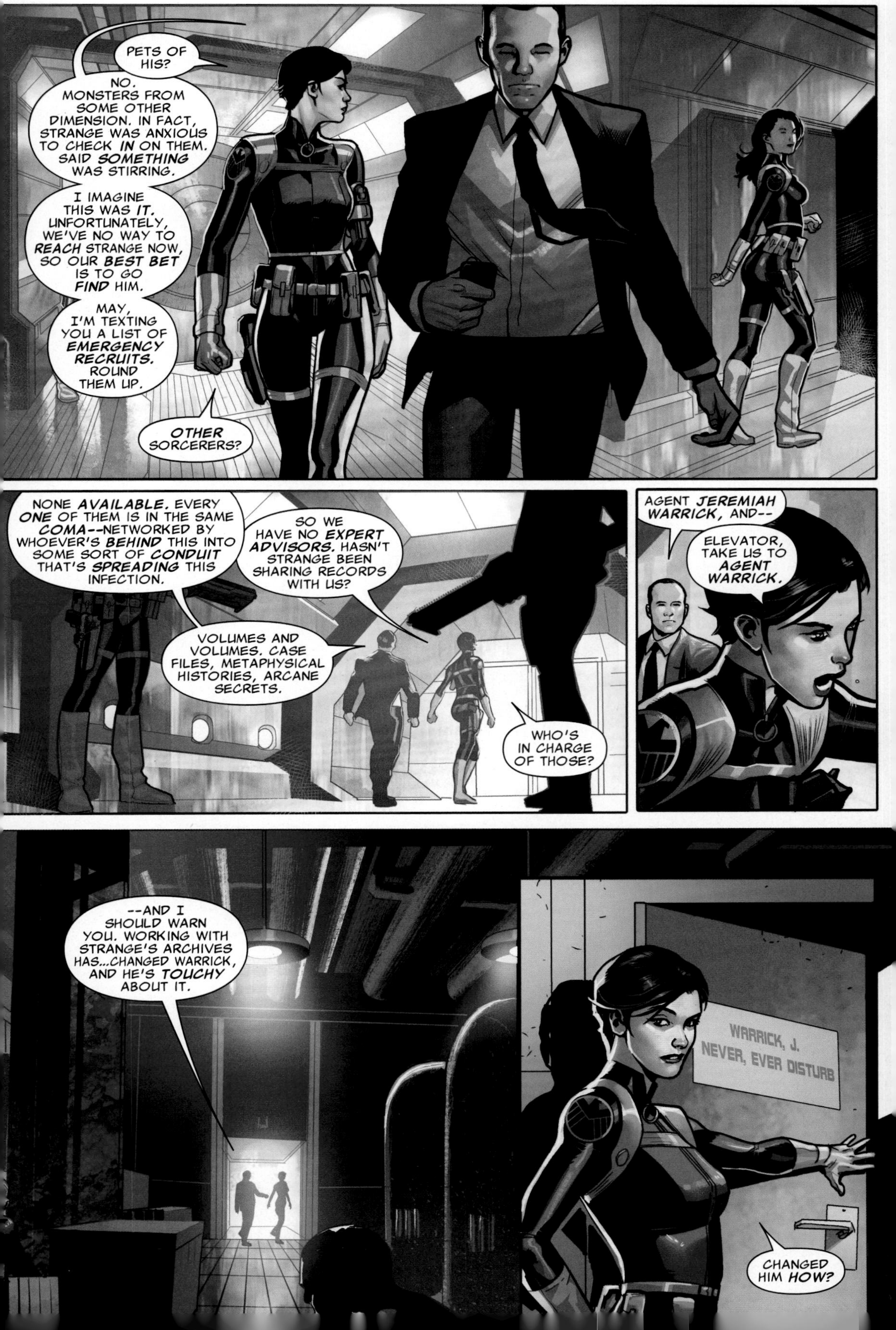
PETS OF HIS?
NO. MONSTERS FROM SOME OTHER DIMENSION. IN FACT, STRANGE WAS ANXIOUS TO CHECK IN ON THEM. SAID SOMETHING WAS STIRRING.
I IMAGINE THIS WAS IT. UNFORTUNATELY, WE'VE NO WAY TO REACH STRANGE NOW, SO OUR BEST BET IS TO GO FIND HIM.
MAY, I'M TEXTING YOU A LIST OF EMERGENCY RECRUITS. ROUND THEM UP.
OTHER SORCERERS?
NONE AVAILABLE. EVERY ONE OF THEM IS IN THE SAME COMA--NETWORKED BY WHOEVER'S BEHIND THIS INTO SOME SORT OF CONDUIT THAT'S SPREADING THIS INFECTION.
SO WE HAVE NO EXPERT ADVISORS. HASN'T STRANGE BEEN SHARING RECORDS WITH US?
VOLUMES AND VOLUMES. CASE FILES, METAPHYSICAL HISTORIES, ARCANE SECRETS.
WHO'S IN CHARGE OF THOSE?
AGENT JEREMIAH WARRICK, AND--
ELEVATOR, TAKE US TO AGENT WARRICK.
--AND I SHOULD WARN YOU. WORKING WITH STRANGE'S ARCHIVES HAS...CHANGED WARRICK, AND HE'S TOUCHY ABOUT IT.
WARRICK, J.
NEVER, EVER DISTURB
CHANGED HIM HOW?

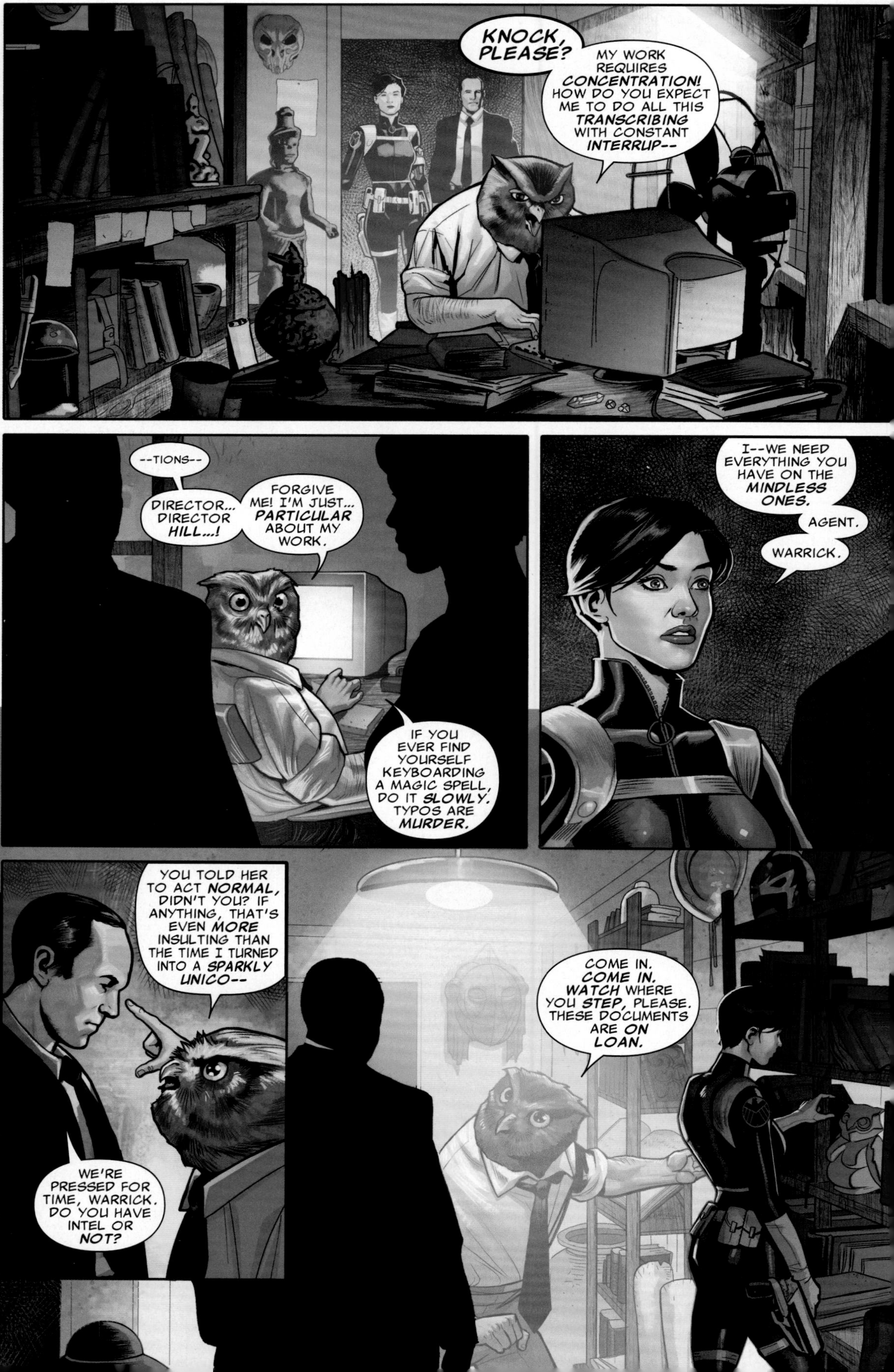
KNOCK, PLEASE?
MY WORK REQUIRES CONCENTRATION! HOW DO YOU EXPECT ME TO DO ALL THIS TRANSCRIBING WITH CONSTANT INTERRUP--
--TIONS--
DIRECTOR... DIRECTOR HILL...!
FORGIVE ME! I'M JUST... PARTICULAR ABOUT MY WORK.
IF YOU EVER FIND YOURSELF KEYBOARDING A MAGIC SPELL, DO IT SLOWLY. TYPOS ARE MURDER.
I--WE NEED EVERYTHING YOU HAVE ON THE MINDLESS ONES.
AGENT.
WARRICK.
COME IN. COME IN. WATCH WHERE YOU STEP, PLEASE. THESE DOCUMENTS ARE ON LOAN.
YOU TOLD HER TO ACT NORMAL, DIDN'T YOU? IF ANYTHING, THAT'S EVEN MORE INSULTING THAN THE TIME I TURNED INTO A SPARKLY UNICO--
WE'RE PRESSED FOR TIME, WARRICK. DO YOU HAVE INTEL OR NOT?

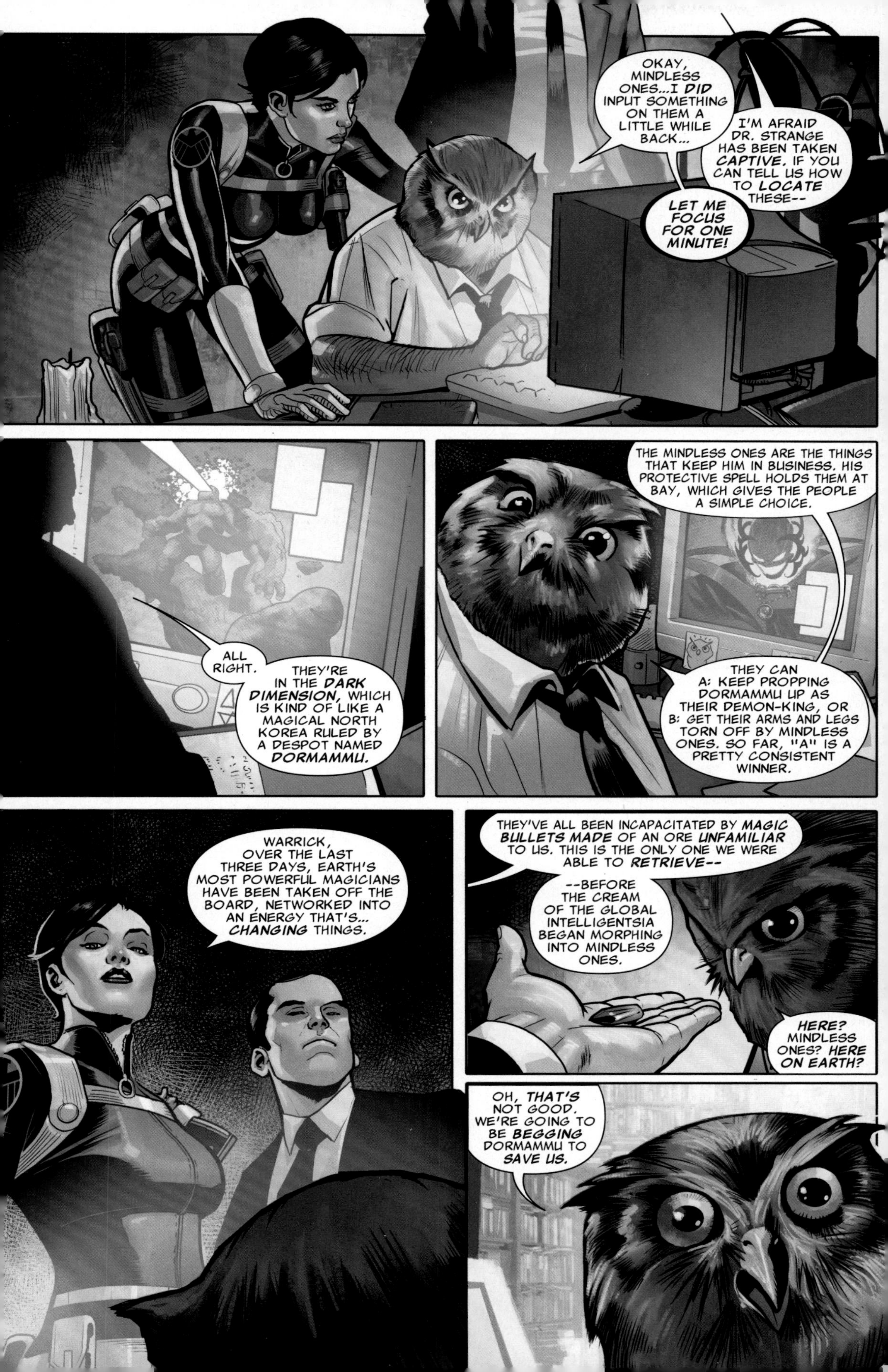
OKAY, MINDLESS ONES...I DID INPUT SOMETHING ON THEM A LITTLE WHILE BACK...
I'M AFRAID DR. STRANGE HAS BEEN TAKEN CAPTIVE. IF YOU CAN TELL US HOW TO LOCATE THESE--
LET ME FOCUS FOR ONE MINUTE!
ALL RIGHT.
THEY'RE IN THE DARK DIMENSION, WHICH IS KIND OF LIKE A MAGICAL NORTH KOREA RULED BY A DESPOT NAMED DORMAMMU.
THE MINDLESS ONES ARE THE THINGS THAT KEEP HIM IN BUSINESS. HIS PROTECTIVE SPELL HOLDS THEM AT BAY, WHICH GIVES THE PEOPLE A SIMPLE CHOICE.
THEY CAN A: KEEP PROPPING DORMAMMU UP AS THEIR DEMON-KING, OR B: GET THEIR ARMS AND LEGS TORN OFF BY MINDLESS ONES. SO FAR, "A" IS A PRETTY CONSISTENT WINNER.
WARRICK, OVER THE LAST THREE DAYS, EARTH'S MOST POWERFUL MAGICIANS HAVE BEEN TAKEN OFF THE BOARD, NETWORKED INTO AN ENERGY THAT'S... CHANGING THINGS.
THEY'VE ALL BEEN INCAPACITATED BY MAGIC BULLETS MADE OF AN ORE UNFAMILIAR TO US. THIS IS THE ONLY ONE WE WERE ABLE TO RETRIEVE--
--BEFORE THE CREAM OF THE GLOBAL INTELLIGENTSIA BEGAN MORPHING INTO MINDLESS ONES.
HERE? MINDLESS ONES? HERE ON EARTH?
OH, THAT'S NOT GOOD. WE'RE GOING TO BE BEGGING DORMAMMU TO SAVE US.

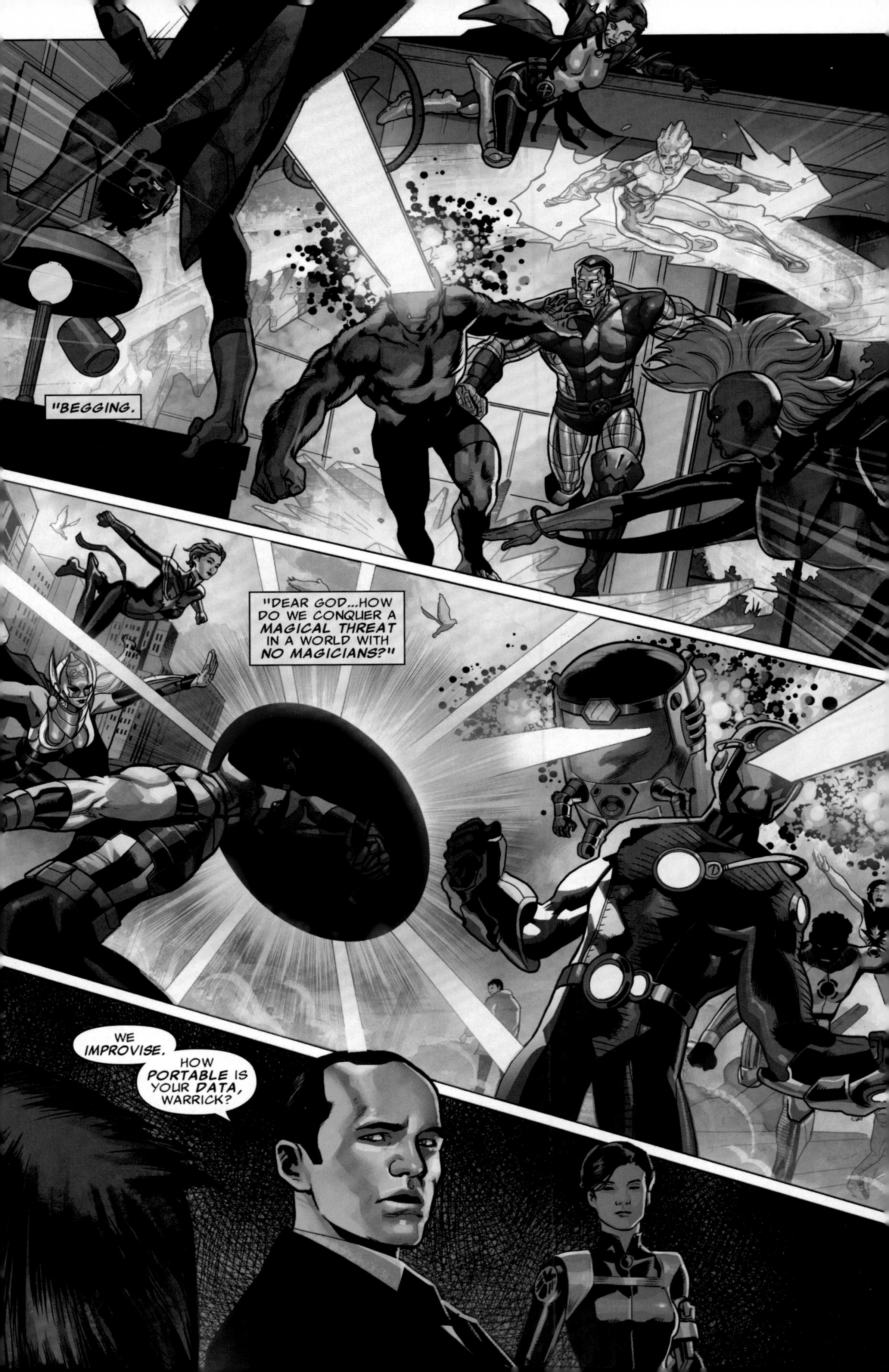
"BEGGING.
"DEAR GOD...HOW DO WE CONQUER A MAGICAL THREAT IN A WORLD WITH NO MAGICIANS?"
WE IMPROVISE.
HOW PORTABLE IS YOUR DATA, WARRICK?

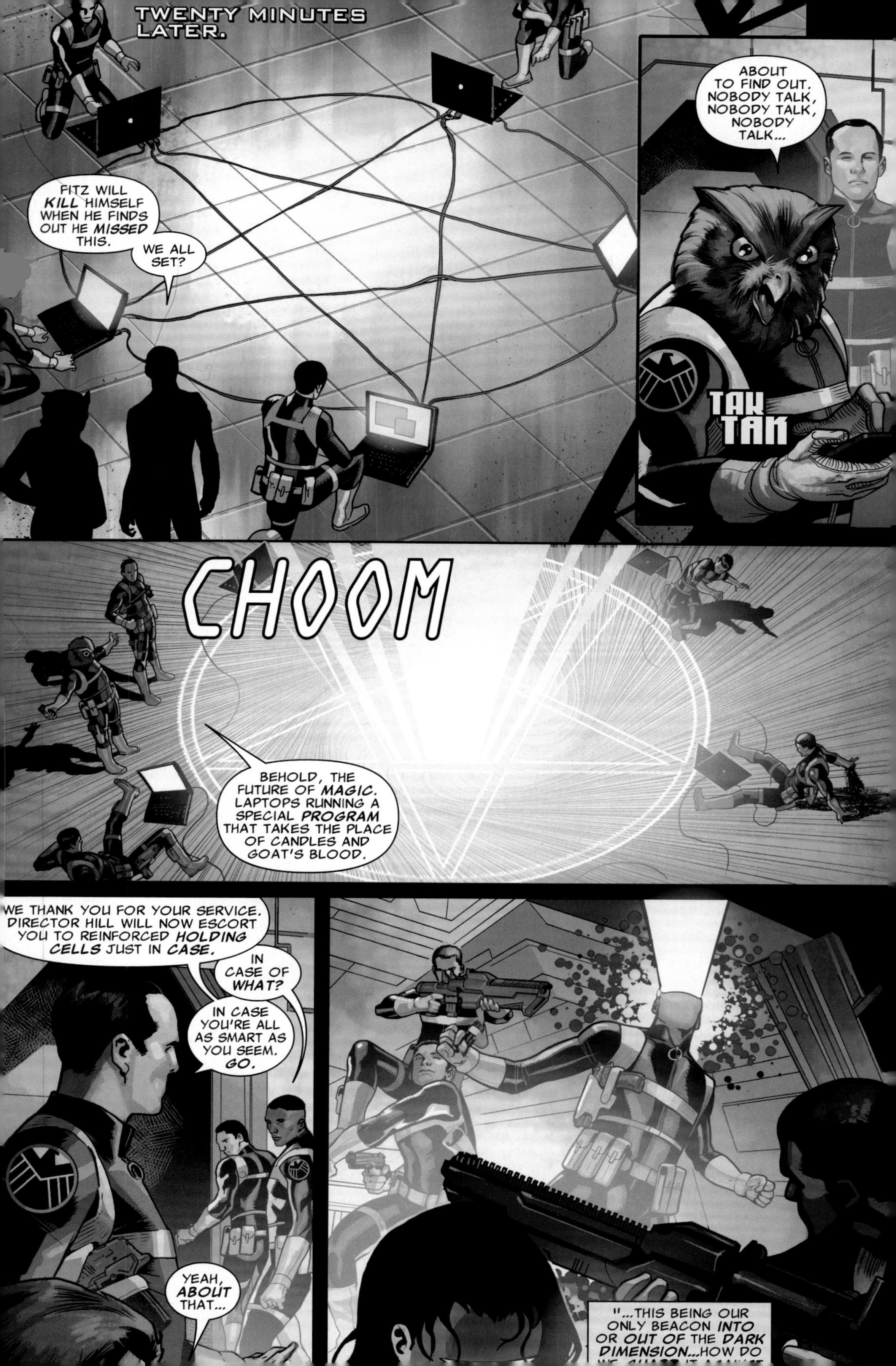
TWENTY MINUTES LATER.
FITZ WILL KILL HIMSELF WHEN HE FINDS OUT HE MISSED THIS.
WE ALL SET?
ABOUT TO FIND OUT. NOBODY TALK, NOBODY TALK, NOBODY TALK...
TAK TAK
CHOOM
BEHOLD, THE FUTURE OF MAGIC. LAPTOPS RUNNING A SPECIAL PROGRAM THAT TAKES THE PLACE OF CANDLES AND GOAT'S BLOOD.
WE THANK YOU FOR YOUR SERVICE. DIRECTOR HILL WILL NOW ESCORT YOU TO REINFORCED HOLDING CELLS JUST IN CASE.
IN CASE OF WHAT?
IN CASE YOU'RE ALL AS SMART AS YOU SEEM. GO.
YEAH, ABOUT THAT...
"...THIS BEING OUR ONLY BEACON INTO OR OUT OF THE DARK DIMENSION...HOW DO

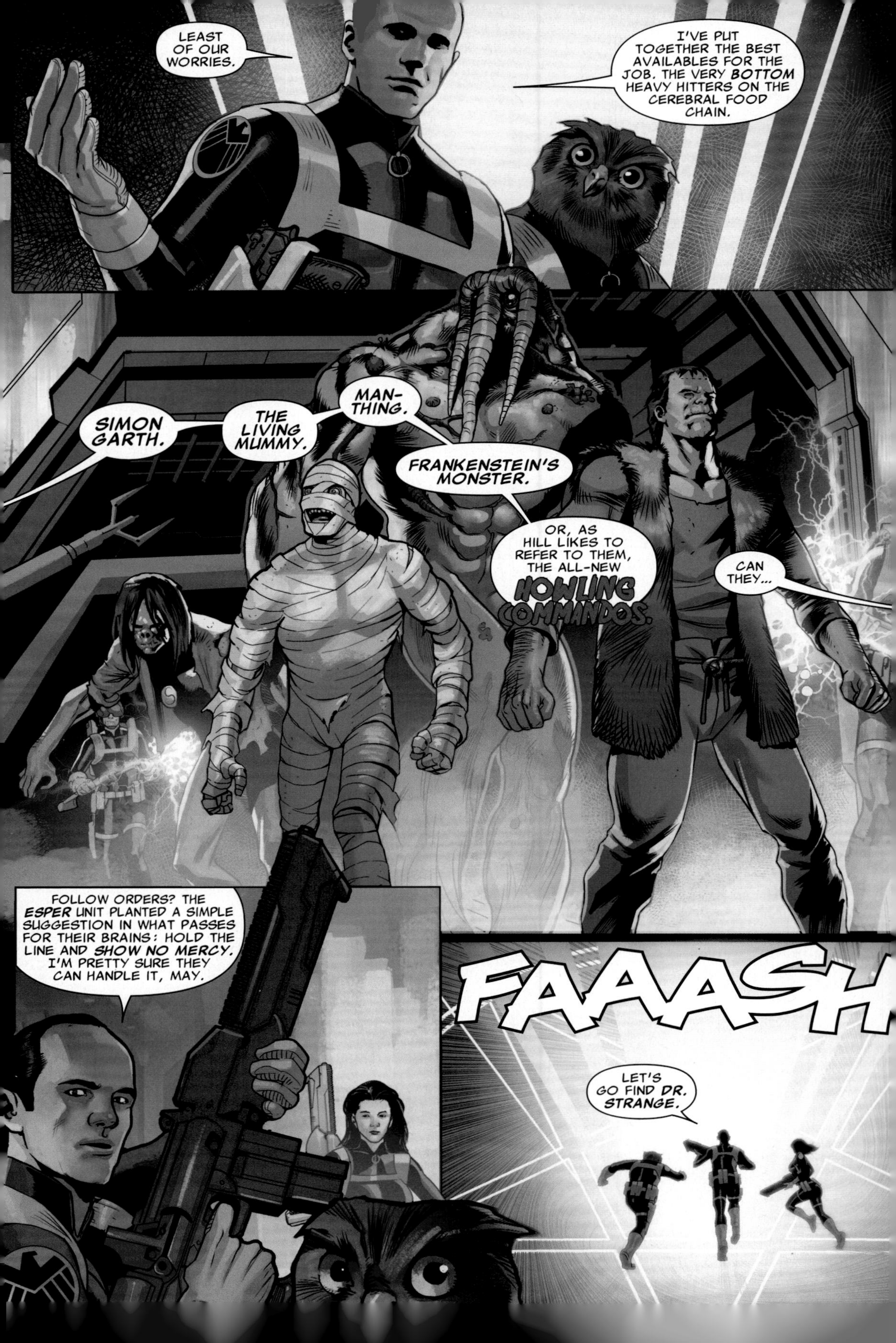
LEAST OF OUR WORRIES.
I'VE PUT TOGETHER THE BEST AVAILABLES FOR THE JOB. THE VERY BOTTOM HEAVY HITTERS ON THE CEREBRAL FOOD CHAIN.
SIMON GARTH.
THE LIVING MUMMY.
MAN-THING.
FRANKENSTEIN'S MONSTER.
OR, AS HILL LIKES TO REFER TO THEM, THE ALL-NEW HOWLING COMMANDOS.
CAN THEY...
FOLLOW ORDERS? THE ESPER UNIT PLANTED A SIMPLE SUGGESTION IN WHAT PASSES FOR THEIR BRAINS: HOLD THE LINE AND SHOW NO MERCY. I'M PRETTY SURE THEY CAN HANDLE IT, MAY.
FAAASH
LET'S GO FIND DR. STRANGE.

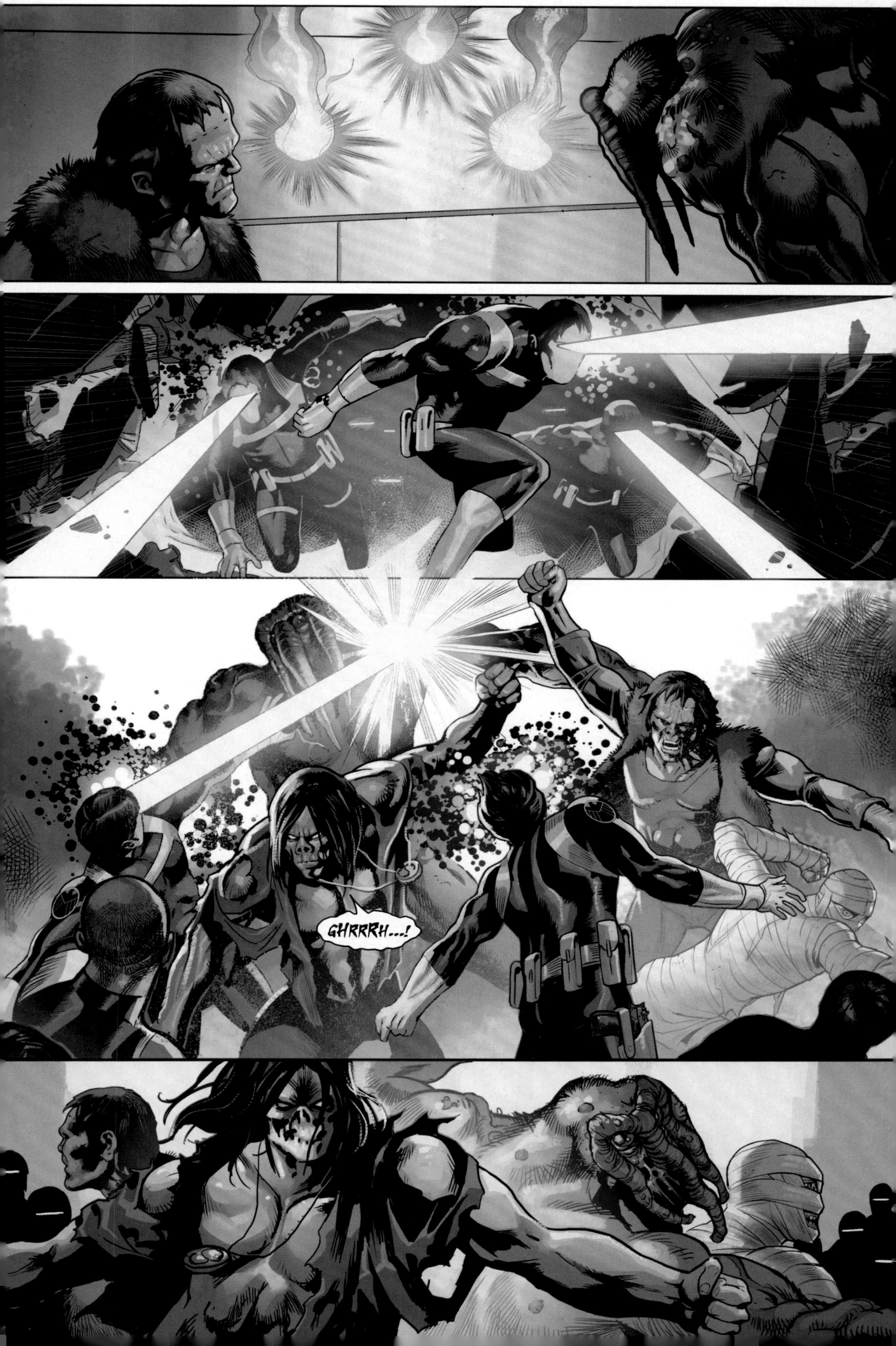
GHRRRH...!

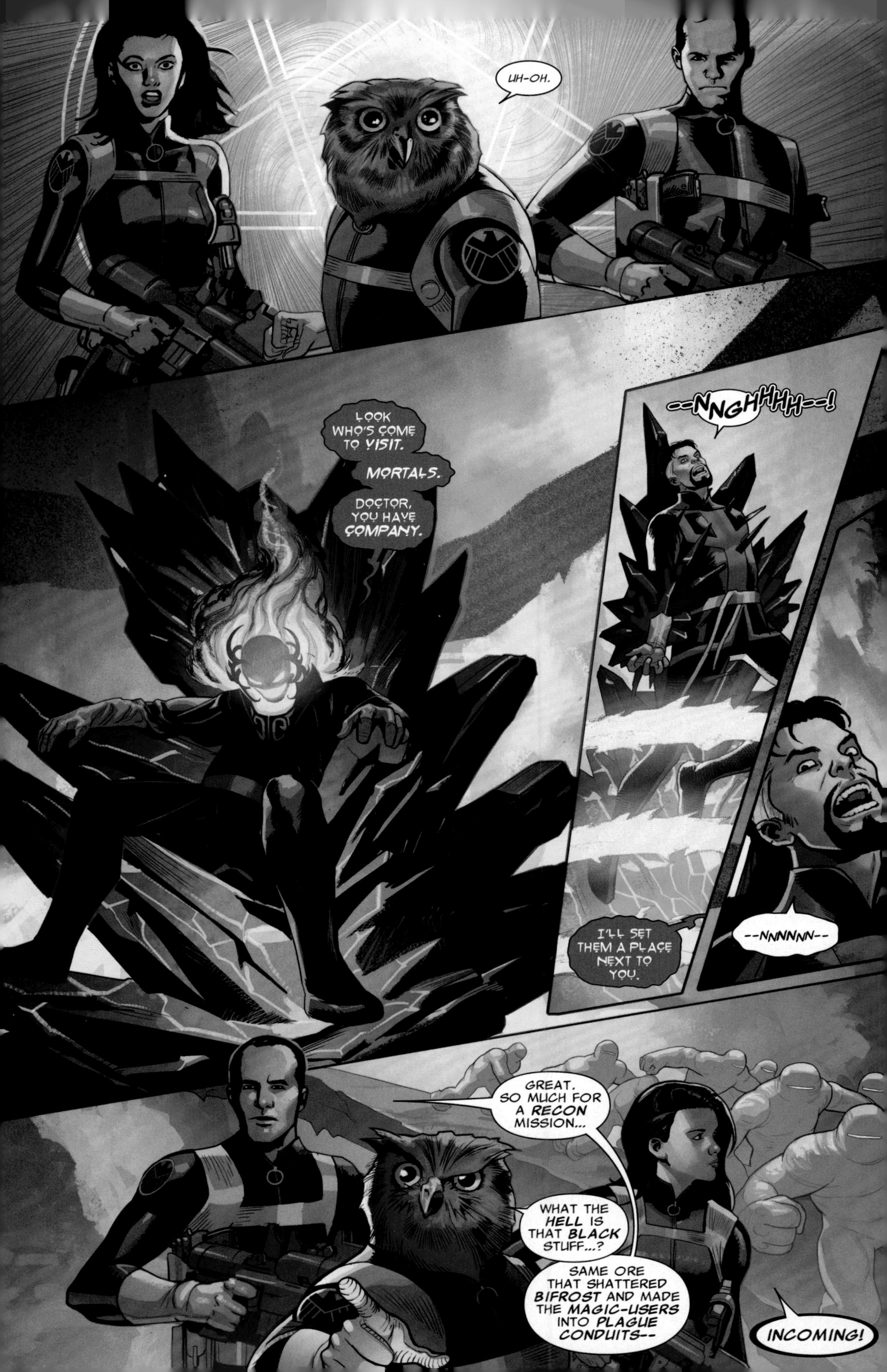
UH-OH.
LOOK WHO'S COME TO VISIT.
MORTALS.
DOCTOR, YOU HAVE COMPANY.
--NNGHHHH--!
I'LL SET THEM A PLACE NEXT TO YOU.
--NNNNNN--
GREAT. SO MUCH FOR A RECON MISSION...
WHAT THE HELL IS THAT BLACK STUFF...?
SAME ORE THAT SHATTERED BIFROST AND MADE THE MAGIC-USERS INTO PLAGUE CONDUITS--
INCOMING!

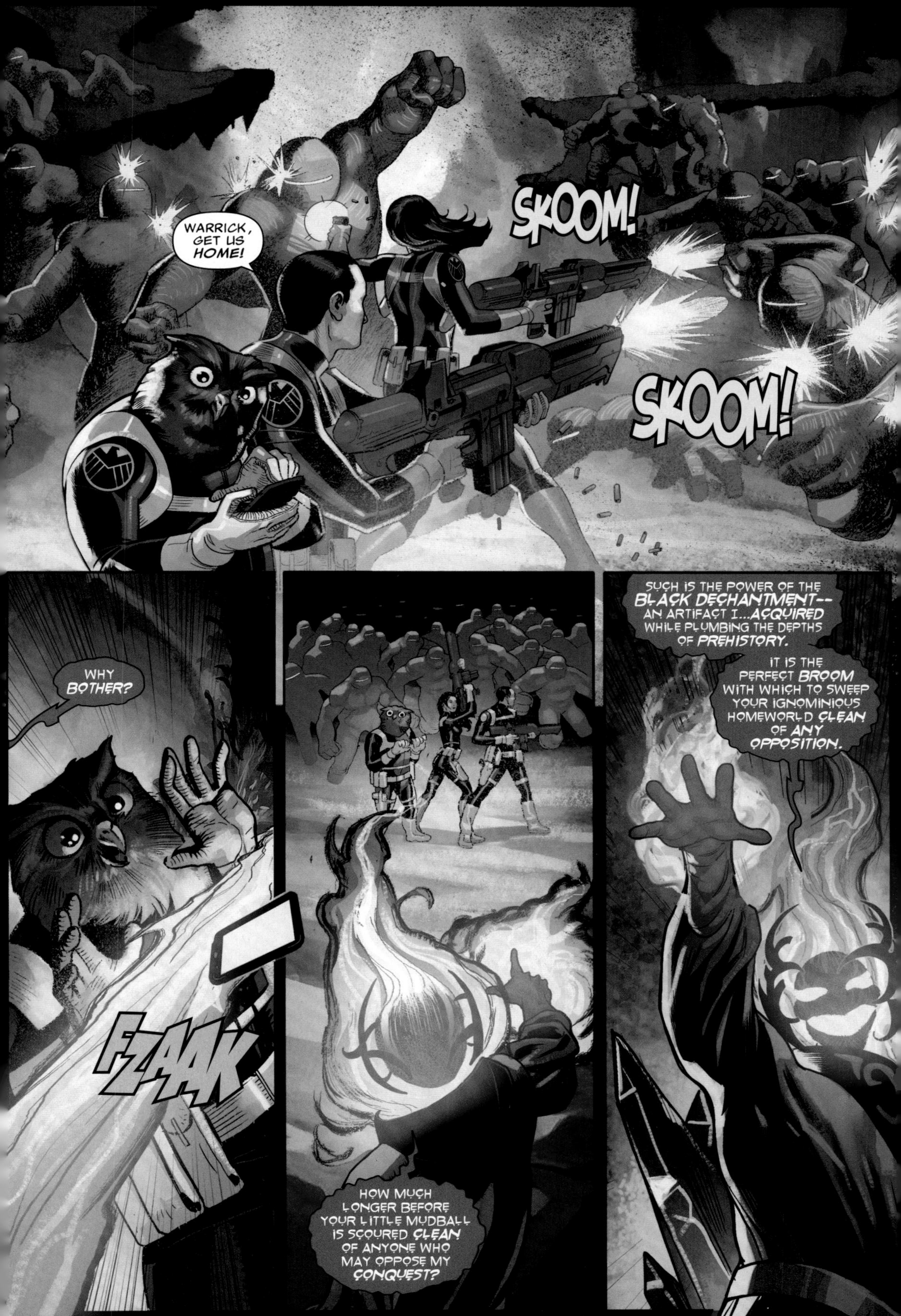

WARRICK, GET US HOME!
SKOOM!
SKOOM!
WHY BOTHER?
FZAAK
HOW MUCH LONGER BEFORE YOUR LITTLE MUDBALL IS SCOURED CLEAN OF ANYONE WHO MAY OPPOSE MY CONQUEST?
SUCH IS THE POWER OF THE BLACK DECHANTMENT-- AN ARTIFACT I...ACQUIRED WHILE PLUMBING THE DEPTHS OF PREHISTORY.
IT IS THE PERFECT BROOM WITH WHICH TO SWEEP YOUR IGNOMINIOUS HOMEWORLD CLEAN OF ANY OPPOSITION.

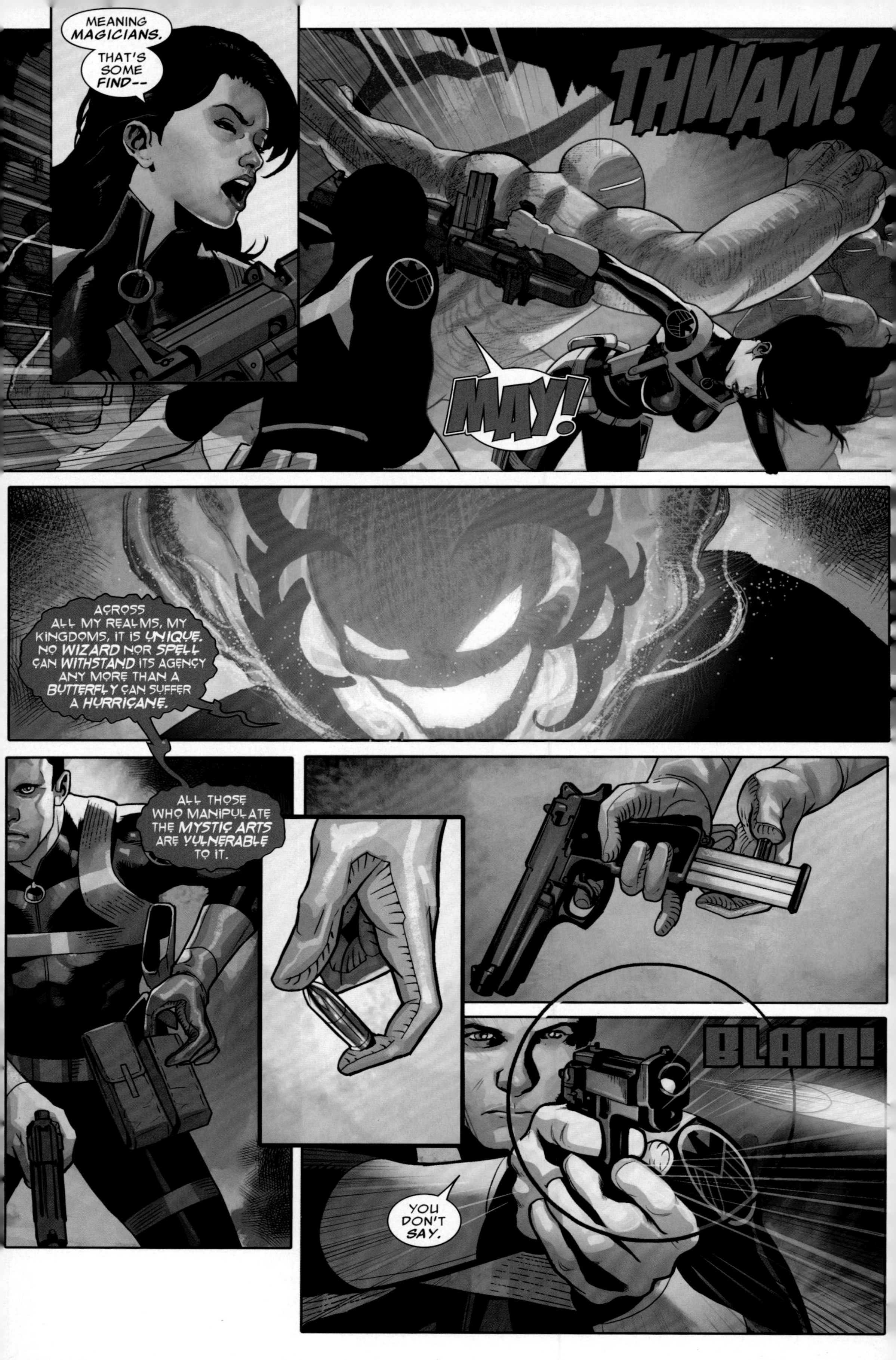

MEANING MAGICIANS. THAT'S SOME FIND--
THWAM!
MAY!
ACROSS ALL MY REALMS, MY KINGDOMS, IT IS UNIQUE. NO WIZARD NOR SPELL CAN WITHSTAND ITS AGENCY ANY MORE THAN A BUTTERFLY CAN SUFFER A HURRICANE.
ALL THOSE WHO MANIPULATE THE MYSTIC ARTS ARE VULNERABLE TO IT.
BLAM!
YOU DON'T SAY.

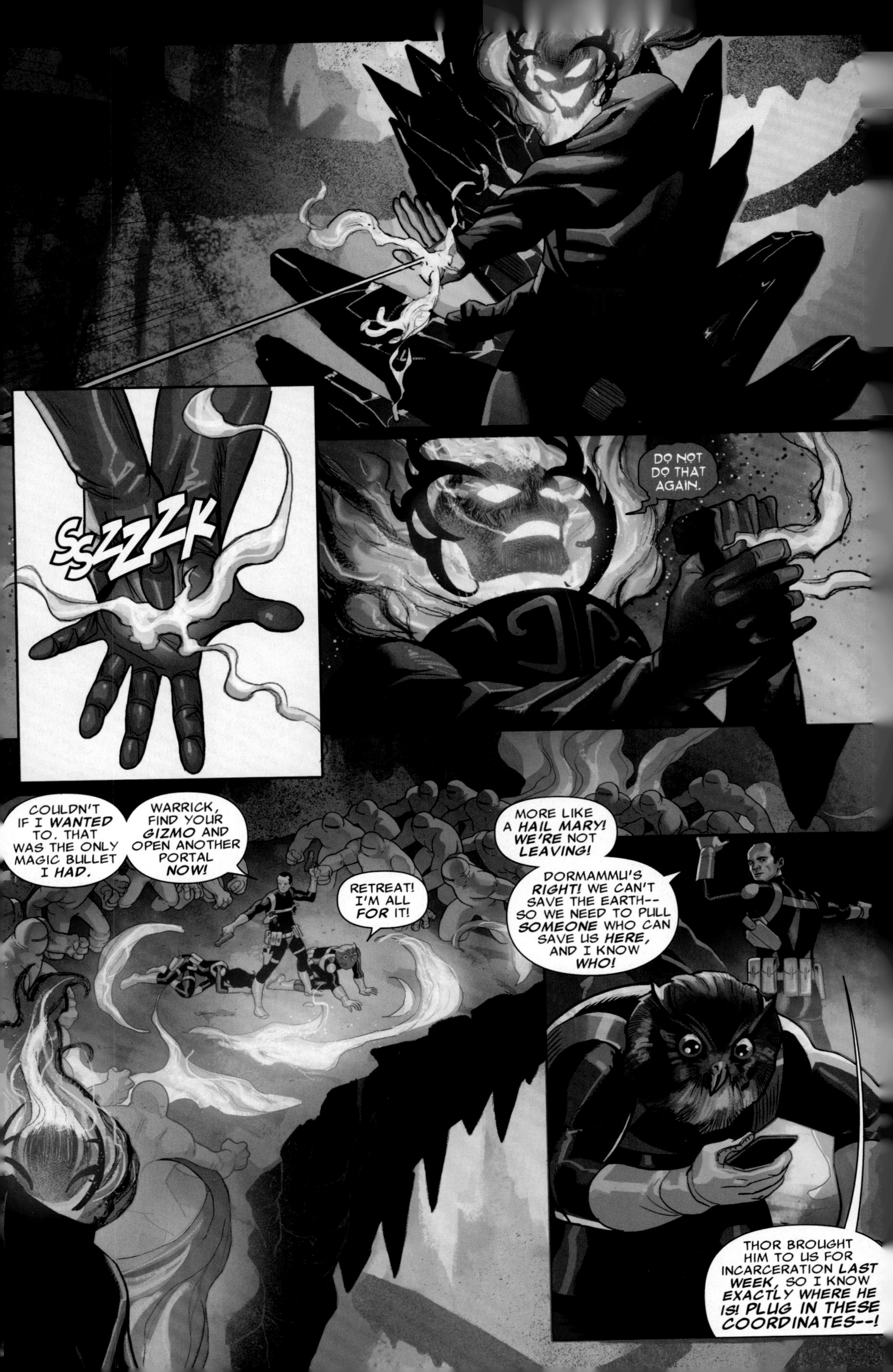

SSZZZK
DO NOT DO THAT AGAIN.
COULDN'T IF I WANTED TO. THAT WAS THE ONLY MAGIC BULLET I HAD.
WARRICK, FIND YOUR GIZMO AND OPEN ANOTHER PORTAL NOW!
RETREAT! I'M ALL FOR IT!
MORE LIKE A HAIL MARY! WE'RE NOT LEAVING!
DORMAMMU'S RIGHT! WE CAN'T SAVE THE EARTH--SO WE NEED TO PULL SOMEONE WHO CAN SAVE US HERE, AND I KNOW WHO!
THOR BROUGHT HIM TO US FOR INCARCERATION LAST WEEK, SO I KNOW EXACTLY WHERE HE IS! PLUG IN THESE COORDINATES--!

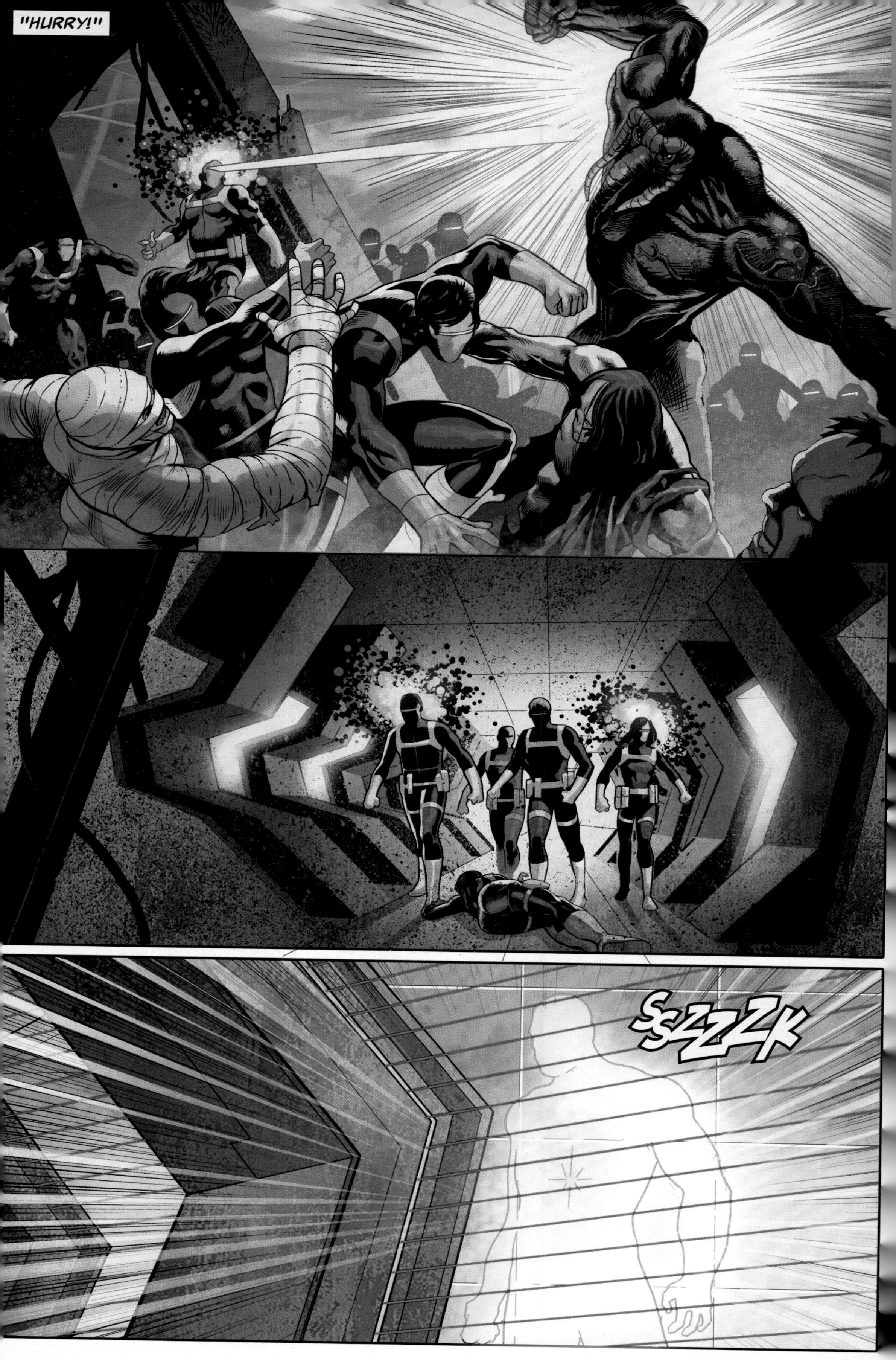
"HURRY!"
SSZZZK

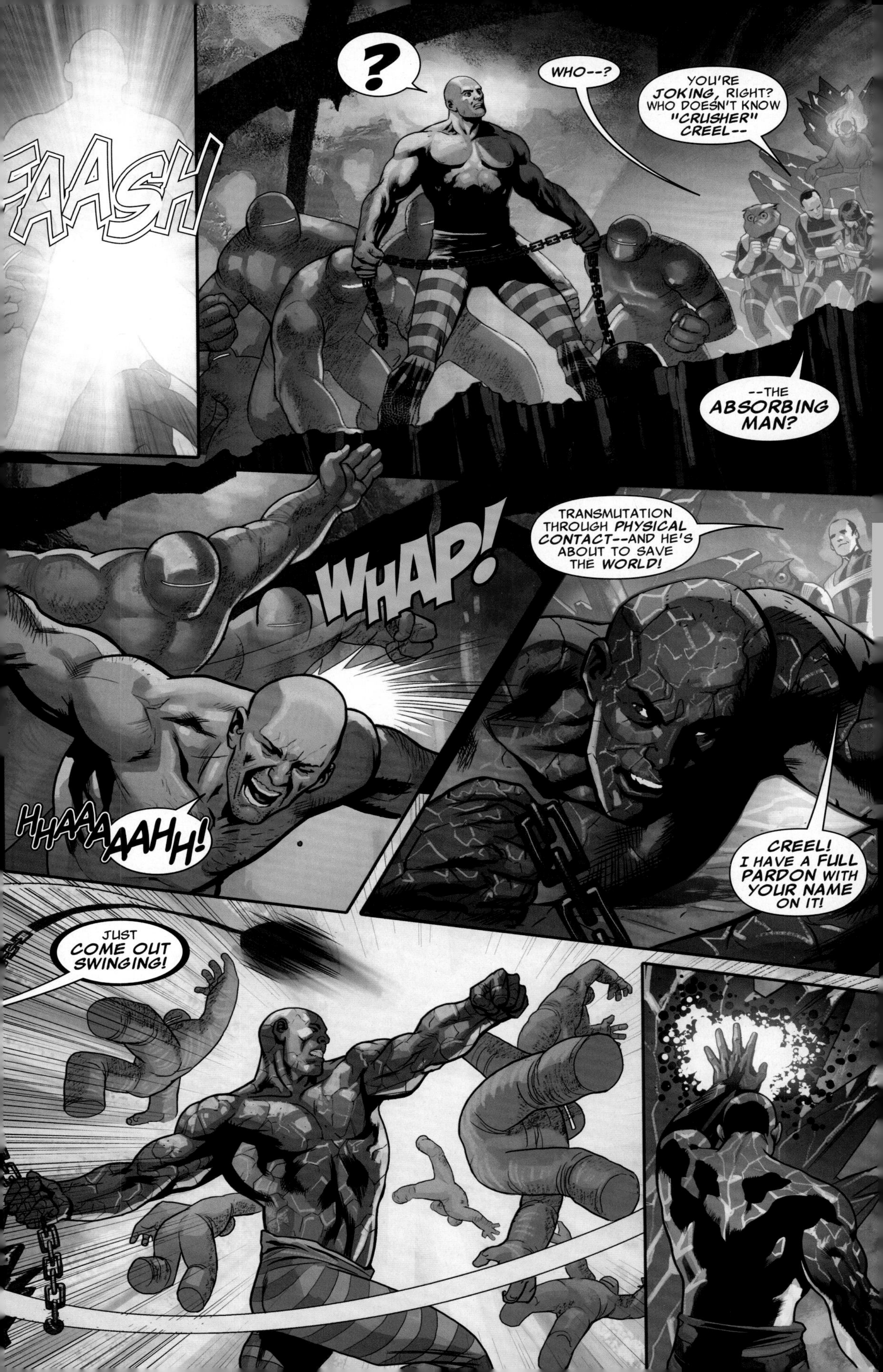
FAASH
?
WHO--?
YOU'RE JOKING, RIGHT? WHO DOESN'T KNOW "CRUSHER" CREEL--
--THE ABSORBING MAN?
WHAP!
TRANSMUTATION THROUGH PHYSICAL CONTACT--AND HE'S ABOUT TO SAVE THE WORLD!
HHAAAAAAHH!
CREEL! I HAVE A FULL PARDON WITH YOUR NAME ON IT!
JUST COME OUT SWINGING!

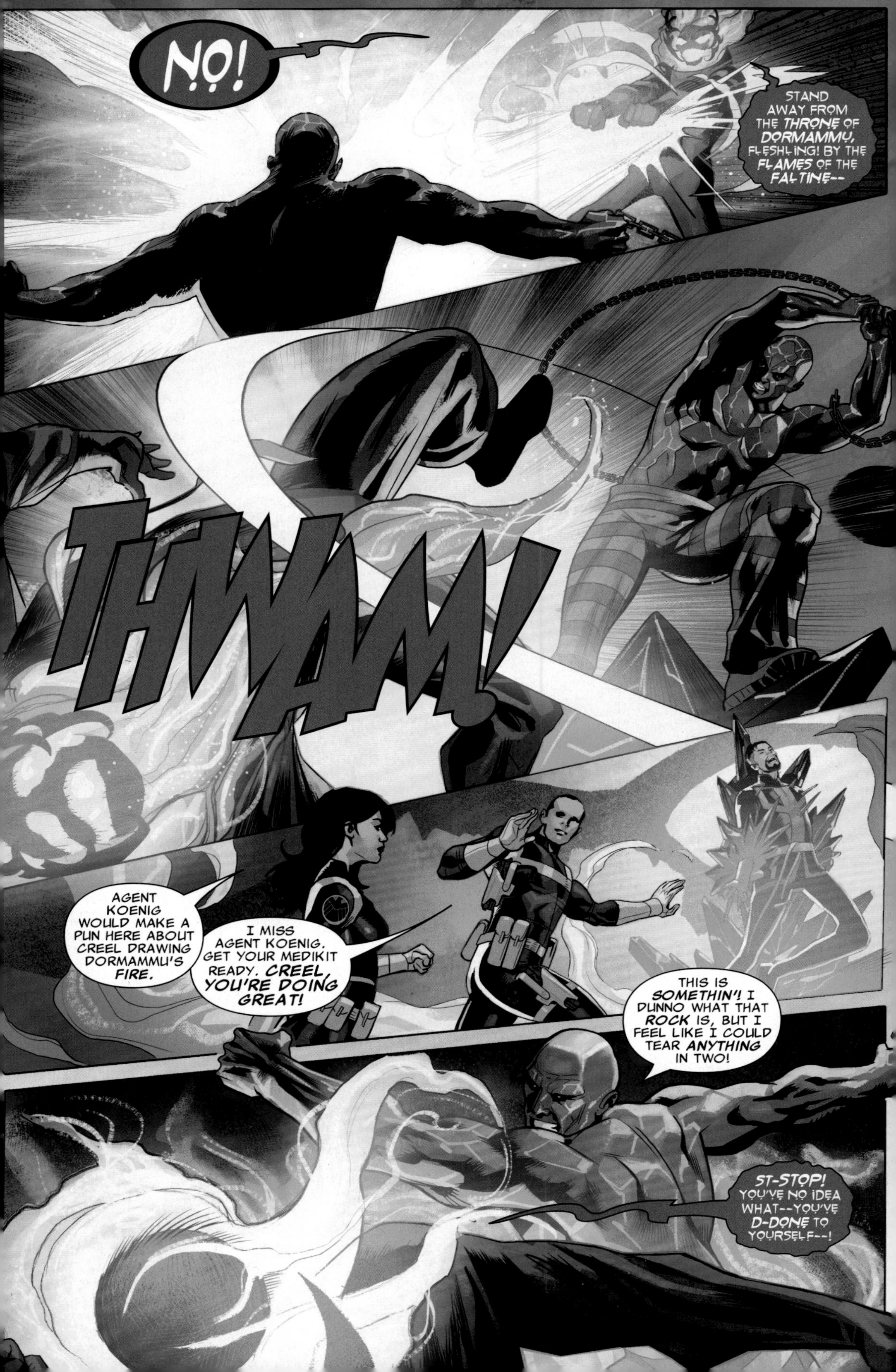
NO!
STAND AWAY FROM THE THRONE OF DORMAMMU, FLESHLING! BY THE FLAMES OF THE FALTINE--
THWAAM!
AGENT KOENIG WOULD MAKE A PUN HERE ABOUT CREEL DRAWING DORMAMMU'S FIRE.
I MISS AGENT KOENIG. GET YOUR MEDIKIT READY. CREEL, YOU'RE DOING GREAT!
THIS IS SOMETHIN'! I DUNNO WHAT THAT ROCK IS, BUT I FEEL LIKE I COULD TEAR ANYTHING IN TWO!
ST-STOP! YOU'VE NO IDEA WHAT--YOU'VE D-DONE TO YOURSELF--!

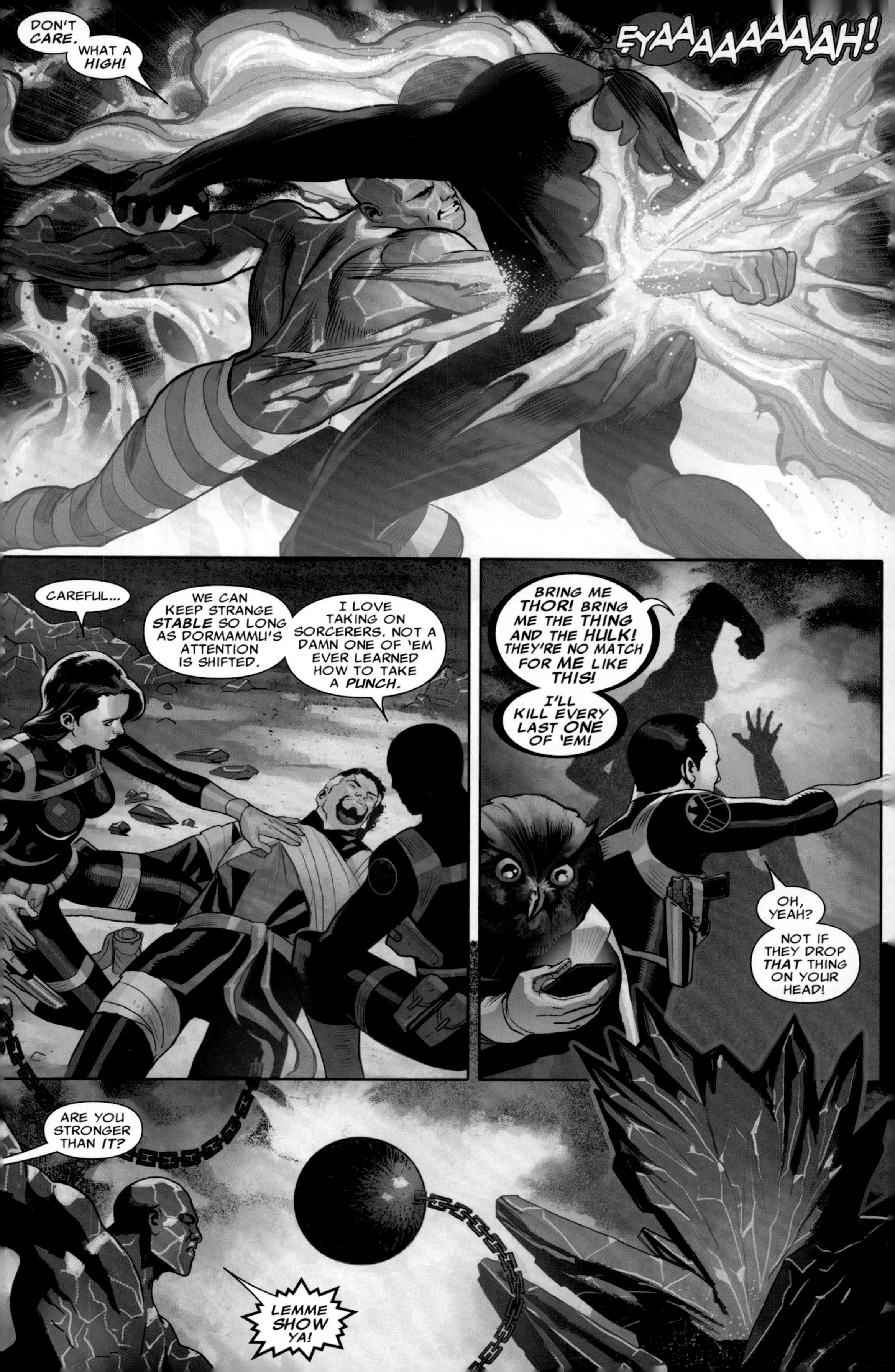
DON'T CARE. WHAT A HIGH!
EYAAAAAAAAAH!
CAREFUL...
WE CAN KEEP STRANGE STABLE SO LONG AS DORMAMMU'S ATTENTION IS SHIFTED.
I LOVE TAKING ON SORCERERS. NOT A DAMN ONE OF 'EM EVER LEARNED HOW TO TAKE A PUNCH.
BRING ME THOR! BRING ME THE THING AND THE HULK! THEY'RE NO MATCH FOR ME LIKE THIS!
I'LL KILL EVERY LAST ONE OF 'EM!
OH, YEAH?
NOT IF THEY DROP THAT THING ON YOUR HEAD!
ARE YOU STRONGER THAN IT?
LEMME SHOW YA!

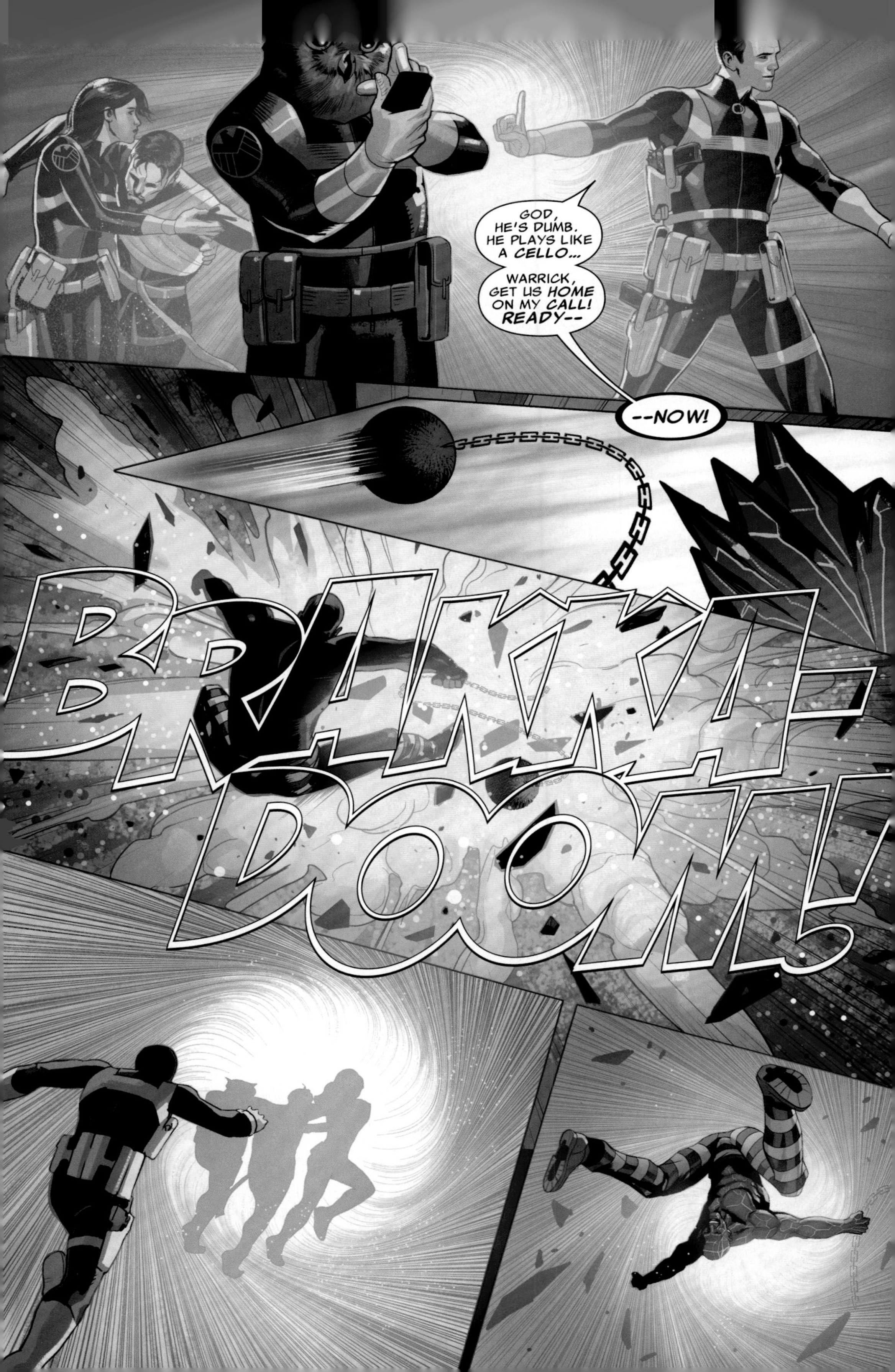
GOD, HE'S DUMB. HE PLAYS LIKE A CELLO...
WARRICK, GET US HOME ON MY CALL! READY--
--NOW!
BRAKA-DOOM!

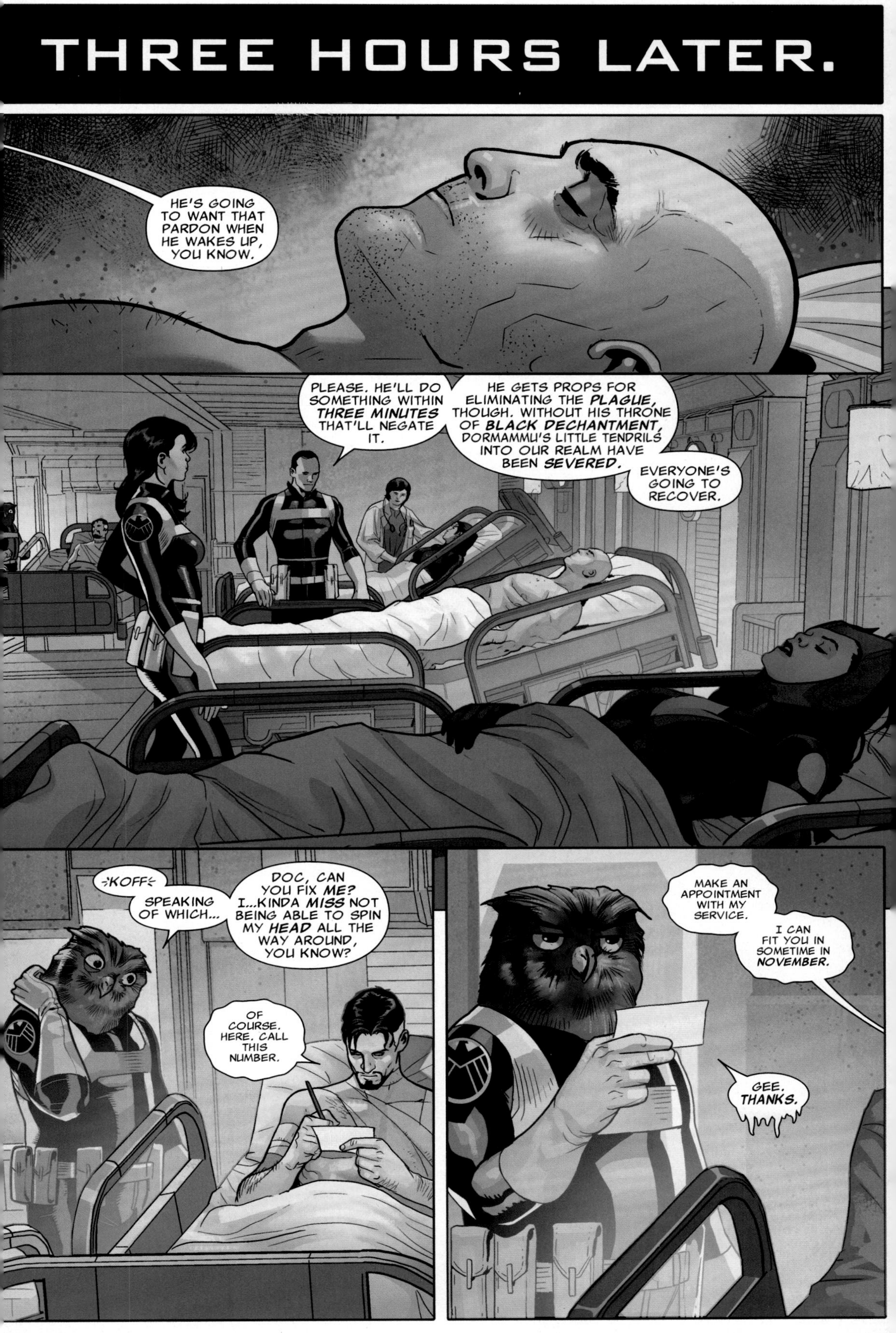
THREE HOURS LATER.
HE'S GOING TO WANT THAT PARDON WHEN HE WAKES UP, YOU KNOW.
PLEASE. HE'LL DO SOMETHING WITHIN THREE MINUTES THAT'LL NEGATE IT.
HE GETS PROPS FOR ELIMINATING THE PLAGUE, THOUGH. WITHOUT HIS THRONE OF BLACK DECHANTMENT, DORMAMMU'S LITTLE TENDRILS INTO OUR REALM HAVE BEEN SEVERED.
EVERYONE'S GOING TO RECOVER.
KOFF
SPEAKING OF WHICH...
DOC, CAN YOU FIX ME? I...KINDA MISS NOT BEING ABLE TO SPIN MY HEAD ALL THE WAY AROUND, YOU KNOW?
OF COURSE. HERE. CALL THIS NUMBER.
MAKE AN APPOINTMENT WITH MY SERVICE.
I CAN FIT YOU IN SOMETIME IN NOVEMBER.
GEE. THANKS.

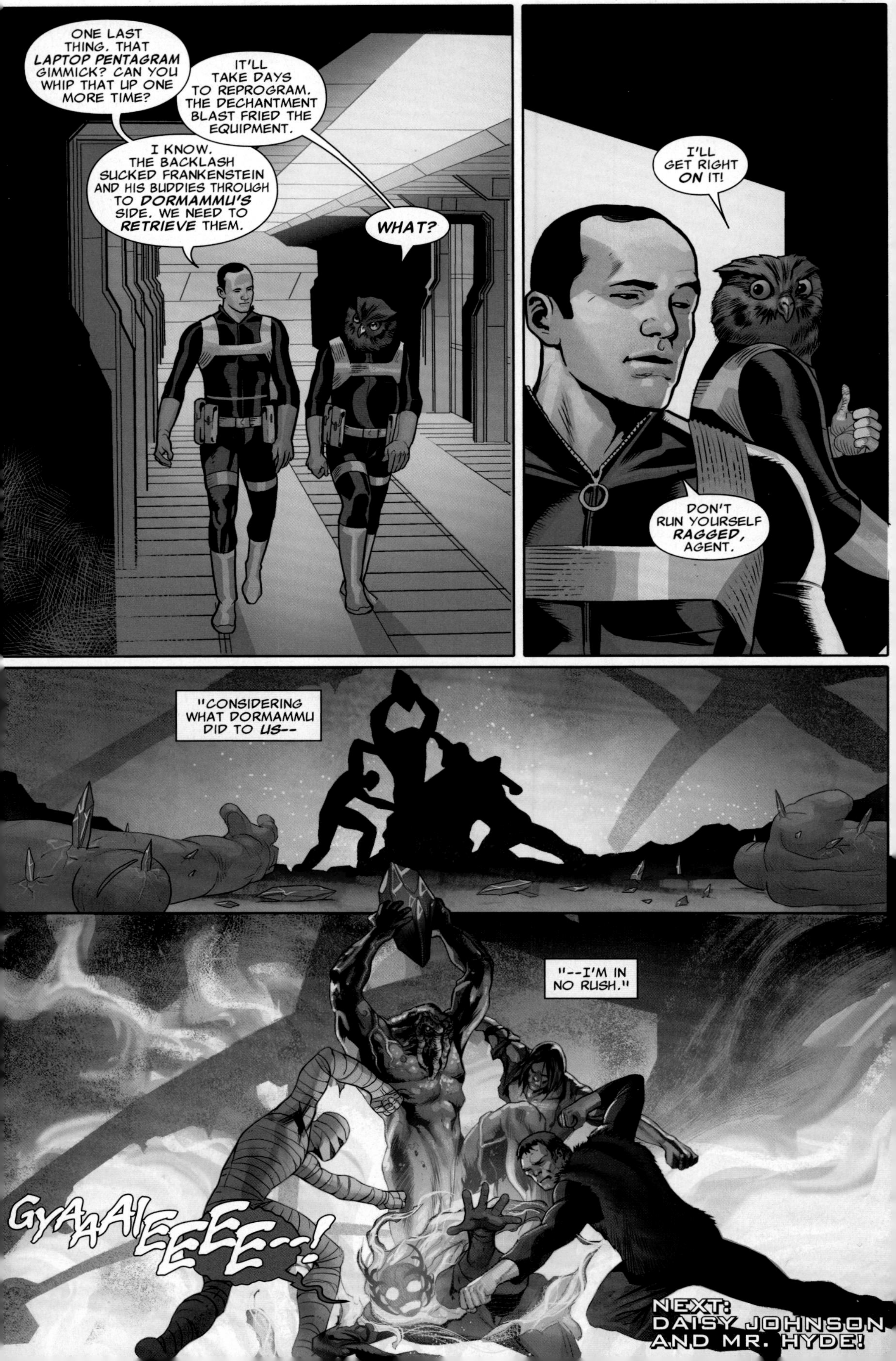
ONE LAST THING. THAT LAPTOP PENTAGRAM GIMMICK? CAN YOU WHIP THAT UP ONE MORE TIME?
IT'LL TAKE DAYS TO REPROGRAM. THE DECHANTMENT BLAST FRIED THE EQUIPMENT.
I KNOW. THE BACKLASH SUCKED FRANKENSTEIN AND HIS BUDDIES THROUGH TO DORMAMMU'S SIDE. WE NEED TO RETRIEVE THEM.
WHAT?
I'LL GET RIGHT ON IT!
DON'T RUN YOURSELF RAGGED, AGENT.
"CONSIDERING WHAT DORMAMMU DID TO US--
"--I'M IN NO RUSH."
GYAAAAIEEEEEE--!
NEXT: DAISY JOHNSON AND MR. HYDE!

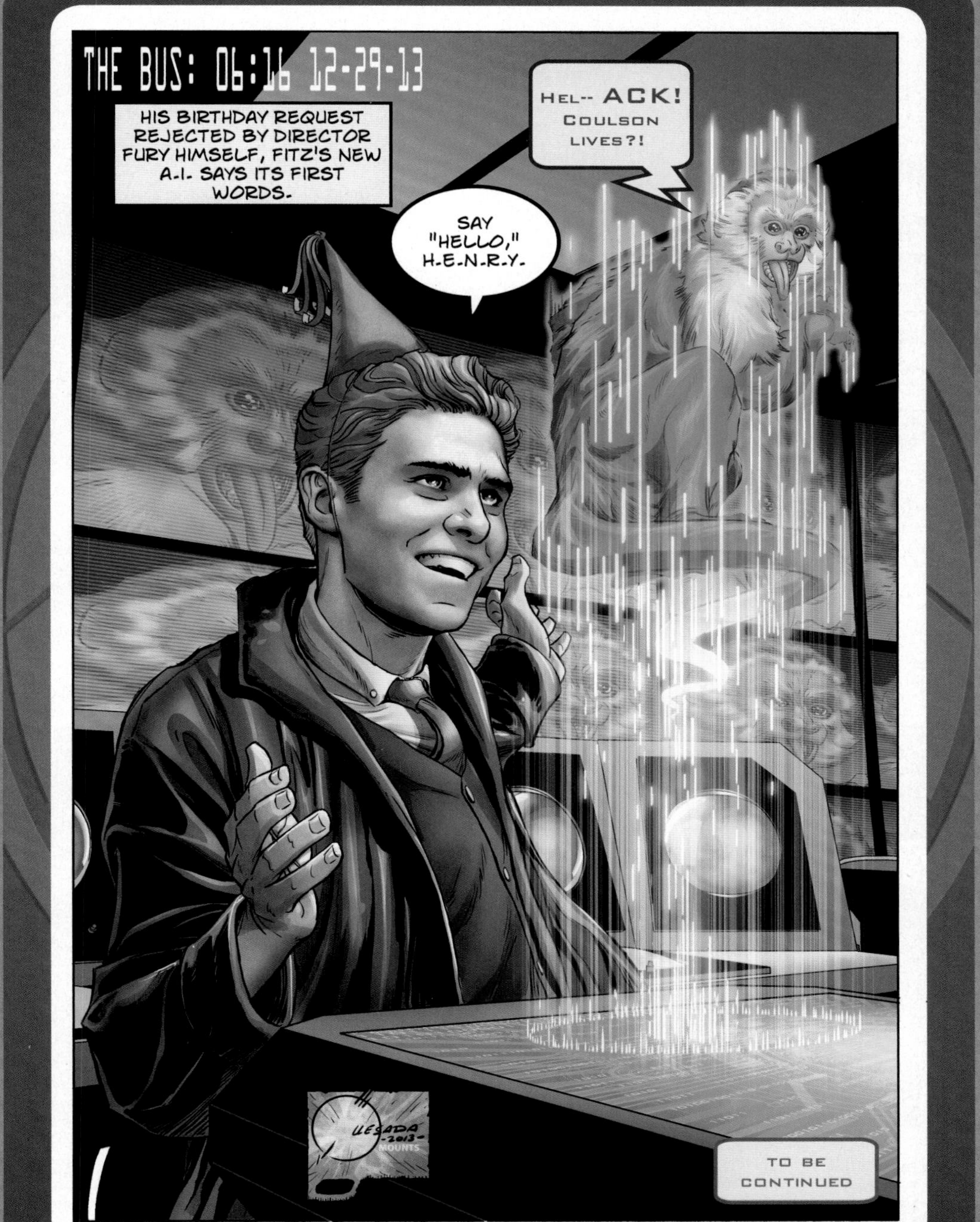
THE BUS: 06:16 12-29-13
HIS BIRTHDAY REQUEST REJECTED BY DIRECTOR FURY HIMSELF, FITZ'S NEW A.I. SAYS ITS FIRST WORDS.
SAY "HELLO," H.E.N.R.Y.
HEL-- ACK! COULSON LIVES?!
QUESADA -2013- MOUNTS
TO BE CONTINUED

PRODUCED BY MARVEL C.C.O. JOE QUESADA FOR THE CAST OF TELEVISION'S *MARVEL'S AGENTS OF S.H.I.E.L.D.*

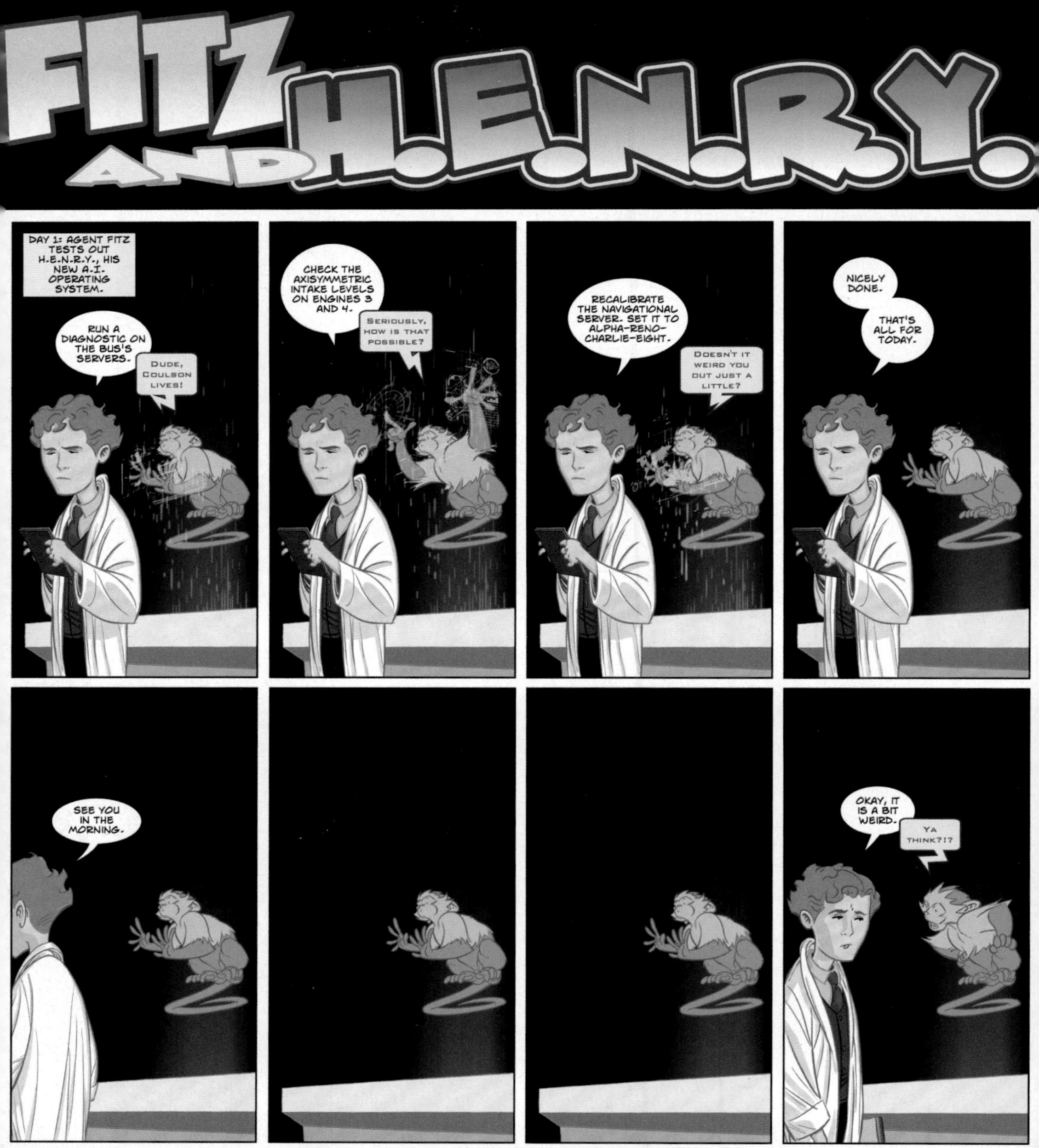
FITZ AND H.E.N.R.Y.
DAY 1: AGENT FITZ TESTS OUT H.E.N.R.Y., HIS NEW A.I. OPERATING SYSTEM.
RUN A DIAGNOSTIC ON THE BUS'S SERVERS.
DUDE, COULSON LIVES!
CHECK THE AXISYMMETRIC INTAKE LEVELS ON ENGINES 3 AND 4.
SERIOUSLY, HOW IS THAT POSSIBLE?
RECALIBRATE THE NAVIGATIONAL SERVER. SET IT TO ALPHA-RENO-CHARLIE-EIGHT.
DOESN'T IT WEIRD YOU OUT JUST A LITTLE?
NICELY DONE.
THAT'S ALL FOR TODAY.
SEE YOU IN THE MORNING.
OKAY, IT IS A BIT WEIRD.
YA THINK?!?

ACCESSING FILES...

FITZ AND H.E.N.R.Y.

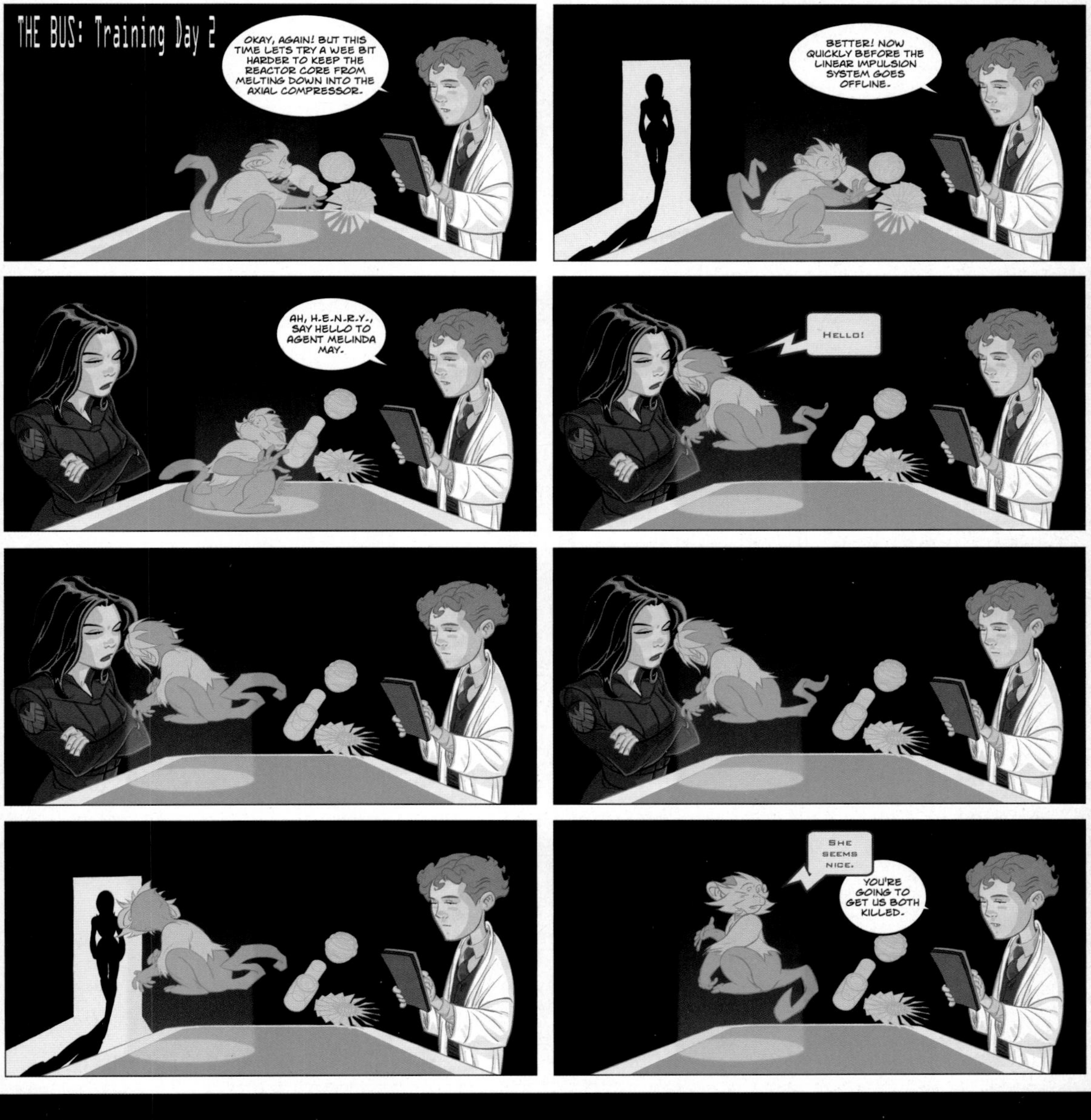
THE BUS: Training Day 2
OKAY, AGAIN! BUT THIS TIME LETS TRY A WEE BIT HARDER TO KEEP THE REACTOR CORE FROM MELTING DOWN INTO THE AXIAL COMPRESSOR.
BETTER! NOW QUICKLY BEFORE THE LINEAR IMPULSION SYSTEM GOES OFFLINE.
AH, H.E.N.R.Y., SAY HELLO TO AGENT MELINDA MAY.
HELLO!
SHE SEEMS NICE.
YOU'RE GOING TO GET US BOTH KILLED.

ACCESSING FILES...

File 1 File 2 File 3

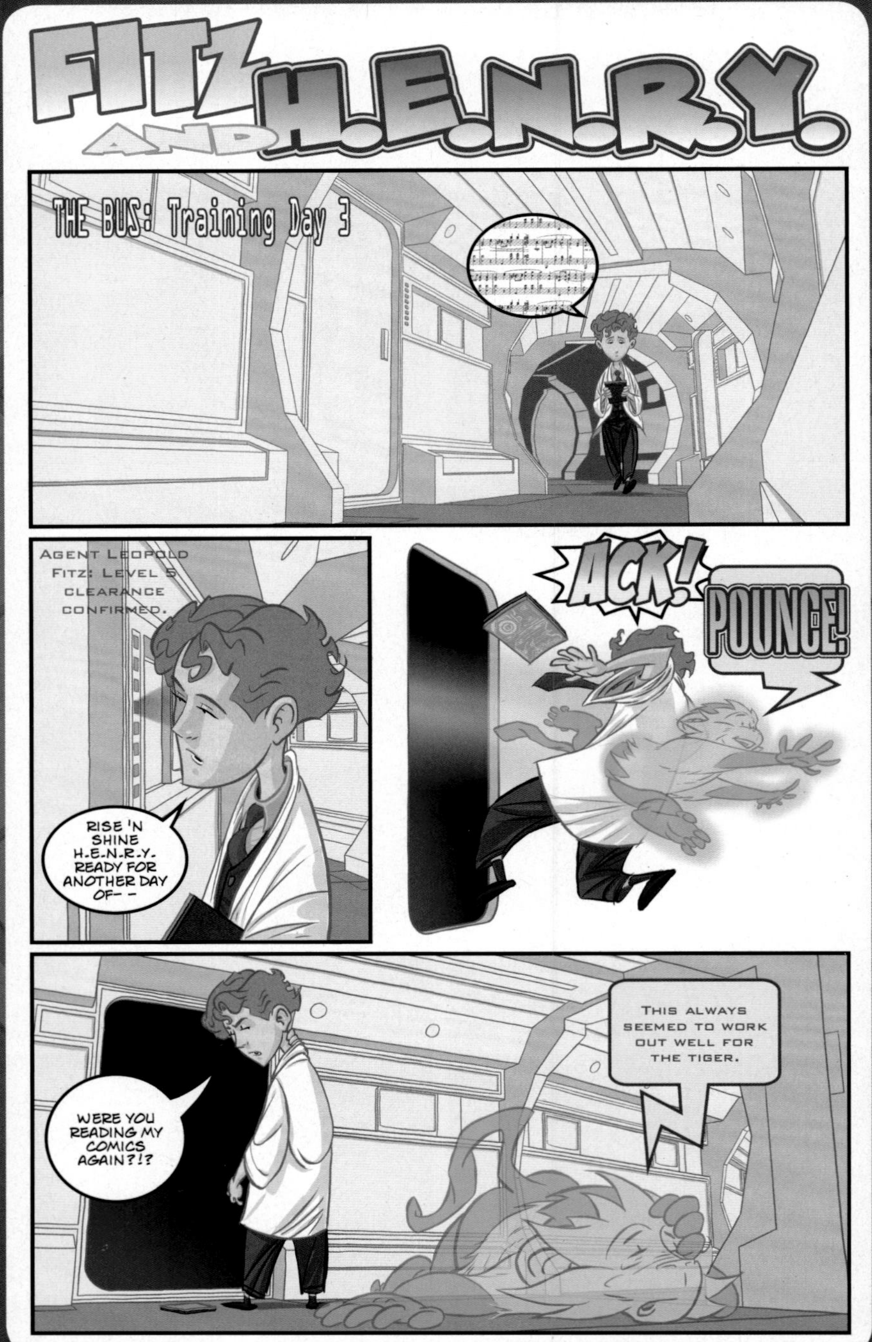
FITZ AND H.E.N.R.Y.
THE BUS: Training Day 3
AGENT LEOPOLD FITZ: LEVEL 5 CLEARANCE CONFIRMED.
RISE 'N SHINE H.E.N.R.Y. READY FOR ANOTHER DAY OF- -
ACK!
POUNCE!
WERE YOU READING MY COMICS AGAIN?!?
THIS ALWAYS SEEMED TO WORK OUT WELL FOR THE TIGER.